Praise for *Lightning Strike*

"Davis masterfully conveys the drama and excitement . . . uncovers new evidence about who actually shot down Japan's top strategist."

—*The Tampa Tribune*

"[Davis] effectively applies his skills as a journalist to this historical drama. He gives Yamamoto a human face. . . . Davis's characters are bound together in an equally colorful narrative."

—United States Naval Institute

"Davis both informs and entertains."

—*Kirkus Reviews*

"An enthralling book that yields new and surprising insights."

—Monika Jensen-Stevenson, former *60 Minutes* producer and author of *Spite House: The Last Secret of the War in Vietnam*

"Exquisitely researched and vividly narrated. *Lightning Strike* puts the reader in the cockpit. . . . Years of confusion shrouding the mission are finally swept away, deftly and conclusively."

—David A. Witts, author of *Forgotten War, Forgiven Guilt*

"*Lightning Strike* is a crisp salute to some of the bravest pilots ever to fly in defense of the United States. Compelling and deeply human, by turns triumphant and profoundly sad, Don Davis's book sheds valuable new light on one of World War II's most pivotal fighter missions."

—James D. Hornfischer, author of *The Last Stand of the Tin Can Sailors*

"A terrific flying story and a great history, *Lightning Strike* strips away the legends and the lies to reveal who really shot down Admiral Yamamoto."

—Stephen Coonts

"*Lightning Strike* is the finest history of World War II in the Pacific, and especially the Yamamoto mission, that I have ever read."

—William H. Allen, president of the American Fighter Aces Association

"*Lightning Strike* is an exciting, well-documented, and masterfully written story. Mr. Davis weaves together the various complex personalities and contradictory facts. . . . It was a delightful read for me, a guy who thought he knew all about the [Yamamoto] mission."

—Bob Manhan, executive director of the Veterans of Foreign Wars

"*Lightning Strike* is a truly wonderful history of the early days of WWII and the desperate fighting on Guadalcanal. The analysis of the air warfare and the great detail about the men who fought in the air in the Solomon Islands is brilliantly done."

—George Chandler, WWII ace, Pacific Theater, and cofounder of the Second Yamamoto Mission Association

Also by Donald A. Davis

The Secret Mission

to Kill

Admiral Yamamoto and

Avenge Pearl Harbor

St. Martin's Griffin

New York

Lightning
Strike

DONALD A. DAVIS

www.stmartins.com

Library of Congress Cataloging-in-Publication Data

Davis, Don, 1939–
    Lightning strike : the secret mission to kill Admiral Yamamoto and avenge Pearl Harbor / Donald A. Davis.
        p. cm.
    ISBN 0-312-30906-6 (hc)
    ISBN 0-312-30907-4 (pbk)
    EAN 978-0-312-30907-7
    1. Yamamoto, Isoroku, 1884–1943—Assassination. 2. World War, 1939–1945—Campaigns—Pacific Area. 3. World War, 1939–1945—Aerial operations, American. I Title.

D767 .D38 2005
940.54'26592—dc22   2004051293

    P1

For Robin

BATTLE OF MIDWAY

MIDWAY

SAN FRANCISCO

HAWAII TO SAN FRANCISCO • 2400 MILES

HAWAIIAN ISLANDS

PEARL HARBOR, HAWAII

CHRISTMAS ISLAND

SAMOA

TONGA

TAHITI

PACIFIC OCEAN THEATRE
WORLD WAR II

TOKYO

TOKYO TO HAWAII · 3800 MILES

ONG KONG

WAKE

MANILA, HILLIPINES

GUAM

YAMAMOTO HQ · TRUK
CAROLINE ISLANDS

MARSHALL
ISLANDS

E A S T   I N D I E S

GAPORE

NEW GUINEA

RABAUL
NEW BRITAIN

GUADALCANAL
SOLOMON ISLANDS

DARWIN

BATTLE OF
CORAL SEA

NOUMEA
NEW CALEDONIA

FIJI

SYDNEY TO HAWAII · 4900 MILES

A U S T R A L I A

BRISBANE

SYDNEY

MELBOURNE

NEW ZEALAND

Contents

Acknowledgments

Jane Dystel and Miriam Goderich, my longtime friends and agents, came up with the idea for this book and were there for me from start to finish. They are the best. Charles Spicer and Joe Cleemann at St. Martin's Press brought their usual boundless enthusiasm and professionalism to the editing table and molded a raw manuscript into a book. Together, we all stepped back into a time of heroes.

Many people went out of their way to contribute information, grant interviews, furnish obscure material, and guide me on this story of a handful of U.S. Army pilots who fought so bravely in the South Pacific during the opening months of World War II, alongside equally valiant members of the U.S. Marine Corps and the U.S. Navy. The sort of war they fought, against a well-armed, well-trained, and determined foe, is inconceivable today.

Among those who helped point the way were Margaret and Shelli Barber, Robert Bollinger, Betty Canning, Joe Childers, Barbara Gratch Cohen, Bill Flynn, Carroll V. Glines, Joe and Helen Hafter, John Houlahan, Frank Mallory, Burnett (Red) Miller, Ian McGibbon in New Zealand, Ann Mitchell, Eileen and Arthur Olson, Robert Pappadake, Professor Irwin Slesnick, and some of the "Old Asia Hands" from the glory days of UPI: the incomparable Bob Miller in Hawaii, Sol and Vic Vanzi in Manila, Miyoko and Pat Killen in Tokyo, Ken Englade in New Mexico, and Al Kaff in New York.

A number of pilots "taught" me about flying in World War II–style combat, including Homer Baker, Bryan W. Brown, Dale Brannon, Larry Graebner, Stewart Gordon, Glen Hart, Vernon Head, Tex Hill, Besby Holmes, Red Inciardi, Julius "Jack" Jacobson, Lou Kittel, Bob McMahon, Jim Morehouse, Frank Olynyk, Stan Palmer, Bill Sharpsteen, John Thompson, Butler Toland, Ray Williams, and John Zink. I also send salutes to all of the men of the 13th "Jungle Air Force," the 347th Fighter Group, the 67th Fighter Squadron, the 68th Fighter Squadron, the 70th Fighter Squadron, the 339th Fighter Squadron, the 12th Fighter Squadron, and the American Fighter Aces Association.

Extraordinary research assistance came from Steve Davenport, reference librarian, San Francisco Maritime NHP Library; Helen McDonald and the staff of the Admiral Nimitz State Historical Site, National Museum of the Pacific War, Fredericksburg, Texas; Laurie J. Thompson and Carol Uhrmacher of the Civic Center Library, California Room, San Rafael, California; David Hays of the Archives of the University of Colorado Library, Boulder, Colorado; the reference staff at the American Heritage Center at the University of Wyoming, Laramie, Wyoming; the Idaho Historical Society, Boise, Idaho; and the U.S. Air Force History Support Office, Reference and Analysis Branch AFHSO/HOR, Maxwell Air Force Base, Montgomery, Alabama.

And special thanks go to George Chandler and Cheryl White of the Second Yamamoto Mission Association, three-war pilot Doug Canning, and historian John Wible. All gave freely of their time and opinions, and we can thank heaven that they have saved many pieces of paper, newspaper clippings, magazine articles, and pictures that no one else wanted.

As always, every word was first critiqued by the best editor in the land, my bride of twenty years, Robin Murphy Davis.

In occasional instances, there were conflicting versions of the same event, and the author had to be a reluctant judge and measure them against other facts and details. So while this book was helped along by many hands, any errors are mine alone.

Lightning Strike

Prologue

The Inland Sea, Japan

Admiral Isoroku Yamamoto, commander in chief of the Combined Fleet of the Imperial Japanese Navy, was not a big man, standing only five-feet, three-inches tall. On the day he died, a Japanese pilot encountering him for the first time stammered in surprise, "Why, the C-in-C is only half my size!" Most Japanese had come to imagine the admiral as a hybrid between a giant and a god, but in reality he was not only small in physical stature, but he spoke softly and his face seemed delicate. The outward, gentle look and a quick smile masked the real man.

Yamamoto was a complex person of stark contrasts: a polite scholar who would stand on his head to entertain total strangers, a sailor who believed in the power of airplanes over ships, a married man and father who had a lifelong passion for geishas, and a gambler who left little to chance.

The ultimate contrast was his relationship with the United States. Although Japanese to the bottom of his soul, he spoke English, read the Bible, had attended Harvard University, been posted to Washington, mastered the games of bridge and poker, loved cigars, was good friends with many U.S. Navy officers, and had probably seen more of America than most Americans. He certainly knew more of the United States than any other serving Japanese officer. Yamamoto considered the United

States to be still a young nation, but already fulfilling a dynamic promise and possessing growing strength. He did not fear Washington's present military ability, but the clattering production lines in Detroit and the thumping pumps that pulled oil from the Texas dirt worried him greatly. Americans were capable of making whatever they needed—skyscrapers or pull toys, ships or planes—at a rate that he knew Japan could not match. And the two countries were on a path to certain war.

In the years after World War I, the government in Tokyo had been taken over by the Imperial Army and its nationalist supporters. The army had invaded China with bloody results and had bathed in the euphoria of easy victories. The United States and other nations demanded that Japan stop its murderous rampage, and when those directions were ignored, Washington responded with an embargo of oil and steel and other vital goods that threatened to strangle the Japanese military machine. To break that grip, the generals decided to go to war against America, and Emperor Hirohito gave his assent.

Admiral Yamamoto had been an outspoken opponent of this plan in the councils of war, urging caution and criticizing the government's expansionist policies and seeming lust for battle.

Yamamoto particularly disagreed with the prevailing xenophobic feeling in his country that Americans were soft and lacked a fighting spirit akin to the Bushido code of a Japanese warrior. From studying the Civil War and biographies of President Abraham Lincoln, he had discerned the singular truth that when the threat was great enough, common Americans would fight, and die, for their country. Carving up a backward nation like China could not be compared to fighting the United States, an industrial giant that was already helping Great Britain and showing it had no fear of the Germans. He advised against Japan's entering the Tripartite Pact, which allied it with Germany and Italy, dictatorships led by men he did not like.

Much of what the admiral said went against the tide of popular opinion, and he made as many powerful enemies as he did protective friends. Earlier, when right-wing fanatics targeted him for assassination, the navy command sent him back to sea to keep him alive and promoted him to command of the Combined Fleet of the Imperial Japanese Navy. There were higher-ups to whom he had to answer, but that was a formality. Yamamoto was on his own, out where he was at his best, on the water, getting his ships and aircraft ready to fight.

Once the emperor agreed to make war against the United States, Yamamoto immediately ended his personal opposition, for he would never speak against the Chrysanthemum Throne. He set aside his feelings and accepted who he was—the sword of the emperor, and the one man in Japan who was capable of bringing the United States to its knees.

"What a strange position I find myself in now," he wrote an old friend. "Having to make a decision diametrically opposed to my own personal opinion, with no choice but to push full-speed in pursuance of that decision." The question for Yamamoto had become not *if*, but *how?*

Established Japanese naval doctrine called for any war with the United States to begin with the Combined Fleet striking straight south, deep into the Pacific Ocean, to capture the distant lands that held the natural resources needed to fight. Not only would that strike obtain the oil and other vital materials needed to sustain a war, but it would also draw the U.S. fleet far away from its home bases and into a battle where it would be crushed. Even the war planners in Washington believed that was the way a war with Japan would develop, except for the outcome of the battle between fleets.

Yamamoto thought it was ridiculous. The move south would be a cautious, time-wasting, and defense-oriented effort that would turn his powerful fleet into mere ferryboats for the army. Once the troops were dispatched to those far-flung grounds, from the Philippines to the Dutch East Indies, then the navy would have to guard thousands of miles of water and hundreds of islands and wait until the Americans gathered their strength and chose a time and a place to attack. The Americans would grow strong, then strike anywhere, at any time, and that was something he could not allow. Time was not a friend. If there was to be a fight, he wanted it on his terms; he insisted that the war had to begin with a swift strike.

The tool Yamamoto would use was the airplane. He was a visionary who believed totally in the power of naval aviation. He had been a careful observer during the past thirty years as many countries experimented with the novel idea that little planes could sink big ships. World War I had brought small aircraft to the front lines, but in the roles of nuisance bombing and scouts rather than as an actual combat force. At sea, most admirals remained wedded to the increasingly musty idea that brute force, sheer tonnage, and the size of a battleship's guns were the ultimate measure of a blue-water navy—broadsides at point-blank range. Yamamoto felt that few people in history had ever been so mistaken.

In 1921, with the Great War over, an American general named William "Billy" Mitchell began advocating an independent air force, and talked the U.S. Navy into letting him bomb some captured German warships to test the effectiveness of the airplane as a weapon against ships. Flimsy bombers appearing like gnats high over the heads of observers off the Virginia coast easily shattered the hapless targets and sank a battleship, a cruiser, a destroyer, three submarines—and centuries of naval thinking.

Three years later, in a mock attack on the Panama Canal, paperweight airplanes flying off the USS *Langley*, a boxy coal ship converted into America's first aircraft carrier, caught the opposing force of battleships at anchor and would have inflicted carnage had the attack been the real thing. But the navy brushed off the incident with a critique that ruled such an attack would not have been effective. In 1929, during another fleet problem, a newer carrier, the USS *Saratoga*, accomplished the same thing, theoretically wrecking both the "enemy" fleet and the Panama Canal locks. Again the navy ignored the possibilities. Under true combat conditions, they said, major warships would blow attacking airplanes out of the sky. Every senior commander in every navy in the world believed that carriers and their planes were meant only to protect the fleet, not to attack it.

Yamamoto, still rising through the ranks, disagreed. His career paralleled the development of aircraft carriers, and he worked with a total determination to force Japan into the future. He captained a carrier, taught naval aviators how to fly, created tactics to maximize their use, and slowly helped convince the Japanese navy to build one big carrier after another. By the eve of World War II, Yamamoto had a fleet unlike any other in the world. With his striking arm of airplanes, all other ships, no matter their size, became nothing more than targets.

Substantial doubt among his critics in the Navy Ministry and Japan's own caste of "big-ship" admirals was finally put to rest on the dark night of November 11, 1940, when outdated British biplanes from HMS *Illustrious* showed up suddenly over the protected harbor of Taranto, Italy, and hit an Italian fleet that believed itself to be quite safe.

Half of Italy's entire fleet—three battleships, a cruiser, and a pair of destroyers—were damaged, and the rest ran away to Naples, which opened the Mediterranean to the Royal Navy. It was an unexpected demonstration of the new truth in modern warfare: Control of the sea depended upon control of the air.

Admiral Yamamoto studied Taranto in detail and decided he could do the same thing to the United States. He would cripple the U.S. Pacific Fleet at Pearl Harbor, sink its carriers, and only then lure the weakened Americans into a final, decisive battle. His tactics were bold, the long-term strategy was sound, and Yamamoto, and not his enemy, would be on the offensive. They would have to react to him!

The Pacific Ocean would become a Japanese lake, and they could pluck the oil fields and rubber plantations in the tropics at leisure and without grave risk, and perhaps even send battleships ranging along the West Coast of the United States to bombard metropolitan areas from Seattle to Los Angeles. Commando forces could reach the U.S. mainland, leaving America so busy defending its own coastline that it could not venture into the Pacific. Washington would be forced to negotiate a settlement.

It had to be the equivalent of a first-round knockout in a prize-fight. If the United States was given time to prepare for war, then its industrial mills and oil refineries would come into play, and Japan would lose everything. Yamamoto advocated the first-strike scenario as fervently as he had once insisted on not fighting the United States at all. This time it was the others who urged caution, but he was having none of that. A furious Yamamoto threatened to resign his command if he could not attack Hawaii, and the admirals, generals, and politicians bowed before his will. So while he thought it was foolish for Japan to go to war against the United States, he ordered his fleet to do exactly that on a chilly morning in early December 1941.

The attack fleet, called the *Kido Butai,* had awaited Yamamoto's final signal in the frigid waters of the Kuriles, a thin and isolated belt of small islands between the northernmost point of Japan and Russia's Kamchatka Peninsula. Under the command of Vice Admiral Chuichi Nagumo, the battle fleet stretched beyond the horizon. At its heart were Japan's six largest aircraft carriers. Hundreds of fighters, bombers, and torpedo planes of the First Air Fleet roosted on and beneath those flat decks, and they would be flown by some of the best pilots in the world. Two fast battleships, a pair of brawny cruisers, and a light cruiser were anchored around the carriers, as were nine destroyers, a picket line of three submarines, and the eight tankers brimming with fuel.

Thirty-one ships slipped away from anchorage undetected, beneath shrouds of heavy weather, on November 30, while Japanese intelligence units kept up a steady flow of false radio traffic that duped eavesdroppers into believing the ships were hundreds of miles away in the Inland Sea or beginning to head south toward targets such as the Philippine Islands.

As negotiations between Japanese and American diplomats reached a stalemate in Washington, Yamamoto messaged the fleet his signal to begin the war, *Niitaka-yama nobore* (Climb Mount Niitaka).

Admiral Nagumo, who had not supported the Yamamoto plan, headed for Hawaii along a northern loop specifically chosen to avoid merchant vessels, an unusual track that was given a practice run earlier by a Japanese passenger liner. The fleet plowed through dense fog and monstrous seas, never slowing down, even when sheets of rain, raging winds, and roaring waters swept several sailors overboard. Radio silence was broken to prevent the fleet from scattering, but the task force somehow remained invisible to American intelligence officers, who interpreted the increased signal activity as involving a long-anticipated movement of naval forces to the south, toward the Philippines, Thailand, and the Dutch East Indies.

Japanese spies and submarines provided final confirmation that although the U.S. Navy's aircraft carriers were not in port, American battleships were anchored like sitting ducks in Pearl Harbor. The decision was made to strike, and the giant fleet sailed on, without even a signal light to mark its position.

Two hundred and thirty miles north of Pearl Harbor, Nagumo brought the Pearl Harbor strike force to life. While mechanics and armorers and other sailors surged to their stations, the just-awakened pilots devoured a hearty breakfast of rice and red snapper and drank toasts of sake. They performed solemn rituals, tucking locks of their hair and fingernail clippings into final letters to loved ones and tying on "thousand-stitch" belts that had been sewn by their families and friends to ward off bullets. Then they buckled into their planes.

Two hundred miles from Hawaii, the carriers were lurching sharply in the heavy seas. To help the attack planes grab more air, they turned into a twenty-knot wind that swept straight down the flight decks. At six o'clock in the morning, green signals flashed, and the 183 planes of the first wave launched as the cheers of the carrier crews matched the roar of their growling, revving engines. Torpedo planes, fighters, dive-bombers, and level-flying bombers clawed off the decks, some so heavily laden that they almost clipped the foamy wave tops before gaining altitude. *Banzai!*

Thirty-nine-year-old Commander Mitsuo Fuchida, a steady veteran of combat in China, had some three thousand hours of flying time to his credit and was an expert with carrier planes when he was picked to lead the attack on Pearl Harbor. He pulled his dive-bomber up through layers of thick, dark clouds until he finally burst into a glorious sunrise that matched the scarlet circles on his plane and the battle flag of his country. Fuchida banked to the south and caught a tailwind. Guided by his unsuspecting enemy's radio beacons, the music-filled frequencies of stations KGO and KGMB in Honolulu, he would reach Pearl Harbor in ninety minutes.

The signal from Fuchida ordering his pilots to attack—*To! To! To!*—was heard clearly all the way back in Japan, some thirty-nine hundred miles away. It was the repeated first syllable of *Totsugeki!* the Japanese word for *Charge!*

Then came a similar-sounding code word—Japanese for *Tiger!*—as Fuchida let Admiral Nagumo, with the carriers, know the attack was actually underway: *Tora! Tora! Tora!*

A five-hundred-pound bomb dropped on Wheeler Field, and the slaughter began.

Yamamoto stood quietly beside the map that dominated the wardroom on his own flagship, the battleship *Nagato,* a forty-two-thousand-ton giant pulling gently at its anchor in Japan's Inland Sea. Staff officers updated a big map that showed every anchorage, airfield, fuel depot, and defensive strongpoint on the island of Oahu. The radio reports from the attacking planes were bouncing off a freak weather layer, and a sense of pride swept through the wardroom. It was an astounding feeling in an era when long-distance communication was difficult, and in most cases, impossible. The admiral's staff could almost *see* the Zeros pummeling every American plane they could find, and the dive-bombers and torpedo planes blowing apart Battleship Row.

A staff officer reported formally to Yamamoto, "Surprise attack successful!" A staccato of astonishing news rushed in . . . direct hit on the battleship *Pennsylvania* . . . *Oklahoma* capsized . . . *West Virginia* sunk . . . *Arizona* sinking. No protective cover of American planes, and little antiaircraft fire. Crackling news programs were picked up from the United States, where shocked American broadcasters confirmed the attack.

It was not a dream. The waves of dive-bombers, low-level bombers, and fighter planes came in small and fast and lethally armed, while the big ships were idle and unprepared. Long torpedoes plowed into gray hulks, and the harbor shook with explosions. The planes swooped and cartwheeled above the American fleet. One after another, the battleships were going down, almost in a fiery, final, and symbolic salute to the admirals who had championed them. The age of naval airpower was crowned on that sunny morning in Hawaii.

Nevertheless, Yamamoto remained skeptical of the scope of the triumph. Young aviators tend to exaggerate what happens in battle, and as a pilot himself, Yamamoto knew things looked different from the cockpit of a fast-moving airplane. While his cheering staff raised toasts of *sake*, the admiral remained stern and aloof, absorbing the incoming details. This was only the first battle of what he knew would be a very long war.

Yamamoto always demanded punctuality, and his staff had nicknamed him the "On-Time Admiral." He had set a very precise timetable to hit Pearl Harbor, for he did not want history to record it as a cowardly blow. Therefore, it was critical that the planes arrive over the target only after hostilities were declared between the United States and Japan. For Yamamoto, it was a matter of both personal and national honor.

The planners designed an incredibly close schedule based upon the expected termination of diplomatic negotiations in Washington so the attack would satisfy international law and still catch the Americans by surprise. If too much time elapsed between the end of diplomacy and the start of war, the Americans might turn Pearl Harbor into a death trap for the attacking Japanese.

The Japanese carrier planes were therefore under orders to attack precisely at eight o'clock, Hawaiian time, on Sunday morning, December 7, 1941, immediately after Ambassador Kichisaburo Nomura gave notice to the U.S. government in Washington. That careful plan broke down when a cipher clerk in Japan's embassy had trouble decoding the lengthy message from Tokyo, and Ambassador Nomura had to request a forty-five minute delay of his meeting with Secretary of State Cordell Hull.

Yamamoto was unaware of the change in schedule, when, at one minute before the time Nomura and Hull were to meet, Fuchida's planes came roaring into Pearl Harbor.

Ambassador Nomura, who did not know of the Yamamoto schedule, was still waiting in Hull's anteroom when an urgent signal from Hawaii informed the secretary of state that Pearl Harbor was under assault. The meeting of the diplomats was brief, perfunctory, and cold.

Aboard his flagship, Yamamoto grew disturbed. Why were the Americans not offering a better defense? True, Sunday was a day of rest in their Christian religion, but the attack seemed too easy, and he worried about the timing. His planes owned the skies over Hawaii.

He asked an aide if the final declaration had been delivered in Washington on schedule. "I suppose the Foreign Ministry's arrangements are all right, are they?" Yamamoto wondered, according to his biographer Hiroyuki Agawa. "From the cables that have come in so far, it looks as though the attack force has kept its side of the bargain. But there'd be trouble if someone slipped up and people said it was a sneak attack. There's no hurry, but bear it in mind, would you, and make a thorough check."

"I'm sure it's all right," replied the aide.

"Nevertheless, I want you to check." When Yamamoto learned the attack had preceded the breaking of relations, he had to have been deeply chagrined. The stigma would bother him for the rest of his life, but there was nothing he could do about it. There was no honor in a sneak attack.

It was immaterial. The war had begun by his design, his friends in America were now his enemies, and they would fight each other to the death.

When the Japanese struck, many of the planes of the U.S. Army Air Corps were still on the ground, parked in tight, neat clusters by commanders who had been more worried about sabotage on the ground than an attack from the air. Parking the planes wingtip to wingtip made them easier to guard.

Crews aboard the ships at Ford Island were getting ready for breakfast and the eight o'clock raising of the colors was under way when the cannon fire of strafing fighter-bombers erupted, drowning out the church bells on shore. Then torpedoes began to slam into the moored battleships. Explosions hammered the area, bullets zinged off steel, and black clouds of oily smoke rose from dying ships and planes. Dive-bombers ripped into the parked aircraft, and Zero pilots strafed clumps of American fighters and took down most of the planes that somehow managed to stagger into the sky. The first wave of Japanese attackers spent ninety minutes turning Pearl Harbor into an inferno, and then the second wave—170 more planes—plunged in with still more bombs, torpedoes, and bullets. The attack caught Pearl Harbor so totally by surprise that ammunition had not even been issued for the army's eighty-six antiaircraft guns, and individual soldiers were helpless because many of their rifles and machine guns were locked up in armories.

The attack left the U.S. Pacific Fleet grievously wounded. Eight battleships had been anchored there at dawn. The *Arizona* was sunk, and the capsized *Oklahoma* would never be repaired. The *West Virginia*, *Nevada*, and *California* would require months of work before they could sail again. Lighter damage was inflicted on the *Pennsylvania*, *Maryland*, and *Tennessee*, but all were out of action. Three destroyers, two auxiliary ships, and a large floating dry dock were sunk or wrecked, while the light cruisers *Helena*, *Honolulu*, and *Raleigh*, a seaplane tender, and a repair ship also sustained substantial damage.

The air bases at Kaneohe Bay, Bellows Field, Ewa, Hickham Field, and the Ford Island Naval Station lay in ruins. The navy lost 112 planes, with only 36 surviving the attack, while almost half of the army's 123 aircraft were destroyed. Overall, 2,388 men were killed and 1,272 wounded. "What a holocaust!" wrote British Prime Minister Winston Churchill in red crayon on the paper that brought him news of the destruction.

The *Kido Butai* task force, intact and undiscovered, had lost only 29 of 353 attacking planes. Commander Fuchida and many of his pilots wanted to return for a second strike to wipe out Oahu's vast oil reserves and then go hunting the missing American carriers. Killing the oil tanks would make it difficult for the United States to so much as send its ships to sea or put planes into the air and could force the country to either ferry fuel all the way from the West Coast or pull the remainder of its fleet back to safer ports there. The war could be forced back to the American continent.

But Admiral Nagumo was hesitant. With the Americans now on alert, future attacks would incur unacceptable losses. He was a brave sailor, but neither a daring commander nor an aircraft carrier enthusiast. He had performed his duty, followed his specific orders to the letter, and that was enough for him. Failure to exploit an opportunity was a weakness that would show up repeatedly among Japanese naval leaders in the coming months. At Nagumo's signal, the mighty task force turned away to the north-northwest.

Aides encouraged Yamamoto to order Nagumo to reverse course for a bold second strike, but Yamamoto also had a dangerous habit for a senior commander. He preferred to trust the man on the scene. It was his habit to protect the honor of other officers, even if they fell short of an objective, and it would repeatedly betray him.

Throughout the morning, listeners to Station One of the Japanese broadcasting service NHK heard reports between segments of Beethoven's Fifth Symphony. The initial special bulletin was issued at six o'clock: "Before dawn today, December 8, the Imperial Army and Navy entered upon a state of hostilities with British and American forces in the West

Pacific." By noon, the newscasters read an Imperial Rescript that officially declared war, then added details of what was being called "a crippling raid" on the American fleet at Pearl Harbor.

Sacks filled with congratulatory mail and telegrams were delivered to the *Nagato* in the following days, and Admiral Yamamoto set about personally answering every one of them. The lights in his stateroom burned until the early hours as he wrote elaborate calligraphy strokes with a bamboo brush, keeping the great victory in perspective. Again and again, he pledged, "I swear I shall conduct further strenuous efforts and shall not rest on this small success in beginning the war."

BOOK I

Dark Days

1

Pilots Three

They didn't look like killers. At the time of Pearl Harbor, Rex Barber, John Mitchell, and Tom Lanphier had never so much as fired a shot in anger. Lanphier and Barber were so new to the military service that the brass bars on their collars showing they were second lieutenants had hardly had time to tarnish, and Mitchell was just happy that he was no longer clerking in his brother's store in Atlanta. All were pilots with the U.S. Army Air Corps, flying what were quaintly called "pursuit" planes in that age before they became more glamorously known as "fighters." Within seventeen months, all three would become hardened warriors who had survived countless deadly battles, led other men into ferocious fights, shot down Japanese planes, sunk Japanese ships, and bombed Japanese soldiers.

The President Johnson

Second Lieutenant Rex Barber was asleep aboard a passenger ship en route to Hawaii, snoring off a hangover, on the morning Pearl Harbor was attacked. The husky twenty-four-year-old pilot with startlingly green eyes had only won his wings about a month before and had only four hours of experience in flying P-40 pursuit planes, but he was headed for the Philippines as part of the headquarters squadron of the

35th Pursuit Group. One squadron of fighters and pilots from the 35th had already reached Manila, where reinforcements were being gathered to defend against a possible Japanese assault. Another squadron was almost there, aboard a second ship that had passed Hawaii. Barber's unit, filled with pilots just as untried as he, was the final group heading over.

They were going in style, sailing aboard the *President Johnson,* which gleamed like a beacon in the Pacific sunlight on Sunday morning as it rode alone, unescorted, on the blue sea. Its deep, wide holds were stuffed with big crates containing disassembled aircraft.

Despite the bright white hull and the single blue band around its stack that gave it the look of exactly what it was, a passenger liner, the *Johnson* had been specifically designed as a C3-type general cargo hauler by the United States Maritime Commission. The American President Lines operated it at a profit on peacetime passenger runs to the Orient, but in time of national emergency the *Johnson* and its sister "Presidents" were leased to the merchant marine to haul military personnel and cargo. The need to improve the defenses of the Philippines for an impending war had qualified as such an emergency.

The *Johnson* sailed from San Francisco on December 6, when the United States was still at peace. By the time the white hull slid beneath the Golden Gate Bridge, the pilots were partying and the first empty whiskey bottle had already hit the water. The ship had retained many of its peacetime accoutrements, and the young men were introduced to the good life at sea, with excellent food politely served by waiters, and there was more than enough booze to fuel card and dice games. Most had never experienced such casual elegance. They wound up portable phonographs and filled the air with popular tunes to help the time speed by. The entire first day of the voyage was a wonderful adventure, and they did not go to sleep until very late, rocking to the unfamiliar rhythms of the moving sea. Rex's schoolteacher mother had demanded that he write, but he could do that tomorrow.

Barber was from a close-knit, churchgoing family that had migrated to Oregon from Illinois on his mother's side, and from Massachusetts on his father's. They helped found the town of Culver, where Rex was born and raised. He had two sisters, but an older brother died as a baby. He would pester the girls but allow no one else to bother them. He might roll Eileen up in a rug and not let her out, but if she were alone in the schoolyard, Rex would break away from playing with the boys and stay with her.

From the beginning the stocky boy was a whirlwind of energy. The physical stamina honed through farm work translated easily into a natural athleticism, and he played football and baseball. Although a popular athlete can easily become outgoing and boisterous, Barber possessed a contrasting, quiet personality, which made his steady regimen of youthful pranks even more surprising.

After high school, Rex spent a year at a nearby small college, then transferred to Oregon State in Corvallis. He was not really interested in studying, for he had discovered a desire to fly through the stories he was told by his uncle, Edgar King, who had been a pilot in World War I. Still, it came as a shock to the family when, only a few weeks shy of getting his degree from Oregon State, he left college and joined the army as a private on the last day of September 1940.

He was accepted as an aviation cadet and left Oregon to learn how to fly Stearman biplanes at the Rankin Aeronautical Academy in Tulare, California. Then he moved up to BT-13s at Moffett Field and took his advanced training at Mather Field, outside of Sacramento. Barber possessed exceptional eyesight, and his boyhood skill at shooting rabbits made it easy for him to become an expert marksman as a soldier. He turned into a dead shot with the machine guns of his airplanes.

Within the 35th Pursuit Squadron, Barber was regarded as a quiet man who preferred to let his actions speak for him. No matter what happened, friends never saw Rex really lose control, although he never backed down from a challenge. When he knocked a front tooth out with a wrench while fixing a motorcycle, he simply got it fixed the next day and went back to work. About the most outrageous thing he would do was break out singing if he got drunk. Barber seemed guided by some sort of inner spirit that made him very confident about what he was doing and where he was going with his life. As one pilot said, "Rex had grit."

On the morning of December 7, he was shaken awake by some of his pals and wobbled topside as he felt the ship slowing down in the water. There was a buzz of news: The Japanese had attacked Pearl Harbor, the destination of their ship. The *Johnson* slid to a halt halfway between

Hawaii and California and bobbed in the Pacific Ocean until new orders were received. Then she turned around and sped for home. The pilots, boisterous the previous day and most of the night, quietly lined the railings, their sharp eyes searching the waters around them for the telltale periscope of a submarine and the horizon for enemy planes.

In so many ways, the party was over, both for those aboard the ship and for their fellow citizens back home. In the space of a few hours, peace had fled and war had come, and nothing would ever be the same.

Charlotte, North Carolina

The United States Army had prepared for war throughout 1941. The previous year, it had only 187,000 men, 488 machine guns, and 28 tanks. From that meager start, it had expanded to an active force of one and one-half million officers and men, although it took a narrow, single-vote majority in Congress to keep many of them in uniform for more than a year. The army spent the summer and fall of 1941 holding the largest maneuvers it had ever staged in peacetime, with mock battles raging from the state of Washington to the swamps of Louisiana. But the exercises lacked realism, due to the shortage of equipment and experience. Some troops used wooden sticks as rifles. Trucks with blaring loudspeakers drove about to simulate the sounds of attacking tanks. Generals fretted that the army just was not ready to fight a war and would suffer heavy losses if it met a competent enemy. A week after the exercises concluded, Japan struck Pearl Harbor.

One major purpose of the maneuvers was to prepare pilots for the roles they would play in combat. Eight pursuit groups of the Army Air Corps and a contingent of dive-bombers on loan from the U.S. Navy sowed confusion during the final war games in the Carolinas, roaring down on the masses of soldiers in simulated attacks. Had it been a shooting war, the planes would have mowed down the ground troops.

Among those flying the blunt-nosed P-40s that roamed the skies and swooped down in make-believe strafing runs on the unwary marching soldiers were First Lieutenant John William Mitchell and nine other pilots of the 70th Pursuit Squadron. The 70th was another squadron of the ill-starred 35th Pursuit Group, which had been staging through

Hamilton Field, outside of San Francisco, en route to the Philippines. The 70th had been formed only ten months earlier out of pilots and enlisted men who were carved from another squadron that had been sent to Alaska.

Throughout 1941, the new unit slowly coalesced into a team as more manpower and planes became available under the command of Captain Henry Viccellio, a square-jawed Virginian with a gift for organization and administration. Viccellio, at the age of thirty when the war started, was older than his charges, and had been around the Air Corps for a while. He had started as a private in 1934 and served as a bomber maintenance crewman in the Panama Canal Zone before being accepted for flight training. He was commissioned as an officer and a pilot in 1937.

By December 7, 1941, most of his experienced fliers had finished their war-game work in the Carolinas and were back at Hamilton, and Viccellio was trying to figure out how to teach the newer men to fly the P-36 Mohawk pursuit plane, in which they had to qualify before they were allowed to fly the more powerful P-40s. Viccellio's problem was that there was only such plane on the base, and it was out of commission with a cracked cylinder. The new pilots, eager youngsters showing up with silver wings on their chests but little experience, were sitting around wasting valuable time because they had nothing to fly.

Back in North Carolina, one of the P-40s also was malfunctioning, and John Mitchell, the unit's assistant operations officer, stayed behind to babysit it. Mitchell had only been promoted to first lieutenant on November 1.

When he learned about the attack on Hawaii, it was if someone had struck him in the face, for to him Pearl Harbor was not just some faraway, exotic place. He had been valedictorian of his high school graduating class in tiny Enid, Mississippi, and had joined the army in hopes of going to West Point, but he flunked the entrance exams and had to begin his military career as a buck private with Battery F of the 55th Coast Artillery in the Territory of Hawaii.

What started off as a failure for the skinny Mississippi boy turned into some of the best years of his life. In Hawaii Mitchell grew taller— although he would never quite reach five-feet, nine-inches in height— and put on some weight; the vision in his brown eyes improved; the constant sun bleached his brown hair almost white; and his confidence grew with a new maturity. He qualified as an expert rifle and pistol shot, handled the brigade's publicity section as the company clerk, and leavened the boring military duty by becoming an instructor in tennis and basketball. There was little that he had not enjoyed as a soldier in Hawaii, and he liked army life so much that he reenlisted. He spent a total of four years and five months in the islands before he got out, became a civilian for a while, then went back in as a fledgling aviator.

Mitchell still had friends in Hawaii and could easily picture the bombs falling on a place he considered paradise. As anger rose in him, he felt cold pleasure that he was an army pilot with a fast plane. He was ready to go to war the moment he read about Pearl Harbor in a Charlotte afternoon newspaper, having just spent a few hours watching Gary Cooper play America's greatest hero of World War I, Sergeant Alvin York.

In a brief telephone call to Captain Viccellio in California, Mitchell promised to get there as soon as his plane was fixed but asked permission to stop over in Texas long enough to marry a girl he had met during his flight school training. Viccellio gave his blessing but told Mitchell to hurry. They had work to do.

San Francisco

As the clock ticked down to war, the army air corps, desperate for pilots, pursued an aggressive advertising campaign that emphasized the ethos of the cocky, swaggering, scarf-in-the-wind fliers of the previous war. An unmarried young man between the ages of twenty and twenty-seven, with some college and able to present evidence of high moral character, could volunteer to become an aviation cadet in a civilian training program. It was an irresistible call for many children of the Great Depression. All of the volunteers were white men, for the military services had not yet integrated, but this was a chance for poor boys to break free, to do something different, and go up there, as the poet John Gillespie Magee Jr. would write, "where never lark, or even eagle, flew." They would spend nine months learning their new trade, three months each in primary, secondary, and advanced training, with planes of steadily increasing complexity. Then the freshly minted pilots would be farmed out to squadrons around the country. The year and alphabetical order of their graduating class, such as 41-E or 41-G, designated their place in the pecking order, and the earlier the better when it came to assignments and promotions.

New bases were needed to accommodate these new men and planes, and one of the best was created in a picturesque hilly area just north of San Francisco. Once the hunting grounds of the Miwok Indians, it passed into a Spanish land grant for Don Ignacio Pacheco and evolved over the years into farmland for settlers before becoming the Marin County Air Field. In the 1930s, it was sold to the U.S. Army Air Corps for one dollar. Engineers built a system of dikes and pumps to hold back the waters of San Pablo Bay, and broad runways were laid out that were actually six feet below sea level. It was unlike any other air base in the United States, not because of its huge, boxy hangars, but for the architecture of its other buildings. The massive edifices, ornate façades, gleaming white stucco walls, and red tile roofs gave it the look of a California mission. It was named Hamilton Field after Lieutenant Lloyd Hamilton, the first American pilot to fly with the Royal Flying Corps in World War I.

Originally laid out to serve two-engine bombers, it was soon deemed too small to be a permanent base for the newer four-engine Boeing B-17 Flying Fortresses and became the home of the 1st Pursuit Wing. The empty California sky was perfect for everything from single-plane training to massed flights of dozens of aircraft. In the coming years, thousands of pilots would pass between the twin towers of the entry-gate arch and go down the palm-lined Casa Grande Real to the tall and regal base headquarters building, with its wrought-iron balconies, arched loggia, and immaculate grounds.

For most of the new, young pilots, the best thing about Hamilton Field was that it was just over the Golden Gate Bridge from San Francisco, and when duty was not calling, they headed downtown in droves. That was exactly what Second Lieutenant Thomas P. Lanphier Jr. had done on the first weekend of December. He was a dashing soldier, slender and handsome in his crisp khaki uniform, with a thick shock of dark hair beneath his garrison cap. Lanphier checked into a hotel, then went out with his buddies in search of a party.

Whereas many of the newer pilots had experienced some sort of epiphany when they had first heard the grumble of an airplane engine overhead, looked up and thought—*That's for me!*—Lanphier had almost been born in a cockpit. He recalled his exciting boyhood in detail when he wrote his autobiography about ten years before his death. Entitled "At All Costs Reach and Destroy," the manuscript was circulated among friends but never published.

His dad was a West Pointer who had fought as a machine gunner in the trenches during World War I before learning to fly and rising to command the legendary 1st Pursuit Squadron. Flying was part of the family tradition, and other aviation pioneers were close friends. General Billy Mitchell, who had taught the world that planes could sink ships, helped young Tommy bury his dog after the animal was run over. The legendary Charles Lindbergh was a frequent guest at the house.

Tom was an army brat, born in Panama City while his father was away on jungle maneuvers, and his childhood memories included falling asleep to the mournful notes of Taps. Later, the family moved to Michigan after his father went to work in Detroit for Henry Ford. Smart as a whip, Lanphier devoured books and graduated from Grosse Pointe High School at the age of fifteen, by which time he already knew how to fly. Secretly instructed by a couple of his father's pilots, the boy had soloed in a rickety Jenny trainer when he was only thirteen. He worked as a copyboy for the *Detroit News* because he was too young to start college, studied Latin and typing on the side, and eventually went to Stanford University in California. Tom Lanphier Sr. had left the army to pursue a business career just in time for the Depression to wipe out his savings, and his namesake son had to intersperse his college years with work as a ranch hand and as a night reporter with the *San Francisco News* before he could graduate with a major in journalism in January 1941.

Lanphier joined the army at the urging of his father. He breezed through flight school, and won his wings exactly one month and one week before Pearl Harbor.

Although he often sat alone, listening spellbound to an extensive record collection of Shakespearean plays, the loquacious and flamboyant Tom loved to be in the middle of things. He was a good athlete, although his desire usually was bigger than his ability. There was one thing besides flying in which he excelled—he towered above all his companions in the storytelling department. He teased his fellow pilots with the story about when he was a newspaper reporter in California and was imperiously summoned to the hotel room of the English actor Laurence Olivier, about whom Lanphier had written a negative review. The door, Tom said, was opened for him by a nearly nude, gorgeous Vivien Leigh of *Gone With the Wind* fame.

His stories could stretch truth and reason, but his fellow pilots gave Lanphier a lot of room, primarily because he was really a good guy, fun to be around, but also because he could fly better than any of them. In the sky, he was untouchable, aggressive and easy with the control stick: They once watched him *bounce* a P-40 over a truck crossing the runway while he was trying to land. It would be good to have a pilot like that up there with them if, and when, they ever went into combat.

Although Lanphier played poker and caroused with the other guys, there was no doubt that he was on a higher social level than the rest of them. Older men of higher rank gravitated to him and fell silent when Tom started speaking in easy, erudite sentences, giving deference to someone obviously worth knowing. Young Tom Lanphier was directly plugged into the world at the top of the army air corps. He knew a lot of generals and famous people, and for an ambitious officer, that fact might someday help a career.

Saturday night, December 6, had been a long and fun episode, and he had returned late to his San Francisco hotel room. The ringing of the telephone at his bedside awoke him a few hours later. In his autobiography Lanphier wrote that his father was on the line, saying, "Turn on your radio. The war is on. They've leveled Pearl Harbor."

Lanphier senior was returning to the army, and would become a lieutenant colonel and the air intelligence officer for Army Chief of Staff George C. Marshall. He told his son to get back to his post at Hamilton Field.

2

War

Washington, D.C.

In the hours after Pearl Harbor, panic swept the United States. Sirens wailed around Los Angeles, where antiaircraft gunners hammered away at empty skies. Boys with BB guns and farmers with pitchforks went to the seashore to help defend the beaches, and deer hunters oiled up their rifles. The *San Francisco Examiner* squealed, "Japanese Invade West Coast." A few fully armed pursuit planes were parked on the runway at San Diego's Lindbergh Field as their pilots slept in the nearby grass.

Americans gathered around radios in their homes, in barber shops, beside potbellied stoves in hardware stores, on dusty ranches, in big city bars, and on street corners to hear the latest news bulletins, and children ran door to door spreading the word—*Pearl Harbor has been attacked!*

Around Washington, machine-gun emplacements were erected, security forces considered painting the White House black, and bewildered citizens walked up Pennsylvania Avenue to stand before the executive mansion and sing "God Bless America." President Franklin D. Roosevelt, whom they had just elected for a third term, met with congressional leaders and his cabinet and prepared to address Congress the next day. A gas mask was hung on the rear of his wheelchair. The country had been instantly united in a common cause, and the America First Committee, which had stridently opposed involvement in foreign wars, abruptly halted its activities and promised to support Roosevelt "until the conflict with Japan is brought to a successful conclusion."

The FBI set in motion what eventually would become a vast roundup of Japanese Americans. Although mass internments did not come for months, the decision to place Japanese Americans in camps had not been made in haste. Five years earlier, Roosevelt had suggested in a secret memorandum that "every Japanese citizen or noncitizen on the Island of Oahu [Hawaii] who meets . . . Japanese ships or has any connection with their officers or men should be secretly . . . identified and his or her name placed on a special list of those who would be the first to be placed in a concentration camp in the event of trouble."

In Tokyo, cheering crowds sang the national anthem and cheered General Hideki Tojo, who had taken over as both prime minister and war minister two months earlier to consolidate the grip of the Imperial Army on the civilian government. They cheered Admiral Yamamoto and his fleet and went to pray at the shrines of their ancestors. Newspapers printed special editions, and radio stations blared martial music. In the American embassy, Ambassador Joseph Grew bristled at the remarks of a U.S. senator who said that America would "lick hell out of the Japanese." Grew, who had watched the long, patient development of the Japanese military machine, commented, "This may be easier said than done."

The Japanese fleet hitting Hawaii had rocked America and fueled an instant hatred of the "Japs." Few Americans could name Emperor Hirohito or Prime Minister Tojo, and neither seemed large enough to carry the wrath of the entire United States of America. That outrage would come into focus only later, after Roosevelt proclaimed that December 7 was "a date which will live in infamy." Americans would learn that Admiral Yamamoto was the man responsible, and they would hate him with an unforgiving passion.

The Inland Sea

Pearl Harbor was not the only place on Yamamoto's mind, as he studied a battle chessboard that covered the entire Pacific Ocean.

To the north, there was no current threat to Japan, for the Russians had been mollified by a nonaggression pact signed in April. The agreement provided a tenuous truce between the old enemies because it allowed both sides to turn their attention elsewhere—the Russians had their hands full with Germany, and Japan wanted to secure its holdings in Manchuria in order to focus on its southward advance. Elsewhere in the north, the Japanese Army had Korea and much of northern China under brutal control. To the east, the defeat at Pearl Harbor had neutralized the Americans, and in the west, the coming land campaign in Burma and Indochina would threaten India, the crown jewel of the British empire, and keep England at bay. That left the south, and what the Japanese called the "Southern Resources Zone."

Japan contained little raw material of its own, and its military and industrial machines sucked up twelve thousand tons of limited oil reserves every day. Ninety percent of its oil had been imported from the United States until President Roosevelt's embargo. Ships could not sail and airplanes could not fly without fuel, so Japan had to find a new source or run out of oil within a year.

The solution lay in the South Pacific, an overflowing treasure house of nickel, chromium, iron, timber, rice, food of all sorts, 98 percent of all the rubber in the world, and, most important, oil. Japan's path to the rich oil fields in the Dutch East Indies and Asia's incredible mineral wealth led through Indochina, Thailand, Malaya, Singapore, New Guinea, and the Philippines, all the way down to Australia. Several of those plums had already been plucked, and the rest were waiting to be snatched from the weakened grasp of absentee British and Dutch government landlords and ruthlessly plundered.

The Philippines

Time added to the fog of war between Japan and the United States, since each new day begins at the International Date Line, which generally follows the meridian of 180 degrees down the middle of the Pacific Ocean. Mariners going east across that line gain a day, and they lose a day when they cross it heading west. Hawaii lay east of that line, so while it was still the morning of December 7 in the ravaged ruins of Pearl Harbor, even further to the east, in Washington, D.C., it was the middle of the same day. West of the line, in places such as Japan, it was already Monday, December 8.

There were no satellite-assisted communications and instant imagery to give faraway commanders and television audiences a real-time view of a battlefield in 1941, for satellites, personal computers, and commercial television did not exist. Throughout World War II the different date and vast time zone differences that spread across the Pacific played havoc with the passing of vital information. Day could be night, and night could be day, depending on where the two people who were trying to communicate were standing. The problem was resolved by reference to Greenwich Mean Time, the time that runs through England, on the zero degree meridian.

At 3:40 A.M. local time in the Philippines, on December 8, the telephone rang in the exquisite Manila Hotel penthouse suite of General Douglas MacArthur. Washington was calling to confirm something he had just found out, that Pearl Harbor had just been struck and that the Philippines might be next.

Manila lay thousands of miles from the United States, but Japanese airplanes based on the island of Formosa (now Taiwan) were only forty miles from the northernmost island of the Philippines, and an easy five hundred miles from Manila. Another task force of Admiral Yamamoto's ships, including two aircraft carriers, a pair of battleships, and eight cruisers, was ready to escort an invasion force of more than forty-three thousand soldiers to the Philippines.

The Japanese expected fierce resistance when they landed, for America's foremost general, MacArthur, was in charge of the defenses. The United States had taken the Philippines in 1898, during the Spanish-American War, and in 1936 the United States Congress had passed an act that would give the country total independence by 1946. Until then, it operated as a commonwealth, overseen by the United

States, and MacArthur was sent to build its defenses in 1935, two years before he retired.

If ever a man and a nation other than the place of his birth were inextricably tied to one another, it was Douglas MacArthur and the Philippines. His father, also a famous general who had won the Congressional Medal of Honor during the Civil War, had served as the military governor of the Philippines after the Spanish-American War. Douglas lived in the Philippines as a boy and served there as a soldier after graduating from West Point before the beginning of the twentieth century. He became a daring young general during World War I, swaggering along the trenches of France dressed in a long fur coat and a flapping scarf, carrying only a riding crop, and disdainful of the German guns. After the war he rose to become the chief of staff of the U.S. Army.

After that posting, MacArthur returned to the Philippines for what he thought would be his final assignment with the army; and when he retired from active duty, he agreed to become field marshal of the growing, modernizing country. A grateful Manila government made him a rich man. MacArthur carried the gold baton of field marshal until the summer of 1941, when he was recalled to active duty as head of the United States Army Forces in the Far East.

It is not unusual for someone in the military services to be retired at a permanent rank lower than he actually carried while on active duty, and the politically controversial MacArthur had ended his tenure with the U.S. Army wearing four stars but with the permanent two-star rank of major general, a development that angered him. Now that he had been returned to active duty and put in charge of defending the Philippines, he would be bumped back up to four stars by President Roosevelt, so there was no doubt of his authority. "By God, it was destiny that brought me here," he exclaimed.

Washington believed the Philippines could not be held in the face of a strong and determined Japanese attack, but MacArthur disagreed. He believed that his fleet of giant B-17 Flying Fortress bombers could shatter any invasion force, speedy torpedo boats would ravage the enemy fleet, and squadrons of sleek American pursuit planes would knock down the enemy's fighters. His Filipino and American infantry units would deal with any Japanese soldiers who might make it ashore.

Give me the planes, the men, the ammunition, and the equipment, he said, and I will hold all of the islands of the Philippine archipelago.

It was a fantasy. MacArthur's vaunted Filipino troops were mostly untrained, he had few combat-ready American units, the Japanese hopelessly outgunned the Asiatic Fleet, and his airplanes were few in number and lacked the necessary supporting infrastructure. What little fighting capability existed was hampered even more by the rainy season, and torrential downpours had turned much of the country into swampy bogs. He had miles of exposed landing beaches that he could not defend.

The general had demanded in August that thirteen squadrons of fighter planes and nineteen bombardment squadrons be sent to Manila, and during the middle months of 1941, ships such as the *President Johnson* began hauling men such as Lieutenant Rex Barber across the Pacific. But it was too little, and much too late.

Then, when the war began, MacArthur froze indecisively while his staff bumbled, and disaster swamped them.

Luck was on the general's side that first morning, because bad weather over the Formosan airfields kept the Japanese planes on the ground, and the Japanese commanders worried that MacArthur's long-range bombers would strike them first. The hours that had passed since Pearl Harbor had eliminated any hope of surprising him.

Japanese carrier aircraft flew a few quick strikes against outlying positions in the Philippines, but the American pursuit planes sent to intercept were unable to find them. Manila was edgy, and the Boy Scouts who cranked air raid sirens sounded three false alarms before regular army soldiers assumed that duty.

Almost two hundred Japanese planes took off when the haze lifted from Formosa about noon, some nine hours after the MacArthur had been alerted. The planes arriving over the Philippines were astonished to find the U.S. bombers and fighters parked close together at several airfields around Manila. They wheeled in for the attack and destroyed most of the American planes on the ground. They bombed fuel storage tanks into blazing ruins and wiped out vital support services. The battle for the blackened skies above Manila was over almost before it started, and it sealed the fate of the big U.S. naval base at nearby Cavite as well.

MacArthur's failure to act led to one of the most tragic military collapses in American history, a sad epic of retreat, defeat, and eventual surrender.

On the same day that Admiral Yamamoto attacked Hawaii and pulverized the Philippines, more of his ships landed Imperial Army troops on the Malayan Peninsula, and, in Thailand, two Japanese divisions crossed from previously occupied Indochina (Vietnam) and subdued the Bangkok government in less than six hours. Japanese bombs rained on the British colonies of Singapore and Hong Kong and on America's three precious island possessions in the Central Pacific—Guam, Wake, and Midway. In response, Great Britain declared war on Japan a few hours before Congress officially did so for the United States, but for the moment those announcements made no difference to the Japanese. For them, victory lay everywhere.

Baton Rouge, Louisiana

War is fluid, and the bigger the war, the more unpredictable the events within it. Armies and navies move slowly, but individual units, people, and equipment are shuffled like playing cards. Someone in a key position or a common soldier can be killed, transferred, promoted, incapacitated, or simply vanish forever, but his job does not end. Someone else steps in immediately to take over.

For now, Mitchell, Barber, and Lanphier were headed back to Hamilton Field, but the three fliers were virtual strangers to each other when the war started, and their destinies lay so far in the future that it could not even be imagined.

While they waited to see action, the hard-luck 67th Pursuit Squadron and its swashbuckling leader, Lieutenant Dale D. Brannon, would move quickly to the front lines of the expanding conflict. It would be the pioneer unit of the army air corps to fly and fight on a bloody island known as Guadalcanal.

Whereas most of pilots in the air corps were green and inexperienced at the time of Pearl Harbor, the same could not be said about

Brannon. He was over six feet tall and had to fold up like an accordion to fit into the cockpit of the small pursuit planes. Skinny and angular, with a sharp chin and a perpetually sardonic grin, Brannon had no nerves at all. He was a natural stick-and-rudder man with a special touch for flying machines. That was what usually got him into trouble— and back out again.

He had come out of a small Ohio town thirty miles from Cleveland, an only child who delivered newspapers as a kid and worked for the local milkman. One day a barnstorming pilot landed his biplane in a nearby field and offered rides for a small price. Brannon, too young and too broke, could only watch from the ground, fascinated, as the pilot took other people up and did all sorts of wondrous things in the sky. He was hooked. Two years at Ohio State were enough to qualify him for aviation cadet training, and he left college in 1937 and never looked back. Flying was easy for him from the first moment, and he coasted through Class 38-A. "I loved it so," he would later recall. "My only question was, 'Where's my airplane and where can I go?' "

Brannon ran through air corps assignments until he became a test pilot at Selfridge Field near Detroit, where he was selected to try out the two original YP-38s that Lockheed had delivered to the army. The builders and civilian test pilots were convinced that the unusually shaped, twin-engine planes called "Yippies" could be the fighter plane of the future, but the aircraft still had to meet tough military standards. Only then would the experimental Y designation be stripped away and the plane could become the P-38, which indeed did prove itself to be one of the best aircraft of the entire war. The relationship between Brannon and the big Yippie was more of a marriage than a job, and he and his pal Lieutenant Ollie Cellini flew the birds in every conceivable way, and liked what they found. Nothing in the skies could touch them.

At an air show held at Selfridge one day in 1941, Brannon and Cellini were instructed to perform a demonstration with their fast new airplanes. An Argentine military dignitary would be present, along with his host, General Henry H. "Hap" Arnold, who was destined to become the top man in the air corps during the war. Brannon was foolishly instructed to put on a show.

As an excited announcer introduced "the Thunderbirds," Brannon and Cellini highballed down from the sky and screamed right across the airfield at almost four hundred miles per hour, only a few feet above the ground. The crowd, punished by the propeller wash and roaring engines, went wild with applause and cheers. Since the first pass went so well, they did it again, but this time with only one engine apiece. Again, there were cheers from the crowd, but horror from Hap Arnold, who thought the two valuable YP-38s were in the hands of madmen.

Brannon was just getting warmed up. Looking over, he saw Cellini still on his wingtip, matching every wiggle, and gave a hand signal. Cellini grinned. The big planes soared up and up, the pilots cut both engines on each plane, and they fell over in slow, silent rolls. Totally without power, they toppled like rocks with wings, and the lack of sound in the sky was matched by silence among those watching from the ground until the pilots hit the switches, kicked the YP-38s back to life, and roared away safely. "We knew the engines would come back up," Brannon said, for they had done the maneuver before as part of the test schedule. "The audience dearly loved it, but I angered a lot of people."

When he landed, Brannon was hauled before General Arnold, who chewed him out. He was grounded, lost his flight pay bonus, and was banished to a desk job at a radar school in Canada. His entire career would fluctuate wildly as his skill as a fighter pilot and ability as a combat leader would almost, but not quite, balance his habit of making important enemies. The Selfridge show would not be his last run-in with Hap Arnold.

But Pearl Harbor put a sudden premium on good pilots in the air corps, and Brannon was allowed to come home from Canada. He flew to Baton Rouge, Louisiana, and joined the 67th Pursuit Squadron, where the word was that he was to be sent as far away as possible, as soon as possible. Brannon didn't care.

Awaiting Brannon and tens of thousands more young Americans just like him was a war of unimaginable magnitude in the South Pacific. At the razor's edge was the Combined Fleet of Admiral Isoroku Yamamoto, one of the most formidable navies ever created. The two men would never meet, but both were immersed in the flow of historical inevitability. Lieutenant Brannon, who would survive the war, was one of the main reasons that Admiral Yamamoto would not.

3

Yamamoto

Sadayoshi Takano was playing a game of Japanese checkers in the crisp April of 1883 when his wife asked what they should name their new baby. He considered the subject insignificant. The poor man worked as a schoolmaster and dairy farmer and was barely scratching out a living; he already had one daughter and five sons and was married to his second wife, the sister of his deceased first wife. Takano hardly paused in his game and curtly instructed her to call the child "*Iso-ro-ku*" (Japanese for the numbers five, ten, and six), since Sadayoshi was fifty-six years old at the time. During World War II, the child who had been so casually named would become known around the globe as he changed the face of modern naval warfare. By then, he would be Isoroku Yamamoto.

Japan closed its doors to the outside world in 1638 after several centuries of contact with foreign "barbarians." Leaders feared that the unique culture of their land was threatened and that the Christian religion being spread by priests and missionaries was undermining the divinity of the emperor, who was the living descendant of the Sun Goddess Amaterasu. A small Dutch trading post was allowed to operate at Nagasaki, but any Japanese leaving or entering the country faced the penalty of death as Japan withdrew into itself for the next 215 years.

Rival clans and shoguns constantly fought for power, but the lack of outside contact condemned the country to remaining a feudal, medieval society. Although quaint and beautiful, Japan steadily fell behind as other nations developed during the Industrial Revolution. Elaborate rituals of common life, strict codes of behavior, and the swagger of the elite class of samurai masked a national decay.

The isolation ended in the summer of 1853 when the young United States was pushing to achieve its "manifest destiny." After taking California from Mexico, America launched into the Pacific Ocean to expand its trade routes, and Matthew Perry, a jowly commodore in the United States Navy, showed up in Edo (Tokyo) Harbor with a squadron of ships. Instead of pleading for entry, the commodore forced the issue, exercised iron-fisted diplomacy, and the Japanese realized their time alone was over. Long swords could not match the big cannon aboard huge ships powered by steam, not oars, not wind. The Japanese chose to accept change, particularly since the new foreigners wanted to export goods, not their religious beliefs.

Imperial rule was restored in 1868, when the Meiji emperor crushed the ruling shogun and set about relentlessly modernizing his country. Japan made lightning advances in almost every field, from education to technology, learning from the outside world it had shunned for so long, but always incorporating the new developments into traditional Japanese ways.

One clan on the wrong side in the civil war against the emperor's new central government was the samurai family of Sadayoshi Takano, who lived in Niigata Prefecture, a bleak land where the Japanese island of Honshu curls north along the Sea of Japan. Regional lords had always provided well for their samurai, buffering such warriors from the travails of a peasant's life. Now the lords were gone, and such men had to fend for themselves, but without their swords. Life became particularly difficult for those families who had fought against the central government and had to eke out a living like the poorest peasant. After the birth of his seventh child, Sadayoshi was pleased to become the headmaster at a primary school in a larger town.

Isoroku embarked on the harsh educational path that awaited every Japanese boy. Foreign nations had shown the need for a strong military arm, and as the Meiji emperor and his countrymen grasped that doctrine, their children became the reservoir of a new militarism.

The education was intellectually stimulating and physically demanding, and even dangerous. In elementary school the teacher at times would extinguish the tiny *kotatsu* that was the only source of heat in the room in order to teach young Isoroku and his classmates to lock out physical discomfort and concentrate on their studies. They wrote calligraphy even as their fingers turned blue with cold.

In middle school Isoroku continued his quasi-military education. Students made long-distance marches in horrible weather, clashed with opposing "armies" of other rifle-bearing teenagers, and slept in open fields. An entire generation of young men, trained in military discipline from their early years, was capable of withstanding incredible hardship to carry out their duties.

A Westernized code of laws was adopted in 1896, and Japan stepped onto the world stage. It reached diplomatic agreement with the United States over control of the Hawaiian Islands and signed a mutual defense alliance with Great Britain against Russia. Czar Nicholas was moving aggressively into Asia, and Japan was uncomfortable with Russian troops and ships being stationed along the China coast and in Korea.

Young Isoroku Takano grew stronger physically as his mind expanded to accommodate new ideas. He ran to and from school, worked hard at gymnastics, and played baseball, a sport imported from America and wholeheartedly adopted by Japan. His conditioning was tested one day when high winds capsized his boat while he was out fishing alone, and he swam through freezing water to the shelter of a cold cave, where he survived for two days before swimming home again.

The Meiji emperor had allowed Christians back into Japan, and a man recalled today only as the Missionary Newall introduced Isoroku to the English language. By first learning to read the Bible, the boy discovered Western literature. Although he was a total product of Japanese training and prized his heritage, he realized there was more to the world than what was between him and the horizon.

In 1901 the country boy from a small town placed second among three hundred students in a competitive examination and won admittance to the Imperial Japanese Naval Academy at Etajima. As a midshipman, he learned the secrets of the seas, winds, and tides while clinging to the ratlines high above the deck of a tilting windjammer under full sail. He graduated seventh in his class, and was immediately sent to war.

The Russian designs on Asia triggered a collision with Japan in 1904. It began with an attack by Japan's powerful new navy on Russian ships tied up at Port Arthur in China, and a brutal ground war began. To the surprise of foreign observers, the modern Japanese army had little difficulty smashing the dispirited Russians, who were far from home, where there was talk of insurrection against the czar. The following year, Japan's foremost admiral, Heihachiro Togo, lured an ineffective Russian fleet into a decisive battle in the waters between Japan and Korea. The Russians, who had sailed halfway around the world, never had a chance. Togo maneuvered his own fleet into an attack formation using the classic naval maneuver of "crossing the T" of the enemy force as it sailed in line, ship after ship, bow to stern. Togo was able to fire all of his guns in deadly broadsides against ships that could respond only with their forward batteries. The Battle of Tsushima Strait was a slaughter. It became a textbook model of naval strategy and sealed the Japanese belief that big naval battles could decide wars.

Admiral Togo became the most famous admiral in Japanese history until Isoroku Yamamoto hit Pearl Harbor. Together, their victories destroyed the myth that a yellow man could not beat a white man.

Ensign Isoroku Takano, twenty-one years old and fresh out of the naval academy, was a gunnery officer aboard the cruiser *Nisshin* in that famous battle. As was the custom, he had donned clean underwear and a fresh uniform when he reported to his battle station. The Russian warships managed to punish the *Nisshin,* and the young ensign was severely injured. He later wrote, "With a great roar, a shell scored a direct hit on the forward eight-inch gun that still remained. Billows of acrid smoke covered the forward half of the vessel, and I felt myself almost swept away by a fierce blast. I staggered a few steps—and found that the record charts that had been hanging around my neck had disappeared, and that two fingers of my left hand had been snapped off and were hanging by the skin alone." His father would save and treasure that blood-soaked uniform.

The revered Meiji emperor died in 1912, and his son Yoshihito assumed the throne as the Taisho emperor. Meiji's eldest grandson, Michinomiya, was invested as crown prince, but was still a child, and walked to the Peer's School through streets lined with awed Japanese citizens who bowed before him. He would become a figure of destiny, known to the world as the Emperor Hirohito.

The aging parents of Isoroku Takano died in 1913, and he was steered into a Japanese tradition in which a family without a male heir could adopt one. At the age of thirty, in a Buddhist ceremony he was formally brought into the well-to-do family of Tatewaki Yamamoto, and the 1916 graduating class of the Naval Staff College included the officer's new rank and name—Lieutenant Commander Isoroku Yamamoto.

Yamamoto was late in taking a wife, for he disdained highborn ladies who could not put up with the demands of a career naval officer. In 1918, he married Reiko Mihashi, a hardworking farmer's daughter who was eleven years younger and one inch taller than he. Only a year after they wed, he left his new bride behind and headed for Washington, D.C., as the new assistant naval attaché for the Japanese embassy. Over the years, the distance between husband and wife grew to be such a chasm that she was almost an afterthought for Yamamoto, and Reiko created a separate life for herself and their children. His biographer Hiroyuki Agawa reported that she never once even went for a private walk with her famous spouse.

Although he was to grow distant from his wife, except for the rare visit home and becoming a father, he exuded popularity and gregariousness. He eventually would become a widely recognized and valued customer at several establishments in the pleasure districts, and would lose his heart to one particular geisha, Chiyoko Kawai.

Where the usual Japanese man was quiet and withdrawn, the

personable Yamamoto was just the opposite. From the moment he set foot aboard the *Suwa Maru* for the trip across the Pacific to America, he befriended fellow passengers. He had already tasted the outside world during naval cruises to Korea, China, Australia, and the West Coast of the United States and felt comfortable around people from different countries. His evolving view of the world also marked him as different from other insular Japanese officers, and he sought out Americans to talk about Babe Ruth and the Bible. Although he was from a land where honor meant everything, Yamamoto thought nothing of making people laugh in the first-class salon by standing on his head, twirling plates, and doing somersaults. No one, however, thought him to be a clown. By the time the *Suwa Maru* docked in San Francisco, he had a circle of new friends, and all of them agreed that the brilliant, entertaining Commander Yamamoto was a man with a future.

The official job station was Washington, but he spent only a week there, playing tourist and seeing the White House, the monuments and the center of American government. Then he traveled to his true duty assignment in Boston, crossing the Charles River to study at Harvard University from 1919 to 1921. About seventy other Japanese students were also enrolled at Harvard, giving him a natural base of support as he plunged into a consuming regimen of study of all things American, particularly the English language. He considered sleep a waste of valuable time, and his lights burned late into the night. Yamamoto was devouring new ideas: The League of Nations was being created, although the United States refused to join; Russia was convulsing in civil war and Czar Nicholas and his family were murdered; and scientist Robert Goddard suggested that rockets could reach the moon. Composers like Fats Waller, Irving Berlin, and George Gershwin wrote toe-tapping music; boxer Jack Dempsey became heavyweight champion of the world; and Sir Barton became the first winner of the Triple Crown of horseracing.

Yamamoto also made every relaxation break worthwhile. He developed a passion for the game of bridge, which required competition, bluffing, daring, and reading the opposition. He said that any Japanese who could master the thousands of ideographs of their own language had no problem keeping track of only fifty-two cards. He also became an expert poker player, always playing for money. If he were broke, he would sometime bet parts of his uniform. American naval officers who sat at his table usually left somewhat poorer, and Yamamoto developed a reputation as a bold, careful gambler who rarely lost.

As a military officer, Yamamoto had kept close watch on the military developments surrounding World War I. Although he was trained for the big ships and had become a hero when he was wounded in a classic naval gun battle, he saw that the future had wings. Admirals in Tokyo still had little use for planes, but Yamamoto was delighted that they had finally agreed to build Japan's first rudimentary aircraft carrier, the tiny, seventy-five-hundred-ton *Hosho*. "The most important ship of the future will be the ship to carry airplanes," Yamamoto predicted.

Few naval officers in the entire world believed as he did. The officer-student noted that the United States and the Western world were making great, fast strides in aviation. Daily airmail service started between Chicago and New York, two aviators made a nonstop flight across the Atlantic, while two others flew from London to Australia in 135 hours, and an inventor named Glenn Martin built a long-range bomber. To Yamamoto, the drumbeat was leading to an age of aerial superiority in military strategy.

He paid special attention to the incredible industrial base that was powering the nation and supporting the technological advances. He watched cars roll off Detroit assembly lines, saw the factories building pursuit planes, and felt the heat of the Pittsburgh steel furnaces. He toured oil fields and became such an expert on the economics of petroleum—the lifeblood of any modern military power—that several American companies extended job offers. Yamamoto concluded that the United States would be able to field a military machine that would dwarf the armaments of World War I. The oil needed to run such a juggernaut was cheap and plentiful, and America's vast agricultural heartland could feed armies. Japan had about one-tenth of the production capacity available in the United States, and years later, not long before World War II began, Yamamoto told some schoolchildren, "Japan cannot beat America. Therefore Japan should not fight America."

Although Japan had sided with the victorious allies in World War I, Washington and London wanted to keep Japan's growing navy in check. At an international naval conference in 1921, Tokyo was forced to accept an agreement under which it would build only three warships for every five built by the United States and Great Britain. The "5-5-3" agreement was regarded as an insult by many Japanese officers who wanted parity with those other nations and felt the treaty relegated the Japanese navy to an inferior status. Yamamoto, however, did not disagree with the result of the conference: If Japan could not defeat America, of what use was parity in naval strength? The differences were sharp, and the navy began to divide into the "fleet faction" that demanded equality, and the "treaty faction," of which Yamamoto was a part. Importantly, Emperor Hirohito also favored the treaty, but the schism would have far-reaching consequences within Japanese politics.

Yamamoto returned to Japan in 1921 and fathered a son to pass on the Yamamoto name, thus fulfilling part of his obligation to his new family. Then he was back at sea aboard a cruiser, after which he attended the prestigious Navy Command School. He was promoted to captain in 1923 and dispatched as an admiral's interpreter on a grand tour that included England, France, Italy, Austria, Germany, and the United States. He delighted in spending some personal time at the gaming tables in Monaco and walked away as a big winner at roulette.

While he was abroad, Japan was rocked for six days and nights by a series of giant earthquakes in 1923 that flattened Tokyo and Yokohama and killed a hundred thousand people. For a nation that was already unable to meet its agricultural needs, and with poverty rife, the earthquake was a severe blow. From London, Yamamoto said his country remained basically strong, and thought people should buy stocks while prices were depressed.

By the time he returned to Japan, Yamamoto was positioned for further advancement, exceptionally well educated and equally outstanding in ship duty, combat, and diplomatic experience. He was clearly moving up in the world.

After a bit of shore duty, he was named captain of his own ship, a cruiser. It would have been the pinnacle of success for many naval officers. Yamamoto, however, wanted to command airpower, not a small ship of the line, and he maneuvered himself into a staff assignment at the home of Japan's fledgling aviation corps.

It was there that he began to create history.

·   ·   ·

The cocky young aviators looked with bemusement at their new executive officer, a forty-year-old with a long record of serving on conventional ships. He could not even fly! The cadets were lithe and athletic, while he was short and pudgy. Yamamoto ignored them and bored in to learn everything he could about naval aviation, taking lessons to become a pilot himself. He did not pounce until he was confident that he knew the subject of flying better than the students.

A sudden burst of strict new regulations on uniforms, discipline, and behavior soon followed. The pilots had enjoyed the feel of their long hair flapping in the wind of an open cockpit; they were shocked when the executive officer, whose own hair was already gray and shorn to the skull, ordered that their hair be cut "just like mine." Flying was not some gift the gods bestowed on a special few, he announced, but a dangerous and deadly business, and they must learn to rely upon instruments, not instinct. There would be intense physical training, difficult classroom studies, impossible navigation problems, an emphasis on night flying, and absolute obedience in the cockpit. Anyone not meeting the new standards was banished and never allowed back on the base beside Lake Kasumigaura.

Over the next eighteen months, Yamamoto transformed the school into an elite camp from which only the most gifted pilots could graduate. As the men came around to his way of doing things, he lowered his wall of reserve and displayed the gregarious manner with which he so easily won affection and loyalty from subordinates. Although he did not drink alcohol, he bought them drinks, mingled at their parties, defended them against their critics, protected them against their own errors, advanced their careers, grieved with them when a brother pilot did not return from a training mission, played cards with them, and listened to their gripes. By the time he was done eighteen months later, the academy was turning out first-rate pilots who swore by Yamamoto's name. When a passenger liner departed Japan in January 1925 to take him back to Washington for a tour as the Japanese naval attaché, the daredevil pilots of Kasumigaura buzzed the ship in salute.

On Christmas Day 1926, the Taisho emperor died. He had long been in ill health and mentally unstable, and for the past five years, his twenty-six-year-old son, the Crown Prince Michinomiya, had legally acted on the emperor's behalf in government matters. With the death of the Taisho emperor, the crown prince finally assumed the throne and became a god, the 124th Son of Heaven. His name would become recognized worldwide—the Emperor Hirohito—and his reign would be Showa, which in English means "Enlightened Peace."

Nothing, however, was as it seemed. Though placid on the surface, Japan was ready to burst; it was the most crowded nation on earth, the islands jammed with people. The population of 80 million was growing at a rate of another million every year, poverty was rampant, and government scandals stirred unrest. As the nation seethed, the strength of its military forces became a source of national pride. Ever since the victory over the Russians, the army and navy budgets had ballooned, and the military was a powerful political force of its own, virtually free of civilian control.

Many young officers wanted to use that power for change.

For the two years following his duty at Kasumigaura, Yamamoto was based in Washington, where he acquired even more Western polish by mingling easily at diplomatic gatherings. On duty, he concentrated his considerable skills on getting to know the U.S. Navy, its ships, planes, and influential officers on an intimate basis. In off hours, he gambled in Cuba, where he bought fine cigars to give to his visitors, attended White House receptions, played poker and bridge with American officers, watched the Washington Senators play baseball, and saw racism directed against the Japanese in California.

He was always near a deck of cards, and always had a book to read. In those years, one of the most popular novels was *The Great Pacific War: A History of the American-Japanese Campaign of 1931–33*, in which the author, Hector C. Bywater, postulated a sneak attack by the Japanese on the U.S. fleet in Manila Bay. The book was required study by the Japanese officer corps.

And aviation was becoming impossible to ignore. Charles Lindbergh flew solo across the Atlantic in 1927.

That same year, Japan launched the sleek, thirty-thousand-ton aircraft carrier *Akagi*, which had been converted from a battle cruiser. It carried seventy-two planes, dwarfing its only predecessor. Another carrier, the *Kaga,* would follow in 1928.

After duty in Washington, Yamamoto was promoted to the naval general staff in Tokyo, then was sent to sea to brush up his sea skills as captain of the cruiser *Isuzu.* On December 10, 1928, the man and his destiny finally met. Isoroku Yamamoto was named captain of the *Akagi.* At last, with a flat deck and an open sea, he would be able to explore naval aviation to its fullest.

Just as he got his wish of a carrier command, however, his country was beginning a long slide into a terrible decade of woe—trouble of such magnitude that the era would be known as the Dark Valley. Despite his own beliefs, Yamamoto and his navy would be swept along like debris in a flooding river.

4

C⁄in⁄C

Within a month of stepping aboard as captain of the *Akagi*, Yamamoto captured the imagination of his crew and pilots. Not only did he prove that he could handle the big ship with consummate skill, but he bantered easily with pilots, flyer to flyer. Discipline was absolute, but he was no martinet; he would watch his officers play *shogi* and chess in the wardroom, chuckling if they made bad moves.

Early in 1929, when he took the carrier into a fleet exercise off the coast of China, the *Akagi* was his ship in every way. The boat was ready, the pilots aggressive, and the brainy staff busy. Yamamoto was supremely confident as he watched his planes tear away from the long, wooden flight deck, one after another, their propellers clawing into the wind. Soon the individual planes joined in orderly formations overhead, silhouettes against gray skies, and set out to attack an "enemy" battleship. The opposing fleet in the maneuvers would never expect him to attack out of a storm front, and as he expected, the *Akagi* planes surprised and "bombed" the target ships. The victory, however, came at a terrible price.

The weather had been bad at launch time and grew steadily worse after the planes took off, then it turned horrific while they searched out the battleship and made their attack. It finally closed around them like a thick dark veil on the return trip. As they bounced through hellish skies, the pilots became disoriented, then scattered, then totally lost. Yamamoto furiously plunged the *Akagi* through the storm, looking for a break in the weather, trying to find a clear spot where he could recover his planes. But every one of them crashed, and every pilot died. Yamamoto stayed on the bridge throughout a futile search that spanned several days. He refused to eat, and at times wept for his lost men.

But what was torture for his soul was a test for his mind. Were there lessons in this disaster? This was a war exercise, after all, and in a war, terrible things happened. He considered death in a realistic training exercise tantamount to a man dying as a hero in real battle. His ships needed better navigation equipment and electronic beacons to bring the planes back home. The planes themselves needed improvements, and his pilots needed more work on trusting their instruments, flying at night, and landing on a storm-pitched flight deck. An aircraft carrier without planes was naked and useless.

Such a catastrophe might have ended the career of a lesser man, for Yamamoto had lost many skilled aviators of the fledgling naval aviation corps, pilots who were believed capable of superhuman feats. But his supporters were able to point out that those pilots also had removed an enemy battleship from the seas. Their sacrifice was a setback, not a waste.

Yamamoto spent less than a year as captain of the *Akagi*. While the Great Depression spread around the world, causing even more economic hardship in Japan, Yamamoto was once again sent abroad. This time he attended the London Naval Disarmament Conference, where the United States, Great Britain, and Japan again attempted negotiations on the size of their respective navies. He was promoted to a rank—rear admiral—commensurate with the diplomatic duty.

Other political and military representatives would handle the actual negotiations, but Yamamoto was needed as a thinker: He knew America as well as any Japanese, spoke English fluently, and could recite the relative strengths and weaknesses of the United States, British, and Japanese fleets. He was popular at cocktail parties, but spoke only Japanese on official occasions, using the translation time to analyze the faces and mannerisms of the person to whom he was talking. For a variety of reasons, the three nations could not agree on how to alter the 5-5-3 treaty, which was about to expire, and the conference foundered. Everything remained the same.

The fleet faction and the treaty faction remained at loggerheads, although this time the emperor had directly intervened to prevent a rupture of the agreement, and the fleet faction obeyed their god-monarch and backed down, but only for the time being. As a minor member of the delegation, Yamamoto had not drawn attention to his own viewpoints, and he was satisfied to leave the political arena altogether when, in 1930, he was named head of the technical division of the navy's aeronautics department.

He had loved the assignment as captain of the *Akagi,* but this particular job ashore was even better. After a career spent watching and obeying orders, Yamamoto was finally in a position to *do* something about naval airpower. His job was to build new weapons systems, and he set about doing so with his usual vision. His ideas almost swamped the drawing boards of the engineers as he began building the most modern naval air fleet in the world.

He worked with industrial giant Mitsubishi to develop a new type of single-wing airplane for use both as the primary carrier plane, a land-based fighter, or—when floats were attached to wings and belly—a combat plane that could operate from an open lagoon. It was called the A6M Zero-Sen (Type oo fighter), and for years to come there would be nothing in the world that could match it. With the Nakajima company, he started planning a new type of torpedo-carrying attack plane, called the Kate, that was fast, tough, and lethal. A twin-engine bomber with an incredibly long range was also needed, because Yamamoto saw the need to be able to cover the vast distances between islands in the Pacific. The fully loaded Mitsubishi G4M Betty could fly a 2,000-mile mission. A dozen years later, Yamamoto would be shot down aboard a Betty.

With the catastrophe that befell his pilots on the *Akagi* in the forefront of his mind, Yamamoto began to improve carriers and to stress rigorous flight training. He formed fourteen new squadrons and created a land-based naval air force to complement the carrier fleet. Anyone trying to attack Japan would now have to wade through a ferocious curtain of naval airpower just to get close.

. . .

That, however, was a defensive mind-set, typical of the treaty faction leaders and contrasting with the aggressive spirit and capability desired by the fleet faction. The political landscape in Japan was becoming volatile. The Imperial Japanese Army was expanding its power in the government, and war was in the wind. In 1931, the Kwantung Army, which had been stationed in China since the end of the Russo-Japanese War, seized Manchuria. That started a chain of events that would give the generals control of the civilian government in Tokyo. The next year, a prime minister was assassinated.

The zealous army generals found allies in the fleet faction admirals who were taking control of the navy. Together, they usurped 43 percent of the national budget and refused to tell the legislature how the money was being spent. Yamamoto was comfortably protected in his backwater technical job as the old-line admirals committed much of their budget to the construction of four superbattleships, each of which would be a seventy-two-thousand-ton behemoth with eighteen-inch guns. They would be the biggest ships in the world. Sheer folly, Yamamoto thought. He said they were like "elaborate religious scrolls which old people hang up in their homes. They are of no proved worth. They are primarily a matter of faith, not reality."

He continued to dodge the political limelight with his next job, in late 1933, when he became commander of the 1st Air Division of the Imperial Combined Fleet. Yamamoto was back safely at sea, his reputation intact, as Tokyo's military and political scene became more and more unsettled. The fleet faction knew he did not agree with them, but they needed his technical and seagoing experience and would put up with him—as long as he remained far from the center of power. Aboard the carriers, Yamamoto plunged into his usual rigorous training for the air fleet and pioneered the tactic of massing carriers for a powerful aerial strike instead of having a single carrier operate alone.

The admiral would have been quite content to stay out there, but the emperor personally requested that Yamamoto be appointed chief Japanese representative in preliminary talks for another naval conference in London. It would vault him to international attention, but at a great price. The treaty faction supporters, he, and even the emperor were about to sell out to the growing power of the ultranationalist right-wingers. Yamamoto was about to show that he was military to the core and could act against his own beliefs when his country called.

To give him rank more appropriate to his mission, Yamamoto was promoted to vice admiral. The ship that carried him on the first leg of his trip to London docked in Seattle, and he once again set out across the United States, this time on the Great Northern Railway. As it rolled through the Rocky Mountains and across the Great Plains, Yamamoto remained secluded in his cabin, passing the hours playing cards with his staff. He had no need to look out the window, for he had seen America before.

After attending a college football game in Chicago, Yamamoto went to New York and stayed at the Astor Hotel, playing a role he described as "the great man" before sailing on to England. He sidestepped all requests for interviews by American newspaper reporters by having aides apologize that their admiral did not speak their language.

Arriving by train at Waterloo Station on October 10, 1934, Yamamoto told newspaper reporters, in perfect English, "Japan can no longer submit to the ratio system. There is no possibility of compromise by my government on that point." His action killed the detested 5-5-3 treaty, which he called "a national degradation," and removed all limits on the size of the fleet or the ships in it.

He returned to Tokyo via the Trans-Siberian Railway in February 1935, after having snubbed an offer to meet Adolf Hitler during a stopover in Berlin. When Yamamoto got home, he was met by misty weather and the thunderous welcome of some two thousand people, including members of secret societies that only five months earlier had considered killing him. Amid *banzai* hurrahs and waving flags, Yamamoto moved through lines of Tokyo citizens to the Imperial Presence, where he received personal congratulations from Hirohito.

After decades of gloom, a sense of pride animated the country. The colorful past finally seemed truly like the past, and the once-revered men who carried swords, dressed in kimonos, and wore pigtails now seemed more like figurines than real people. The Meiji emperor had been worshipped, and Admiral Togo had gained prominence during the Russo-Japanese War, but those days were also part of history. It was time for a new hero, a man of the times, someone who could match the barbarians on every front, whether in international negotiations or man-to-man or as a warrior. Emperor Hirohito, though beloved, was bland; he was a marine biologist and looked more like a rumpled professor than a god. Politicians were considered cheap; the army was powerful, but generals and political leaders were constantly being changed, forced out of office, killed, or ignored. There was only one man whom the public could openly embrace as a living symbol of the spirit of Bushido—the way of the warrior. Isoroku Yamamoto was a hero to match his day.

The adulation, plus the obvious support of the emperor, frightened the fleet faction and the army: Yamamoto might begin speaking out. While he had done their bidding by breaking the 5-5-3 treaty, the admiral was known to advocate peace, and his new public standing could provide a platform for his views. A not-so-gentle shove was made to push Yamamoto into retirement.

He was given a job with a nice office in the Navy Ministry, and nothing to do. The admiral spent several idle months with his family and began to frequent geisha houses in the Roppongi District, where he was treated as an honored guest. That meant he didn't have to pay, because his presence drew other, wealthier customers. "Admiral Yamamoto was no saint," wrote Sokichi Takagi, whose observation was published by biographer Agawa. "Few men could have been as fond of gambling and games of chance as he . . . *shogi, go,* mah-jongg, billiards, cards, roulette—anything would do." In the scalding baths, the girls soothed the admiral's body, which had been horribly scarred by the explosion in the Russo-Japanese War, and teased him about his two missing fingers. The geishas would hold up ten fingers to tease him that they usually charged one hundred sen for their company but said he could have a twenty percent discount. The nickname "Eighty Sen" pleased him.

He worked with the ministry to further strengthen the naval air arm and encouraged the building of more aircraft carriers for the Imperial Navy. In a unique victory, one of the new superbattleships was to be turned instead into the world's biggest carrier. But Yamamoto was on the sidelines at a critical moment in February 1936 when aggressive young army officers attempted a coup that turned bloody, then failed when the emperor personally intervened.

The militarists had overextended their reach, and a period of political quiet settled over troubled Japan. The emperor chose a civilian to be prime minister, and Admiral Mitsumasa Yonai was made the navy minister in the cabinet. The expansionist, aggressive fleet faction was displeased, for not only was Yonai a moderate, but he selected Admiral Isoroku Yamamoto to be his vice minister. The Navy Ministry had slipped from the grasp of the fleet faction and stood as a balance to the Imperial Army's ambitions. Yamamoto, who had avoided the political arena, was squarely in the middle of things.

His office in the red brick ministry headquarters soon became a popular hangout for newspaper reporters, who would drink and joke with him. They became unabashed supporters, freely writing about his view that Japan would be "extremely foolish" to go to war against Great Britain and the United States. Asked if he thought the Japanese navy could win such a war, he answered, "No, I do not."

The right-wingers howled against Yamamoto's open advocacy of peace. When hate mail and death threats poured into his office and young officers spoke against him, Yamamoto laughed and said he was as patriotic as any Japanese and willing to die for his beliefs. Sometimes he pushed his own way through angry demonstrators. The army provided bodyguards when he went out, but they were loyal to the generals, so Yamamoto always made sure that he had navy bodyguards along who were loyal to him.

There was nothing the navy could do, however, to stop the army in 1937 when it suddenly slashed deep into China after a questionable ambush of Japanese soldiers at the Marco Polo Bridge, south of Peking. The generals unleashed hell in several Chinese cities, particularly in Nanking, where soldiers murdered and pillaged at will, using captured Chinese men for bayonet practice, raping women, and slaughtering children. A quarter of a million Chinese died there.

The navy's fleet faction supported the action on the spot, and Japanese planes sank a U.S. gunboat, the *Panay*, on the Yangtze River. It was an intentional act of war, but Yamamoto leaped into action and put his reputation on the line to diplomatically smooth things over with the Americans. Hawks within the navy saw that only as another illustration of his pro-American stance.

As cabinets rose and fell, the army reasserted its power. Although the army had no one of Yamamoto's popularity or stature, it did have one general who had steadily risen higher and higher. His actual battle experience was minimal. General Hideki Tojo was known as the Razor because of his sharp tongue. He was humorless, smoked as many as sixty cigarettes a day, worked harder than anyone else in his command, wore horn-rimmed classes, and was totally dedicated to the army way of doing things, for his father had also been a general. While Yamamoto had studied in America and appreciated its potential military might, Tojo spent his overseas time as a young officer in Germany, where he enjoyed the Teutonic efficiency of that nation. On his only brief visit to the United States, Tojo concluded Americans were indolent, unsophisticated, and of no importance militarily. To the general, the main threat was still on land, from Russia. Yamamoto saw any Pacific war as primarily a naval battle against the United States.

Tojo was commander of the Kwantung Army in China when he was recalled to Tokyo and entered the higher councils of government. He seemed to progress another step upward with each governmental shakeup.

Yamamoto and Tojo—who together would push Japan toward the most disastrous war in its history—were as different as night and day. Navy against army; one popular with his men and the other a bitter disciplinarian; one seeing the United States as a formidable foe, the other seeing it as nothing to be concerned about.

When Admiral Yonai lost his job as navy minister, one of his last acts was to send Yamamoto back to sea. It probably saved his life, but was a positive move for the militarists, who would need him at the helm of the Imperial Japanese Navy in the coming conflict.

On the hot day of September 5, 1939, Admiral Yamamoto nimbly climbed aboard the battleship *Nagato*. The Order of the Sacred Treasure, First Class, was among the many decorations on his dress white uniform when he took command of the Combined Fleet. On October 17, Tojo rose to prime minister and simultaneously took the portfolio of war minister. The next year, Yamamoto was promoted to full admiral. His reluctance to fight America finally overcome by loyalty to his country, he struck hard and fast, starting with Pearl Harbor.

After the initial series of decisive victories, the admiral and his

Combined Fleet dominated the vast blue Pacific Ocean. But he was wrapped in melancholy so deep, even the exquisite set of sake cups that the emperor had sent along with a personal letter of congratulations failed to lift his spirits. Yamamoto was aware that many long and costly battles lay ahead and that victory over America would be impossible.

He had somberly written a friend months earlier that Washington and the American people would not simply give up once war began, no matter what the militarists in Tokyo believed. "It is not enough that we should take Guam and the Philippines or even Hawaii and San Francisco. We would have to march into Washington and sign the treaty in the White House." That pessimistic note would be twisted into Allied propaganda that claimed Yamamoto planned to personally march up Pennsylvania Avenue and dictate peace terms to President Roosevelt.

After Pearl Harbor, the Americans identified him as the personification of its foe, and *Harper's Magazine* declared, "Perhaps our chief individual enemy, next to Adolf Hitler, is leather-faced, bullet-headed, bitter-hearted Isoroku Yamamoto."

5

Running Wild

Hamilton Field

Lieutenant John Mitchell arrived back in California to find that his home base, Hamilton Field, had changed quite a bit while he was gone. When he had left for the North Carolina war games, the pace for the pilots had been slow, the day usually beginning with a leisurely fourteen-cent breakfast of eggs, cereal, potatoes, toast, coffee, milk, and fruit, then some studying, flying, and routine work around the squadron. It was not a hard life.

That seemed like some distant era now. Antiaircraft guns bristled along the long runways, men were filling sandbags, tanks were parked around the perimeter, and pilots carrying .45-caliber pistols pulled guard duty at the gates. The blue sky buzzed with training flights, while some planes, fully armed, ran patrols off the northern California coast. At night, bright searchlights probed the darkness. More planes and men were coming in from all over the country every day; rows of wooden barracks, warehouses, and mess halls were under construction; and the beautiful white stucco walls for which the base was known vanished beneath hurriedly applied coats of green and brown camouflage paint.

As much as the physical changes to the landscape, there also had been a change in attitude, and the pure joy of flying a plane had been leavened by a combination of determination and an unspoken touch of fear. If those Japanese carriers could hit Hawaii, what was stopping them from striking San Francisco?

The hell-for-leather barracks bragging of newly minted pilots was more subdued as the young men realized that flying was a deadly serious business. Sitting in the cockpit of a slick pursuit plane during peacetime training was not the same as being up there alone in a war, with someone trying to kill you. The men who chose such a job were special, even among the other fliers, and most trainees could not wait to sign up for combat duty. But at another base, where a new group of pilots was about to graduate, the instructor asked for volunteers to fly pursuit planes in the South Pacific. Only one man stepped forward.

Mitchell had been assigned to Hamilton shortly after getting his pilot's wings in July 1940. He started with the 55th Pursuit Squadron of the 20th Pursuit Group and drew assignments such as assistant squadron engineering officer, assistant squadron armament officer, assistant squadron supply officer, assistant squadron athletic officer, and the squadron's skeet officer. That had been before December 7, 1941. Now the country, the air corps, and Hamilton Field were at war, and Mitchell was no longer just another unknown officer doing routine deskwork when he was not flying. He was an experienced pilot who would have to lead other men into battle.

It had been a close call. Mitchell had failed to get into aviation cadet training the first time he tried and almost washed out when he was finally accepted. At Love Field in Dallas, he earned a "barely passing" grade of D, but the army air corps badly needed pursuit plane pilots. He struggled through the classroom work, and the more he flew, the better he got. Finally, he won his wings.

By the time he was peeled away from the 55th to help form the 70th Pursuit Squadron, the lieutenant was considered an old hand. New fliers coming into the 70th found him to be a confident officer. Despite his student years at the University of Georgia and Columbia University in New York, and the service as an enlisted man in Hawaii, he still spoke with a slow Mississippi drawl. They learned through the grapevine that Mitchell spent part of the summer of 1941 in England flying British Spitfires and Hurricanes and witnessing the horrible reality of the German bombing of London. The youngsters believed in John Mitchell.

Captain Henry Viccellio, the commander of the new squadron,

was glad to see Mitchell back at work, for the unit was rapidly expanding as the war beckoned. Nothing could replace time in the sky to give the new boys experience, but they did not have such training time, for the squadron already had orders to go overseas. They managed some gunnery practice with low-powered P-39s and practiced dive-bombing by attacking silvery streaks of glass and aluminum powder that were dropped into the waters off Oakland. The pilots were lucky to get even a couple of rides in the tougher, faster P-40.

When they were not flying, the squadron assimilated newcomers and packed its gear and planes for the long boat ride to some unknown place in the Pacific Ocean. Viccellio, Mitchell, and the small team of other experienced officers knew that no matter how hard they worked to improve the skills of the young pilots, some would not make it back alive. They included themselves in that grim assessment.

Guam

After World War I, Japan's reward for fighting alongside the Allies was three island groups that previously had been controlled by Germany in the central Pacific Ocean—the Carolines, Marshalls, and Marianas. Guam, the southernmost of the Marianas chain and the largest island between the Philippines and Hawaii, remained an American property, and another task force of Yamamoto's ships and planes struck there right after Pearl Harbor. By dawn on December 10, the garrison of four hundred American sailors and one hundred and fifty-five marines was overrun, and Japan had captured its first American prisoners of war. Guam's civilian governor was forced to stand at attention in his underwear as the Rising Sun flag was raised to replace the Stars and Stripes.

Singapore

All was not lost in the Pacific, for the British bastion of Singapore at the tip of the Malayan Peninsula had tens of thousands of British, Australian, and Indian Army troops on alert, with another British division coming from the Middle East. Rings of antiaircraft batteries and giant naval guns capable of destroying any enemy fleet protected the harbor complex. The city shrugged off a slight bombing raid on the first night of the war. It was said that Singapore could hold out for months.

Great Britain immediately struck back at the Japanese. As the sun set that first night, England's newest and most powerful battleship, the *Prince of Wales*, accompanied by the formidable cruiser *Repulse* and four destroyers, sailed from Singapore on a mission to raid Japanese troop convoys and smash invasion beaches. "We're off to find trouble!" came the signal from the *Repulse*. The big ships were to strike, then hide among the islands of the southern Pacific and emerge unexpectedly to hit the Japanese again and again. In command of Task Force Z was Rear Admiral Sir Tom Phillips, a personal friend of Winston Churchill and the former deputy chief of staff of the Royal Navy, a man so tiny that he was called "Tom Thumb." Once clear of the Johore Strait, the force turned northeast and increased speed to seventeen knots. Phillips stood on a box so he could see over the armored bridge of his mighty flagship.

Despite Britain's own aerial victory at Taranto, England remained married to the dreadnought, and Churchill was confident that the mere presence of the *Prince* in the area should deter Japan. "There is nothing like having something that can catch and kill anything," he said of the thirty-five-thousand-ton battleship that was affectionately known to its sailors as the HMS *Unsinkable*.

Admiral Yamamoto had a favorite proverb of his own, one that favored planes over ships: "The fiercest serpent may be overcome by a swarm of ants." Task Force Z sailed to its doom.

Before the British ships could make any difference at all, more than a hundred Japanese fighters and bombers found them the following day and beat them to death. Both rolled over and sank, taking down more than eight hundred officers and seamen. The defeat left the Royal Navy with only seven major ships worldwide, and it would be strained just to protect the convoy routes in the North Atlantic that were a lifeline to America. In both the Indian Ocean and the Pacific, Churchill glumly observed, "Japan was supreme, and we everywhere were weak and naked."

On December 11, Germany and Italy declared war on the United States.

Wake Island

Some twenty-three hundred miles of ocean separates lonely little Wake Island from Hawaii, and there is no other land around. Less than four square miles of total land area curves like a pair of narrow arms around a lagoon, and the whole island is just big enough to accommodate a small military airstrip at one end. At Wake, five hundred U.S. Marines, ready when the Japanese invasion force arrived, turned back the initial assault. Then Japanese bombers methodically wrecked everything aboveground.

A powerful U.S. Navy strike force, built around the aircraft carrier *Saratoga* and three heavy cruisers, sailed from Hawaii on December 16 to reinforce Wake. It was to deliver the 4th Marine Defense Battalion, supplies, spare aircraft engines, ammunition, and eighteen F4F Wildcats of Marine Fighting Squadron 221.

While the imperiled island endured constant attacks, Rear Admiral Frank Jack Fletcher dawdled en route, repeatedly slowing to refuel his escort destroyers. He was still hundreds of miles away, refueling again, when the Japanese captured Wake on December 22. Fletcher never reached Wake; he turned around and returned to Hawaii with his task force unscratched by battle.

Sydney, Australia

Admiral Yamamoto's fleets sailed from one impressive victory to another, and Allied leaders had no problem envisioning the Rising Sun flag being hoisted in a vast semicircle from the cold shores of Russia all the way down to New Zealand. Australians watched with dread as the Japanese headed south into the Philippines and down the Malay Peninsula, straight toward them. Three of Australia's own combat divisions, and one from nearby New Zealand, were off fighting Germans in the deserts of North Africa. The only other Aussie division was tied up in the defense of Singapore. Australia was militarily bare, and the loss of the *Prince* and the *Repulse* decapitated British naval power in the area. Churchill's promise of protection rang hollow. Former Australian

Prime Minister Robert Menzies groused, "What Britain calls the Far East is to us the Near North."

Washington

More bad news seemed to arrive on every tide.

The job of stopping the onrushing Japanese fell to a fragmented command structure of civilian leaders, generals, and admirals representing the United States, England, the Netherlands, and their allies. Two days before Christmas, 1941, Churchill arrived in Washington with a British delegation to meet Roosevelt and his staff for a series of strategy conferences to define the course of the war. While Churchill abhorred the bloody attack on Pearl Harbor, he was immensely pleased that war-weary England finally had the strong ally it had wanted for so long. More than thirty years earlier, he had compared the United States to "a gigantic boiler. Once the fire is ignited under it, there is no limit to the power it can generate."

His primary mission was to keep America focused on Germany as the primary enemy, despite headlines across the United States that howled for revenge against the Japanese. The prime minister insisted that the Nazis must be brought to heel first. Roosevelt and the American leadership, after fierce debate, agreed with the British, and the Pacific Ocean instantly became a secondary theater of war. Europe would have priority.

In September 1941 General George C. Marshall, the U.S. Army chief of staff, promoted a bright colonel named Dwight D. Eisenhower to brigadier general; in December he brought him to Washington and made him the deputy chief of war plans. The situation in the Philippines was desperate, and Eisenhower was the right man to give Marshall a candid opinion. "Ike" had worked with General MacArthur for years, including a long tour in Manila, and he predicted the Filipino cause was doomed. The prowling Japanese fleets made American reinforcement convoys to Manila, eight thousand miles from San

Francisco, impossible. Eisenhower advised that Australia would have to be the main Allied base in the Pacific. "Do your best to save them," the chief of staff instructed his new deputy, who knew little could be done to help the Americans, who were already in retreat in the Philippines.

A lesser-known addition to Marshall's staff was Thomas Lanphier Sr., who had come out of retirement to be an air intelligence officer on the general staff. In his autobiography, Tom Lanphier Jr. wrote that his father and Eisenhower were old friends. While they were both West Point cadets, Lanphier asked the girl he was going to marry to a dance, but was suddenly confined to his room in a disciplinary incident. He coaxed his buddy, Dwight Eisenhower, to be her escort that evening.

Ambitious officers who worked with Lieutenant Thomas Lanphier Jr. would never ignore the fact that his father was directly connected to the highest halls of power in Washington.

Pearl Harbor was the worst thing to happen to the United States since the Civil War, and an immediate change was made in the navy. Admiral Husband E. Kimmel was at the helm when his command was wrecked in Pearl Harbor. For decades to come, arguments would rage over whether he was made a scapegoat for failures elsewhere, but there was no denying he was unprepared, as evidenced by the battleships parked in neat rows, and crews not being on alert when war clouds had been on the Hawaiian horizon for weeks.

The hatchet man was Secretary of the Navy Frank Knox, who was fully capable of making such a decision, for he had been a lightning rod many times. In 1936 he had run as the Republican vice presidential candidate on a ticket with presidential candidate Alf Landon *against* the Democratic incumbent, President Roosevelt. Four years later, FDR persuaded Knox to be secretary of the navy.

In his younger days, Knox fought in Cuba as one of Theodore Roosevelt's Rough Riders. A newspaper publisher in civilian life, he never shied from a fight. After a quick trip to Hawaii, he returned to Washington and fired Admiral Kimmel. Knox then plucked Chester W. Nimitz, a snowy-haired Texan with piercing blue eyes, away from his desk as chief of the Bureau of Navigation and gave him command of the Pacific Fleet.

Nimitz would report to Admiral Ernest J. King, a naval airpower enthusiast who was elevated to command the entire U.S. fleet in both oceans. One of King's first decisions was to change the military acronym of his new job. Henceforth, he ordered, his office would be known as COMINCH (COMmander IN CHief) and not Commander in Chief, United States, known as CINCUS, and pronounced "sink-us."

King, in turn, reported not through the general staff, but directly to the president. He made no attempt to cover his distaste for the "Europe First" decision that had come out of the Churchill conference. Hitler had no aircraft carriers that could attack America. King would work with the British, but the eyes of the navy's tattooed, crusty leader would be on the Pacific, where he had once commanded a carrier group.

Hong Kong

Hong Kong fell on Christmas Day. The British colony off the coast of China had been under siege since December 8, and the island's water supply from the mainland was severed on the first night. A long and bloody battle ended without mercy as Japanese soldiers slaughtered helpless civilians, mutilated children, raped nurses, and bayoneted wounded men lying in their beds.

The Philippines

Manila also fell that day. Soon after the initial attacks, Japanese invasion forces had come ashore in great numbers and rushed toward the capital in a giant pincer movement. General MacArthur declared Manila to be an open city. The Japanese could have occupied it without further resistance, but they bombed it anyway.

MacArthur had regained his balance and conducted a masterful withdrawal, carefully holding vital bridges until they could be blown up in the face of the advancing enemy, but the flash of his military genius came too late, for his cause was already lost. He could slow the Japanese but not stop them.

The Japanese chased the faltering Filipino and American forces down the narrow, jungled Bataan Peninsula. Only four battered P-40 pursuit planes were still in operation, so, other than the men needed to keep those few planes flying, the remainder of the army air corps pilots and enlisted men in the Philippines picked up rifles and joined the infantry in the retreat. Thousands of American troops were fighting and starving, without support and in constant contact with the enemy.

MacArthur shifted his command to the fortified island of Corregidor, in the mouth of Manila Bay, where he lived and worked in a huge tunnel that had been carved out of solid rock. Many of those fighting on Bataan were furious that "Dugout Doug" was not sharing their hardship, and their pathetic anthem was:

We're the battling bastards of Bataan,
No mama, no papa, no Uncle Sam,
No aunts, no uncles, no nephews, no nieces,
No rifles, no planes, or artillery pieces,
And nobody gives a damn!

In China, U.S. General Joseph W. Stilwell took stock of how the Allies were being slammed by one hammer blow after another and scribbled in his diary, "My God, worse and worse."

"If you tell me it is necessary that we fight, then in the first six months to a year of war against the United States and England I will go wild, and I will show you an uninterrupted succession of victories," Admiral Yamamoto had written to a friend shortly before the war began. "But I must tell you that if the war be prolonged for two or three years, I have no confidence in our ultimate victory." True to his word, he was indeed running wild.

But always at the back of his mind was the knowledge that he did not have much time. He could not allow America to catch its breath and bring its industrial power to bear against his fleet. His nightmare was that on some afternoon in the future, he would look up and see a horizon filled with American warplanes that had been launched from a fleet of brand-new U.S. carriers. He would be the serpent. They would be the ants.

6

"They're Yanks!"

Few Americans could render a hearty "Happy New Year" as 1941 came to a close. Along the Atlantic coast, Nazi submarines stalked U.S. ships and sank tankers within sight of people on the beach, and the Pacific was a sea of defeat, as Admiral Yamamoto's fleets and planes ranged from one target to another. The average American was bewildered. Everyone knew the location of London and Paris and Rome, but where were Timor, Tarakan, and Truk? How could you even pronounce Kwajalein and Tjilatjap? What was the difference between Bataan and Borneo? Where was the Molucca Sea? The Pacific Ocean was home to such an array of odd names and places that military planners hustled to dig up old *National Geographic* magazines and oil company maps to find the landmarks of disaster.

The new year did not begin any better than the old one ended. In early January 1942, a Japanese submarine torpedoed the aircraft carrier *Saratoga* southwest of Hawaii and sent the badly wounded "*Sara*" stumbling home for extensive repairs. The incident awakened an interest in submarines among senior Japanese naval leaders, since, under Yamamoto's influence, they had been focused more on airplanes than undersea craft and viewed submarines primarily as defensive weapons to protect the homeland, not as specialized ships that should take an attacking, offensive role. Yamamoto was so pleased that a sub had wrecked an American carrier, he awarded his torpedo staff officer seventy bottles of beer, and the morale of the long-ignored submarine fleet soared. There would be more critical submarine victories in the months to come.

On the same day the *Sara* was hit, Japan declared war on the Dutch and invaded the Netherlands East Indies to grab the region's mineral wealth. Far to the east, the capital of American Samoa was shelled, and the critical harbor city of Rabaul in the Bismarck Archipelago was bombed. It seemed as if a giant umbrella were closing, darkening the South Pacific.

By turning her attention to plundering the Southern Resources Zone, Japan gave America the respite that Yamamoto most feared, time to recover from the shock and prepare to fight back. In striking Pearl Harbor and the Philippines, the admiral had cut the heart out of the American forces in the Pacific, but instead of capitalizing on those victories by finding and killing the other American aircraft carriers, he was required to support the headlong stampede to subdue the southern regions. Yamamoto was almost alone in understanding that if he slew the U.S. Navy in the Pacific—and within a very limited time—then the rest of the area would fall with little trouble.

A national accord had energized the United States, as Yamamoto feared. For the rest of their lives, every American would remember where he or she was when they learned of the attack on Pearl Harbor.

Manpower would never be a problem, for thousands of men had rushed to join the armed forces and fight for their country. Some were stuffed into uniforms so fast they did not have time to be trained; these men found themselves aboard ships heading west, out to the islands with names no one could pronounce, and to the suddenly endangered continent of Australia. The army needed bodies fast; it would figure out what to do with them later.

Some help had already arrived Down Under. Convoy 4002 had left San Francisco on Thanksgiving Day, before the war started, and dashed for the Philippines, a string of seven fat merchant ships jammed to overflowing with airplanes, tanks, and troops and shepherded by the heavy cruiser *Pensacola*. They were nine days out of Hawaii and had just crossed the equator when the Japanese hit Pearl Harbor. Washington decided it was too risky to try to punch the convoy of reinforcements through to General MacArthur in Manila. If Yamamoto found it, he would sink it.

Near Fiji, the *Pensacola* convoy changed course and headed southwest, dodged some Japanese ships, and pulled into the big harbor in Brisbane, Australia, two days before Christmas. Seventy crates of planes were unloaded, as well as 4,600 men of two National Guard field artillery regiments and some 2,400 troops of the army air corps. Local citizens turned out to cheer the dapper young Americans who marched smartly from the Dalagata Pier to big tents that had been erected at the Ascot Race Track. Delighted Aussie girls whispered to one another, "They're Yanks!" The new troops would immediately be thrown into the fight.

A makeshift force of American, British, Dutch, and Australian troops was cobbled together to defend the Malay barrier, which included the Malay Peninsula, Sumatra, Java, and the islands stretching eastward to northwest Australia, but had no chance of stopping Yamamoto. Japanese planes, ships, and naval landing forces maneuvered freely throughout the area, and Japanese army troops were plunging south. Singapore and the northern coast of Australia were threatened, and if Australia was lost, or isolated, neighboring New Zealand could not be defended. American forces might have to fall all the way back to Hawaii or the West Coast.

Before Admiral Nimitz left Washington in late December, Admiral King gave him a final briefing. He slashed a long line across a map of the South Pacific, extending from Midway Island south for some two thousand miles to Samoa, and then passing through the Fijis and down to Brisbane, on the eastern coast of Australia. Safeguard Hawaii first, King ordered Nimitz, then reinforce Samoa and extend the defensive arc to Fiji and New Caledonia. Those were the stepping-stones to Australia for ships and planes coming from the United States, an invisible front line that had to be guarded at all costs.

It was a bold statement, for Yamamoto might burst through that perimeter anywhere and at any time. Nimitz needed to get ground troops on those islands and cover them with combat planes, for he did not have the carrier strength to do the job.

The navy pulled the *Hornet* and *Yorktown* out of the Atlantic and sent them through the Panama Canal to join the *Saratoga, Lexington,* and *Enterprise* in the threatened Pacific Theater. But the loss of the *Sara* left Nimitz with only four carriers to cover the wide Pacific. Yamamoto had ten—all six of the big carriers that had attacked Pearl Harbor, plus four smaller ones, and as a gambler, he had to like the favorable odds.

Australia needed every plane it could put in the air to defend its own northern boundaries, and New Zealand had only a few older planes in service. The primary air defense of the vital islands would have to be assigned to land-based planes of the U.S. Army Air Corps and the Marine Corps. Orders were cut to start them moving westward.

The Thomas S. Barry

D. D. Brannon and the 67th Pursuit Squadron were sardined aboard a troop train for a jolting trip from Louisiana to Fort Dix, New Jersey, where doctors put them all under quarantine in unheated barracks with no lights and no cots for several days. When released, they rode more crowded trains to Brooklyn, and they climbed the gangway to the *Thomas S. Barry*, a passenger ship that normally plied the New York-Cuba run. As the last unit to board, they had little choice about where to bunk, for all of the best sleeping quarters were already assigned. Brannon and the officers were stacked tightly in the ship's library, and the enlisted men were herded deep below, into what had once been the ship's refrigerator, and it was still cold. Brannon and his officers took every wool blanket they could find and gave them to the men.

The *Barry* sailed on January 23 and dashed south through the Atlantic coastal waters that were the hunting grounds of German submarines. Once safely into the tropics, the men below decks sweltered in the deep, unventilated refrigerator space. Each man was allowed only two canteens of water per day for washing, shaving, and drinking. The enlisted men had to wait at least an hour in line for meals that featured bread slathered with orange marmalade, while waiters disappeared into the officers' mess bearing platters of steaming turkeys. Brannon, helpless to change things, could only tell everyone they would all be off the ship soon. Stay tough, he said.

Thirty-eight days after leaving New York, and having pitched and tossed across the rough Tasman Sea, the *Barry* arrived in Melbourne, Australia. The men of the 67th were marched and trucked to the nearby town of Baxhous Marsh, where they collapsed on large burlap sacks filled with straw. Within a week, the expanding squadron was given about fifty untrained soldiers and a dozen pilots who had volunteered to fly in China but instead found themselves stranded in Australia. They all went to sea again in a voyage that carried them a thousand miles back in the direction from which they had come, to a narrow island called New Caledonia. A French colony only 236 miles long, it rested on Admiral King's invisible perimeter around the Pacific, and the rampaging Japanese were always somewhere just over the blue horizon.

For months to come, the 67th would be the only air defense assigned to this important island, which shielded the eastern coast of Australia. But they were a confident unit, particularly since they had been issued new pursuit planes that lay crated in the holds below, and the squadron expected to arrive on New Caledonia ready to fight.

They had no idea the airplanes they had been given were of a type that most of the pilots had never even seen, much less flown, and the mechanics would have no idea how to put together.

Singapore

After only two months of resistance, the storied bastion of Singapore fell on February 17 to a powerful Japanese army that fought overland for six hundred miles, something British planners had thought impossible. Its sixty-two thousand defenders were trapped. The island's most feared weapons, huge Vickers cannon, all faced the sea and were useless against the ground attack. "All I want from you is *yes* or *no*," Lieutenant General Tomoyuki Yamashita told Britain's General A. E. Percival when they met to discuss surrender terms.

Darwin, Australia

The primary weapon available to the U.S. Army Air Corps in Australia was the Curtiss-Wright P-40 Kittyhawk single-seat fighter-bombers that came in aboard the *Pensacola* convoy. Many of them arrived with parts missing. None of the pilots had more than four hours' experience in flying such aircraft, and even those skills had eroded during the weeks spent at sea. The aircraft were assembled as fast as possible, and the greenhorn pilots climbed in and flew them north to join the bitter fight against the onrushing Japanese. Their destination was the port city of Darwin, on the northern edge of Australia, the jumping-off point for the allies fighting in the Netherlands East Indies, Java, and New Guinea. Just ferrying the planes up to Port Darwin was risky, because the pilots and planes were both unsteady. The Americans fell from the sky in appalling numbers. "You won't have any trouble finding your way to Darwin, mate," a grim Aussie corporal at a refueling station told a pilot. "Just follow the trail of crashed Kittyhawks. You can't go wrong."

On the morning of February 19, ten P-40 pilots took off from Darwin on a combat mission, only to be turned back a few minutes later by a severe weather front. While they were landing, a single Japanese Zero appeared out of nowhere, but they chased him off and began settling onto the airstrip. Before they could even get out of the cockpits, a crew chief yelled, "The Japs are here!" Zeros swept in with their guns winking, butchering the Americans, who were pushing their throttles forward, trying to get back in the air.

It was the opening blow in the Japanese assault. The forty-six ships huddled in the Darwin anchorage, a farm of oil tanks, and a nearby bomber base were the main targets of the Japanese assault. Four of Yamamoto's large aircraft carriers parked a safe distance away and hurled almost 190 fighters and bombers against the city, which they bombed and strafed with impunity. The Civil Hospital, Government House, the police barracks, and the post office were destroyed in the first attack. Then another wave swept down to continue the carnage.

Hundreds of people were killed, including the governor's Aboriginal housekeeper and the postmaster and his entire family. At least seven ships were sunk, and one vessel filled with ammunition detonated with an earthshaking roar. An accurate count of the dead and damage was impossible, and censors blocked reports of their extent, for to let the information out would have cast a pall of gloom throughout Australia. An American pilot who flew in the following day gave the benediction: "Darwin is no more. . . . It is a scene of utter desolation."

The Java Sea

When a massive Japanese invasion convoy surged forward to take Java one week later, on February 26, the Allies could send out only five cruisers and ten destroyers to stop it. Within an hour of leaving port, the little fleet ran headlong into the oncoming enemy. Although the Battle of the Java Sea lasted several days, and extended over hundreds of miles, it was not much more than a deadly pursuit by the Japanese. In still another disaster for the Allies, all five cruisers and six of the destroyers were lost. Among the several thousand Allied seamen who perished were seven hundred and eighty Americans aboard the cruiser *Houston*. The last twenty Allied planes in Java were destroyed on the ground, several more Allied ships were sunk trying to escape, the Dutch admiral commanding the fleet went down with his ship, and the British general commanding the coalition force fled to India. The wealth of the Dutch East Indies, including its oil wells, was falling into Japanese hands as fast as the troops could get ashore.

Australia now lay open to a ground invasion, but headquarters in Tokyo did not want that. Establishing control of the air and sea around the huge continent, and perhaps staging commando raids near the main cities, should be enough to prevent any effective Allied buildup there. With the Southern Resources Zone under control and the battle in the Philippines drawing to a close, Yamamoto could again turn his attention to finding and killing the American aircraft carriers. He knew they were still out there, and still dangerous.

The President Monroe

Lieutenant Rex Barber walked up the gangway of the passenger ship *President Monroe* and looked out in wonder at the teeming San Francisco waterfront. Seagulls screamed, pulleys creaked, and long-shoremen shouted as pyramids of boxes containing everything from toilet paper to ammunition were hoisted aboard navy and merchant ships. Thousands of uniformed men were being moved through the port, heading off to war. A month had passed since he had been aboard the *President Johnson* out in the middle of nowhere on the morning Pearl Harbor was hit. That ship had turned around and fled home as fast as it could.

This time he was heading west with 43 officers and 217 enlisted men of the 70th Pursuit Squadron. Because of the extravagant losses the Allies were enduring around the Pacific, all available forces were being rushed into the fight as soon as possible, in piecemeal fashion, and the men of the 70th found that they were the only passengers aboard the spacious liner. There was still plenty of room to spare belowdecks after big boxes containing almost three dozen Airacobras P-39s were safely stashed in the holds. One was lost while being loaded. The next time the *Monroe* made this crossing, she would be packed to the rails with about two thousand men, and the holds would bulge with cargo.

Because he had been on a ship only a few weeks before, Barber was more comfortable than his buddies. As Henry Viccellio, John Mitchell, and the other senior officers hustled to make sure everything was ready, Barber, Tom Lanphier, and the other pilots gathered at the rails and waved to those below. Life had been good for this handful of fliers since Pearl Harbor, for duty had been light at Hamilton Field as the squadron got ready to move, which meant a lot of time to party in San Francisco. Stepping out sharply down Market Street—in a pressed uniform with silver wings gleaming on their chests and shiny Sam Browne belts across their shoulders—meant they could hardly buy a drink on their own.

Someone looking up at the khaki-clad lieutenants on the deck of the *Monroe* would be impressed by how they all looked so much alike. They were lean, they were young, and they were confident and carefree, bantering back and forth as the lines let go and the big ship edged into the channel, then threaded its way through the submarine nets at the mouth of the harbor.

Silence fell over them as the spire of Coit Tower and the broad Embarcadero faded and San Francisco's stair-step hills grew dim. Many stood there until they could no longer see the red towers of the Golden Gate Bridge, each knowing this might be the last time he would ever see his homeland. Five pilots at the rail that evening would never return.

The *Monroe* joined two other troopships that were taking the 49th Pursuit Group to Australia. A light cruiser and a couple of destroyers formed around them for protection, their bows kicking up bones of white water and crews standing at their guns.

Among those taking in the sights from the *Monroe* was Lieutenant Doug Canning, a compact twenty-one-year-old pilot from Wayne, Nebraska, whose broad grin made him everybody's pal. He had decided to fly after a neighbor, who had become a pilot, landed his plane in Wayne and let Canning sit in it. That was enough to make him volunteer as an air cadet. He pinned on his wings at Kelly Field in Texas four days before the end of September 1941. Before he was done, Doug Canning would fly in three wars over the next thirty years. As part of Class 41-G, he underwent an abbreviated training course because of the demand for new pilots. After graduation, they all got leave time before having to report to the 35th Pursuit Group at Hamilton Field. Most of the class took only five days of leave, but Canning took ten and bought a new car so he could drive through Nebraska and visit his family. The visit threw him slightly behind the training schedule of his classmates.

The 70th Pursuit Squadron to which he was assigned at Hamilton had only two P-36 single-seat planes; all new pilots had to check out in them before going overseas. His friends shipped out earlier because they arrived at Hamilton earlier, and as Canning waited his turn in a P-36, most of his classmates had departed for the Philippines. Now he was aboard a ship, too, aware that his friends had been part of the convoy that had been diverted to Australia. He hoped to catch up with them somewhere out in the Pacific.

Meals aboard the *Monroe* were elegant events, with food befitting a four-star restaurant served by waiters in formal ties and swallow-tailed coats, peacetime attire for those who catered to the whims of the very rich. They still politely presented the fresh officers with six-page menus of gourmet cuisine, such as squab and baked Alaska. But as it grew apparent that the war had replaced the ladies and gentlemen with a bunch of rowdy soldiers, the waiters were displeased.

Captain Viccellio decided to let the good times roll, for he knew that hard months lay ahead. Marathon poker games went on belowdecks among the enlisted men, although one prickly captain frequently ordered the pilots to go down and stop the card playing. Since the fliers would soon be putting their lives in the hands of those mechanics and technicians, they ignored such a peacetime chickenshit order. Let 'em play, the pilots said, and rigged up an advance warning system with the sergeants below. Anyway, they had their own poker games going.

As the snout of the *Monroe* bucked through the long swells rolling across the Pacific, a sense of brotherhood was being born among the young pilots. Other fliers would join and leave the 70th in the coming months and years, but the few who sailed aboard the *Monroe* shared the unique experience of being present at the start. The trust they developed on the trip created an unspoken measure of respect, and when it came to future combat missions, a pilot wanted an old-timer on his wing.

The ship's bar had been closed, but one lieutenant, the rambunctious son of a Baptist preacher in Texas, had smuggled aboard several cases of whiskey. That fueled marathon talking sessions among the pilots, when they were not pulling torpedo watches at night or scanning the skies for enemy aircraft during the day. The squadron's flight surgeon held court as the ship's philosopher, and a New Zealand pilot, returning home after flying in the Battle of Britain, told harrowing tales of fighting above London. The Americans could not get over the fact that he had a personal servant along, an enlisted fellow called a batman, who politely woke the New Zealander every morning at six o'clock with a steaming pot of tea and tiny triangles of toast on a tray. His three roommates thought that was a grand idea, but none dared suggest it to any of his own men.

During three weeks at sea, the long talks ranged over every conceivable subject. But mortality was rarely discussed, for they had the impenetrable belief of strong young men that they would survive. Unknown to them, fierce air battles were already taking place in the skies north of Australia, and American pilots were suffering losses of up to 75 percent. Those men in combat were not thinking about going home again, but rather about how they would die—in a fiery crash, by being blown up, or being machine-gunned by the enemy while dangling helplessly in a parachute. They just prayed it would be over quickly.

After a week at sea, the *Monroe* left its convoy and headed off on a zigzag course under the watchful eye of a single Australian cruiser. With a maximum speed of only sixteen and one-half knots, close watch was kept for Japanese submarines, but the sense of danger faded with time, and enlisted men came up from the holds to sleep soundly on the main deck in the warm tropical nights. Halfway over, the 70th had eaten everything in the larder; after that the officers dined on C rations at linen-covered tables. After two more weeks, the *Monroe* shuddered to a stop in a crystalline bay lined by palm trees. White clouds towered into an incredibly blue sky, and the smell of coconut oil drifted on the air.

"Where are we?" Doug Canning asked a ship's officer.

"Fiji," came the reply.

The Java Sea

After Canning's classmates from 41-G arrived in Australia, they were shipped around to Freemantle, on the country's west coast, and reloaded aboard the USS *Langley*, which was to ferry them closer to the fighting in the north.

Twenty years before, the boxy *Langley* had been the first aircraft carrier in the United States Navy, created by hammering a short, blunt deck atop the hull of a coal-carrying ship. By 1941 she was an antique, and the flight deck had been sawed off by about a third to make a kind of floating parking lot for seaplanes. She had been based in the Philippines when the war began, and all of her planes were destroyed. The *Langley* herself escaped and was put to work hauling emergency cargo into the war zone, living up to her nickname of "The Old Covered Wagon."

This time she was taking American troops through the waters of the Indian Ocean south of Java. Along with thirty-three pilots and many more enlisted men, she carried a load of P-40 Kittyhawks that were lashed to her deck. When a Japanese scout plane found the old *Langley* early on the sunlit morning of February 27, the pilot saw the flat deck crowded with planes and took the old ship to be something it wasn't. He thought he had found a frontline aircraft carrier, but actually had discovered only a sturdy old mule of a ship that was chugging along at a top speed of just over eleven knots.

A short time later, nine twin-engine Japanese bombers in arrowhead formations dived out of scattered clouds and, ignoring the defending destroyers, took dead aim at the lumbering *Langley*. She dodged their first pass by making a sharp turn at the last moment, but the enemy squadron patiently lined up astern the second time and slammed their 250-pound bombs into and around the creaky ship. Steel plates buckled from the violent shock waves of near misses, allowing seawater to flood into the hull, then direct hits marched along the flat deck, shredding metal and men. Zeros finished the job with strafing runs. It took only thirty-nine minutes from the moment the boat was sighted until hundreds of men were in the water, scrambling for debris and rafts and being plucked from the sea by the shepherding destroyers.

The shocked survivors were transferred by motor launch through rough seas the next morning to an oil tanker, the *Pecos*, for the trip back to Australia. But two of the big Japanese aircraft carriers in the area had been alerted that an American flattop was around and wanted to make certain she had been sunk. A *Pecos* lookout shouted, "Here they come!" and clouds of Japanese planes roared in to whip the blocky oiler for four hours before it sank stern-first. They mercilessly strafed the survivors in the water. Another seven hundred American servicemen died in the massacre, including all but one of the pilots.

Among the dead were Doug Canning's eighteen friends from flying school. He was alive and on Fiji only because he had missed the boat. It was a shame, but the war would not allow anyone time to stop and grieve. Canning was already with another group of men, new buddies with whom he would fly into battle, and to whom he would trust his life.

7

Islands

The Inland Sea

The huge gray shape of the superbattleship *Yamato,* a mammoth testament to the art of shipbuilding, entered the Hashirajima anchorage on a rainy Sunday morning. Sailors were awed. The *Yamato* weighed more than 75,000 tons, had belts of thick armor plating and a huge stack that raked back away from its control bridge, an elegant pagoda-shaped tower the size of a small skyscraper, overlooking a deck made of teak. She bristled with pods of antiaircraft guns amidships, even the secondary guns were bigger than those aboard a destroyer, and the main guns were three huge cannon set in each of three low turrets. The nine 18.1-inch guns could hurl shells weighing more than one and one-half tons more than twenty-two miles. The big ship dropped anchor just west of the *Nagato,* dwarfing the battleship from which the C-in-C was then running the sea war.

Six years earlier, Yamamoto had argued strongly against building the *Yamato,* because he considered such an expenditure of effort and treasure to be folly. Where others saw an ultimate weapon, he saw a dinosaur, and he had proven his point by ravaging the American battlewagons at Pearl Harbor nine days before the *Yamato* was commissioned.

Yet here it stood, magnificent, so roomy that it was scathingly referred to elsewhere in the fleet as the "Hotel Yamato." It was to become the admiral's new home and headquarters. Yamamoto transferred his flag aboard, and was pleased to find his spacious cabin was air-conditioned. He was displeased when the biggest ship in the world almost ran aground while trying to dodge a sailboat. The *Yamato*'s brief, militarily useless existence would come to an end on April 7, 1945, when American carrier planes sank it with ease.

But in early April 1942, optimism in the Imperial Navy bloomed like the springtime cherry blossoms. The Japanese counted three enemy carriers as being off the board. Planes had sunk the *Langley*. The *Saratoga*, damaged by the submarine torpedo, was back in Bremerton, Washington, for extensive repairs. And the British carrier *Hermes* had been destroyed near Ceylon. Yamamoto, having missed the carriers at Pearl Harbor, was now picking them off one by one.

The Southwest Pacific victories concluded the initial phase of Japan's campaign, and the senior army and navy staff debated what to do next, including the possible invasions of Hawaii and Australia. Yamamoto considered such talk to be nonsense until the remaining American aircraft carriers had been destroyed. He had a bold plan of his own: attack the vital American island of Midway and draw the U.S. carriers out of hiding so he could crush them. Army and navy planners considered the scheme reckless, but Yamamoto pressed the issue, once again threatening to resign if he was not given his way. The C-in-C was at the zenith of his power, highly regarded by the emperor, and the rush of victories had elevated his popularity at home to rarified levels. He had been right so far, but all he could get this time was a compromise.

Even Yamamoto was answerable to others. The commander in chief of the Combined Fleet was only part of the chain of command, technically reporting through the naval chief of staff to the minister of the navy and the Imperial Joint Staff, although he demonstrated that he could override it in most things. Usually, whatever the admiral wanted from the naval general staff, he got, for he also was a favorite of Emperor Hirohito.

But things became muddled when the navy had to work with the army, for the commands were sharply divided on leadership, history, and outlook. The distance between the two services would greatly hurt the Japanese war effort and constrain Yamamoto's freedom of action.

When General Hideki Tojo became prime minister, some thought that Yamamoto might be summoned back to become navy minister. It probably would have been a death sentence for the admiral, who had been sent to sea because of his outspoken stance against fighting the United States. The last person the War Cabinet and the Imperial War Cabinet wanted in that job would be Yamamoto, who might become a powerful voice for reason and peace. To the generals, this was a time for conquest, not diplomacy.

Although Yamamoto had been correct in his audacious war plans so far, the decisions concerning the steps to be taken during early 1942 were made above his head, in high-level negotiations in Tokyo. In May, attacks would be made to capture Port Moresby on the southern tip of New Guinea, the big lizard-shaped landmass just above Australia. From Port Moresby, Japanese planes would be only about two hundred miles from the Australian mainland, a short hop over the Great Barrier Reef. That would help consolidate Japanese positions in the south, but it would also divert precious resources from Yamamoto's drive to hunt down the American carriers.

Only after Port Moresby fell would Yamamoto get his wish and be allowed to pluck Midway. Further invasions of Fiji and Samoa were planned for July to snap the U.S.-to-Australia supply line. Then the Pacific Ocean would belong to Japan.

Australia

Douglas MacArthur left the Philippines under direct orders from President Roosevelt, who feared the general was too much a symbol of American resistance to risk his being captured. Japanese propaganda broadcasts had promised that MacArthur would be hanged in public in Tokyo. At sundown on March 11, he turned over his doomed command to General Jonathan Wainwright and walked to the south dock on Corregidor's destroyed waterfront. He wore a soiled uniform, with checkered socks and wingtip shoes. He had lost twenty-five pounds sharing the meager diet of his men. Standing amid the stench of the dead harbor, MacArthur raised his hat in final salute, and stepped aboard a fast torpedo boat to run the Japanese blockade. Thirty-five hours later, after a horrendous ride that severely punished the sixty-two-year-old general, he stepped ashore at a pineapple plantation on the island of Mindanao. From there a B-17 Flying Fortress ferried him to Australia. During a long train ride across the vast, empty Outback, his health and iron will returned. "I came through," he told reporters. "And I shall return." He was presented the Congressional Medal of Honor. Two months later, Corregidor fell, and the Japanese had the Philippines.

Nouméa, New Caledonia

On March 15, 1942, D. D. Brannon came on deck as the 67th Fighter Squadron sailed into New Caledonia's spacious main harbor, where the French tricolor flapped atop the lighthouse. Free French forces had chased out the pro-German governor and held their ground until a division of U.S. soldiers arrived. Now it was up to Brannon's inexperienced squadron to provide the airpower, and there was not a minute to spare. New Caledonia was one of the western anchors of the Allied line that stretched across the Pacific, and the 67th had to get its birds up as soon as possible to defend against a possible Japanese attack.

Rugged mountains heaved up from the coral coastline, and columns of yellow smoke rose from nickel-mining docks where dark-skinned men, many wearing wraparound skirts, worked in the hot sun. Rooftops of varying pastel shades dotted the shore, and brightly colored buildings reflected the heat that baked the colonial town of Nouméa. Wrought-iron balconies, the imposing façade of the Catholic Church, and the genteel L'Hôtel du Pacifique evoked thoughts of the Riviera and New Orleans.

Every leg of the trip from Louisiana had been a challenge for the 67th, and another lay before them, for the squadron's new home was not to be this nice little city that looked like a South Seas paradise, but Tontouta, thirty miles away over the hills, where the French had carved a 6,000-foot-long runway several years earlier, and the Australians had recently added another 4,000-foot strip. Getting there was a problem.

Each of the squadron's forty planes was packed in a ten-thousand-pound crate. Workers used squealing pulleys and cranes to lift the boxes off the ship and onto the combination truck and trailer in Nouméa. The rig then had to be driven over the treacherous, curving route, following a jeep with a red flag as officers called out to the locals, "*Gardez! Un grand camion là-bas!*" Because the truck could carry only one boxcar-sized crate at a time and the drive took eight hours, a full week passed before the first plane made it from the ship to the base.

The troops disassembled the crate as soon as it was delivered, ripping down the sides, unpacking the loose gear, and unwrapping the fuselage as if going after a giant birthday present. Then they stood back in dejected surprise. What lay before them was not the expected, familiar P-40 Kittyhawk, but a little Bell P-400, which most of them had never even seen. It was the export model of the P-39 Airacobra.

Brannon later discovered that when Pearl Harbor was bombed, a cargo ship called the *Athenia*, carrying this load of P-400s, had been crawling toward Russia. The Soviets loved the plane, for although it was slow and could not climb high enough to dogfight enemy planes, the nose of the P-400 was studded with a big cannon and four machine guns that made it a lethal low-level attack plane useful against German troops and tanks. The Russians wanted all the P-400s they could get, but when the United States suddenly needed planes for its own defense, the *Athenia* was diverted to Australia.

Regular P-39s entering the South Pacific were being refitted in Australia with British-style oxygen systems that allowed them to reach high altitudes, and the P-400s were supposed to have a similar upgrade. But the need for fighter cover on New Caledonia was so great that the *Athenia* was dispatched to the island before the retrofit was made, and the perplexed mechanics of the 67th Pursuit Squadron were now looking at a tank buster built for the European theater, not a dogfighter for the Pacific. There were no instruction books.

Since the mechanics had no choice, they figured it out. In wretched conditions, the pilots and ground crews worked side by side to assemble the planes, sometimes sitting in six inches of water, rain cascading down their faces while they took turns with the few available wrenches. The only good thing about the torrential rain was that it kept away the mosquitoes. When it wasn't raining, the thirsty insects attacked without letup. Tents were forbidden because of the need for camouflage, so enlisted men slept either in the open or beneath lean-tos while the officers were jammed into the basement, parlor, and bedroom of a broken-down farmhouse. Everyone slept in soggy clothes, fully buttoned up, and covered by wet blankets to defend against the biting insects. Mosquito netting was a prized possession.

Six days after the initial crate was popped open, the first P-400 was ready. It was do-or-die time for D. D. Brannon, who would not let anyone else make the initial flight. Ground crews watched nervously as he wiggled his lanky body into the small, shark-shaped fighter. They had created this airplane by guess and by golly, and did not know whether it would fly. Brannon gunned the Allison engine, released the brakes, and let the plane roll forward on its tall tricycle gear. It gradually gained speed, the nose tipped up, and somehow it lifted into the sky. The 67th was in business.

As soon as the squadron was operational, it spread out to smaller bases elsewhere on New Caledonia so the planes would be dispersed in case of enemy attack—a bitter lesson learned at Pearl Harbor and in the Philippines. Brannon and the headquarters unit remained at the main facility of Tontouta. His number two, Lieutenant John Thompson, a blond, square-jawed Oregonian, settled another flight in at "Patsy," a grass runway shared with a herd of cows and bordered by a hill at one end and power lines at the other. A third base, appropriately called "Dust Bowl," was in a windy wilderness at the southern end of the island. A few others would be added later.

Other senior officers would rotate in for a short time and assume command, then move on to other assignments. The men of the 67th saluted whoever was acting as CO, but acknowledged as their real leaders the two guys who would take them into battle—D. D. Brannon and John Thompson.

Fiji

Halfway between New Caledonia, the new home of the 67th Pursuit Squadron, and American Samoa, where some five thousand U.S. Marines were digging in, were the Fijis. All were targets because they were the vital hubs of the supply route between the United States and Australia, and the enemy knew when the 70th Fighter Squadron had arrived.

The Japanese employed a number of women radio announcers who lobbed daily propaganda programs at the Allies. The announcers, with lilting, feminine voices, were known collectively as "Tokyo Rose." Lanphier would write later that when he, Mitchell, Barber, and the rest of the 70th Pursuit Squadron pulled into Fiji, Tokyo Rose mentioned in her broadcast that she was sorry that a 70th airplane had been wrecked while being loaded in San Francisco. The startling comment made them feel they were being watched.

They were. The easygoing native Fijians welcomed the newcomers warmly, but the other half of the population was downright hostile. The latter, originally immigrants from India who had been imported as plantation labor, had risen over several generations to become merchants, skilled workers, and money changers, and many of them wanted to see Japan win the war and drive the British out of India. Tokyo Rose and Japanese intelligence operatives received a lot of information about the 70th on Fiji.

The squadron settled down, twenty miles from the capital city of Suva, at a short airstrip that had been a sugarcane field until the Royal New Zealand Air Force chose it for an air base. The P-39s were hauled out of their crates, but this group of planes also lacked assembly handbooks. By chance, one mechanic had brought along a ragged copy of a *Popular Mechanics* magazine that had an exploded view of the planes. It was passed around for a quick study, and the planes were put into the air in rapid order. To mark the completion of each new aircraft the pilots took the crew chief up for a test ride. The practice was good insurance, and the 70th Pursuit Squadron was up and flying.

The American pilots who were gathering on the various islands did not seem much to match against the experienced Japanese pilots whom they would soon face in combat. They were mostly raw kids, new to their jobs, who had been rushed to the South Pacific because no one else was ready to go. Their hometowns, education, and backgrounds were a cross section of America, and they were bound together by a desire to fly. But each was competitive by nature, on a football field or in an airplane, and they had not come out to these distant islands to lose.

For the time being, they would hold that line of islands with whatever they had at hand, and if the Japanese attacked, they would fight, for they never believed they were outmatched. Eventually, they knew the United States would swing onto the offensive, and that's when they would be able to show their skills and courage.

The first big fight would be Guadalcanal, and it was there that D. D. Brannon and his 67th Pursuit Squadron, now in New Caledonia, would blaze the way for the army air corps. They would hand off a thriving and aggressive operation to John Mitchell, Tom Lanphier, and Rex Barber and their mates of the 70th, who were now flying in the tropical skies of Fiji.

More eagles were gathering elsewhere. Far away on Christmas Island, a speck of coral about a thousand miles south of Hawaii, the 12th Pursuit Squadron took up station near the equator in March 1942. The squadron was known as the Dirty Dozen.

The man who would rise to command the 12th, and later the 70th, was Captain Lou Kittel. By any measure, he was an unusual guy who took life with an even, easy hand. He had been one of the early army flying cadets and had vomited from airsickness the first three times he went up in a trainer, but he had stuck it out to become part of the first expansion-era graduating class, 1940-A. After that rocky start, Kittel became a daring pilot who could land in cow pastures as easily as he could fly under a low bridge. If it had wings, Kittel could fly it. His fellow pilots of the Dirty Dozen would all become equally proficient in the air, for they would have a lot of time to practice before being sent close to combat.

When Kittel arrived on Christmas Island, he felt he might be in for a long stay. While the others pitched tents, thinking they were only passing through, Kittel made himself comfortable. He guessed right, for the squadron remained on Christmas Island for almost a full year.

Their airstrip was between the island's two native settlements, known as London and Paris, and Kittel prowled the beaches and the bushes to collect driftwood, abandoned wooden crates, and discarded nails, which he used to build a hut and some furniture. His makeshift accommodations slowly improved until they were the best on the entire 222-square-mile island. When generals passed through, Lou Kittel would be kicked out of his house for the night so the brass could stay there.

When they had sailed from Pearl Harbor, the pilots of the 12th were ordered not to take along radios, booze, or cameras, so Kittel took some of each. Boredom led him to grow a thick beard that he trimmed to accommodate his oxygen mask. He talked an old fraternity brother who was a navy clerk into assigning him a motorcycle and got a friend in Hawaii to send him a dog. This peculiar animal—it looked like a cross between a German shepherd and a dachshund—liked to ride on the motorcycle with his master. It growled at women and children.

A benefit of living on Christmas Island was that seafood was fresh and plentiful. Pilots of the 12th would fly small spotter planes out over the coral reefs, searching for schools of giant fish that moved like dark shadows through glassy water. They would land on an atoll, catch a few, and fly back to base with fish strapped to the outside of the plane or carried in the lap of a backseat observer. When the army sent them crates of Spam, they sent it back. But their repeated requests for transfers to combat were denied, and they instead became instructors, training other pilots and sending them along the pipeline to New Guinea and Guadalcanal while the Dirty Dozen sat on Christmas Island going nuts.

Besby Frank Holmes, from San Francisco, was a slight, short man with a crooked grin. He graduated from flight school in Class 41-H on November 1, 1941, pinned on his wings, and went straight to Hawaii for gunnery training with the 47th Pursuit Group. It turned out to be the real thing. On December 7, he was wearing a brown pin-striped suit and attending mass when the bombs started falling. As he rushed to Wheeler Field, he heard a radio announcer confirm the Japanese were attacking and say there was no need for panic because the army had everything under control.

When Holmes got to the field, a crew chief slapped a .45-caliber pistol in one hand and a parachute in the other as they ran toward a parked P-36, the outdated little planes being used as trainers for the gunnery students. A Japanese plane came in on a strafing run, and Holmes, still in his civilian suit, popped away at it with his pistol as it flew by. The crew chief had to start the unfamiliar aircraft for him, but Holmes was in the sky a half hour after leaving church. The Japanese were gone, but nervous American gunners were not: They tried to shoot him down, so he landed.

After rotating through various assignments, Holmes arrived on Guadalcanal to fight with the 67th Pursuit Squadron, and he then moved in with John Mitchell's flying circus. Besby Holmes would become an ace, a pilot with five aerial victories, but he would be better remembered for challenging both the official and unofficial histories of the Yamamoto mission.

Lieutenant Ray Hine was a tall kid with sandy brown hair and such dark good looks that his radio call sign was "Heathcliff," after the brooding hero of the classic novel *Wuthering Heights*. He was not one to chitchat with strangers.

Hine, holder of a degree in civil engineering from Purdue University, had signed up as an air cadet while still a student. He won his wings five days after Pearl Harbor in Class 41-I. By Christmas, he had caught up with the 68th Pursuit Squadron, another of the new units that had been created to expand the air corps. Within months of being formed, the 68th went from Selfridge Field, outside of Detroit, down to Baton Rouge, Louisiana, then by troop train to San Francisco, in January 1942, and on by boat to Brisbane, Australia, where it arrived in March, with no planes and little training.

Heathcliff and the squadron's other thirty-two pilots climbed aboard the Dutch freighter SS *Maetsuyeker* two months later and spent a week at sea, trundling halfway back across the Pacific before the ship tied up at a short wharf on a foot-shaped island called Tongatabu. When the squadron commander told the pilots they were in Tonga, nobody had any idea where that was. They were about four hundred miles southeast of Fiji, near the intersection of the Tropic of Capricorn and the International Date Line. They unpacked their twenty-five P-40 Kittyhawks and got busy flying patrols out of a grass airfield.

Hine, once he shoehorned his six-foot frame into a cockpit, knew what he was doing with a plane and grew comfortable at the controls as he made long sweeps out over the deepwater anchorage where big navy ships, including carriers, would stop to get supplies. That was one of the few contacts the 68th maintained with the real war, because Tonga was far away from the fighting front. As the months passed, however, the unit moved closer and closer until it, too, ended up fighting on Guadalcanal.

8

Raid

Task Force 16

Admiral Yamamoto was haunted by the possibility that the Americans might try a surprise attack on the homeland in retaliation for what happened at Pearl Harbor, and that dread spurred him to take rigid precautions to protect the Imperial Palace and the emperor. The admiral established a screen of ships in an arc a thousand miles from the coast, brought the entire 21st Air Flotilla back from Southeast Asia to a base near Tokyo, recalled two aircraft carriers, dispatched scout submarines, and planted antiaircraft batteries everywhere.

But a man such as Yamamoto, with the thorough knowledge of the quick-strike capabilities of aircraft carriers, must have known no defense would be perfect. Even as he prepared his defenses, two American aircraft carriers—the venerable *Enterprise* and the brand-new *Hornet*—were heading straight for Tokyo, with America's best carrier admiral, Bill Halsey, in command.

William F. Halsey was an Airdale to the core. His pugnacious attitude, combined with bushy eyebrows and a craggy face lined by years of staring into the sun bouncing off the sea, had inspired reporters to bend his real name of "Bill" to the more evocative sobriquet of "Bull." He was coming to Japan with a score to settle. Halsey had seethed with anger when he brought the *Enterprise* into Pearl Harbor shortly after the Japanese attack. The *"Big E"* had been only two hundred miles away, coming home to Pearl after delivering a squadron of marine planes to Wake Island, but he missed the entire fight. When he saw the devastation, he growled, "Before we're through with them, the Japanese language will be spoken only in hell!"

Early in the gray morning of April 18, 1942, as his Task Force 16 pounded through heavy seas only 688 miles from Tokyo, the carriers were spotted by a fishing boat that was also doing patrol duty on the outer perimeter of Yamamoto's warning line. The fishermen managed to radio warnings to Tokyo before being blasted apart by an American cruiser.

The alert arrived on Yamamoto's desk at 6:30 A.M. and the defensive net came to life. The staff checked the reported position and believed there was plenty of time for an interception, for the Americans needed to travel several hundred more miles before even the best fighter-bomber in the U.S. Navy could launch with any hope of reaching Japan. Four Japanese battleships sortied from Yokosuka, and a dozen Zero fighters and thirty-two medium bombers dashed toward the Americans.

The admiral's staff did not know that navy planes would not be making the strike that day. Instead, twin-engine B-25 medium-range attack bombers of the U.S. Army Air Corps did.

Revving up the engines of the lead B-25 was Lieutenant Colonel James H. "Jimmy" Doolittle, whose name was almost a household word in America. He was a daredevil barnstorming pilot, racecar driver, and champion boxer; he was also a thoughtful scientist with a doctorate from the Massachusetts Institute of Technology. Doolittle never gambled, and would act only when the odds were better than fifty-fifty in his favor. This mission, he believed, was a good bet.

When the task force was discovered, it was still some two hundred miles east of the originally planned launch point, but Halsey gave the signal to go. Leathery Marc Mitscher, captain of the *Hornet* and an aviator himself, turned his carrier into the wind. The ship bit into thirty-foot-high waves, and it surged from side-to-side as well as up-and-down. Doolittle stood on the brakes to hold his plane steady as a fifty-knot wind howled straight down the flight deck, which seemed to twist before his eyes. He lifted a hand from the yoke only long enough to wave to Mitscher, who was standing on the wind-lashed bridge. Mitscher solemnly returned the salute.

The launch officer circled a checkered flag overhead, and Doolittle applied even more power, until his bomber shuddered with the vibration. The B-25, overloaded with extra gasoline and two thousand pounds of bombs, was a ton beyond its maximum weight. The bow of the carrier dipped into the steep trough of a wave, and as it slowly rose up the next wall of water, the launch officer dropped the flag, Doolittle released the brakes, and the B-25 shot forward, the nose wheel following a white line to stay centered, and the wingtip missing the ship's bridge by only six feet. The bomber jerked sharply into the air at 8:25 A.M.

Once all sixteen of the big, brown planes were on their way, Task Force 16 circled about and headed for safer waters, executing the tactic commonly known as "Haul Ass with Halsey."

The bombers would not be coming back aboard, but were to fly straight on to China. They arrived over Japan at wave-top level. When they emerged from the cloud cover, fighters chased a few of them, and antiaircraft guns chattered, but they had appeared overhead and were gone so quickly that accurate fire was impossible. Rice paddies and beautiful countryside slid past in the morning light.

The crews were under strict orders not to attack the Imperial Palace, for hitting the home of Emperor Hirohito would unify the Japanese even more. Each bomber had a military target, and Doolittle dropped his incendiary bombs on a Tokyo factory. He flew on to China and safely bailed out before his plane ran out of gas and crashed. Of the eighty crewmen involved in the raid, three were killed when their planes crashed, eight more were captured (three of whom were beheaded), and several were interned when they landed in Russia, which was neutral in the Pacific theater after having signed the nonaggression pact with Japan. The others eventually made it back to the United States.

Tokyo and six other cities sustained bomb hits but received only minor damage. The raid may have been a strategic fleabite, but in the United States, morale soared at the news of the first significant American success of the war. President Roosevelt hinted that more attacks might follow, and teased reporters that the bombers had flown from a secret base called Shangri-La, a fictional land in James Hilton's popular novel *Lost Horizon*. When Doolittle came home, the president gave him the Congressional Medal of Honor.

The psychological factor was exactly the opposite in Japan, where Admiral Yamamoto and his staff stood shocked. Their disbelief turned to puzzlement, then to anger—Tokyo bombed! The C-in-C was embarrassed, shamed, and coldly furious. He did not believe the attacking planes had come from some mysterious Shangri-La, nor even from secret bases in China, Russia, or Alaska. They had been brought aboard carriers, and he was more determined than ever to rid the ocean of those floating enemy bases.

Even Yamamoto's most strident critics fell into line after the Doolittle raid, finally agreeing that the American carrier fleet had to be destroyed. Operation Midway was on.

Pearl Harbor

Despite the success of the one-of-a-kind raid, the war was going badly for the desperate Allies. The Germans seemed on the edge of toppling Russia, and panzer columns rumbled through Egypt. Japan was driving through Allied ships and planes with brutal efficiency, controlled most of the sixty-four million square miles of the Pacific Ocean, had wrecked the U.S. fleet and snatched away British and Dutch possessions. They were close enough to Australia to see the kangaroos. Only a thin line of American and Allied troops and planes on the little islands protected the supply route from California to New South Wales. That was not much in the way of resistance, but it was all that was available.

In a pair of basement rooms beneath the 14th Naval District Administration Building at Pearl Harbor, some unlikely warriors were about to make a huge contribution to the war. Admiral Yamamoto did not know it, but Joe Rochefort was reading his mail. Not the letters and personal notes the admiral constantly wrote to his friends and admirers, but military information and orders that were transmitted to his far-flung command by radio. The Americans had broken the Japanese operational naval code.

Commander Joseph J. Rochefort always believed that a man had to be a little nutty to get into the intelligence business, a line of work that attracted people who were hopelessly addicted to crossword puzzles and couldn't look into a bowl of alphabet soup without seeing a message. Most cryptanalysts closed their minds against anything but the riddle of the coded message before them, often skipping lunch and forgetting family engagements, and even entire days.

Rochefort led a little band of analysts who operated Station Hypo (the H stood for Hawaii) in what was known as the Dungeon, for the offices were chilly even in Hawaii's tropical heat. A few desks were jammed into a larger room that was festooned with maps, while IBM punch-card sorting machines clanked away in the smaller room. Rochefort padded about in carpet slippers and wore a tattered red smoking jacket over his uniform. He lived off sandwiches and coffee, caught a few hours of sleep on a small cot when he was about to collapse, and was occasionally expelled from the Dungeon and told to take a bath.

A brilliant perfectionist, the slender Rochefort was indifferent to personal comfort. He was also fighting a couple of wars. One was with the Japanese, whom he knew extraordinarily well, having lived in their country. The other was with Washington, where his caustic attitude toward senior officers was the stuff of bitter legend. He said flatly that he worked for Admiral Nimitz, not for anyone in Washington, where envious competitors wanted to take over the Pearl Harbor intelligence operation. His comment did not go unnoticed by Admiral King, the COMINCH, whose office was in the nation's capital. Only Rochefort's reputation as the navy's foremost cryptanalyst and Japanese linguist kept him in the game.

Station Hypo not only decoded and translated the Japanese messages intercepted by special monitoring stations, but also went the extra step of trying to figure out the *intent* of the messages in order to provide the Pacific Fleet commanders with an active tactical picture of what the Japanese would do next. Analysts in both Washington and Hawaii missed forecasting the Pearl Harbor attack, but Station Hypo had failed because it had been prevented from seeing all of the relevant information. Rochefort spent no time feeling sorry for not making a correct forecast; he concentrated instead on whatever was coming next and on sending his findings up the chain of command to his old friend and protector, Commander Edwin T. Layton, the fleet intelligence officer. The busy team in the Dungeon had grown more efficient at combat analysis during the early months of the war, and they were even able to say that individual ships, planes, and officers were operating in certain places, thus indicating buildups, possible attacks, or withdrawals.

By March, Station Hypo had solved about 30 percent of the mysterious Japanese naval code in which five-number groups represented the words, phrases, and letters used most frequently by the Japanese navy. That was the month that Admiral King sought Rochefort's opinion for the first and only time during the war. The COMINCH wanted an estimate of Japanese intentions in the coming few months.

By combining fragments of information, the conclusions of the Hypo analysts, and his own famed sixth sense, Rochefort came up with an astonishingly accurate prediction. It was as if he had seen the Japanese battle plan. The Japanese were done with their operations to banish the British fleet from the Indian Ocean, he said, and had no intention of operating nearer to the United States than Hawaii, but they would advance farther down the southern islands toward Australia. In addition, Rochefort predicted, another major operation was coming, and it would be separate from the thrust in the south. He was precisely correct on all four points.

That analysis, Rochefort later said, was about the most important combat intelligence message he ever sent. When it reached Washington, the message vanished without a trace. But at Pearl Harbor, where Admiral Nimitz believed in his quirky analyst, more radio intelligence steadily brought confirmation that Rochefort had figured right. Something was afoot in the Coral Sea, a pearly body of water that washes onto the Great Barrier Reef along the northeastern shoulder of Australia.

The Japanese also operated a substantial radio intelligence-gathering network, with its central control base in the town of Owada, about fifteen miles from Tokyo. Data was gathered through networks of distant listening posts throughout the sprawling empire of islands and fed back to cryptanalysts and linguists for processing. In combination with ship sightings, reports from spies, and other sources of information, the

Owada teams were excellent at interpreting many Allied military moves. But their code-breaking abilities did not match the levels of their American counterparts.

While the Owada center had sent out many unconfirmed alerts that an attack might be threatening the Japanese homeland, the Doolittle raiders achieved complete surprise. The Japanese radio-interception analysis would also fail to accurately predict the coming battles in the Coral Sea and at Midway.

To the Japanese, such analysis was only part of a strategy that was drawn up at the highest levels of command. In the hands of a true believer such as Admiral Nimitz, it was a tactical, immediate weapon.

The Inland Sea

Admiral Matome Ugaki had become the powerful chief of staff to Admiral Yamamoto five months before the Pearl Harbor attack. He had risen swiftly through the ranks of the Imperial Navy, taught at the Naval Staff College, served on the Naval General Staff, and captained the battleship *Hyuga*. Although a big-ship veteran, he quickly came to accept Yamamoto's belief in the power of the airplane. He was devoted to his leader. The tall, lean, and imperious Ugaki willingly played the flinty-eyed bearer of bad news from the C-in-C to the staff, and oversaw much of the general strategic planning for Yamamoto. He kept a private diary in which he recorded everything from the weather to major events, wins and losses, and the mood of his chief. After the Doolittle raid, he painted a picture of a naval staff that was distracted from one of the important jobs at hand. That included Yamamoto.

For days, they were obsessed by how the Americans got those long-range planes within striking distance of Japan and then, for the most part, got away clean. "Work harder to resolve the riddle!" Ugaki demanded of himself. New plans were drawn to further improve defenses so as to prevent another such attack. Then, by the time of the celebration of the emperor's birthday on April 29, the staff was involved with meetings, plans, and war-gaming for the coming Midway operation, with mock battles being played out on large tables built on the fore mess deck of the *Yamato*. The giant battleship itself sortied out of the anchorage for gunnery practice.

As a result, Yamamoto and his chief advisers were focused on a minor bombing raid and a battle that had not happened at the cost of overlooking one that was about to explode in the Coral Sea. A Japanese invasion fleet was heading for Port Moresby—part of the trade Yamamoto had made in order to be able to strike Midway—and he was convinced those forces were more than adequate for the job. He probably would have preferred to include the two big fleet carriers that were part of the Port Moresby operation in the Midway strike force, but the deal had been made. He would have to fight Midway with four carriers instead of six.

The strategically pivotal city of Rabaul, at the tip of New Britain Island, had been captured in January and converted into a major air and naval base, from which the Japanese could attack farther south while also supporting the operations on New Guinea. More airstrips would be needed in the area, after Port Moresby was taken, in order to isolate Australia and even bomb Sydney. Therefore, the first step of the Port Moresby operation would be to land troops and engineers in a small harbor town on Tulagi, in the Solomon Islands, and establish a forward seaplane base there.

After that, the main invasion force of troop transports would sail for Port Moresby, guarded by cruisers and the small carrier *Shoho*. The planners hoped to lure the American carriers toward the invasion force and trap them in a pincers movement that had the fleet carriers *Shokaku* and *Zuikaku*, both veterans of Pearl Harbor, sweeping around from the northeast.

Pearl Harbor

Admiral Nimitz knew a fight was brewing somewhere in the Coral Sea, but he did not have much with which to answer the Japanese threat. The man he would have liked to have leading the American task force was Bill Halsey, who was still returning from the raid on Tokyo with the *Enterprise* and the *Hornet* and much too far away to help. That left

Nimitz with only the *Lexington* and *Yorktown,* under the command of the temperamental Rear Admiral Frank Jack Fletcher. Both Nimitz and Admiral King had reservations about Fletcher's ability to run an aggressive carrier operation, for, as a former cruiser commander, Fletcher had a habit of wanting to keep his ships filled with fuel in readiness for a traditional naval battle. It seemed that he would rather spend days bobbing around, refueling, than going out to hunt. There was no other choice, however, and Nimitz ordered Fletcher and his two carriers out to stalk the Japanese moving south.

The Battle of the Coral Sea was a confused affair from the start. Some of Fletcher's planes arrived over Tulagi on May 4, the day after the Japanese unit landed there, and they sank a destroyer, a transport, and two patrol boats, then shot up a nest of parked seaplanes, but by doing so alerted the enemy that American carriers were in the area.

The opposing fleets brushed near each other during the night of May 7, and joined battle the following morning when Zeros pounced on a pair of U.S. ships, mistakenly thinking one was a carrier. Machine guns stuttered and bombs thundered as the Japanese sank the destroyer *Sims* and damaged the fleet oiler *Neosho* so badly that it was later scuttled. There was no carrier.

Then a full strike of American planes—launched in response to an earlier mistaken American report—swarmed down on the lightly armed *Shoho* and slammed her with thirteen bombs and seven torpedoes in twenty minutes. The *Shoho* burst into flames and sank within minutes, taking down 545 crewmen with her. "Scratch one flattop!" came the word from the enthusiastic American pilots.

The duel between the big fleet carriers the next day was more a matter of luck than of tactics. In history's first naval battle in which the opposing ships never saw each other, U.S. Navy planes—Wildcat fighters, Dauntless dive-bombers, and Devastator torpedo planes—damaged the big *Shokaku* with three bombs and decimated the air wing from the *Zuikaku.* But Japanese Zero fighters, Val dive-bombers, and Kate torpedo planes found the *Lexington* and blew it apart so badly with bombs and torpedoes that she had to be intentionally finished off. Two hundred and sixteen crewmen died, but more than two thousand were rescued. *Yorktown* caught a bomb deep in her guts and pulled away, badly hurt. Thick clouds of smoke from destroyed ships and burning oil smothered the battle area, and debris and bodies bobbed in the water as the crippled distant fleets disengaged, their fighting done.

The Inland Sea

Some four thousand miles to the north, Admiral Yamamoto and his staff posed for a photograph aboard their superbattleship on the last day of April, just as the fight in the Coral Sea was beginning. Little news had reached them from the Coral Sea.

Initial reports seemed positive and did not interrupt a four-day table exercise of the Midway plan. But as more signals were received, Yamamoto turned sour, and then frustrated. When he learned that the Port Moresby invasion force had turned away from its goal, and an obviously crippled American carrier was getting away, he personally ordered a resumption of the chase to catch the grievously wounded *Yorktown*, but it was too late.

Still, Japan had gained a clear tactical victory. The little *Shoho* and a few smaller ships had been sunk, the *Shokaku* damaged, and the air component of the *Zuikaku* torn apart. The Americans, however, had lost one frontline carrier, the *Lexington*, and a second, the *Yorktown*, had been crippled. A destroyer and a tanker also were sunk. The strategic edge, however, went to the Americans, for the cautious Japanese admirals had not pressed their advantage, a habit that Yamamoto detested. This time, caution had cost more than planes and ships, because the Americans had stopped the Japanese southward plunge. The shaky Allied southern perimeter had held.

May 8 dawned fair, the blood-red rising sun clearing away the rain clouds. In his stateroom, Yamamoto was in a private, turbulent storm. *Another chance lost!* He took no comfort from the Imperial congratulations, nor from the army in taking the final surrender of the stubborn island of Corregidor in the Philippines and capturing some seventy-five thousand prisoners. On the surface, things were still going Tokyo's way, but Yamamoto saw a crack in the surface; he recognized that his fleet had been checked in the Coral Sea. It left him enraged, as if somehow he knew that the Japanese would never advance farther than that.

Irresponsible reports of American battleships being sunk, enemy ships able to steam around within reach of his carriers, the annihilation of Japanese planes and pilots, admirals ignoring orders to attack, the Port Moresby invasion force running away, and a heavily damaged American carrier escaping without even scout planes tracking it! Dismal defeatism! No matter how the propagandists framed the news, Yamamoto considered the battle a major setback.

Admiral Ugaki agreed, and wrote in his diary, "A dream of great success has been shattered."

Yamamoto felt he had personally to make up for the back-to-back blows, the bombing of Tokyo and the Coral Sea error, and threw himself into planning Operation MI, the invasion of Midway Island. This time he would lead the expedition himself.

9

Midway

Pearl Harbor

Admiral Nimitz counted his carriers. He had lost three frontline flat-tops since the start of the war: The *Lexington* was gone for good; the *Saratoga* had been under repair since being torpedoed four months ago; and the *Yorktown* was limping back from the Coral Sea trailing an oil slick ten miles long. That left Nimitz with only the *Enterprise* and the *Hornet*. The balance of carriers was tilted about five-to-one in favor of the Japanese, and now his favorite skipper, Bill Halsey, was out of the fight, too, hospitalized with an agonizing case of dermatitis. Nimitz had no choice but to give tactical command once again to Fletcher, who had stalled on his mission to relieve Wake Island, narrowly missed both defeat and victory in the Coral Sea, and seemed to prefer refueling to fighting.

Nimitz knew that his best bet for blocking the Japanese now lay with Joe Rochefort and his oddball, pasty-faced code breakers. If the gnomes in the Dungeon could figure out *where* the next battle was to be fought, he might be able to figure out *how* to fight it.

The Japanese had been scheduled to change their special naval code on May 1 but had not done so. The conquest of so much territory, so fast, had made it impossible to distribute the new codebooks to everyone who needed them by that date, so the switch was postponed for a month.

The delay was a fatal error, for it allowed the Station Hypo cryptologists and analysts at Pearl Harbor to crack about 90 percent of it. In one of the biggest intelligence coups of the war, Rochefort and his gang predicted the Japanese fleet was about to attack Midway.

Part of the guess was based on the Japanese code for the target, indicated by the letters AF. But was AF Midway? The analysts devised a means of finding out. Station Hypo directed the marines on the island to transmit a false message complaining that their freshwater condensers were causing trouble. When Midway complied, Japanese eavesdroppers intercepted the seemingly routine piece of information and promptly relayed it by code to higher headquarters and the Combined Fleet: AF was low on water. *That* message was heard in turn by the Americans, and it confirmed Midway was the target.

Washington reviewed the same radio intercepts and came to a startlingly different forecast: The enemy fleet might be heading for the island defense chain in the south, even Australia, and could not move against Midway until the middle of June. One Hypo analyst snipped, "If we listen to Washington, we will all end up as Japanese POWs." Nimitz placed his faith in his own people at Pearl and set about organizing an ambush.

He might have only two carriers, but he had the forces needed to turn little Midway into a fortress. Nimitz made a quick personal visit to the island, then dispatched orders to pack it with five thousand troops, a hundred planes—there was no room for more—and thickets of guns. If the Japanese tried to come ashore, it would cost them.

The Inland Sea

Admiral Yamamoto had so many ships that he could not see them all at one time. The massive, soaring superstructures of eleven battleships seemed to needle the low clouds, and the flat decks of four large aircraft carriers looked like islands. Ships at anchor spilled over the horizon, more than two hundred of them preparing to head out for Midway and the grand quest to lure the American carriers to their deaths. It would be a bloody business, but Yamamoto wanted to deal the U.S. Navy a horrendous loss and force the Americans to consider negotiations for peace.

The First Air Fleet was aboard the carriers, with 272 bombers and fighters that would be flown by some of the best pilots ever to enter combat. Cruisers and destroyers would slice alongside the big ships as escorts, and submarines were stationed in an early warning belt off of Hawaii. Transports would waddle along carrying an invasion force of some five thousand troops. The Americans had nothing that could match the Combined Fleet.

The battle plan was overly complex. It would begin with a diversionary attack high in the North Pacific on the Aleutian Islands of Attu and Kiska. When the Americans dashed in that direction to block an advance toward their mainland, the middle of the Pacific would be left exposed, allowing Yamamoto to capture Midway and take over the island's airstrip. That would be tantamount to adding a fifth aircraft carrier to his already superior strike force. The Americans would be forced to wheel back from the Aleutians to face the crisis and run into the waiting Combined Fleet.

Yamamoto wanted the looming battle to be one-sided, brief, and final. He would pound the U.S. ships with the air groups from his carriers, then slaughter whatever was left with his powerful battleships. That would be the end of the American navy in the Pacific. The southern operations could resume, and his ships would roam the sea like hungry sharks, slashing at America until Washington sued for peace.

The plan was flawed from the start, but because Yamamoto championed it, the critics had fallen silent. Still, signs of ill fortune swirled around the fleet like the seabirds looking for bits of garbage.

The Coral Sea battle had shaken the Imperial Navy's feeling of invincibility. That the little carrier *Shoho* had been sunk was unimportant. However, when the big *Shokaku* hobbled into Kure harbor for repairs, it was a clear symbol that the enemy could fight back, and when the *Zuikaku* arrived a few days later with her air group in tatters, it was difficult to view the Coral Sea as any sort of victory. Still, Yamamoto remained confident that Admiral Nagumo—with the *Akagi, Kaga, Hiryu,* and *Soryu*—had more than the firepower he needed for the coming showdown.

Bad omens followed. Yamamoto learned that Commander Minoru Genda, the planning genius behind Pearl Harbor, lay abed, stricken with a high fever, and Mitsuo Fuchida, the pilot who had led the aerial assault on Hawaii and was to spearhead the Midway air attack, was recovering from an emergency appendectomy. Yamamoto himself was suffering from severe stomach cramps brought on by intestinal parasites. Things he could not control were bedeviling him.

His friend Admiral Ugaki had skewed the war games that tried to foresee the outcome of the battle. At one vital point in the games, an unlikely roll of the dice punished the Japanese carrier force with severe losses, but Ugaki, acting as the senior umpire, simply changed the rules in a misguided cockiness born of previous success. It was called "victory disease."

While Yamamoto might stroll the teak deck of his superbattleship with confidence, his heart was troubled after the four melancholy days he had spent on shore leave in Kure with his geisha mistress, Chiyoko. She was so seriously ill with pleurisy that doctors had almost given her up, but she insisted on going by train to see Yamamoto. He met her at the station in disguise, with a mask to cover part of his face, and wearing civilian clothes so no one would recognize him. The admiral in mufti toted his sick sweetheart on his back from the train to his car. While his flagship was being readied for battle, Yamamoto stayed with her at an inn, nursing her as doctors gave her injections. In a farewell poem that he left behind, the admiral confided that, while at sea, he would press kisses upon her picture.

Beneath the dress uniform and towering image of the forceful commander in chief was a man worried about a woman.

Pearl Harbor

On May 27, the same day Admiral Nagumo's carrier force sailed away from Japan, Admiral Nimitz approved his own Midway plan during a staff conference in Hawaii, then went down to visit the battered *Yorktown.*

It sat in the vast dry dock like a mauled, helpless colossus. Nimitz went through it carefully, examined the severity of the Japanese bomb damage, and made a crucial decision. He would not to wait for full repairs, which might take three months. Nimitz just wanted her seaworthy and at least able to throw some kind of punch, not fitted out for a white-glove inspection. "We must have the ship back in three days," he ordered, and hundreds of shipyard workers worked marathon shifts to perform a miracle, somehow patching the carrier enough so that she was able to sail out again in only forty-five hours. Repair crews would sail aboard her, still mending damage, but the *Yorktown* would be able to fight at Midway.

Nimitz now had three carriers instead of two.

He also had a crystal ball in Joe Rochefort and his Dungeon acolytes, who had been so busy that Edwin Layton, the Pacific Fleet intelligence officer, was able to predict that the Japanese would attack Midway at six o'clock in the morning on June 4, approaching from the northwest on a bearing of 325 degrees, and an hour after they launched, the enemy planes would be spotted 175 miles from Midway. When contact actually was made and the battle commenced, that analysis was off by five degrees, five miles, and five minutes. The Japanese finally switched to their new code a few days later, but the damage had been done.

Slender, dark-eyed, and brainy Rear Admiral Raymond A. Spruance, who had never commanded a carrier in his life, was chosen to replace Bill Halsey. Spruance had been in charge of the cruisers that protected Halsey's flattops and knew the tactics and the admiral's staff. Even better, as far as Nimitz was concerned, Halsey had recommended Spruance for the job. Spruance sailed from Pearl Harbor with the *Enterprise* and *Hornet*, five heavy cruisers, a light cruiser, and nine destroyers on May 29. He was followed two days later by Fletcher, with the wobbly *Yorktown*, two heavy cruisers, and six destroyers. They would rendezvous at sea.

Task Force 16 under Spruance and Task Force 17 under Fletcher joined at Point Luck, an imaginary dot northeast of Midway, and by the first day of June were sending out scout planes and submarines to hunt the Japanese.

Midway

Rain and heavy fog swallowed the battleships and left Admiral Yamamoto blind. Not only could he not communicate with the carrier force several hundred miles ahead of him, because of radio silence, but the dirty weather prevented him from even being able to see the ships around the *Yamato*. The refueling tankers had gotten lost, and navigation throughout the force became so difficult in the fog that ships turned on bright searchlights as beacons. Attempts to fly reconnaissance planes over Hawaii failed, analyses of radio intercepts were spotty, and he had no true idea of the location of the American carriers. He stayed with the established plan, which was designed to draw them out, wherever they were.

His force, incredibly powerful as a single unit, was dispersed over the wide sea. And while he exercised overall command, that was merely a title, because tactical decisions were in the hands of the individual commanders. All Yamamoto truly had under his command was Battleship Division 1, made up of three mastadons trundling along far behind the carriers. Instead of striking with a clenched fist, the plan unfolded more like individual fingers reaching out tentatively.

The Japanese diversionary group captured two of the frigid Aleutian Islands without problem, in a victory of no importance, far from the central battle zone.

The Midway invasion force of transports and escort ships hung back until the air threat from the island could be neutralized. Nagumo's main carrier strike group, operating as an independent task force, would attack Midway first, then prepare for the American response. The battleship group lurked far in the rear, ready to pounce.

In the Pearl Harbor operation there had been bad weather and radio silence, and both had worked to Yamamoto's advantage. This time, however, there would be no element of surprise. He received sketchy reports from the Owada intelligence complex that a large enemy force had sailed from Pearl Harbor, but to maintain radio silence, the staff did not pass the warnings along to Nagumo. The Combined Fleet entered the waters around Midway as the weather cleared and showed up exactly where and when the Americans anticipated, and the trap was sprung.

The biggest battle between aircraft carriers to that point in history began on June 3, but Admiral Yamamoto was so distant from the fight that he might as well have been with Admiral Nimitz, who was playing horseshoes and taking target practice with his pistols in Hawaii. Both had issued their orders, and it was up to their subordinates to carry them out, win or lose.

Midway Island was savaged by Japanese bombers just after dawn, and some three hundred Americans were killed there, most of them from the marine garrison. But pesky American fighter planes made the Japanese bombers misjudge the actual damage they had caused—it was substantial—and Nagumo was persuaded to launch a second strike on the island. It was a critical error.

The carrier battle that followed was a colossal duel in which pilots on both sides dropped by the dozen as they pressed attacks to deliver their bombs and torpedoes through walls of antiaircraft fire and enemy fighters. Some sacrificed themselves as decoys so their squadron mates could get through. Opposing commanders made critical decisions, right and wrong, in a matter of minutes, even seconds.

The Japanese commanders were surprised by the number of American planes in the sky, many more than could have possibly come just from Midway. There had to be American carriers out there, but how many, and where?

Nagumo had been readying a new wave of planes with torpedoes to fight the American fleet when he was persuaded to launch the new strike against Midway. The first attack force had returned to be refueled, and all four carriers became a hive of frantic work. Aircraft were lined up wingtip to wingtip along the decks, carrying bombs or torpedoes and filled with volatile fuel. The complex operation was almost complete when American planes caught the ships just as they were turning into the wind to launch.

U.S. Navy Dauntless dive-bombers rammed two direct hits into the *Akagi*, and although neither normally would have been a serious blow, fire raged through the planes on deck, and they exploded like a long series of devastating bombs. Flames swept through the passages, burned along the deck like a prairie fire, and climbed the command bridge, forcing a stunned Admiral Nagumo to escape to another ship from which he could retain command of the fight. Among the few effective orders Admiral Yamamoto issued that day were, first, not to scuttle the *Akagi*, which had been his first carrier command, and then reversing himself several hours later, to do so and prevent her from falling into American hands. Japanese destroyers put a fan of torpedoes into her and she went under, exploding beneath the sea. The *Akagi* captain tied himself to an anchor and went down with his ship. Oily smoke hung like a black tombstone above their final resting place.

Six bombs from Americans chewed into the flight deck of the *Kaga* during the same attack. The captain was killed almost immediately, and a holocaust rampaged until the ship became a listing, burning hulk. Dense smoke towered black above the length of her flight deck until she blew apart with tremendous explosions. She vanished beneath the waves nine hours after first being hit.

The *Soryu* also was struck about the same time, with three American dive-bombers walking direct hits along her flight deck. In five minutes, the massive ship was awash in bright fires that triggered explosion after explosion, and within twenty minutes the order was given to abandon ship. Captain Ryusaku Yanagimoto refused evacuation, even when his men ordered a giant seaman who was a wrestler to bodily pick up their popular skipper and carry him to safety if necessary. The big man, unable to bring himself to touch his steely superior, turned away in tears. The last voice heard aboard the *Soryu* as it sank was that of her captain singing the Japanese national anthem.

The fourth carrier, the *Hiryu*, escaped the deadly bombs and torpedoes that sent the other three to the bottom, and Rear Admiral Tamon Yamaguchi, one of the bright minds in the fleet, immediately counterattacked. A scout plane from one of the doomed ships landed aboard the *Hiryu* and brought the first word that three American aircraft carriers had been found. That explained why there were so many American planes in the sky, but it also meant that the odds had significantly changed. Instead of having a statistical advantage, the Japanese were now outnumbered three big carriers to one.

Hiryu pilots located and torpedoed the *Yorktown*, and the aggressive admiral was about to launch another strike at dusk with the few planes he had left when the Americans found him. Four bombs slammed into the deck around the bridge, followed by the usual deadly progression of flame and explosion. The ship lost momentum and tilted to one side like a staggered boxer. After it was abandoned, Japanese destroyers slammed in torpedoes to sink her. None of the four defeated carriers was allowed to fall into American hands. Admiral Yamaguchi and the ship's captain waved from the bridge of the *Hiryu* as it slid from sight to the steady drumming concussion of multiple explosions.

In an incredible forty-eight hours of furious fighting, death, and destruction, the invincible auras of the Imperial Japanese Navy and its storied leader, Admiral Isoroku Yamamoto, were shattered.

For the Americans, the price was steep. The *Yorktown*, which had barely made it to the fight, was sunk. A destroyer also went under, and about 150 American planes were shot down. Three hundred and seven sailors and aviators died.

But the price was ghastly for the Japanese. All four of their big carriers, a heavy cruiser, and fourteen other ships, plus more than 250 planes and 2,200 men. Among the losses were many of the elite pilots and talented mechanics and technicians of the carrier force, who carried years of training and experience down with them. Experienced commanders willingly went down with the ships, wasting their skills. It was a disaster in every way. Admiral Nagumo had to be persuaded not to commit ritual suicide in his shame over the first major Japanese naval defeat of the war.

Yamamoto played no significant part in the engagement, other than covering the agonizing retreat. The fighting was over before the battleships even got there. His overall plan had worked, for he had finally drawn the American carriers into a decisive battle, just as he had wanted to do for so long, and the power of the airplane over ships would never again be questioned. But he had lost! The radio reports of his carriers going up in flames staggered him.

Yamamoto was incredulous at the scope of his losses but knew the Battle of Midway had changed everything.

He retired to his spacious stateroom, emotionally drained, sweating profusely, and in agony from the worms in his belly. The heart had been ripped from his fleet, and he gave orders that no one criticize Nagumo. "I am the only one who must apologize to His Majesty," he told his officers.

Washington

JAP FLEET SMASHED BY U.S.
2 CARRIERS SUNK AT MIDWAY,
NAVY HAD WORD OF JAPAN PLAN TO STRIKE AT SEA.
KNEW DUTCH HARBOR WAS A FEINT

The headline roared from the front page of the *Chicago Tribune* on Sunday morning, June 7, and was reprinted by the *Washington Times-Herald*, the *New York Daily News,* and several other newspapers. The highly detailed story beneath the headline all but acknowledged that the secret Japanese code had been broken.

Navy Secretary Frank Knox managed to persuade the newspapers to drop the story after the first day, but the reports persisted. Popular broadcaster Walter Winchell announced that intercepted radio messages had been used to save Midway, and an intemperate congressman revealed: "Somehow our navy had secured and broken the secret code of the Japanese navy." There was a brief congressional hearing, and legal action was threatened against the Chicago newspaper, its publisher, and the reporter who wrote the story but had never signed a security pledge.

Initially, the Japanese missed the news, but eventually grew suspicious. Admiral Ugaki noted that the Americans "must have succeeded in decoding, which was the cause of our defeat at Midway." The code was changed again, and once more the cryptographers started all over.

In Washington, COMINCH was furious. Admiral King considered the publication of such vital information to be pure treason and ordered that henceforth the incredibly valuable secrets of code breakers must be protected at all costs.

10

The Quiet Time

The army pilots helping guard the islands that stretched from California to New South Wales did not even know about the Battle of Midway until weeks after it happened. The knife had been removed from their throats, but censorship was so tight that they were unaware of the reprieve. They went about their training still thinking the Japanese fleet might show up at any time. But there was a new jauntiness to their step, a bright addition to their already considerable egos, thanks to a simple semantic change made on May 1, 1942. The U.S. Army Air Corps became the U.S. Army Air Forces, and the antiquated World War I designation of single-seat combat aircraft as "pursuit" planes was replaced by the dashing new term "fighter." Pursuit meant to chase something. Fighter meant to catch it and shoot it down. To a man, they liked the new term: They were *fighter pilots!*

On New Caledonia, Dale Brannon and his executive officer, John Thompson, seemed to be everywhere as the 67th Fighter Squadron spent weeks trying to master the strange P-400 airplanes that had been pulled from the crates. In a bizarre assembly line, soldiers and officers started before dawn, worked shoulder to shoulder all day, and returned to work after dinner in colossal rains and among clouds of ravenous insects. They labored through bad weather, invasion worries, dysentery, and disease, many times until exhaustion buckled their knees. All of the work was done by muscle power in a blistering summer sun, for there were no trolleys, lifts, or automatic pumps. Conditions were so primitive that the squadron clerk set up the commander's office in an old chicken coop.

Each P-400 was a puzzle. They called one the "Rube Goldberg Special" because it was so strangely configured that when the switch was pressed to lower the flaps, the guns fired instead. When the engine was tested on another P-400, the plane spun around with one locked wheel as its guns blazed away, blowing out the back of a building. But there was a junkyard pride in getting them together, and sometimes the worse they were, the better the men liked them.

Brannon and Thompson had their hands full coaxing and advising the young fighter pilots on the peculiarities of the P-400. On low-level flights, it zoomed above the water without effort, rock-steady and reliable. The problems began when they ventured higher. At ten thousand feet, with throttles to the firewall and the engines straining, spots danced in front of the pilots' eyes because they had no oxygen supply. By the time they reached fourteen thousand, the planes just hung limply on their twirling propellers as the pilots grew ever more woozy and had to come back down. Brannon knew the Japanese Zeros regularly flew above thirty thousand feet! The enemy would be able to loiter upstairs and jump his boys anytime they chose.

Ever so slowly, the pilots learned the P-400, and felt that at least by determining its severe high-altitude limitations, they would know what to avoid. The lessons, however, came at a price. A colonel commanding the Tontouta Air Base died when his plane drilled into the ground at the end of a steep dive. Another P-400 stalled on takeoff, hit the beach, and exploded. One pilot died when he did a victory roll over the field after attacking what was thought to be a submarine, but was really a whale. He clipped the treetops and pancaked into a fireball. Dead pilots were the price of realistic combat training.

Mechanics scrounged and salvaged every part they could when a plane went down and used it again. Since there were so few P-400s in service, every cannibalized part could keep another plane flying. The favorite P-400 on the island was a battered aircraft that had skidded to a halt one day after landing on its belly because its wheels collapsed. It came to rest with a wing crumpled and the propeller bent, making it an open source for spare parts. However, the need for flyable aircraft was so great that mechanics nursed it back to health. One wing was U.S. Army olive green and the other was British camouflage. Instruments were plugged into gaping holes in the cockpit panel. The three-bladed propeller contained two blades from one wrecked plane and one blade from another; it was balanced by pouring in lead until it spun almost correctly. The aircraft took on a strange personality all its own and would outlast every other plane in the squadron. It was proudly christened "The Resurrection."

Brannon and Thompson dreamed up unique ways to train their young fliers, most of whom were so inexperienced that they had yet to learn such basic things as flying in formation, a critical skill in combat. Flying without another American plane at your side for protection was an invitation to disaster. To practice navigation, the pilots flew around and around the familiar island to pick out landmarks from the air. Gunnery practice included Brannon and Thompson flying at a medium altitude along the beaches, casting their own planes' shadow on the sand below while other planes flying beneath them fired at the moving black silhouettes. It was better than nothing, but not much.

Life was better 812 miles to the northeast, on Fiji, where the 70th Fighter Squadron was guarding another leg of the convoy route. Things were so tranquil that John Mitchell, Tom Lanphier, Rex Barber, and the other pilots had trouble believing the world was indeed in flames. Distances were great, and news was scarce. They were 2,500 miles from California, some 1,700 miles from Australia, and about halfway between New Caledonia and American Samoa. There were plenty of uniforms around, and planes and ships, but the tropical oasis still did not have the grim look of a combat zone. "It was like an adventure," said one pilot. "We were aware of the war, but we could not see it or hear it. We were almost like a group of college youths on a field trip."

Once their P-39s were flying, things settled into a pleasant, boring routine. When not on duty, the fliers sampled Suva's quiet colonial lifestyle, which seemed straight out of a novel. From the spacious veranda of the Grand Hotel, they could look out over the bustling harbor, drink Tanqueray gin, and be cooled by overhead fans.

Doug Canning had a tailor rework his khaki uniform into the British-style tropical outfit of shorts and a short-sleeved shirt—something more suitable to the scorching weather—and a number of other pilots soon copied him. The short pants were unusual to the Americans, but could not compare with the white skirts decorated with seashells that were worn by local Fijian policemen, large black fellows with wild stacks of bushy hair and precise English accents.

There was plenty of company, for five companies of American ground troops, including the advance ground echelon of the 70th, had arrived several weeks before the pilots, another five thousand New Zealanders had been protecting the place on their own since the war started, and more Americans seemed to arrive with every boat. The pilots were disappointed when their silver wings and boyish charm failed to impress the pretty daughters of the families of the British colonial administrators and wealthy planters. The girls preferred to help civilian Red Cross workers spend their lavish cash allowances.

The delights of Suva became harder to reach when engineers finished a mile-long all-weather landing strip on the far side of the island. The pilots strapped on their P-39s and flew over ancient volcanic peaks and dark jungle to the new air base, and the others came by truck convoy.

The squadron commander, Henry Viccellio, organized the same sort of routines as the leaders of the other island squadrons to bring the pilots up to combat standards. But he also allowed the men a lot of freedom, as long as they got their jobs done, for no one knew when their turn would be called, and ready or not, they would have to go.

A *bure* boy cleaned their palm-thatched huts and ran errands. They worked on planes and did their flying in the mornings and played baseball every afternoon, the hot sun bronzing their bodies. Officers and enlisted men fielded separate teams to play pickup squads from other units. For the officers, Lanphier was at third base and Barber was at shortstop. It was the same stuff day after beautiful day. Even the food, invariably mutton shipped up from New Zealand, was boring. Fijians, who lived off the bounty of the sea and teeming forests of fruit, thought the soldiers' diet was strange. Bomber crews passing through from the States sold Coca-Cola for five dollars a bottle. The local mouth-numbing liquor called kava, made from fermented coconut juice, was popular, and the nearby town of Nandi became the alternative to hanging around the base.

There was even a touch of humor out on the flight line. A painter sketched a cartoon of Emperor Hirohito on the tail of one P-39 and drew a little blue devil with a pitchfork on the adjacent rudder. Every time the rudder moved, the devil stuck the emperor in the butt. That was about as close as they got to the war. As week after week passed, all they did was train, train, and train some more. Few of the younger pilots realized that the effort was paying off, that they were becoming a unit honed to a fine, sharp edge.

John Mitchell shopped through the ranks for a wingman, someone who could keep up with him in the sky no matter what he did, and settled on Julius "Jack" Jacobson, a smart, whippet-lean sharpshooter who had been in these parts before. Jacobson was descended from a Russian family that immigrated to the United States in the early 1900s and settled in New York, where his uncle found work sewing insignia on naval uniforms. When the navy opened a base in San Diego, Jacobson's family moved there, arriving in the coastal town in 1919 with twenty dollars among them. He was three years old at the time. In high school Jacobson excelled at math and Latin, but his goal of becoming an accountant derailed when he and a friend stowed away on a British freighter and headed around the world. The captain made his unwanted passengers spend their first eighteen days at sea chipping paint, then allowed them to help the cook. Dumped in the Philippines, they spent a night in jail before joining the crew of a passenger ship as kitchen helpers. By the time the cruise ended, the teenager from California had sampled the ports of Singapore, Ceylon, Bombay, and Marseilles before landing in New York and making his way back to California. To John Mitchell, that kind of experience added up to a reliable guy who did not scare easily. Jack Jacobson would ride on John Mitchell's wing. They both made it through the war alive.

Such personal histories were surfacing frequently as the men spent so much time together, and there simply was not much else to do but talk after the work, the flying, the baseball, the swimming, and hanging around doing nothing. Bull sessions dwelled on any topic that could hold their interest and pass some time. The hours spent talking combined with the sense of trust being sowed as they flew together to give the pilots confidence in the abilities of the men flying beside them. The sense of brotherhood and bonding unique to members of combat units was becoming stronger with each passing week. Most would remember the names of their fellows and stay in touch with them for the next sixty years. They were beginning the most important phase of their young lives, and nothing would be held back.

On one calm South Seas night, Rex Barber had finished writing another letter to his mother and wandered over to a coconut log to sit and sip some whiskey with his friend Tom Lanphier. Rex was a quiet sort, but being with Lanphier was almost like turning on a radio. He might talk longingly about his fiancée, Phyllis Fraser, whom he called Phoebe and whose family was well connected back in Idaho. Or he might reel off some adventure from his famous father's days as commander of the old 1st Pursuit Squadron in the 1920s. And sometimes he would just exaggerate a story until it stretched beyond belief.

Tom was easy to listen to, and his friends enjoyed his company so much that they brushed off his tall tales. They had no doubt that he was a superior pilot; he had only recently flown beneath a bridge just for the hell of it. But his bragging grated even on his longtime friends. "He was the greatest name-dropper in the world," recalled Jacobson, who had lived next door to Lanphier in a barracks during flying school. "He would say, 'Well, I talked with, or I know this guy and that guy,' and it turned out later that he didn't know them. I used to tell him, 'Tom, you're so full of bullshit,' and he'd laugh."

But sitting on that log in Fiji on that night, Lanphier had something on his mind. Henry Viccellio had been promoted to major and given a staff job with wider responsibilities. Captain Waldo Williams had taken over the 70th, and Lanphier was shifted into Williams's position as leader of the A Flight. It was a step up the ladder, and Lanphier was so delighted that he allowed Barber a glimpse of the demon that was pushing him so hard to do reckless things in order to draw attention and to succeed.

It was no surprise that Tom was ambitious, but Barber had never before heard him admit that he actually had a plan! Everyone else in the squadron just wanted to get this war over with, go home, and get on with life. For Tom, that wasn't enough. Lanphier said he was looking forward to going home, too, but not yet. With careful logic, he explained that an ordinary military record was not going to be enough for him; he needed a sterling combat record to fuel his future career. He needed glory.

"I'm going to be the most famous pilot to come out of this war," he announced.

Why? Rex wanted to know.

Lanphier responded, with all seriousness, "I'm going to be president of the United States."

Tulagi

The war had not stopped, and despite the unexpected victory at Midway, the Allies remained desperate in the summer of 1942. A German summer offensive had pushed deep into Russia and was driving on Stalingrad. Nazi U-boats were choking the lifeline to England by sinking merchant vessels coming from the United States faster than replacements could be built. In Africa, the port of Tobruk surrendered to the Afrika Korps of Field Marshal Erwin Rommel. America was gathering forces along the eastern United States but had not yet put to sea for the invasion of North Africa. The invasion of France, D-day, was two years off. In the Asia-Pacific theater, Japan controlled millions of square miles of conquered territory and remained threateningly close to Australia. Midway only stabilized the naval balance; it had not retaken any territory, nor had it given the United States mastery of the sea. Admiral Yamamoto might be temporarily dispirited, but he had plenty of ships left with which to fight, planes to scour the skies, and marinelike units of sailors, called naval landing forces, with which to attack island outposts.

The northern coast of Australia was being bombed, and its giant island neighbor of New Guinea was turning into a bloody, frantic battleground. Supporting those Japanese operations were the big air and naval bases at Rabaul, which had been captured in January. But Yamamoto wanted new airstrips even closer to the fighting on New Guinea, to prepare for another thrust that could finally capture Port Moresby, so Sydney could be bombed, Australia isolated, New Caledonia and Fiji captured, and the American supply line cut. Success in the south would balance out the disaster at Midway.

The Japanese troops who had gone ashore at Tulagi before the Coral Sea fight recovered quickly after the single attack by American carrier planes. Tulagi had been the administrative center for the British Solomon Islands Protectorate, and while it had a nice, small port, the new Japanese owners were interested in bigger game.

Tulagi was suited only for use by seaplanes, so a working airstrip would have to be located elsewhere, and scouts found another island just twenty miles away, directly across Sealark Channel, a place where dormant volcanoes dropped abruptly into deep ravines and thick jungle dominated a good coastline. Ninety miles long and some twenty-five miles wide, it offered good natural harbors and commercial plantations that Europeans had groomed on the flat terrain near an area called Lunga Point. That smooth area would be ideal for air operations.

The name of the island was Guadalcanal.

BOOK II
Guadalcanal

11

Guadalcanal

A thousand miles off the eastern coast of Australia, an uneven line of islands is sprinkled along the upper right quadrant of the Coral Sea. On a map it is hard to distinguish one from the other, and the many curious names, some impossible to pronounce, are legacies of indigenous natives and explorers from many lands. The upper point of the volcanic chain is the Bismarck Archipelago, almost on the equator and directly east of the rump of the big New Guinea lizard. From there the islands fall away like rungs on a ladder to New Caledonia, 1,578 watery miles to the southeast. The tip of the New Guinea lizard's tail points directly to the midpoint on that ladder, to the Solomons, one of which is Guadalcanal.

It is not a kind place. The first European to arrive in that harsh tropical land was Spanish explorer Don Alvaro Mendaña of Spain, in February 1568. He boldly named the islands after King Solomon, but instead of finding treasure, discovered only heat, disease, and rot. A group of Austrian explorers found out the hard way that not only was the climate a killer, but some of the Melanesian inhabitants were cannibals. Author Jack London took a look at the crocodiles and poisonous spiders, giant lizards and vicious white ants, towering mountains, thick jungles, suffocating heat, and torrential, drowning rains, and declared, "If I were a king, the worst punishment I could inflict on my enemies would be to banish them to the Solomons."

Nevertheless, civilization inexorably marched into the area, and the British and Australians had governed the Solomon Islands for a hundred years prior to World War II. White planters worked with the natives to till the rich soil, missionaries arrived, and a small cluster of government buildings was constructed on Tulagi. Most of the Europeans, Australians, and New Zealanders pulled out as the Japanese approached, but a few stayed behind and took to the jungles throughout the Solomon Islands to become hidden eyes for the Allies. Under the administrative control of the Royal Australian Navy, which had trained and equipped many of them for just this purpose, they were known as coastwatchers, and were worth their weight in gold.

Curious Melanesian natives, friendly and loyal to the white people with whom they had worked for many years, had watched impassively as the first small unit of Japanese soldiers came ashore on May 3. Several reported back to the coastwatchers, who had taken up life in hidden huts, that, "Japan-man he come along Guadalcanal." By the end of June, rows of tents had been erected, and ships were bringing in more troops and construction equipment. Plumes of dark smoke rose above the Lunga Plain, where trees and brush were being burned, and workers hacked a runway out of the kunai grass near the coast. The coastwatchers passed along the word by radio, and the Solomon Islands became the unlikely center of the Pacific universe.

Admiral Yamamoto could not have put his finger on any weaker point in the Allied command structure. Washington had divided the Pacific neatly into two major sections. General MacArthur, headquartered in Brisbane, was in charge of the Southwest Pacific Area, which included Australia, New Guinea, and the Philippines. Admiral Nimitz ran the Pacific Area, with responsibility for most of the islands. Each Allied nation, such as the Dutch and Australians, had its own commander, who was the under the overall direction of the respective American headquarters.

The Solomon Islands sat squarely on the boundary separating the areas, along longitude 159° east. Since the supply route to Australia was so important, Washington also created a single subarea of operations to handle what was called the South Pacific Area. Chosen to lead in that vital territory was Vice Admiral Robert L. Ghormley, a popular fifty-nine-year-old Oregonian.

Ghormley was a large man who possessed an extraordinary intellect, and his career seemed to make him singularly suited for the hard task ahead. He had held important senior staff jobs, including chief of the War Plans Division, and had spent time in the high diplomatic circles of London. The flaw was that his sea experience had been aboard destroyers and cruisers before he became the executive officer of the battleship *Nevada* and captain of the battleship *Oklahoma*. He was sailing a desk in Washington when the Japanese attacked Pearl Harbor and took out both of those big ships. The *Oklahoma* was capsized and sunk, and the *Nevada* was so badly damaged that it had been run aground to keep it from going under. Ghormley, a big-ship admiral in the dawning age of the airplane, would be overwhelmed by his new job in the South Pacific. Instead of just protecting the island bases of the convoy route, he found himself in charge of the complex and gruesome fight for Guadalcanal and its sea approaches, where ships would die in such large numbers that sailors nicknamed the waters "Ironbottom Sound."

Ghormley was a gift to Yamamoto. Instead of having to deal with the boldness of a recovered and vengeful General MacArthur, or the strategic skills of Admiral Nimitz, or the bulldog bite of Admiral Halsey, he would face Ghormley, who secluded himself aboard his flagship and became a timid hermit.

Wellington, New Zealand

Marine Major General Alexander Archer Vandegrift, the soft-spoken Virginian who commanded the 1st Marine Division, didn't even know where Guadalcanal was when he got orders to invade it. The instructions to launch the operation came to him while he was still aboard a ship bound for New Zealand. The invasion was to take place on August 1, in just five weeks, a clearly impossible assignment, but despite heated arguments and impassioned pleas, Vandegrift was given a delay of only one week. Ready or not, his marines would hit the beach on August 7.

Not only was part of the division still at sea, and the rest spread out in temporary camps all over New Zealand, but the marines were nowhere near prepared for such a major amphibious operation. Many had enlisted right after Pearl Harbor, were given a few weeks of recruit training, and sent along to North Carolina to join the 1st Marines. Since then, their experience had consisted primarily of taking a long boat ride to the South Pacific. They carried bolt-action 1903 Springfield rifles, and their mortars had been packed away in grease since World War I. Their standard machine gun was the 1917 Browning, which could fire only one hundred and fifty rounds per minute and was described by one officer as "a cross-eyed old bitch that kicked, jerked, and jolted like a jackhammer gone mad." Their canvas leggings were twenty-three years old. When the army learned the marines had no machetes at all with which to cut through the jungle, it helpfully donated eight hundred cavalry sabers.

The 1st Marines initially had been sent out to train for some unspecified minor amphibious operations in 1943, but that timetable had been thrown away. The Japanese had moved too far, too fast, until they finally overstretched their military capabilities. They could not be everywhere at once. Their drive on Port Moresby had been stymied, substantial damage had been inflicted on them in the battles of Coral Sea and Midway, and the Allied commanders could not sit idly by and let them regroup. Plans for the first Allied ground offensives were rushed forward, both to stop the Japanese southward thrust and to crack their main line of defense. That could turn the whole war around. It would be a double attack, with a reinvigorated General MacArthur striking back against New Guinea, while the navy and marines set about retrieving Guadalcanal and capturing the airstrip under construction there.

Later in the war, island assaults would become finely meshed operations, but the attack on Guadalcanal was patched together from the start.

Before they even set out from the United States, a naval supply officer refused to recognize that marines landing on hostile shores needed sturdy crates for their food and supplies, not the flimsy pasteboard cartons that were adequate for storing food to be cooked for sailors on ships that also had refrigeration. The supply officer ignored all requests and issued the standard cardboard boxes, which melted into slush when stacked on docks in the winter rains of New Zealand and rotted apart

on the beaches of Guadalcanal. Marines went to war wading in corn-
flakes.

The transport ships were so improperly loaded at the U.S. ports
that much of the equipment most needed in combat—ammunition and
food and vehicles with which to move them—had been stored at the
bottom of the deep holds of the transports instead of on top. In New
Zealand, the tightly unionized longshoremen, called "wharfies," staged
so many work stoppages that the marines took over as stevedores along
Aotea Quay to rearrange the cargoes themselves. Someone scrawled on
an outhouse wall "All wharfies is bastards."

The division was not up to full strength in manpower, since five
thousand of its men had been stripped away to protect Samoa. Then,
even as the Guadalcanal landings were being organized, an abrasive and
arrogant midlevel admiral arbitrarily weakened the 1st Marines even
more by scheduling the division to also capture a small island that was so
useless no one wanted it, not even the Japanese.

Vandegrift had no accurate maps of Guadalcanal except for a few
outdated navy prints, a questionable German document of World War I
vintage, some fuzzy *National Geographic* cartographic work, hand-
drawn sketches made by people familiar with the islands, and a single report from an officer who was almost shot down during a flyover of the
island.

While the marine general had little idea of what the landing beaches
looked like, the U.S. Army actually had fine maps of Guadalcanal.
Richard Tregaskis, a correspondent who would write the famous book
Guadalcanal Diary, reported after the war that a lazy American army
transportation officer in Townsville, Australia, had been ordered to send
current air reconnaissance maps over to the marines three weeks prior
to the attack. "He stalled around for ten days before forwarding the A-1
priority shipment," Tregaskis wrote. When the box of maps reached New
Zealand, it was lost during a dispute with the wharfies.

Koro, Fiji

On July 27, the sky didn't seem so empty—or the war so distant—to
John Mitchell, Rex Barber, Tom Lanphier, Jack Jacobson, Doug

Canning, and the rest of the army pilots of the 70th Fighter Squadron. The largest amphibious task force ever assembled by the United States had gathered off the southern island of Koro to practice the invasion of Guadalcanal. Nineteen navy transports packed with two marine combat teams bobbed at anchor under the close escort of a force of destroyers, cruisers, and a brand-new battleship, the *North Carolina*. Three aircraft carriers—*Enterprise, Wasp*, and the repaired *Saratoga*—were supplying the air cover, and buzzing clouds of blue navy planes dotted the clear Fijian sky.

To the superstitious, it seemed that bad luck dogged their trail. The "*Big E*" had lost its first plane just as it left Hawaii, when an F4F Wildcat crashed while trying to land on the broad deck. Then the cruiser *Boise* ran aground. The island of Koro, chosen because it was in a secure area, was discovered to be fanged with coral reefs that would rip the bottoms out of landing craft. Only a third of the marines were able to get ashore at all in their practice invasion. As the top brass boarded the *Saratoga* for a final strategy conference, one admiral was showered with rancid milk flushed from a garbage chute. That, thought General Vandegrift, set an appropriate tone. The rehearsal was a miserable failure.

Then it got worse. Ghormley, the overall commander of the South Pacific Area, was so tepid about invading Guadalcanal that he stayed aboard his flagship, anchored at distant New Caledonia, and sent his chief of staff to lead the final invasion conference. It was a significant error, for it meant Ghormley was represented at the meeting by an underling who was outranked by Vice Admiral Frank Jack Fletcher, the overall tactical commander of the operation. Fletcher, after the battles at Midway and in the Coral Sea, looked tired and nervous. Never a risk taker, he was determined not to lose any more aircraft carriers. He announced that his carriers would take up a position distant from the invasion area and provide air cover for only three days before pulling out to avoid attacks by Japanese planes.

Vandegrift could not believe his ears. Fletcher intended to leave the marines exposed on a hostile beach, possibly while locked in heavy combat. Fletcher brushed aside the protest, and Ghormley's outranked chief of staff remained silent. After three days, the skies above the marines were to be given over to the Japanese.

. . .

The convoy raised anchor in the dark of night on July 31 and started the weeklong journey from Fiji to the Solomon Islands. Mitchell, Barber, Lanphier, and the rest of the army pilots of the 70th Fighter Squadron would not be going along, but the time for some of them would come sooner than they thought.

The marines were ill prepared for combat in almost every area. Air cover would be limited, supplies were questionable, their weapons were old, and many of the recent enlistees were virtually untrained. Perhaps the single advantage they did have was a core of good officers and solid, experienced sergeants who had fought before, in stations from China to Haiti. This "Old Breed" didn't give much of a damn who they fought or where, whether on a beach or in a bar. Just get us there, they told the navy, and we'll do the rest. Their rugged spirit rubbed off on the kids they were about to lead into battle. America was sending its tough guys to storm the Solomon Islands in the first U.S. offensive of World War II.

Guadalcanal

The assault force stole around the northwestern end of Guadalcanal at 1:33 A.M. on the morning of August 7. United Press reporter Robert C. Miller, a reed-thin, gregarious writer who would become one of the premier war correspondents of the next half century, spoke for many of those on board when he wrote in his private diary, "I'm going to be closer to death within the next few days than I have ever been before. Sort of have the butterflies caroming around my midriff already. . . . I am apparently still sleeping with Lady Luck. Hope to hell she doesn't desert me when the bombs begin falling."

The convoy moved undetected past Savo Island, which guarded the northwestern entrance to Sealark Channel like a cork in a bottle. One group of ships split off to attack Tulagi, and the second group headed for Lunga Point on Guadalcanal. The battle opened with a salvo from the cruiser *Quincy* and strafing attacks by carrier planes, and after the preparatory bombardment the marines went ashore. Bitter fighting erupted on Tulagi, but on Guadalcanal the Japanese defenders and construction workers abandoned a hot breakfast and faded into the jungle, allowing the marines to come across the beach unchallenged.

The sudden arrival of the U.S. Marines and American warships was radioed to the huge Japanese base at Rabaul, 565 miles to the north, and in a few hours, a flight of dive-bombers, fighters, and torpedo planes of the 25th Air Flotilla lifted off and headed for the invasion force. An Australian coastwatcher saw them pass overhead and sent a warning to Guadalcanal, "Twenty-four torpedo bombers headed yours."

American carrier planes climbed to a high altitude and were waiting when the enemy arrived at midday, penetrating white clouds that were starkly beautiful against the blue sky. The first aerial battle above Guadalcanal was a ballet of fire and death, and plane after plane, American and Japanese alike, fell in flashes of fire and smudges of smoke that trailed down into the green jungle and hungry blue sea. The Japanese lost fourteen bombers and two fighters, and the Americans lost eleven Wildcats and one dive-bomber. Most of the pilots died.

By nightfall, some eleven thousand U.S. marines had landed on Guadalcanal. Another six thousand were slugging it out on Tulagi and two smaller islands, where most of the fanatical Japanese soldiers they encountered defended their fortified caves until they were killed. Japanese servicemen had been raised in a culture that preached duty to the emperor, and they were only a few generations away from the legendary samurai who thought nothing of dying for one's lord and master. In World War II, that same attitude led common soldiers to endure great hardship and prefer death to the dishonor of capture. Of the two hundred and fifty Japanese defenders on Tulagi, only three surrendered.

Across the channel, on Guadalcanal, the boxes of supplies were piling up on the beaches as the American transports hurriedly unloaded. The ferocious air battle over their heads convinced the sailors to work fast.

Day One of the invasion had not been without casualties, but it was more of a success than anyone had dared expect. Although it was not apparent at the time, the Japanese would consistently underestimate the number of U.S. marines who actually landed, and many future attacks would be poorly planned, based on that error.

The Yamato

Light rain gilded the steel superstructure of the battleship *Yamato* before dawn as a staff officer hurried to report to the commander in chief of the Combined Fleet that the Americans were attacking Tulagi.

In the month since the Battle of Midway, the Combined Fleet had been licking its wounds, performing maintenance, and planning future operations. Admiral Ugaki, the chief of staff, noted, "We can't do anything for the time being but take a nap." The only significant movement had been to start troops marching from the northern coast of New Guinea on a dangerous trek south over the rugged Owen Stanley Mountains for a Singapore-like attack on the rear of Port Moresby.

Yamamoto still had a powerful fleet, and he estimated that he still owned a two-to-one advantage over the American aircraft carriers. "There is no need to worry, as competent Yamamoto is commanding," reflected the Emperor Hirohito. But Midway had been a disaster for the commander in chief, and he had been even more reserved than usual as he gathered his wits and confidence.

The report of a new American offensive galvanized Yamamoto and plunged him back into work. Just by spinning the huge globe he had bought in England and presented as a gift to the *Yamato*, he could read the entire story of the Pacific theater. The little gravel-and-clay runway the Japanese had built on Guadalcanal, no more than a dot on the map, was never meant to be anything other than another stepping-stone in the drive to the south. Now it had become vitally important. It had brought the Americans to fight.

Safely kept in Japanese hands, Guadalcanal and its airstrip would be tantamount to an unsinkable aircraft carrier. If it fell into the grasp of the Americans, they would use it as a springboard to attack to the north. From a strategic standpoint, it was a bit of pleasant news for him, for the Americans had committed themselves to a pinpoint position.

They would need carriers to support the invading ground troops, which meant he finally knew exactly where they would be. He would not have to hunt them all over the ocean.

Yamamoto decided to fight for Guadalcanal.

12

Cactus

Guadalcanal

Day Two was about the same as Day One on Guadalcanal. Japanese planes set a transport ship afire and torpedoed a destroyer, at the cost of most of the attacking Japanese bombers. The marines encountered minimal resistance and seized control of the almost completed airstrip, along with a treasure trove of supplies, including a refrigeration plant, Ford and Chevrolet trucks, mosquito nets, and plenty of food, from dried kelp to candy. The place had been abandoned so swiftly that a copy of the latest Japanese codebook was left behind. The marines had the feeling that this was all coming too easy.

Despite the lack of stiff resistance, Admiral Fletcher threw in the towel, concerned that the enemy torpedo planes that had struck the transports might soon come after his carriers. He radioed the faraway Admiral Ghormley for permission to withdraw as planned, made his usual claim that his ships were low on fuel, and pulled out.

A screen of cruisers was left behind to guard the transports, which worked all night to off-load supplies, so they, too, could leave. But while the American commanders worried about air attacks, the real danger was approaching by sea. Ugaki happily wrote in his diary that the Japanese navy was again on the move. "The Eighth Fleet is going to surprise the enemy in Guadalcanal tonight. Come on, boys! Do your stuff!"

Marines in their foxholes saw the black sky light up out at sea shortly after midnight on August 9 when a Japanese raiding force of five heavy cruisers, two light cruisers, and a destroyer slammed into the line of un-suspecting Allied cruisers. Brilliant flashes colored the low clouds in bright slashes of yellow and silver and orange and red, and a constant low grumble of big guns echoed across the dark waters. Marines drifted down to the beach and stood watching the sky change color and listen-ing to the deep thunder of ships fighting for their lives. Australia's *Can-berra* was smashed to bits, and a torpedo tore off the bow of the American cruiser *Chicago*. Huge salvos ripped into the *Astoria*, and the *Quincy* was violently sunk. The *Vincennes* was caught and destroyed, and the way was clear for the Japanese strike force to plunge into the un-protected transports supporting the marines. But unaware that Fletcher had pulled out of the battle zone, and fearing a daylight attack by carrier aircraft, the Japanese did not want to be caught in the open, and they fled north before dawn.

The Battle of Savo Island was one of the worst sea defeats ever in-flicted on the U.S. Navy. One thousand and seventy-seven American and Australian sailors were killed, and another seven hundred were wounded. Their blood spilled into the sea and drew hordes of sharks that feasted on men who had jumped into the water.

The one-sided battle rekindled the spirit of the Imperial Japanese Navy. "Those conceited British and Americans who regard the battles of the Coral Sea and Midway as supreme victories cannot say anything now," Ugaki gloated, unaware that they had just missed winning the battle for Guadalcanal by breaking off the action instead of plunging ahead to destroy the unprotected American transports and savaging the invasion beach itself.

Next day, the U.S. transports got back to work unloading on Red Beach, and dumped the boxes and crates in such a clutter that landing craft carrying more material were turned away from the shore. Then the transports fled, because they had no cover in the air or on the sea. They still contained tons of supplies and even units of fighting marines who were supposed to be put ashore. When Japanese search planes and submarines came snooping, they found neither planes nor ships. The marines on Guadalcanal had been abandoned.

.   .   .

Although the Battle of Savo Island was a crippling blow to U.S. naval power in the area, airplanes were going to be what settled the ownership of Guadalcanal. The marines knew that finishing the little airstrip was a paramount task, because it would free them from depending on the whims of Fletcher and Ghormley. Sooner or later, Japanese land forces were going to show up, and air support was going to be vital for survival.

Any doubt about the kind of fighting that could be expected was erased early in the campaign when a marine patrol went out to accept the surrender of a Japanese unit thought to have waved a white flag. It actually was a Japanese flag, but a whipping wind had hid the red sun in the center of the white field, and the approaching marines were massacred. Survivors told of seeing sunlight glint upon swinging swords as their buddies were chopped up. After that, neither side showed mercy, and neither expected it.

On August 17, ten days after the Americans landed on Guadalcanal, a huge shadow moved through Japan's Kudako Channel as the mighty battleship *Yamato* once again sailed away from the home islands, this time heading for the advance base at Truk so Admiral Yamamoto could be closer to the action. Lookouts kept sharp watch for lurking American submarines, and radio silence was maintained as the huge vessel ploughed south through the moonless night. The C-in-C, remaining in his stateroom to write letters, missed the opportunity to say good-bye to his homeland.

Strategically, Yamamoto faced a problem. The Japanese army, not the navy, was tasked with recapturing Guadalcanal, and the arrogant army generals believed they could easily sweep away the American troops on the island. They estimated there were only two thousand marines on Guadalcanal when in fact five times that number had been landed. The army's lassitude and unrealistic expectations reached into Yamamoto's own staff, which was still euphoric over the Savo Island victory. The navy was ordered to ferry new troops to Guadalcanal and "mop up the enemy remnant, rescue the garrison and repair the airfield."

Lieutenant General Harukichi Hyakutake had more than enough troops for the job in his 17th Army, but his fifty thousand men were scattered over a wide section of the Pacific, and he had been concentrating on Port Moresby and New Guinea. He assigned the job of dealing with this new problem at Guadalcanal to Lieutenant Colonel Kiyono Ichiki, who led a force of only about a thousand men. They were tough veterans who had been scheduled to take Midway, and with their aggressive spirit, the Ichiki detachment was deemed strong enough to subdue the Americans.

It took about a week to shuttle the Japanese force to Guadalcanal, and the troops sometimes brazenly went ashore in broad daylight, within sight of the U.S. Marines, who had no airplanes with which to fight back and no guns that could reach them. Bloody clashes erupted along the Tenaru River, only about a mile from the airstrip, and in the major attack screaming Japanese troops threw themselves against American strongpoints for three days, where point-blank machine gun and cannon fire mowed them down like waves of grain. Those who made it through the barbed wire found themselves locked in bayonet-thrusting, sword-swinging combat with the unexpectedly tough marines. The entire Japanese detachment was annihilated, with only a handful of prisoners taken. Colonel Ichiki, shamed by the loss, committed suicide.

Through it all, work continued on the airstrip, which had been incomplete when it was captured. Engineers working with Japanese equipment filled in a 180-foot gap in the middle, then smoothed it out with a small steamroller they had found. They repaired craters, cut down trees, and expanded the runway until it was about 3,500 feet long and 150 feet wide, all the while with combat marines at the edge of the jungle pushing out the defensive perimeter and shooting back at the snipers. When it was ready, the bumpy airstrip was christened Henderson Field, after Major Lofton Henderson, a marine dive-bomber pilot killed at Midway. On August 20, marine pilots flew in nineteen Grumman F4F Wildcats and a dozen Douglas Dauntless SBD-3 dive-bombers. The ground troops were alone no more.

The call for the army's 67th Fighter Squadron to move up to the combat area had come quickly back on New Caledonia. An enlisted man who drove a jeep on a two-day courier run between bases returned to his starting point to find the entire camp was gone. He said that a baby goat and a pig that had been adopted as pets scampered up to beg for food, and "the three of us just looked at each other." Everyone was gathering at Tontouta, heading for Guadalcanal.

Captain D. D. Brannon brought the first bunch of five P-400s to the embattled island. They had flown more than a thousand miles in a series of hops because they did not have the range to do it in a single bound. Without adequate navigation devices, the fighters huddled behind a guide B-17 bomber.

After almost four solid hours of flying the final leg, Brannon was still over blue water, with no land in sight, when the radio crackled and the bomber's navigator said, "Hold this course for twenty miles. When you get there, check the flag on the pole at the edge of the field. Make sure it's American." The B-17 curved away to return to its base, followed by a second B-17 that had been tailing along to throw a rubber raft to any P-400 pilot who might have to ditch. No safety margin had been allowed.

The fighters were only two hundred feet above the water when the green island of Guadalcanal, code-named "Cactus," came into view. A narrow white beach gave way to a deep jungle that rose into a distant, hazy high country called Mount Austen. Sealark Channel was calm, devoid of ships. From a distance, the place looked peaceful.

As Brannon turned to make his landing approach to Henderson Field, he was happy to see an American flag was in fact fluttering on a pole. Beside it, a flimsy, oblong building stood on a slight rise a short distance from the long, pale runway that stretched east to west on a flat plain between two dark rivers and edged by lines of shattered coconut trees. He dropped his wheels and the covey of P-400s touched down.

Brannon taxied to the edge of the runway, shut down his engine, and climbed from the tight cockpit, sweating and with his muscles cramped after the long hours, during which he had never taken his eyes off of the B-17 until it left them. His gas tanks were almost bone-dry. "Where are the Japs?" he asked a marine who came out to meet him. The man pointed to the sluggish Tenaru, about two hundred yards away, and replied, "Just on the other side of that river." The stench of death rose from over there, for hundreds of Japanese bodies still lay unburied after the ferocious three-day battle that had ended only the night before. A navy unit came out to work as the ground crews for the P-400s.

The five army pilots of the 67th Fighter Squadron were greeted like long-lost brothers by the tired marines, because anybody with a gun was welcome, and pilots who could provide air cover were particularly welcome, no matter what uniform they wore. "We were all marines as far as they were concerned," Brannon said. The gathering ragtag multiservice group would become one of the most famous aerial out-fits of World War II—the Cactus Air Force.

Brannon checked in with the commanders at the wooden building near the runway. Called the Pagoda, it had been built by the Japanese, and was converted by the marines into the island's air operations head-quarters. Then he and his boys settled down for their first night in a palm grove at one end of the Henderson runway, beneath leftover Japanese tents that had been strung between tree trunks. Deep foxholes covered with planks, metal, sandbags, and tree trunks pockmarked the area.

Marine pilots, already looking tired and older after having been on the island for only two days, instructed them to dive for a hole quickly when they heard the bark of naval guns offshore: Those big shells came in every night, trying to destroy Henderson Field and the planes on it. Nobody got any sleep, the marines said, a problem aggravated by one particularly irksome Japanese plane that came over each night, easily recognized by unsynchronized motors that made a horrible racket. It was never just one pilot or plane, but the names of Washing Machine Charlie and Louis the Louse stuck to the nightly visitors, who would make a single noisy pass and drop a few aimless bombs, just to make sure everyone was awake. No matter what happened during the night, the American pilots would be up at dawn and ready to fly by the time a full Japanese air attack showed up around lunchtime.

When Brannon lay back on a straw mattress that had been made soggy by the hard rains that swept the island daily, he heard, for the first time, the strange night sounds of Guadalcanal—unknown things making noises in the jungle and the scuttle of land crabs, sporadic rifle fire, and the whipping bursts of machine guns around the perimeter of the field. The night was never quiet.

He was concerned about the performance of his five streamlined little army fighters that were scattered along the edge of the Henderson runway. The P-400s were tank busters built for the European theater, not dogfighters for the Pacific, so they were headed into a type of battle they were totally unsuited to fight. Then a Japanese submarine started shelling the field, and he jumped for a hole in the ground.

A loud, jarring explosion came rolling across Sealark Channel, where the Japanese destroyer *Kawakaze*, delivering infantry reinforcements to Guadalcanal, caught the American destroyer *Blue* with a torpedo and blew off its stern. Flames reached toward the stars. The marines sharing the foxholes told the army pilots that tonight's shelling had been nothing compared to a bombardment by a battleship. A small shell just screams in and sort of goes *bang,* and if you are below ground level, chances are that nothing will happen to you. But a battleship throws a punch that arrives with a deep and throaty roar, followed by a stupendous explosion that seems to shake the world, and if it lands close enough, it will flatten your world, no matter where you try to hide.

They went back to bed when the submarine went away, heard the coughing arrival of a Washing Machine Charlie, and awoke before dawn as a torrential rain slashed the jungle. Henderson Field was covered with a thick, gray-brown mud that clung like glue to the wheels of planes and the boots of the men. The marines took them to the mess tent, where they got some breakfast and found a safe spot to wolf it down before a sniper could locate them. There wasn't much to eat, since the navy had halted the supply train. The marines were already down to two meals a day and living off captured Japanese rations, dehydrated potatoes, Spam, and whatever else the cooks could sling together. They shared their leathery food with their new buddies from the army.

While they ate breakfast and readied the planes, the sun popped out and dried the muck of the airstrip into a thick layer of choking dust, a coarse powder that worked its way into everything. Marine dive-bombers, escorted by fighters, went out hunting Japanese ships. They returned and were rearmed as noon approached, when everyone kept an eye on a pole outside the Pagoda. It took a Japanese plane from Rabaul all morning to reach Guadalcanal, and a black flag would be hoisted if the coastwatchers sent word that another air raid was on the way. That only worked if the Japanese flew over a coastwatcher, and on the first full day for the army fliers, the attack formation went around them. The black flag went up only when the sound of incoming bomber engines could be heard.

The American pilots scrambled to get off the ground. The whirling propellers of the Grumman F4Fs marine fighters and two of the P-400s threw up storms of dust as the planes rose from the runway, while Zeros swooped in to make daring strafing runs beneath a falling canopy of bombs from planes up high.

Dale Brannon took off so quickly that he did not have time to plug in his earphones, fasten his parachute harness, or hook up the safety belt. He and his wingman pushed their throttles to the firewall and climbed, straining the engines, trying to reach the nine bombers that cruised lazily above them. They couldn't do it. Marine Wildcats zipped by the P-400s and shot down eight of the bombers. The pair of army pilots did catch one low-flying Zero and shot it down. The fight only underlined what Brannon already knew—the P-400s were not going to be of any help in the cartwheeling world of high-altitude dogfights.

The Yamato

The day after Brannon's baptism in combat, a Japanese naval strike force leading Admiral Yamamoto's oncoming Combined Fleet made contact with the American carrier force, far to the northeast of Guadalcanal. It was a battle that either might have won, and neither did.

Two large Japanese aircraft carriers and a small escort carrier that was only one-quarter the size of its big cousins were under the skittish command of Admiral Nagumo. Groping toward them was the equally reluctant Admiral Fletcher, who had the carriers *Saratoga* and *Enterprise*, but had dispatched the carrier *Wasp* to the rear for refueling. Both admirals were still wary after Midway.

The small Japanese carrier *Ryujo* sent its planes to hit Guadalcanal in a surprise raid that culminated in a spectacular fight with the Wildcats and P-400s. It was an intentional sacrifice of the carrier, and when the American task force took the bait and moved in to pummel it, the big Japanese carriers flung seventy-three planes at them. While the

Ryujo drew away the American planes, the Japanese pierced the protective screen around the venerable *Enterprise* and in only four minutes smashed it with three bombs that penetrated the flight deck and went deep into the carrier to detonate stores of gunpowder and set large areas aflame belowdecks. Near misses by other bombs hammered the ship with volcanic concussions that broke apart steel plating, damaged crucial systems, and started even more fires. The expendable *Ryujo* was sunk. Although the *Big E* was rendered ineffective, it managed to stay afloat and set off for Pearl Harbor to be repaired. Nagumo and Fletcher were both refused the opportunity to grab a decisive victory and ran for safety, although each still had plenty of weapons. The costly fight left Admiral Nimitz just as frustrated with Fletcher as Admiral Yamamoto was with Nagumo.

The pleasant quiet of Fiji was driving Tom Lanphier crazy. He was tired of training and tired of waiting; he wanted to touch the war, so he volunteered to be a messenger to the bomber base up on Espiritu Santo.

The B-17s there were running frequent attack and reconnaissance missions into the war zone, and he hitched a ride as a sightseer. When the plane happened upon a cluster of Japanese ships, Zeros attacked it.

"I cowered in the belly of the bomber while the top turret, waist, and tail gunners stood off the Japanese fighters," Lanphier would write later in his autobiography.

He did not cower for long. In his autobiography, Lanphier described how, driven as much by the urge to occupy himself so he could ignore his fear as by a wish to "take up arms for the first time against Japan," he stepped over a wounded and unconscious gunner and took over the soldier's station. He wrote that, while he doesn't believe he could possibly have hit any of the attacking fighter planes, the bomber crew insisted that he get credit for a "probable."

"I have always appreciated the thought, but they and I both knew I had only gone through the motions of firing. I've never had the gall to claim that 'probable.' "

Others recall him describing the mission in great detail. The bomber crew would not confirm the story.

Once back on Espiritu Santo, Lanphier decided to go take a look at Guadalcanal before returning to Fiji. He was not the only fighter pilot on the advanced bomber base on the morning of August 26, for Captain John Thompson, the operations officer for the 67th Fighter Squadron, was leading a group of ten more P-400s to Henderson Field to rejoin Brannon's lead element, which had gone in two days before. They had flown up from New Caledonia and spent the night at Espiritu Santo. Lanphier walked over to talk with them, take a look at the strange P-400s, wish them good hunting, and tell them he hoped to be flying a fighter on the Canal soon himself.

Second Lieutenant Bryan Brown of the 67th did not pay much attention to the guy from the 70th, because Brown, a quiet, boyish-looking pilot, was making sure that the space behind the seat of his P-400 was stuffed with carton after carton of American-made cigarettes, which were valuable commodities on Guadalcanal.

The P-400s took off, and John Thompson formed them up on the tail of the guide bomber, like a bunch of chicks behind a mother hen. Tagging along was a DC-3 transport carrying supplies, with Tom Lanphier riding as a passenger.

The pilots of the 67th were happy to finally be on the way to rejoin the other guys from their squadron who had left earlier. Already a few P-400s had been lost, and reinforcements were badly needed. They all shared a quiet confidence that everything was going to turn out okay. "I never, ever had the feeling that I wasn't going to come back," said Thompson. Some of them did not.

The B-17 actually took them all the way into Henderson, as Japanese soldiers hiding in the jungle popped a few shots at the arriving planes. The P-400s touched down smoothly, and when the pilots opened their cockpits, they found the strip to be eerily quiet. Thompson had no idea what that black flag flapping on a tall pole near the runway meant. It had been waving over the Pagoda for half an hour before they arrived, and, except for some pilots who had scrambled out to meet the incoming Japanese afternoon raid, everybody was hiding in foxholes.

Bryan Brown stood on the wing of his plane and loaded his arms with cartons of cigarettes. He was walking across the runway when he finally understood some of the shouts—people yelling for him to take cover because an air raid was coming. He dropped the cigarettes and ran.

Tom Lanphier had stepped out of the DC-3, which had begun unloading, when the bombs began to fall. In his autobiography, he would write that he was terrified and jumped into a deep foxhole and lay there like a lamb awaiting slaughter, "flinching and cringing" as the explosions detonated. He said the moment defined his life and made him want to fight for democracy.

Immediately after the raid ended, Bryan Brown hurried back out on the runway to retrieve his precious cigarettes, but quicker men had beaten him to them. One thing he did find was a small shaving kit with the name LANPHIER stenciled on the side.

Its owner was nowhere around, he said. The DC-3 had already sped away, taking Tom Lanphier with it.

Often, cargo planes never stopped their engines when they landed at Henderson, so they could take off again at the first sign of trouble rather than becoming a fat target. This would not be the last time that a Tom Lanphier story came in different versions, with different interpretations.

13

Jagdstaffel

Truk

The American marines held a small part of Guadalcanal, but the sea and the sky still belonged to Admiral Yamamoto, who was sending fast convoys filled with ground troops down through what was known as the Slot—the channel that separated the double chain of the Solomons. He wanted to ferry enough troops to the island so a successful attack could be launched against Henderson Field while his ships and planes cut the supplies and reinforcements to the marines. The place would fall like a ripe plum.

He gathered his forces not only at the big base on Rabaul, but also in the great anchorage of Truk, one of the Caroline Islands in the Central Pacific, halfway between Japan and Australia. The Carolines had been under German control until the Japanese took them over at the end of World War I—a prize for fighting as an ally of Great Britain, France, and the United States. Over the years, the Japanese turned Truk into a major base from which the Imperial Navy could control the Central Pacific. Just as important as the prime location was the secrecy it afforded. Protected on all sides by hundreds of square miles of water, Truk was well beyond the reconnaissance range of any Allied plane, an empty hole on the map for the Allies. Other than what could be picked up through radio intercepts, the Americans had no idea what was there, and more ships of the various arms of the Combined Fleet were arriving daily, preparing to fight at Guadalcanal.

Yamamoto arrived in Truk on Friday, August 28, aboard the *Yamato*, which dominated the surrounding waters with its big guns and towering masts. That warlike appearance masked the fact that life was still quite luxurious aboard the admiral's battleship, even as preparations were made around it for a life-or-death fight that would involve thousands of men.

The sailors and officers worked day and night to keep the ship antiseptically clean to protect the sensibilities of their leader. Men wounded in battle were not to be brought aboard, because the staff worried that Yamamoto might be upset by the sight of blood. Nothing adverse was allowed to influence his judgment. The ship was under direct orders from the emperor not to go near the battlefront, where Yamamoto might be endangered.

The admiral enjoyed the best food and spotless uniforms and in Truk could even visit a "naval restaurant" that was really a house of prostitution. He used his underwear only once; each morning he would open a porthole of his splendid cabin and drop the previous day's soiled loincloth into the sea. Hours were spent conferring with his staff and visiting senior officers, but he still had plenty of time to host dinners, play poker and chess, answer his mail, and do calligraphy for admirers.

Things were going well, in his opinion. Only a few days after he arrived in Truk, he received the good news that a Japanese submarine had slammed a spread of torpedoes into the American aircraft carrier *Saratoga* and mauled the flattop, which had only recently rejoined the fleet after repairs from being torpedoed seven months earlier. In the space of a week, two of the largest enemy carriers—*Enterprise* and *Saratoga*—had been taken from the board, which meant even less support for the beleaguered Americans trapped on Guadalcanal. Yamamoto was pleased.

Guadalcanal

Americans on the island were feeling the Japanese choke hold. The navy could not bring in enough supplies to feed the troops, who were still eating abandoned Japanese rations. Sweat-stained uniforms disintegrated in the rotten climate, and captured Japanese loincloths, one size fits all, replaced GI underwear. Cuts and sores would not heal, and malarial mosquitoes swarmed onto the men, causing frightening chills and sharp fevers, turning their skin yellow and felling them as surely as a bullet. Dysentery caught from eating unclean food made a man constantly shit feces, blood, and mucus. Two men, carrying their weapons, would go into the jungle together so one could stand guard while the other defecated, and out would come blood.

The human organism simply broke down under the extreme tropical conditions. Even the strongest men suffered substantial weight loss and aching joints, and their thinking could become so clouded they might even lose the will to live. Many grew listless, felt abandoned, and lost hope.

Every day, cargo planes flew into Henderson Field. They brought in enough drums of gasoline to keep a dozen fighters in the air for a single hour and then flew out loaded with casualties, either thirty-six seated men or eighteen stretcher cases.

The drenching daily rains brought no relief from the heat, and air raids during the day and naval bombardments at night prevented sleep. Hollow-eyed and gaunt marines on the perimeter of Henderson Field, diseased and combat-weary, looked back over their shoulders and felt sorry for the pilots.

The Cactus Air Force fliers were going through the same physical hell as the ground-pounders, but they also had to fly every day, then return to Henderson and hunker down overnight as sitting targets. For them, Guadalcanal was sleeplessness, fatigue, unrelenting strain, disease, and poor food as they tried to operate in a hostile sky where instant reactions were the difference between life and death. It was impossible to fly a plane while sick with malaria or dysentery, and some pilots lasted only a few days before falling wretchedly ill. A pilot who was mentally exhausted was just as easy a target as one who was physically worn out.

Every pilot in the Cactus Air Force felt his stamina seeping away, almost from the moment he arrived, and D. D. Brannon watched the abrupt physical changes scour his 67th Fighter Squadron. Already slender, Brannon himself had lost weight from exhaustion and inadequate food. Combat flying required physical endurance, and the Americans could not operate at maximum efficiency on a meager diet of dried fish and cold rice. But the captured food was usually all they had.

Then there was the problem with the planes. The same day Yamamoto arrived in Truk to plan further destruction, the army pilots on Guadalcanal again discovered just how lousy their P-400s were in aerial combat. They scrambled to meet the noon air raid, but were once again blocked at their fourteen-thousand-foot ceiling. Reduced to being aerial combat tourists, they could see the attacking Japanese bombers and Zeros going at it with the Wildcats above them, and when they looked down, they saw Japanese bombs exploding like flowers of dirt and fire on and around Henderson Field. John Thompson shot a Zero that was chasing another P-400, only to find another Zero right behind him. The Japanese pilot put seventeen bullets into Thompson's plane, including two that went through the thick glass of his canopy, one through the top of his shoulder. He circled down to a safe landing, and as he coasted to a stop, the propeller quit. Another bullet had gone through the regulator on the side of the engine. The plane never flew again. Thompson was patched up and returned to flying status.

All of Henderson Field seemed to be ablaze that afternoon, and men shoveled dirt onto burning planes to keep them from exploding, while other crews beat out grass fires with blankets and litter bearers hunted for the wounded. Crates of ammunition cooked off in relentless explosions, brave men rolled drums of volatile fuel away from the fires, and pilots ducked behind their planes for cover as snipers picked at them.

The army pilots felt they were somehow partially responsible for this carnage because they could not get up high enough to help kill off the Zeros and bombers. But what could they do with those damned P-400s?

Things got worse. Sleep was impossible as enemy destroyers came down the Slot at midnight to land more Japanese troops and lob shells their way, and Washing Machine Charlie made his irritating bomb runs. As explosions steadily chewed at Henderson Field, the pilots sat in their foxholes and were showered by dirt falling between the beams of their overhead cover. They emerged at dawn, cold and wet, and went up on patrol, although their bodies begged for sleep and nourishment.

They worked out a new plan with the marines so the ten P-400s still able to fly would get a piece of the action. Marine Wildcats would go high after the bombers, and flush the Japanese fighters and dive-bombers down to lower altitudes. There, six P-400s would lurk in ambush among the cumulus clouds to jump the descending enemy. Another four army planes would loiter still lower to nail diving Japanese planes at the vulnerable moment when they were pulling out of their dives.

The trap was sprung on August 30, and it was a miserable failure. The cumbersome P-400s were themselves ambushed by Zeros that slashed in from every possible direction, and had to be rescued by marine fighters. More Zeros tore apart the lower formation of army planes. The army pilots were learning the hard way about the swift, nimble Zeros and the daring men who flew them. The bastards could climb straight up, make square turns, and be on your tail in a blink. A P-400 simply could not quarrel with a Zero. Only six army planes made it safely back to Henderson that day, although two of the missing pilots eventually showed up. While marines were becoming "aces"—which required shooting down five enemy planes—the P-400 was derided as nothing but a P-40 with a Zero on its tail.

At 3:30 P.M. on the same day, the black flag went up again, but the Japanese bombers chose to sink a destroyer offshore rather than hit the field. An hour and fifteen minutes later, two earthquakes jolted Henderson. That night, the routine started all over again as Japanese ships brought in more infantry reinforcements and laid an awful offshore bombardment on the Americans.

Within a week of the arrival of the 67th Fighter Squadron, only three of the original fourteen planes were still able to fly. "We thought we were a fighter outfit, but if you got into combat with a Zero, you were done," Brannon said. About the only way a P-400 could shoot down a Zero was with the help of the Japanese pilot. Now when the black flag went up, the army pilots were told to take a reconnaissance jaunt around the island and stay out of the way. Two of their pilots were dead, others were wounded, most of their planes were out of commission, and their mission was virtually worthless. "What good are we?" they asked. They begged army headquarters on distant New Caledonia for permission to fly the marine F4F Wildcats. Some pilots even sat in the cockpits of the big Grumman fighters while marines leaned over their shoulders and explained the controls and instruments. The request was denied, and an army general at headquarters, hundreds of miles away, grumbled that the 67th pilots were just a bunch of bitching malcontents.

Of the original nineteen navy Wildcats that had arrived, only five could still fly, and the army planes were useless. Vandegrift, the marine commander on Guadalcanal, did not question the courage of the army pilots, for he had seen them at work, but their machines simply could not get the job done. He needed more fighter planes and pilots in a hurry, but he told headquarters not to bother sending any more P-400s.

New Caledonia

The marines had learned that asking Ghormley for assistance was wasted effort. Cloistered aboard his flagship *Argonne* in the harbor at Nouméa, New Caledonia, he had grown increasingly nervous and distraught trying to command the volatile South Pacific war zone. Naval losses were piling up at sea, the marines were in a terrible meat-grinder battle, and planes were falling like autumn leaves. He had never been enthusiastic about the Guadalcanal operation and felt that time was running out for the men on the island, and perhaps for himself. Ghormley worried that the Japanese might strike south and even show up outside of Nouméa harbor at any time.

His dwindling confidence received another blow when he learned that Admiral Frank Jack Fletcher was among the wounded on the torpedoed *Saratoga*. Although Fletcher had been worn thin by the battles at Coral Sea, Midway, and Guadalcanal, Ghormley had needed him to run the American aircraft carriers. He messaged Nimitz to send a replacement. The aggressive Bull Halsey was out of the hospital after recovering from his terrible bout with skin disease, and Nimitz immediately named him to replace Fletcher. It was one of the best decisions he ever made.

Fiji

In answer to the plea from Guadalcanal for more airplanes, Ghormley managed to scrape up a few army P-39 Airacobras, and when his staff looked around for someone to fly them, the call went to the 70th Fighter Squadron on Fiji. Captain Henry Viccellio drove over from headquarters and told John Mitchell to pick fourteen other pilots and head out on temporary assignment to the exhausted 67th. They were to spend a few days at New Caledonia, then fly up to Guadalcanal. They were going to war.

One pilot recalled that when Mitchell asked whom he should take, Viccellio replied, "Anyone except Tom Lanphier. You can't take Lanphier."

During the past months on Fiji, the former squadron commander had become quite a fan of the flamboyant young lieutenant. As Viccellio had become more of an administrator than a day-to-day flier, a small coterie of officers had begun to follow him everywhere, as if Viccellio were the locomotive of a train. One car on that train was Tom Lanphier.

Now Lanphier, possibly the best flier in the squadron, was spared from the first round of 70th pilots being sent into Guadalcanal. "Tom has connections," said the pilot who overheard Viccellio's comment, with a touch of envy. The connections went both ways, because a rising star in the army air force could always use a friend whose father was plugged into the senior staff in Washington.

Yamamoto had come to Truk, and now John Mitchell and his team packed their gear and headed over to New Caledonia.

Henderson Field

Just when things seemed blackest, the 67th Fighter Squadron on Guadalcanal found its niche. The P-400 was no dogfighter, but it packed a lot of firepower—a cannon in the nose, two .50-caliber machine guns, four .30-caliber machine guns, plus bombs—and the pilots finally figured out a way to use it: The 67th gave up trying to perform high in the sky. Just as the Russians loved the little plane's ability to destroy German tanks, the Americans experimented down around the treetops and waves, buzzing so low that they were within the reach of enemy rifle fire.

On September 2, four P-400s took off in swirling dust clouds, carrying full ammunition trays and five-hundred-pound bombs. They caught a Japanese landing force only twenty miles from Henderson Field. "They were trying to come to shore, and we strafed right through them. In a crowd like that, you can't miss," said John Thompson. The army planes came in low and fast, bombing and strafing landing barges and troops who were wading through the water, and created hell below their wings. One crisscross attack by two planes on frantic enemy soldiers left a giant, bloody X in the water. The P-400s flew back to Henderson, rearmed, refueled, came back, and did it again.

The 67th soon became specialists in delivering such devastating attacks, flying so close to the palm trees that their propellers sometimes clipped the fronds. The ground marines loved to watch the swift little planes roll in with guns blazing to destroy everything before them. The pilots started going up early to look for smoke from breakfast fires, followed tire tracks along roads, dive-bombed landing barges. When they ran out of bombs, they dropped navy depth charges wrapped in chains, which smashed through overhead tree cover and exploded upon hitting the jungle floor, spraying steel fragments everywhere. Marine patrols later found circles of dead Japanese soldiers who had been shredded by those depth charges.

The pilots of the 67th regained their swagger and confidence and gave themselves a German-sounding nickname, the *Jagdstaffel*, the word for "fighter squadron." They flew every available plane they had, every day.

Along with the new name came a new home, a two-thousand-foot-long airstrip carved from a bumpy patch of kunai grass a mile east of Henderson. It lacked metal matting, and was usually muddy, but it could handle the light fighter planes, while the heavier bombers stayed over at Henderson. The place was christened Fighter I, and the Japanese were unaware that it existed. They continued targeting the Henderson Pagoda, increasing the survival chances of the American fighters at Fighter I.

Truk

The conflict simmered at a low boil in early September as both the Americans and Japanese licked their wounds and counted the growing losses in men, planes, and ships. Neither side could disengage, so both kept pushing reinforcements toward the bloody sinkhole of Guadalcanal.

High-ranking Japanese officers paid regular visits to the floating headquarters of the C-in-C. At one glittering dinner, Yamamoto hosted the commanders of the Second, Third, Fourth, and Sixth Fleets, as well as a member of the emperor's family who was the vice chief of the Army and Navy General Staffs and visiting from Tokyo.

Their briefings were no longer just lists of victories but included reports of serious setbacks. A garrison trapped at Rabi, on New Guinea, was being mauled, and the attempt made by infantry troops to march over the Owen Stanley Range to reach Port Moresby had been blocked by tough Australian soldiers. Storms that regularly ripped the sea between Rabaul and Guadalcanal continued to thwart Japanese pilots trying to reach that island battleground.

Therefore, the briefers told the gathered luminaries, it was essential that Japanese ground troops capture the airfield on Guadalcanal. Planes and ships could attack and support but could not occupy anything. For a new attack, reinforcements were being landed each night by fast minesweepers and destroyers.

They all agreed on a new and vigorous assault that was to begin in the middle of September, and this time the army and the navy had to have better coordination. Since the soldiers reported to generals, and the sailors and naval land forces reported to admirals, cooperation had been lacking. In Yamamoto's opinion, the generals, over whom he had no control, were still looking to take Port Moresby instead of concentrating on the strategic prize of Guadalcanal. Sending troops into the island piecemeal had been a disaster. This time everyone agreed to work together and push the attack to success, no matter the losses.

Major General Kiyotake Kawaguchi had no intention of failing. He was on Guadalcanal with sixty-two hundred battle-hardened troops who had captured Borneo and had been slated to invade Fiji until Midway changed the schedule. The general thought he had the Americans outnumbered, but the Japanese intelligence services had, once again, greatly underestimated the defending force. There were thousands more marines on the island than reported, but even so, the

American defensive perimeter had to cover a wide arc around Henderson Field. It was vulnerable.

Yamamoto decided to open the fight with a merciless bombardment by air and sea to soften resistance to the coming ground assault.

Guadalcanal

The black flag went up on September 11 even as the high-pitched singsong of incoming bombers gave way to the *swissshhh* of falling bombs. Men dived for foxholes as the first bomb struck in the distance, then the explosions stomped closer and closer, and each man thought the next one was meant for him. Prayers went up as bombs came down, muscles tensed until they ached, and men screamed. It seemed to last forever.

So many bombs fell in such a wide pattern that both Henderson Field, which was the primary target, and Fighter I, of which the Japanese were still unaware, were repeatedly struck and burned fiercely. Ammunition exploded with jarring concussions, men were killed and wounded, and another P-400 was blown to bits. The marine squadrons, which had been augmented by planes from the two damaged aircraft carriers, were left with only a dozen Grumman F4F Wildcats that could fly.

D. D. Brannon and two other pilots of the 67th had rushed to their favorite foxhole when the attack began, then three marines also piled inside with them. It was twelve feet by twelve feet and covered with metal plates three-eights of an inch thick, coconut tree logs, and sandbags. The protection only worked if you were inside. Brannon decided to stand near the entrance to watch the show for a while. Suddenly, he spotted the huge blob of a thousand-pound bomb heading straight for him. "I think it's here!" he yelled, and dived headfirst into the bunker. The bomb exploded about five feet away and sent sandbags, thick metal plates, dirt, and all six men flying in a blinding blast of heat and light. The concussion stopped Brannon in midleap and "oozed" him back out of the foxhole as the bomb dug a crater twenty-five feet across. The marines were unhurt, but all three army pilots were wounded. Brannon took a deep cut in the jaw from a bomb that should have killed him.

The fight went on.

14

Bloody Ridge

Guadalcanal

D. D. Brannon and John Thompson, mere captains, were the highest-ranking U.S. Army officers on Guadalcanal, where the marines and the navy were locked in mortal combat both ashore and at sea. The army's mauled 67th Fighter Squadron, however, would spell the difference in the coming fight for a ripple of high ground only two thousand feet away from the Fighter I airstrip. If the Japanese came through there, the battle for Guadalcanal would be over. The place would earn the name "Bloody Ridge."

General Vandegrift, the marine commander, had been expecting the inevitable attack by the Japanese, who had been bringing in thousands of fresh troops. The target obviously was going to be Henderson Field, and Vandegrift's lines were spread thin, all the way from Alligator Creek in the east, across the Lunga River, through the jungles and swamps and back to the coastline on the west. Some of the line was manned only by roving patrols, which made it porous.

General Kawaguchi was about to fling sixty-two hundred highly trained Japanese soldiers at the airfield in a three-pronged attack, but he did not take adequate time to scout the American positions, nor did he appreciate the ferocious terrain his soldiers would have to slog across just to reach their attack positions. Both sides were discovering that Guadalcanal itself defied anybody's timetable.

The dwindling number of American fighter planes somehow continued to thwart Japanese attempts at aerial surveillance, and while Japanese ships might roam freely in the channel at night, neither planes nor ships could count troops hidden in the dark. Neither General Kawaguchi, nor any other Japanese commander, knew that some nineteen thousand American marines were now ashore on Guadalcanal and had become experienced fighters. The island was large enough so that Japanese could land at one end undetected even as American troops landed at the other, equally invisible.

On September 12, the eve of one of their biggest battles since landing on the island, the American marines were dug in and well armed but weakened by disease and spread out in a long loop that could not be strong at every point. At that critical moment, Vandegrift received a handwritten letter from Ghormley back in New Caledonia. Because of his heavy losses at sea, the admiral said, he could no longer support Guadalcanal. With that terse message, Ghormley washed his hands of the marines.

Vandegrift was visibly angry, madder even than when the navy pulled back its carriers in the opening days of the invasion and left his marines stranded on the beach. Ghormley might be giving up, but the marines did not. Vandegrift had no intention of surrendering and handing the Japanese the awful opportunity to stage another Bataan Death March. As a military realist, however, he had to recognize that, without naval support, Henderson Field might fall to a concerted Japanese attack. He ordered his staff to prepare a plan for the possible abandonment of the airfields and a fighting withdrawal into the jungle. They would continue to fight, somehow, somewhere. The marines then settled down for the night with a sense of desperation.

The deadly clash began on September 13 and lasted all day and throughout a moonless night. It went from hand-to-hand combat in the thickest jungle positions to the sky overhead, where Zeros and Wildcats tumbled about in dogfights. The marines faltered in some places, held until they were outflanked, pulled back, reorganized, and held again as screaming Japanese soldiers rushed forward, continuing the onslaught over the dead bodies of comrades who had piled up before the American guns.

Finally, the gigantic battle rolled onto the grassy ridge that overlooked the airfield, defended by fewer than a thousand exhausted marines.

Brannon and Thompson led the 67th flights on alternate days, and with Brannon injured, Thompson was on duty during the night of the pitched battle for Bloody Ridge. Sleep was impossible with all of the shooting that was going on, so he sat with a few pilots in a large, well-protected foxhole beside the flight line on Fighter I and listened to the man-made thunder. The night sky was bathed in the ghostly artificial light of red and white flares and the bright streaks of tracer ammunition. They heard the marines and Japanese cursing at each other, the crump of grenades, and so many rifles firing so fast that they sounded like machine guns. The unrelenting Japanese charges bent the marines back into a tenuous U-shaped line.

About three o'clock in the morning, a messenger found Thompson and told him he was wanted over at the Pagoda. As he was driven to the ramshackle building, the pounding of the guns on the ridge was a loud, incessant roar. Thompson found a couple of senior officers talking to a marine captain beside a table made out of a box. Blood streamed down the captain's face from a head wound. His helmet had a hole in it. "We can't hold that area much longer," the marine told Thompson. "We need some strafing out there." He sketched a quick map with the stub of a pencil. The marines still held the top of the ridge, but Japanese soldiers were massing on the back side and across several acres of meadowlike area that fanned off into the jungle. "They want that ridge," said the marine. "When it gets to be daylight, there's going to be another charge. If you can get out there and disrupt them, it may be enough to delay the attack."

Thompson returned to Fighter I, and the ground crews got busy readying the only three P-400s that could still fly. Back in the foxhole, speaking above the sound of gunfire, he told Lieutenants B. E. Davis and Bryan Brown to saddle up. He showed them the map. "The situation is critical. If they break through, they're going to be on the field."

He explained that the three of them would take off and head out to sea, flying low so the Japanese could not watch them. Then they would climb, spread out enough not to interfere with one another, and turn back in for strafing runs. If they did it right, they might catch the enemy out in the open—prime targets for the low-level tactics of the *Jagdstaffel*.

Dawn was just breaking when they spun up their engines. From the cockpits, the three pilots could see the flashing of guns along the ridge. The Airacobras took off with the first flicker of daylight, when there was just enough brightness to let them see what they were doing. They sped out over the water and swung hard into a line, one after the other. Thompson led, followed by Brown, followed by Davis.

The planes banked around, dived down to the level of the trees, and headed for the ridge. When Thompson popped up for his strafing run, he saw the marine's map had been perfect. A thousand or so Japanese soldiers milled about below him, gathering to charge the hill again. He pressed his trigger, and machine guns rattled and his cannon coughed, vibrating the entire plane as he swept right over their heads, and his bullets mowed a bloody path through the startled soldiers. Instead of scattering, however, the soldiers recovered from the initial surprise and started shooting back. Bullets pinged off Thompson's fuselage and wing, and he was sure every Japanese rifle down there was firing at him.

The men at Fighter I watched the attack unfold like spectators at football game. They cheered as Thompson zoomed away in a climb to make room for the next plane. Marines on the ridge yelled obscenities at the disoriented Japanese as Brown roared in. His guns wreaked more havoc, butchering more of the Japanese force, which still fought back. A bullet hit his radiator. By the time the third plane popped over the treeline, and Davis opened up with his guns, the Japanese were spraying the sky with bullets. He flew right through the storm, combing the hillside with his guns, and the Japanese finally began to break. They didn't know how many more of the brown shark-shaped planes were headed their way.

As the pilots gathered for a second run, Brown saw a trail of light smoke coming from Thompson's plane. "You better look behind you, Tommy, because you're on fire," he radioed. Thompson responded, "You better look behind you, because you're on fire, too."

Brown shut down his engine and used his speed to curl back in for a dead-stick landing on Fighter 1 while Thompson made one more pass over the ridge, once again chewing into the ranks of Japanese soldiers. The field was strewn with bodies, but the return fire seemed just as intense. He was forced to land his damaged plane, but the show was still on. The Japanese did not know there was only one plane left, for it seemed an entire squadron was after them, diving down one after another, and the soldiers bolted for cover in the jungle. Davis made his second pass and then came around for a third sweep across the killing ground. Out of ammunition, he finally landed, with his guns red-hot. Rearmed, he went out again.

The marines that morning found more than five hundred Japanese bodies stacked before their positions on the ridge and carpeting the back of the hillside, all the way through the meadow. The marines on the ground had stopped the initial assaults, and the three army pilots from the 67th Fighter Squadron had shattered the gathering enemy forces that might have broken the line.

General Kawaguchi would remember Bloody Ridge as the graveyard of the Japanese army. His force was utterly destroyed. The U.S. Marines suffered high casualties, but Japanese losses were ruinous.

The smoke cleared with Henderson Field and Fighter 1 still in American hands. Vandegrift himself came over to congratulate the pilots of the 67th, slipped a bottle of whiskey to Thompson, and said the P-400s had saved Guadalcanal. Thompson was given a Navy Cross and Davis and Brown were awarded Silver Stars.

The I-19

The day after Bloody Ridge, the crew of the Japanese submarine I-19 heard loud propeller noises around them as they hovered underwater near the Solomon Islands. When Commander Takaichi Kinashi looked through his periscope, he could barely believe his eyes. His submarine somehow was inside the protective circle around the American aircraft carrier Wasp, and he grasped the opportunity. Seldom has one submarine wreaked such havoc at a single stroke and gotten safely away.

His first torpedoes struck the vital ammunition and fuel storage areas of the Wasp, and the big carrier was ripped apart by internal explosions and engulfed in raging fires. She was abandoned and scuttled.

Another torpedo blew a thirty-foot hole below the waterline of the battleship *North Carolina*, which limped away in dire need of repairs, and still another torpedo damaged the destroyer *O'Brien* so badly that it sank several weeks later before reaching safe harbor.

Thanks to the work of that single submarine, Yamamoto's grip on the sea lanes became much stronger.

But for Admiral Ghormley, it was a demoralizing setback. The loss of still another American aircraft carrier and the crippling of a battleship was more than he could take.

Guadalcanal

Help finally arrived for the battered 67th Fighter Squadron in the form of a bunch of borrowed pilots. John Mitchell and six of his fliers from the 70th Fighter Squadron had loaded onto a navy cargo plane and were flown up to Henderson Field. As they approached, they could see smoke curl up through the jungle from Japanese breakfast fires, not far from the runway. Despite their recent losses, the Japanese were that close.

As soon as the door opened, the fliers recoiled at the miasmal stink, a foul combination of rot and mud and steamy jungle and death, for enemy bodies were decaying not far away. As Mitchell headed for the Pagoda, Doug Canning climbed down from the plane, niftily clad in the smart, cut-off khakis he had ordered hand-tailored in Fiji. Someone he knew was coming across the runway to guide them to their new home, a former college football star known to all as "Tiger Jack." Lieutenant Bob Kerstetter, now a rowdy pilot with the 67th, had been on the island for just a few days. Canning saw that his friend had already lost weight, was unshaven, and wore marine boondocker boots and a filthy uniform. Around his waist drooped a cartridge belt with a holstered pistol on one side and a long machete slapping against the other leg.

"Is that what I'm going to look like in a week?" Canning wondered. "Jeez, what have I gotten myself into?"

New Caledonia

Admiral Nimitz flew out from Pearl Harbor in late September for a firsthand look at the command situation and did not like what he found. Pessimism hung like dark curtains over Ghormley, who had not left his flagship in Nouméa harbor for a month. Transport ships rode at anchor, fat with supplies and army infantry reinforcements who were available to join the battle, but they had not yet been dispatched to the island. During one meeting, Ghormley received more bad news from the front and moaned in his commander's presence, "My God, what are we going to do about this?"

Nimitz ordered Ghormley to send those transports and the army's 164th Infantry Regiment right away, then he personally flew up to Guadalcanal, something Ghormley had never done. He toured Bloody Ridge and the other marine positions, handed out decorations for bravery, and spent a typical wet, noisy, uncomfortable night on the island. He was almost killed when his plane had trouble taking off from mud-caked Henderson Field during a pelting rainstorm. The admiral returned to Pearl Harbor and pondered whether Ghormley had the guts needed to continue running this show.

Espiritu Santo

Hap Arnold, commander of the army air force, was also on a tour of the South Pacific. He hopped to various bases and gave pep talks but remained firmly wed to the "Europe First" strategy. The invasion of North Africa was imminent, and the Atlantic and European theaters had priority on planes. The boys in the Pacific had to make do with what they had.

With that in mind, he was extremely impressed by the gallant fight being waged off the northern coast of Australia and over New Guinea by army pilots. Because of their records with P-39s and a handful of twin-tailed P-38s, Arnold felt that there were enough planes already in the region to do whatever was necessary.

He also wanted to hear about Guadalcanal, but he did not go there.

Instead, he summoned D. D. Brannon, the senior army officer on the island, down for a private meeting at the bomber base on Espiritu Santo, where the air force had established an area headquarters. It was the second time Brannon had personally encountered the bombastic Arnold, and he hoped the general did not remember him as being the pilot who had been disciplined for showing off in a P-38 during the Selfridge Field air show in Michigan before the war.

Walking into the headquarters made Brannon uncomfortable, for most of these officers had stayed far from the fighting, and they had brushed off his squadron's complaints about the dreadful living conditions and the limited abilities of the P-400s. It seemed that as far as the army air force was concerned, the 67th Fighter Squadron had become an unwanted stepchild because, on Guadalcanal, they actually worked for the marines.

Brannon was taken to a small room and closed the door behind him. He saluted Arnold and took a seat directly across a table from the four-star general. He had rehearsed what he wanted to say in his first-hand briefing on the combat situation. Instead, the general apparently had been listening to the headquarters critics of the 67th, had read the reports of poor performance, and was angry that the army pilots on Guadalcanal were not doing as well as those fighting over New Guinea.

"What the hell is going on with your people?" Arnold shouted.

Brannon, caught completely off balance, stammered an answer about the problems of the P-400s. Arnold brusquely cut in: "They're doing a fine job in Australia!"

"They have P-39s in Australia, sir, not P-400s, and they have oxygen," Brannon said, wanting to explain how his unit had been given a boatload of awkward planes that originally had been bound for Russia. "We don't—"

"That's not the case at all." General Arnold was in no mood for excuses. To him, the problem wasn't the aircraft, but the pilots! The marines were getting headlines for shooting down Zeros on Guadalcanal, the army fighter pilots were handling the enemy over New Guinea just fine, despite tremendous odds, and he demanded similar results on Guadalcanal. He was in no mood to hear about this *Jagdstaffel* nonsense or how the P-400s had become feared by the Japanese as a ground-attack aircraft. He did not even ask about the big bandage taped across Brannon's chin as the result of the bomb blast.

Arnold came to his feet, leaned across the table and smacked it so hard with his fist that it jumped. "The problem is that you're a coward!" he snarled, looking Brannon squarely in the eye. "You have a whole squadron full of nothing but cowards!"

D. D. Brannon was shocked into absolute silence, and Hap Arnold spun on his heel, stalked from the room, and slammed the door behind him. *Cowards?* Brannon touched the bandage, and possible responses flooded to his mind, but it was too late. What about the entire flight of four P-400s that had taken off one day and was never heard from again? What about all the pilots who had died or been wounded? What about the ground crews who endured daily bombings and nightly bombardments and worked through hellish conditions and the scourge of disease? What about the tree-nibbling attacks made into cauldrons of enemy fire, dive-bombing down right into the very smell of the jungle? What of the Zeros that *had* been shot down by those inferior P-400s? And what of Bloody Ridge? Cowards? The *Jagdstaffel?*

But a captain cannot argue with a general, even when he thinks the man is an idiot, so Brannon stuffed his rage and flew back to Guadalcanal, almost shaking in furious silence. Until 2002, the year before he died, he never let his men know their commanding general called them cowards.

Arnold returned to Washington without ever setting foot on Guadalcanal, but he did stop by Christmas Island on the way home. Lou Kittel of the 12th Fighter Squadron was kicked out of his little handmade house so the general could spend the night in it.

In an equalizing twist of fate, air force bureaucrats created a new fighter squadron for the South Pacific while General Arnold was away from Washington. Called the 339th Fighter Squadron, it would be equipped with powerful new twin-engine P-38s, and its first personnel would be drawn from the veteran pilots and crews of the 67th Fighter Squadron.

A leader was needed, and one candidate stood head and shoulders above all others, particularly since many pilots had never even seen a

P-38. This officer had been one of the test pilots for the plane, commanded a combat squadron, had shot down Zeros, and had been wounded. Unaware of Arnold's pique, they picked the man whom the general had just chewed out for being a coward.

To his total surprise, Captain D. D. Brannon was promoted to major and given command of the 339th.

15

Battleships

Truk

Admiral Yamamoto had not felt well in the month after the last big attack on Guadalcanal. He did not like failure. Mood swings gripped him as he considered what to do next, for there was no question of giving up the fight. He picked at details normally delegated to his staff members, rambled on about unimportant things, and felt every one of his fifty-nine years. He even remained withdrawn and pensive during a special dinner aboard the *Yamato* with a couple of old friends, both admirals, who had come to visit. They ate fresh fish off sparkling plates that sat on polished tables of black lacquer; the silverware gleamed. Afterward, they retired to his stateroom, left tactics and strategy outside, lit some English cigarettes, and spoke of more personal matters. Yamamoto, who did not drink alcohol, made certain his guests were provided with good scotch whiskey. When they were settled, he was asked what he planned to do after the war.

The commander in chief was well aware that things were no longer going easily, or well, for Japan. Almost a year had passed since the war began, and America was obviously getting its mighty production lines in gear. Their untrained masses were becoming soldiers. The supply convoys were getting through to Australia, and, in the opinion of many, New Guinea was a lost cause, a sinkhole into which valuable fighting strength was being recklessly poured. The American airplanes on Guadalcanal were still annoyingly capable of defending the island, and Chief of Staff Ugaki admitted in his diary, "They bring up planes as fast as we shoot them down. It is a problem." Proof of improved American fighting ability was evident in the fact that the marines still held that little perimeter around Henderson Field. They were besieged but still in control. Victory for Japan must come soon, or it might not come at all.

Yamamoto tapped a long ash from his cigarette as the history of France came to mind, the rude justice meted out in the revolution and Napoleon's death in exile. What would happen to him after the war? If Japan won, there would be no problem, and he could retire in comfort. But if the Americans won, he probably would not have much choice, for surely they would treat him as a war criminal for his attack on Pearl Harbor. "I imagine I'll be packed off either to the guillotine or to Saint Helena," he said.

The protective bubble in which Yamamoto lived aboard the luxurious *Yamato* had done him a disservice, because this admiral, so badly wounded in an earlier war, was out of touch with the reality of the men on the ground. They were army troops, not his, but Yamamoto was shocked to his soul on September 24 when an army officer finally managed to get in to see him. The troubleshooter had been sent out from Tokyo to find out why things had stalled on Guadalcanal. His report snatched Yamamoto out of the doldrums and back into the reality of the moment.

The tattered Japanese garrison on Guadalcanal was literally starving, reduced to eating grass and insects, grubbing like animals in the dirt, the officer reported. "Ants, lice, but no rice," one soldier wrote. Supplies were not getting through in sufficient quantities to keep the men from hearing "the sound of hunger," and they were being ravaged by the terrible existence in a hot, wet jungle that seemed to be alive with deadly diseases. Any supplies left stacked on the beaches by an overnight run of what Ugaki called the "Tokyo Express"—fast, small convoys that could reach Guadalcanal under the cover of darkness and be gone before daylight—became easy targets at dawn for those low-flying American planes that rose from Henderson Field.

Tears filled the admiral's eyes. Yamamoto had not realized things were so bad. He promised that the navy would not abandon those soldiers. He vowed to bring in food, medicine, ammunition, guns, supplies of every sort, and fresh troops, even if he himself had to lead the way to Guadalcanal aboard the *Yamato*.

Having secured the personal pledge of Yamamoto, his visitor then went off to push the generals to cooperate with the navy and commit enough forces and equipment to get the job done on Guadalcanal. A new and forceful battle plan emerged in which the army and the navy would at last work hand-in-hand. This time, Lieutenant General Harukichi Hyakutake, the commander of the 17th Army, would go ashore himself to assume command.

True to his word, Yamamoto put his efforts into resupply during the coming weeks, and thousands of fresh soldiers from the 17th Army's elite Sendai Division were ferried to the island by the Tokyo Express, along with stocks of supplies, and, for the first time, 150-mm artillery pieces and tanks. It seemed that perhaps the army finally grasped what he had been saying for so long, that Guadalcanal was important. But he had believed that before.

He was still displeased that the generals withheld their own fighter planes from the battle in the South Pacific, saying the aircraft were needed in China, and in case Russia decided to attack. That left the air battle up to the navy, and this was where the disaster at Midway was having a lingering effect. The reservoir of highly trained naval aviators was running low. The training schools were turning out new pilots, but there was a shortage of both experienced leadership and the time needed to truly teach the boys the deadly trade of war. His naval air force was not the formidable presence it was once was, but he still had plenty of combat pilots who knew how to fight. The question was, Which side would last longest?

In the new battle plan, a change in tactics would make up for some of that lost experience. He knew the enemy had secreted spotters, the men called the coastwatchers, on the islands between Rabaul and Guadalcanal, and those spies had been tremendously effective in warning that air raids were coming toward Henderson Field. So this time the planes would fly around, not over, those prying eyes, and attack in two large waves from unexpected directions. The first group would decoy the American planes into the air and then depart. When the defending American aircraft landed to refuel, the second wave of Japanese attackers would strike.

That same night, Yamamoto would send in battleships to pound Henderson Field to rubble, lock down the island with a naval blockade, and take on any American ships that tried to rush to the rescue. With Henderson Field neutralized and the U.S. Navy kept at a distance, the ground assaults could begin.

The army planners this time expected certain victory. General Hyakutake of the 17th Army carried with him the dress uniform he intended to wear when he accepted the American surrender. Imperial General Headquarters had a personal representative at the battlefront, and an army inspection team from Tokyo promised to visit Yamamoto on its way back to Japan after touring the recaptured Guadalcanal.

Yamamoto's period of disappointment had vanished when he came onto the weather deck of his flagship on the beautiful Sunday morning of October 11 and put powerful binoculars to his eyes to watch the Combined Fleet uncoil like a huge viper from its resting position at Truk. Five big aircraft carriers, four battleships, nine cruisers, and twenty-eight destroyers pushed off to take their new stations, kill Henderson Field, and annihilate what was left of the U.S. fleet.

Henderson Field

Things were happening so fast, involved so many people, and covered such a large area that the air force units involved with Guadalcanal remained snared in the web of divided commands. Army pilots flew with navy pilots as part of the Marine Air Wing, under the direct command of a marine general, but they also had to answer to an army general twelve hundred miles away in New Caledonia. There was no such thing as a well-coordinated premission briefing, and many postmission debriefings simply vanished. Confusion reigned as men, planes, squadrons, and responsibilities were constantly shifted around, and the paperwork could not keep pace.

To help bring some order, the 347th Fighter Group headquarters was formed in the first week of October as an administrative unit to oversee the various army squadrons on Guadalcanal, but the change would be in name only for the next month. Pilots and crews still fought and lived together, and the army still shared missions with the marines and navy. On many mornings, who flew which plane on what mission depended solely upon who was still able to climb into a cockpit and what planes had been patched together enough overnight to be able to take off. Through necessity, instructions relied quite a bit on what was called "verbal orders of the commander," or VOCO. The idea was to get the fighting done, and let the paperwork catch up later. It never did.

Mitchell and his batch of new pilots from the 70th Fighter Squadron had only a short time to learn the ropes, because they were fighting almost as soon as they arrived. Experienced veterans of the 67th passed along the advice they had received from the marines and other army pilots who had come before them: Don't be lured into a dogfight with a Zero, because a Japanese pilot could spin on a dime and be on your tail before you knew it. Instead, the favored tactic was to gain some altitude, dive down in a single pass on the Japanese fighter, then get out of there as fast as possible. Keep your head on a swivel, and constantly scan the skies. The enemy pilots were fearless, and many had been fighting for years. They often removed the radios from the Zeros to make them lighter and quicker, and didn't wear parachutes because they would never bail out over enemy territory anyway. They would rather die than be taken prisoner.

The trade-off for that cat-quickness was that the Zero carried no armor. While a U.S. fighter could soak up bullets and still fly, a good hit would turn a Zero into a fireball. The twin-engine Betty bomber was also vulnerable, but very fast, and it could take a lot of hits.

The P-39s arriving on Guadalcanal were the big brothers of the clunky P-400s, and although they looked the same on the outside, there was one major difference. They had an oxygen system that could take the pilots through the invisible ceiling that had plagued the P-400s and up as high as twenty-seven thousand feet. But by now, the *Jagdstaffel*'s mission had become primarily supporting the marines on the ground, thus freeing up marine and navy Wildcats to tangle with the Zeros, which they did almost every day. John Mitchell's pilots joined in dive-bombing and strafing enemy positions and escorting bombers and torpedo planes, and they still got in an occasional shot at a Zero or a Betty that dropped within range.

His first time out, Mitchell led a flight of four P-39s to escort a torpedo-plane strike against Japanese vessels 150 miles away. Zero floatplanes, which wore pontoons that allowed them to operate from the water instead of requiring a runway, rose to challenge them, and Mitchell shot down one, and two other members of his flight scored "probables." One pilot was cut by flying glass when Japanese bullets shattered his cockpit, but everybody made it safely back to Fighter I. Mitchell realized that his boys had done well in their first taste of combat. The long, hard training back on Fiji had paid off. He had finally met the enemy, done the job, killed a Zero, and brought his men home alive. Nothing more could be asked of a flight leader.

Cape Esperance

Both sides were pumping reinforcements onto Guadalcanal as fast as they could. While the Japanese were bringing in a major part of the experienced Sendai Division on their part of the island, the Americans, spurred by Admiral Nimitz's trip to New Caledonia, were rushing in three thousand fresh troops of the 164th Infantry Regiment. The opposing convoys moved under tight bands of escort warships, and those task forces collided in the dark of night on October 12, four miles off Cape Esperance, the northwestern tip of Guadalcanal.

The Japanese boldly sent three heavy cruisers and two destroyers down through the Slot to cover the troop landing and bombard Henderson Field. The Americans came curving around the western coast of Guadalcanal with four heavy cruisers and five destroyers. As soon as the shooting began, the formations broke apart, plans were abandoned, and every ship on the water blasted away.

The Americans claimed a tactical victory in the encouter, because they didn't lose outright. They suffered 163 killed and another 125 wounded, the destroyer *Duncan* was sunk, and the heavy cruisers *Boise* and *Salt Lake City* were forced to withdraw because of substantial damage. The Japanese considered the battle a draw, although the commanding admiral and 450 other Japanese sailors perished, many while struggling in the shark-infested waters, and about 100 more were taken prisoner. They lost an old cruiser, the *Furutaka*, and the destroyer *Fubuki*. The heavy cruiser *Aoba* had to return to Japan to be mended before she could fight again.

The fight did not stop the flow of heavy reinforcements to the island by either side. The Japanese cruiser force failed to bombard Henderson Field that night, but when the Americans pulled out, they left the northern gate to Guadalcanal unguarded against the approaching Japanese battleships.

Guadalcanal

The U.S. Army pilots watched a small marine ceremony with a mixture of pride and envy as the last standing pilot of marine dive-bombing squadron VMSB-232, one of the two original squadrons to arrive on Guadalcanal, was sent to the rear. Of the nineteen pilots in that squadron, seven had been killed, four were wounded, and the rest had fallen to the island's diseases. The army pilots believed the only marine aviator left out of that group certainly deserved all the rest and medals that might come to him, but they also realized this marked a passage. The marines were rotating out of the combat area as entire units, some even going back to the United States. But the army's 67th Fighter Squadron wasn't going anywhere. A guy might get some leave time or a brief stay in the hospital, but he would be coming right back to Guadalcanal.

The 164th Infantry Regiment of the Americal Division, strong young men from the Dakotas and Minnesota, were totally raw when they reached Guadalcanal. The first battalion of the National Guard troopers to set foot on the island were called "the Stevedores" because they had spent the past six months being used as labor, loading ships. Guides met them at the beach and steered them through the nightmare landscape of slashed brown and green vegetation, past the marine cemetery. The boys from the rich farmlands of the Midwest were mentally stunned even before reaching their positions around Henderson Field. They had received no jungle warfare training, but that did not really matter, because no training could have prepared them for what they were about to endure within a few hours.

Fighters and dive-bombers ran their usual morning mission from Fighter I, attacked some landing barges that had beached during the night, then flew home. The missions had been easy, and they were arming up to fly again when the black flag was suddenly hoisted. The newly arrived infantrymen watched from their foxholes as the army P-39s, P-400s, and marine Wildcats clawed into the sky.

This was the start of the new Japanese offensive, and twenty-seven Betty bombers and eighteen Zeros were overhead at thirty thousand feet almost before anyone knew they were there. Following the plan approved by Yamamoto, they had flown a wide route around the northern islands and avoided the coastwatchers. By the time the Americans could get into the sky, there was little left to fight. One Zero, one Betty, and one Wildcat were downed.

The bombs fell instead, with wicked precision, on Henderson Field. A parked B-17 blew apart in a fireball. A fuel dump containing five thousand gallons of precious aviation gasoline exploded in a thunderclap, and flame and black smoke rolled into the sky. Other bombs damaged eleven fighter planes that had been caught on the ground, and the metal matting on the main runway was cratered and twisted into nightmarish steel sculptures. Shrapnel sliced through trees and flesh with equal ease, and the army infantrymen began digging their foxholes deeper.

When the Japanese raiders left, the American fighters flew back to the grassy strip of Fighter I and were in the midst of refueling when Yamamoto's second wave of attackers, eighteen Bettys and another eighteen Zeros, swept in unopposed. A dozen Wildcats took off through the rain of bombs and strafing, but the airfield was again pummeled. By the time the Japanese flew away, Henderson Field was out of action. Storage dumps were destroyed, and hungry fire gobbled up aviation gasoline. More wrecked planes were pushed into the boneyard at the far end of the runway. "I think a chance of turning the tables has been grasped at last," Admiral Ukagi cheerfully wrote in his diary.

The Americans were still cleaning up when the Japanese opened fire with a pair of 150-mm howitzers that had recently been brought ashore and carefully hidden high on Mount Austen. This, the first serious use of land-based artillery since the campaign began, posed an immediate menace. The gunners would fire a single shell at the airfield, wait until repair crews rushed out to repair the damage, and then send another shell whistling into the same spot. American spotters could not find the well-camouflaged guns that became known as "Pistol Pete." Pilots waited in foxholes with their parachutes on and ran to their planes between explosions.

That evening, veterans nodded sagely over the double air raid, then those big guns firing from Mount Austen. Something was definitely up. The fires burned all day, and the stench of smoke hung heavy, giving their food an oily taste.

A purple cloak of darkness settled over the tense island, and the army fliers, done for the day, kept close to their hiding holes. A few managed to catch some uneasy rest before a Washing Machine Charlie hiccupped his way across the destroyed airfield at 1:30 A.M. on Wednesday, October 14. In addition to his usual stick of bombs, Charlie popped some green flares that drifted slowly down, brightening the sky with a peculiar light.

The men on the ground knew something bad was about to happen.

The fast battleships *Kongo* and *Haruna*, a cruiser, and a covey of nine destroyers had sailed down the Slot and entered Ironbottom Sound unchallenged, and when they were about a mile from shore, they opened fire with their huge fourteen-inch guns. Japanese soldiers lit three fires at the edges of the target area, and a gunnery officer hidden up on Mount Austen would guide the accuracy of the naval barrages. Four spotter planes hummed overhead and dropped more colored illumination flares.

The first big shell from *Kongo* slammed into Henderson Field and spewed out four hundred and seventy incendiary bomblets, as the

Americans dived for their bunkers. A storm of naval cannon fire raked through their base, explosions and fires erupted, and the new infantrymen wondered what in the hell was happening. Marines out on the front lines facing the jungle counted themselves lucky that night as they watched the barrage crawl through the area behind them. Japanese spotters on the island viewed the deadly show with fascination, and sailors aboard the booming battleships cheered what looked like a giant fireworks show.

Each roaring shell was a minor earthquake. The big guns fired in lazy synchronization into the parked planes and then reached into the palm groves where the aviators and enlisted men crouched in their holes like frightened animals. Brannon and Mitchell and the other veteran pilots were burrowing in as deeply as any scared private. Tents were flattened and shredded. A single shell killed five dive-bomber pilots crouched in the same hole. The Americans prayed and cursed God, wept, called for their mothers and shook uncontrollably. Some were reduced to making pitiful animal noises. One of the new army sergeants crawled about begging for someone to shoot him, and others tore off fingernails while digging with their bare hands. Erupting clouds of dirt and dust choked the men, foxholes collapsed, and soldiers tried to hide beneath each other, fighting to get deeper and deeper as the ground shook and hellfire razed the world outside.

Ammunition exploded with terrific detonations, razor shrapnel the size of car doors scythed through the trees, and almost the entire stock of aviation gasoline was set afire, coloring the night with grotesque orange and red flames and sucking, heated winds.

The first pass lasted forty-five minutes, then the guns stilled as the two Japanese battleships turned about. In the momentary quiet, some of the stunned Americans commandeered vehicles or ran toward the water to escape the killing zone around the airfield. Then the barrage started again, and when all of the high explosive shells were expended, the battleships switched to armor-piercing rounds that screeched in and exploded with deafening thunder.

The two Japanese battleships paraded with a deadly nonchalance, rocking easily with the recoil of their booming guns, while the destroyers chimed in with their five-inchers. American artillery popped without effect at the ships, all of which were beyond their reach, and the only navy ships around were four little PT boats that were no more than gnats to be dealt with by the screening destroyers.

After a barrage of almost a thousand shells, the battleships shut down and hauled majestically out of the channel, building up speed to get beyond the range of American planes by dawn.

Admiral Yamamoto had stayed awake aboard his flagship that night to learn the result of the day's synchronized raids, and about three o'clock in the morning, the observers on Guadalcanal reported that Henderson Field was burning fiercely and still being rocked by secondary explosions. For at least a few days the tiresome American planes would be no threat. Reinforcements and supplies would be strengthening the growing ground attack force, and Yamamoto was determined not to squander this rare opportunity. "I now have confidence that we can't lose this battle," he told an aide, and ordered Admiral Nagumo to go and find the American fleet. It was now his turn.

16

2100 Banzai

Guadalcanal

The pilots crawled from their foxholes at daylight to find huge flame devouring supply dumps and aviation fuel storage areas burning hard and bright. Roiling black smoke blocked the morning sunlight and detonating ammunition baroomed and clattered. Forty-one Americans had been killed, and the cries of another hundred wounded pierced the morning air. Men lurched about like zombies, almost deaf from the barrage.

Debris hung from treetops, and even the jungle seemed to have been crippled by the shrapnel that gouged through the stands of banyan, palm, rosewood, and mahogany trees. Many planes were completely blown apart. Of the thirty-nine Dauntless dive-bombers parked on Henderson the previous evening, only five were intact. A few B-17 bombers that could not get into the air were intentionally destroyed that morning to keep them from falling into Japanese hands.

Over at Fighter I, things were not any better. The Japanese did not even know the strip was there, but with such a saturation bombardment of the Henderson Field area, it was inevitable the nearby fighter base also would take a beating. Only twenty-four Wildcats survived, as did a pair of army P-39s and four of the doughty P-400s. With the dawn, Pistol Pete began lobbing in shells. A bulldozer was sent out to raze the Pagoda beside the Henderson runway, which had been the main aiming point for the bombardment.

There was no time to mourn the dead, and their bodies were put aside for burial later. A friend who was killed was just suddenly gone, as if he had left a party without saying good-bye, a presence no longer around except as a snapshot of memory. Pilots did not get a free pass just because someone died. Weakened or not, dispirited or not, if it was time to fly, you flew.

The battered 67th Fighter Squadron was undergoing significant changes. The two men who had been the lynchpins of the squadron and had brought it over from the States had gone to other jobs—D. D. Brannon was organizing his new 339th Fighter Squadron back on New Caledonia, and John Thompson had been scooped into a fighter group headquarters job. Several temporary skippers followed, and the latest left abruptly on the morning after the battleship bombardment. The nervous commander, who had fought in the Philippines before coming to Guadalcanal, had simply had enough. He jumped aboard one of the B-17s departing after the Night of the Battleships. From the hatchway he called to a nearby officer, "Hey, Holmes! You're acting commander of the 67th!" Then he was gone.

Lieutenant Besby F. Holmes, who less than a year earlier had pinged away at a swooping Zero with a 45-caliber pistol at Pearl Harbor, had built a reputation as a good pilot after he arrived on Guadalcanal with the 67th. He was a shooter, but for the moment he had nothing with which to shoot. He stood amid the remains of a squadron that had almost ceased to exist. The first thing he did was to steal an overturned marine jeep, get it running, drive it under a tent, and have it painted army green. His one-car motor pool almost matched the number of planes left in the squadron.

Then he went the skeletal remains of the command post at the jungle's edge, where a shredded tent flapped like dirty laundry, and found John Mitchell. They blended what was left the 67th with the guys who had come out with Mitchell on assignment from the 70th Fighter Squadron into a single group. Mitchell, who outranked Holmes, took charge, and would come to regard Holmes as the kind of a fellow you wanted along on challenging missions. Before the war was done, both would become aces, with credits for shooting down at least five enemy planes each.

Throughout the day, despite the shelling by Pistol Pete and a noon raid by several dozen Japanese bombers, a few American aircraft got off the ground. Ground crews sucked out every drop of aviation gas they could scavenge from destroyed planes, and someone remembered a long-forgotten cache of aviation gas, a gift from the war gods, that kept the planes aloft for a few more missions. But the pilots came back to report that enemy ships were surging unimpeded down the Slot and infantry reinforcements were making brazen daylight landings. Zeros blocked the Americans from getting at the troop transports.

Nineteen replacement Wildcats arrived just as Japanese planes were blowing up a barge ferrying in more aviation gas and attacking an American destroyer out in the channel. Eighteen of the Wildcats landed, but the final pilot spotted the Japanese dive-bombers working over the destroyer and shot down four.

But such victories were small in comparison with the overall threat to Guadalcanal. The Japanese had taken iron control of the air and sea. The day of reckoning was at hand on the ground, and everyone knew it.

As the few remaining army planes readied their final mission of the day, a lieutenant colonel brought them grim orders from marine head-quarters. "I want you to pass the word along that the situation is desperate," he told a group of three pilots and one mechanic. "I don't know if we will be able to hold the field or not. There's a Japanese task force of destroyers, cruisers, and transports headed this way. We have enough gasoline left for one mission against them. Load your airplanes with bombs and go with the dive-bombers and hit them. After the gas is gone, we'll have to let the ground troops take over. Then your officers and men will attach themselves to some infantry outfit." He gave them a lost look. "Good luck and goodbye."

The Cactus Air Force was too weak to stop any new Japanese attack, and the men of the fighter squadrons did not know whether they would be alive, dead, or prisoners of war by the same time next day.

That night the pilots burrowed below ground again. For years thereafter, they would remember exactly who was sweating it out in the bunker with them, exactly how they were positioned, exactly how close the bombs and shells exploded around them. In the world of dirt, dark, and danger the man beside you became your brother, for you might die together right there in that hole. "Nothing compared to those ship bombardments," said pilot Doug Canning. "Nothing."

Two Japanese cruisers slammed the airfield with another eight hundred shells, and several thousand more Japanese troops landed. The next day, more Japanese planes staged devastating attacks, and Pistol Pete kept popping. On the ground, the inexperienced American army infantrymen and haggard marines braced for the coming human-tidal-wave assaults.

But when dawn broke the next morning, they were still alive, and still ready to fight. The big attack had not come. They did not question why the Japanese troops had not stormed the barricades, but were thankful that they had not. Enough gas was found in the buried cache and drained from wrecked planes to put some fighters up again, so the pilots were not converted to infantrymen. Emergency shipments of fuel were on the way by cargo plane and fast ships. If they could hold out for a few more days, maybe things would get better.

Truk

Yamamoto was waiting for the attack, too. The strategy had worked out so successfully that he virtually held Guadalcanal in his fist, owning the sea and the air so totally that the Tokyo Express was landing troops on the island within sight of American marines, who could do nothing to stop them. The Japanese army, which now had about twenty-three thousand men gathered on the island, boasted that the marines would be conquered no later than October 15.

That promised deadline had passed two days earlier, and the land attack had not even begun. Yamamoto's patience had worn thin. He did not want to hear slogans. He wanted action, for he knew that the current level of superiority could not be maintained forever. The weather was turning bad around Rabaul, and that would hamper air operations. Valuable pilots and planes were being lost daily in the air raids, and at sea, Admiral Nagumo and his carriers had not found the Americans, while the Japanese fleet was sucking up oil reserves so fast that tankers were siphoning fuel from battleships. The army had to move!

But the Japanese army had again underestimated the evil nature of Guadalcanal itself. Before soldiers could strike, they had to reach the assault positions, and every passing hour seemed to make even that modest goal impossible. The Americans were not just waiting to be hit. Marine and army ground troops went searching for trouble and attacked whenever they had a chance, while the American planes still rose from Guadalcanal to attack anything that moved in the daylight hours. So the Japanese marching had to be done at night. The advancing troops were hampered every step of the way by impenetrable terrain, grasping green jungle, and unrelenting storms that were followed by blistering heat. Heavily laden soldiers worked their way forward until they wobbled in exhaustion. They had expected a much swifter advance, but their allotted food ran short, and rations were cut in half. The artillery pieces that had seemed so important a few days earlier were abandoned in the jungle because they were too heavy to push. Strength leached from the soldiers' bodies, and disease ravaged them. Communications between units degraded, and the mighty Japanese force staggered, became separated and uncoordinated, and divided into smaller, ineffective units.

A new start date of October 22—a week behind the original schedule—was pushed back another day, and then Yamamoto was notified by telegram that the offensive had to be put off for still another day. The jungle, the weather, and the stubborn opposition of the Americans had all been underestimated, and the elaborate plan to attack simultaneously in three separate ground assaults, with continuous naval and air bombardments, folded.

Washington

Things had deteriorated to such a state that even the Joint Chiefs in Washington, D.C., were finally paying attention to Guadalcanal. While they had geared up for North Africa and adhered to the "Europe First" doctrine, Admiral Yamamoto had thrown the Pacific into chaos. President Roosevelt, alarmed by the reports about what was happening on

Guadalcanal, personally intervened with a terse memo to the men running the war: "My anxiety about the Southwest Pacific is to make sure that every possible weapon gets into that area to hold Guadalcanal, and that having held it in this crisis, that munitions and planes and crews are on the way to take advantage of our success."

The attention was welcome, overdue, and of no immediate help.

Pearl Harbor

Another decision, however, did have an immediate impact. Admiral Nimitz took the crisis of Guadalcanal as final proof that his area commander had surrendered the sea. Ghormley had to be replaced. The choice was easy. Bill Halsey was back on duty after a three-month hospital stay and was already in the area, preparing to replace the wounded Fletcher in command of the carrier force. New orders were rushed to Halsey on October 18. When he received them, he blurted out, "Jesus Christ and General Jackson! This is the hottest potato they ever handed me!" Instead of just taking over the carriers, Halsey was to replace Ghormley instead, thereby assuming command of the entire South Pacific.

The soldiers and marines on Guadalcanal, facing what might be their darkest hour, reacted instantly to the news. "One minute we were too limp with malaria to crawl from our foxholes, the next we were whooping it up like kids," wrote General Vandegrift. The troops knew Halsey was a fighter, and with his bushy eyebrows and barrel chest, he seemed ready for a brawl. He commanded like one, too. He did not believe navy ships should be coddled far away from a battle zone. They were built to go in harm's way, and he would put them there. Halsey immediately pledged that the navy would no longer stand by idly while marines and army soldiers were dying on that godforsaken island.

Carrying out the promise would be difficult. He had only one aircraft carrier, the *Hornet*, but the *Enterprise* was due back from repairs by the end of the month, along with the battleship *South Dakota*. His force was substantially inferior to the Japanese fleet, but Halsey believed the biggest challenge in the South Pacific was not of steel, but of spirit. Soon his hard-nosed personal slogan would spring up on rough banners across the South Pacific: KILL JAPS! KILL JAPS! KILL MORE JAPS!

Guadalcanal

The Americans on the island did not know why the big attack had not come, but every minute of postponement helped them recover. As the Japanese delayed their synchronized attack, enough dribs and drabs of aviation fuel and ammunition were reaching the island to keep the Cactus Air Force flying. On the ground, the marines began pushing out farther, hunting the enemy, and savage fighting erupted, further skewing the Japanese timetable.

The handful of marine pilots and some navy fliers on loan from the damaged carriers went against the Zeros and bombers, fighting right over Henderson Field, and occasionally spiraled down to dead-stick landings when they ran out of gas. The few brown U.S. Army P-400s and P-39s continued roaming the jungles in dangerous close-support missions for the ground troops.

The monsoon season was approaching, and hard rains turned Fighter I into a bog. Every landing and takeoff became as dangerous as a dogfight as thick mud grabbed at the wheels and caused accidents. Some pilots were burned to death in the cockpits of planes that nosed over and exploded before they ever got off the ground.

The tension on the island was as tight as a wire late on the afternoon of October 23 when John Mitchell led a flight out on patrol. He and his longtime wingman, Jack Jacobson, took off side-by-side from one end of the runway, with mud splashing against their planes, and as soon as they lifted off, two more P-39s started rolling from the other end. In those days, it did not take long to find trouble. After they had bombed and strafed Japanese positions, some Zeros swooped down on them through the dark storm clouds. Mitchell found a shot, took it, and a Zero exploded in a ball of fire. Then he led his guys back to Fighter I, made a splash landing in the syrupy mud, dodged around bushes that ground crews placed in the runway to mark shell craters, handed the plane back to the crew chief, and waded away through the pouring rain, his work done for the day.

There was no use running, for there was nowhere to run. The Japanese were all around, and the relentless rain soaked everybody. Mitchell hoped the chills he was feeling were due to the cold temperature at night, and not to the fatigue, dysentery, and malaria that were crippling his small team of pilots. They seemed to be wasting away into scarecrows.

Like everyone else, he carried a spoon in his shirt pocket, because without a spoon, you might not be able to eat. No cooking fires were allowed, so he dug into a cold can of Spam. Then he bedded down for the night beneath a dank blanket, hoping to get some sleep before the Japanese ships showed up to shoot at them some more. Washing Machine Charlie came by with his usual nightly load of noise, and John Mitchell woke up long enough to realize how much he hated that little son of a bitch. At dawn, he had to fly again.

No combat situation remains static, and the Japanese gradually lost any hope of launching a coordinated attack. Although the opposing forces on Guadalcanal were, for the first time, evenly màtched in manpower—about twenty-three thousand on each side—the continued delays, the wicked jungle, the fading strength of the Japanese as they advanced through extreme hardships, and the continued American resistance dissolved any strategic advantage the Japanese may have had.

Nevertheless, when the fight finally began, it was of nightmare proportions, even by Guadalcanal's bloody standards.

Over the course of two nights, bitter clashes from regimental size down to individual bayonets raged all along the perimeter that guarded Henderson Field. Wave after wave of fanatical Japanese troops, supported by tanks in some areas, crashed into the weary, but determined, Americans. The marines and army soldiers had targeted their machine guns and artillery on areas over which the Japanese had to pass, and were waiting with nervous triggers. Slashing monsoon rain soaked them all, the mud turned red with blood, and still the attacks continued unabated.

Japanese troops poured through breaks in the line, and in some places the American defenders rolled back, reorganized, and continued the fight. Insults were screamed, grenades were hurled, rifles were used as clubs, knives slashed. Marine cooks and clerks were pressed into the line. Some Japanese soldiers broke through to the edge of the airfield, and several stormed the tent where General Vandegrift sat studying a map. Marines shot them dead. The attacks continued.

Truk

Early in the morning of Sunday, October 25, Yamamoto received the message from the army for which he had waited so long—*2100 BAN-ZAI*—the code words that meant Henderson Field had finally fallen. Matome Ugaki, recently promoted to vice admiral, happily savored the news as he paced the moonlit weather deck of the flagship. He wrote in his diary, "This settled everything! March, all forces, to enlarge the result gained!"

Yamamoto went to sleep believing that Guadalcanal was back in Japanese hands, that his destroyers were plunging down the Slot to add their firepower and bring in more infantry troops, and that Admiral Nagumo was thundering south with his carriers toward the outnumbered American fleet.

17

Homesick Angels

Truk

Yamamoto was misinformed. The report that Guadalcanal had fallen had been sent in error. The Americans continued to hold and to fight.

There was only one place where a Japanese victory could still be achieved: at sea. A decisive defeat of the American fleet could strangle the troops on the island by blocking their supplies and reinforcements until the Japanese army could finish its job.

Yamamoto turned his attention to that final piece of the overall plan, only to be disappointed again, for instead of dashing forward to snare the U.S. warships, Nagumo wasted valuable hours refueling his ships and loitering north of where he was supposed to be. Yamamoto personally sent orders for him to boldly head south, toward the enemy!

On October 26, a major carrier battle erupted off of Santa Cruz Island, well to the southeast of Guadalcanal, and the U.S. fleet indeed took heavy losses. The *Hornet* was sunk, and the *Enterprise* wobbled away, once again crippled. Eighty-one American naval aircraft were lost.

For the Japanese, the big carrier *Shokaku* and the smaller carrier *Zuiho* were put out of action, and ninety-seven planes went down. A number of escort ships on both sides traded body blows.

At that point, although the Americans had no carriers anywhere in the entire Pacific Ocean, Nagumo once again turned away, missing a golden opportunity to take total control of the sea. Yamamoto decided that the Battle of Santa Cruz would be the last time he would endure Nagumo's reluctance to deliver a killing blow. The commander in chief hosted an official dinner aboard the flagship to honor Nagumo and then sent him back to Japan to take a desk job.

Meanwhile, the ground fighting on Guadalcanal tapered off in what had been a defeat of staggering proportions for the Japanese. The army was paying dearly for its refusal to abandon antiquated frontal assaults against the American artillery and machine guns. Incredibly heavy casualties had been sustained, and to underline the humiliation, even Hyakutake's dress uniform had been captured. Yamamoto would have agreed with one common soldier's assessment that it "was truly a foolish military operation."

One of the most disturbing aspects of the battle, in Yamamoto's opinion, was the information from a captured American pilot that more ships of every type, including carriers, were being launched. That meant the production lines in the United States were not only running, but were working even faster than expected. Japanese shipyards would be strained just to replace his losses, much less increase his force. America had moved to a war footing. The admiral no longer could miss any opportunity to crush his enemy, for eventually those new generations of ships would reach the South Pacific in a never-ending buildup of power and strength.

Japanese planners immediately set to work for still another major attack against the Americans on Guadalcanal, to end the battle once and for all. They based their work upon the tactics of the last offensive, which had come so close to victory. Air raids would increase, then battleships would again bombard Henderson Field, and a strong naval task force would be sent on the prowl. Fighters and bombers would operate out of a new, forward airstrip that cut the time they needed to reach the combat zone. Ten thousand fresh troops would be ferried into Guadalcanal via the Tokyo Express, along with more big guns and mountains of supplies.

Yamamoto was skeptical of the army's new promises of success, and he was particularly irked that despite his losses of aircraft, they still refused to release army planes to fight alongside his dwindling force of navy pilots. The generals remained queerly obsessed by the belief that their aircraft would be needed in future battles far to the north, against its traditional foe, Russia. Yamamoto futilely argued that he needed the help immediately, in the grinding aerial battles of the South Pacific. Japan wasn't even at war with Russia!

Prior to the war, the Japanese Naval Air Force demanded that its pilots be virtual supermen. Saburo Sakai, Japan's leading ace, recalled that he was among fifteen hundred men who applied for flying school in 1937. Only seventy were accepted. Those who were chosen endured a brutal ordeal of physical training and exhaustive mental conditioning that drove out all but twenty-five cadets.

A JNAF pilot had to be the best of the best, in every way. He had to hang from a tall pole by one hand, hold his breath for ninety seconds underwater, balance on his head, and leap from a high platform, flip several somersaults, and land on his feet. The handful of graduates who possessed such incredible physical stamina and impossible reflexes were able to see stars in the daytime and could maintain equilibrium in the most extreme dogfight aerobatics. In the cockpit of a fighter plane, they were as good as any pilots on earth, and better than most.

Now, as those extraordinary fliers dwindled in number, the JNAF was paying a terrible price for its policy of graduating only the cream of the crop. The unintended result of the harsh training was that the reservoir of naval pilots was never deep. The loss of even one pilot of such high caliber was felt, and the wholesale slaughter of the corps in 1942 had been disastrous. New Guinea, Midway, and Guadalcanal were eating them alive, and many more were killed because they refused to wear parachutes. So ill-trained youngsters were now being rushed through an accelerated flying program with lower standards. The result was a high casualty rate.

Both at sea and in the air, the Americans were winning the battle of attrition.

Fighter I

The ferocious fighting during October had bought valuable time for the Americans on Guadalcanal.

Halsey was pushing through the supplies and reinforcements necessary to change the status of the island from an exposed forward position to a bastion of American strength. The battle-weary Cactus Air Force was able to make up its losses. More fighter planes made the long flight from New Caledonia to the Canal, and the fresh pilots arrived well trained and ready to fight. Another airstrip was created to the west of Henderson, on the other side of the Tenaru River and parallel to the coast, and was christened Fighter II.

Captain John Mitchell had shot down his third Zero on October 23 and was discovering the administrative side of his job as a commander was as difficult as fighting the enemy. Replacement pilots were pressed into service almost as soon as they arrived, for the Japanese had only pulled back to regroup, and everyone knew they would be coming again. It was just a matter of time. The signs were clear that another major offensive was coming, and it might be the pivot of the entire campaign.

Japanese scouts had finally discovered Fighter I. One night, Mitchell went to bed with eighteen planes in service, but at daybreak, after another all-night naval bombardment, he had only two planes still able to fly. Pistol Pete then began to hammer the strip, and Mitchell moved his planes over to Fighter II to at least get out of Pete's range.

New Caledonia

Halsey turned Nouméa, the capital of New Caledonia, upside down as he reorganized Ghormley's old command into his own tough image. Refusing to be locked aboard a flagship, he set up headquarters in the former Japanese consulate overlooking the harbor, some nearby Quonset huts, and an old house that became known as Havoc Hall. Unlike his ascetic counterpart Yamamoto, this admiral ordered ten cases of scotch and five cases of bourbon each month, for his own pleasure as well as for entertaining.

Then Halsey headed up to Guadalcanal, where Ghormley had never visited. He was shocked by the haggard appearance of the troops. But when an officer asked for another regiment of reinforcements, Halsey smacked a sandbag so hard that it split open. He had already put several convoys in motion, and was frustrated that he could not give more. "Hit with what you've got, son," he barked. "That's what I have to do."

Guadalcanal

The crucial battle opened on November 12, when Japanese planes swarmed down on American transport ships and destroyers off of Lunga Point and the Cactus Air Force roared up to meet them. In minutes, trails of smoke and blossoms of fire tarred the beautiful blue skies. Planes and pilots of both sides died.

Wild as it was, there was something uniquely different about this particular fight. Amid the somersaulting fighters were twin-tailed aircraft with a pair of roaring engines that could rip through the sky at better than four hundred miles per hour. Only that morning, D. D. Brannon had brought the first dozen P-38 Lightnings of his 339th Fighter Squadron to Guadalcanal, and this was their curtain-raiser.

The P-38 looked like no other plane in the sky, for it had a peculiar shape, somewhere between a square with wings and a flying capital letter H. The pilot's cockpit was located in a nacelle sitting in the middle of a long, knife-thin wing. On either side were two powerful engines housed in long fuselage booms that tapered down to rounded rudders linked by a single horizontal stabilizer and elevator.

The pilot's armored cupola had two inches of bulletproof glass in front of his face, and the bathtublike cockpit had a bewildering array of thirty-six switches, twenty-one dials, twenty levers, six thumb buttons and radio controls, five cranks, and two plungers. When he pulled the triggers, the guns on the nose of the plane spit out bullets so tightly focused that most of them would hit in a seven-foot-diameter circle a thousand feet away. This was an astonishing flying machine—responsive, bristling with firepower—and it had the wonderful ability to climb like a homesick angel. It had self-sealing fuel tanks to minimize the danger of fire, could fly incredible distances, and, if necessary, could come home from a long mission on just one engine.

The P-38 had a pedigree even before joining the Cactus Air Force. The plane had seen action in the Aleutian Islands; it had been the first American plane to knock down a German Luftwaffe fighter in Europe; and it was in the thick of things over New Guinea.

This new fighter squadron had come to Guadalcanal on the first leg of what would be an historic journey. In coming months, they would help turn the tide in the fight for Guadalcanal and take the their awesome destructive ability deep into territory that once was owned by Admiral Yamamoto.

Just as important as the new birds were the men flying them. When Brannon pieced together the 339th Fighter Squadron back at Tontouta Air Base on New Caledonia, he had a number of Guadalcanal veterans among the 33 pilots and 102 enlisted men. This was no batch of rookies, and they were quick to pick up what they needed to know.

By the afternoon of their first day on the Canal, the P-38s joined the big dogfight upstairs, going even higher and faster than the marines and speeding through Japanese formations with their guns blazing. Their 20-mm cannon shells broke red against enemy planes, and bullets from the four .50-caliber machine guns hit with white flashes. The smell of gun smoke seeped into the cockpits.

One Lightning was lost in action on that first day of combat, but the planes were there to stay.

The fifth and final major fight around Guadalcanal was at hand, another gigantic, merciless brawl in which men died in the jungle, pilots were blown from the air, and sleek warships were smashed into rude, wrecked steel coffins for the hundreds of sailors who went down with them.

On the ground, American marines and the new army units dug in even deeper after patrols found evidence that the Japanese were gathering in strength, preparing for another assault. In the afternoon, a big air battle took place right over U.S. Navy ships that were unloading men and supplies. Something was definitely afoot.

As night fell on November 12, the Japanese navy moved. Eleven transports filled with troops moved to bring in reinforcements, and the battleships *Hiei* and *Kirishima* sailed to bombard Henderson. Japanese cruisers and destroyers nosed down the Slot in search of American ships, with Rear Admiral Hiroaki Abe pushing hard through the rain and darkness.

Since the Americans had no carriers left for support, the air group of the *Big E* had been transferred to Guadalcanal, adding to the strength of the Cactus Air Force. So, if the Japanese could shut down the fields again, there would be no air cover at all.

The U.S. Navy, however, was not helpless. It had a force of cruisers and destroyers in the immediate area, under the command of Rear Admiral Daniel J. Callaghan, and two American battleships were also heading for the combat zone. All that separated the enemies was a storm that had also moved into Sealark Channel off Guadalcanal.

The Americans had the advantage of using a radar that could penetrate the bad weather, and it picked up the oncoming Japanese force, which was vulnerable at that moment. Admiral Abe's battleships were loaded with antipersonnel high explosives to bombard the airfield when a lookout saw the American ships. Instead of firing immediately, Callaghan stalled and approached closer to the Japanese, giving Abe eight precious minutes in which to reload with armor-piercing shells for a ship battle. The opposing ships were at point-blank range before they began firing, and confusion grew as big shells and torpedoes flew like steel hail.

Guadalcanal seemed to shake beneath the tense men huddled in foxholes as the explosions and thundering retort of big guns reverberated across the water and the night sky was illuminated into a ghostly sheen and balls of fire ballooned over dying ships. The fight broke off before daybreak, and when the fighters and dive-bombers rose from Cactus at daylight, they found the channel to be a nightmare scene of wrecked and burning ships and of bodies floating in the water.

Unrelenting fighting in the air, on the ground, and at sea continued for several days. Casualties on both sides were enormous, and several admirals died with their ships. Washington again worried whether the island could be held.

When the sea fight was done, the Americans had lost two cruisers and seven destroyers; three cruisers were seriously damaged, and one battleship was battered. But the fleet had managed to keep the enemy battleships from closing Henderson Field and to cover the landing of another entire regiment of marine reinforcements. Army and navy planes had also crushed the Japanese landing force.

By any accounting, the Japanese had suffered still another disastrous setback. Two battleships, a heavy cruiser, and three destroyers were lost, and another six warships sustained damage. Their landing attempt was a catastrophe, with only two thousand men and a fraction of their supplies making it ashore, much of that only because four transport ships were intentionally driven aground.

It was the beginning of the end for the Japanese on Guadalcanal.

The bloodied 1st Marine Division, the victors of Guadalcanal who had gone in as poorly equipped boys and grown with honor into seasoned combat veterans, was pulled out in December after sustaining three thousand battle casualties, with almost triple that number falling victim to disease and being invalided out of the action. The remnants of the division were transported to Australia to rest and recuperate. But instead of being assigned to nice beaches and pleasant surroundings, they were relegated to open tents in a swamp in the middle of a sweltering summer. The mosquitoes were as plentiful as on Guadalcanal. Hundreds of marines went to the hospital with malaria.

As the marines were leaving Guadalcanal, United Press correspondent Bob Miller, who had been on the island during the early, mean months of the fight, returned for another tour. He hardly recognized the place. While interviewing one general, the newsman was even offered a rum collins with ice in it. Planes, jeeps, and trucks were everywhere, and roads reached into the jungles. "Back home again," Miller wrote after touring the muddy island. "It was quite a thrill to drive around the place this morning over the old battle grounds, each acre of which is sowed with rows of memories."

He did not file a news report about one especially significant incident, but wrote it in his diary a few days after he got back. Eleven Japanese destroyers had come down the Slot, but were smoothly intercepted and turned back by small, maneuverable American PT boats based across the channel in Tulagi. "We had full information of their coming, as we have been breaking their codes again for several weeks," Miller said.

Even before 1942 ended, it was no secret on Guadalcanal that American code breakers were reading Japanese communications.

D. D. Brannon's time was up. He had brought the 67th Fighter Squadron in back in August, when all they had were the wretched P-400s, and then worked to transform them into deadly weapons that flew low and hit hard. After being appointed the first commander, and creator, of the 339th Fighter Squadron, he led the first P-38s into Guadalcanal and fought with them. With his deep pool of combat experience, Brannon departed to continue his career elsewhere, but he would always be something of a rebel, and get into even more of his trademark scrapes as the years passed.

He handed the 339th off to John Mitchell. The squadron never lost a beat.

Even before he started driving P-38s, Mitchell already had three confirmed kills and more probables to his credit. He led daring dive-bombing missions, escorted bombers to distant targets, took off in mud and fog, and returned home without navigational equipment to dark, rain-swept fields that had no landing signals because the Japanese would use the lights as targets. The thoughtful and serious former enlisted man from Mississippi had a reputation for knowing how to run a successful mission and bring his men back alive. He had been promoted to major.

Tom Lanphier and Rex Barber arrived on Guadalcanal on December 21, 1942, as part of a flight of eleven P-39s of the 70th Fighter Squadron. Confined to Fiji and day after day of training, they had missed much of the hottest fighting and were eager to show what they could do. After hauling their gear up to the ridge called Strafer Heights, they were ready to fly and itching to get into battle.

Three days later, Tom Lanphier took off in his P-39. Bucking a crosswind off the ocean, he led eight planes from the 70th to escort B-17 bombers attacking a new strip the Japanese were building in the jungle at Munda, on New Georgia Island, some two hundred miles away. In his autobiography, Lanphier would recall spotting a Zero sliding in on one of the B-17's and peeling away from the formation to curve in behind the enemy fighter. While the Zero pilot concentrated on the bomber, Lanphier steadied up and pulled the trigger. His P-39 shuddered with the recoil of the hammering machine guns, and the bullets lanced out in flashes of fire, with the periodic flaming tracer rounds making it easier to track them. The first shots were low and behind the Japanese plane, and he eased the nose of his own aircraft up until the trail of bright tracers went gleaming into the Zero. The enemy plane exploded in his face, and bits of debris rattled against the P-39 as he flew through the fireball.

Lanphier landed on Guadalcanal in a howling Christmas Eve rainstorm. He claimed that, on the way back, he had also downed a second Zero. In Lanphier's view, he was well on his way to achieving one of his most coveted goals, becoming a fighter ace, the elite title awarded to a pilot who shot down five enemy planes. But only one had been recorded as an official victory, because no one had seen the second one happen. Just like the Zero he claimed to have shot down while acting as a gunner aboard a bomber, it was never confirmed.

Another career-enhancing boost had taken place that was not quite as obvious, but certainly as helpful. He shared a tent with three other officers, including his good friend Major Henry Viccellio, his old squadron commander, who was now holding down an important slot in headquarters.

Christmas of 1942 on Guadalcanal was like a day off in hell. The fighters and bombers took off and landed, and that night the bright beams of two searchlights swung through the sky above Henderson Field, probing for enemy planes that might try to sneak in for an attack. On Christmas Eve, the troops sang "Silent Night" and "O, Come All Ye Faithful," and "I'm Dreaming of a White Mistress." Santa Claus came around in a captured Japanese car dragging an effigy of General Tojo and distributed Red Cross packages containing woolen scarves and knitted sweaters. A military policeman accidentally set off the air raid siren and didn't know how to turn it off, scaring everyone. Little trees decorated with junk made the men homesick. Beer and whiskey and crude sorts of alcohol, drunk from old Clorox bottles, boosted their spirits. A chaplain conducted midnight mass.

"The moon shining through the palms on a clear blue background, the roar of the Flying Fortresses pulling their loads of death and destruction into the air, the candlelit expressions on the faces of the men, the chant of the mass—all very storybookish," Bob Miller noted in his diary.

It was only an interlude, for the war waited just on the other side of the Christmas trees.

Within a week, on December 28, Rex Barber also got on the scoreboard with a spectacular victory.

Nine years before, in 1933, while Yamamoto was chief of the technical division of the Japanese Naval Bureau of Aeronautics, he helped prepare for the particular needs of a war in the Pacific. One project he pushed was development of a long-range bomber that could cover the long distances between islands. The result was the twin-engine Mitsubishi G3M, a huge aircraft with a wingspan of more than eighty-two feet and a crew of five. The Allies called it the "Nell."

Barber was prowling the skies around Munda in his P-38 when he saw a Nell easing in for a landing. He figured "this was as good a time as any to shoot him down." He dived on the bomber, only to find that his fighter was sluggish. An external fuel tank that gave him extra range, still attached to the belly of his plane, was acting as a brake, so he popped the silvery container loose just as he opened fire. Bullets chewed into the big plane.

The Nell erupted in a ball of fire just about the same time Barber's spinning fuel tank tumbled into the expanding sphere of flame. An astonished Australian coastwatcher on the island below witnessed the attack and radioed back to Guadalcanal that he had just seen the most amazing thing—an American fighter had actually bombed a Japanese plane right out of the air!

Truk

The Japanese recognized at last that they had lost Guadalcanal and decided a few days before Christmas to abandon it. Admiral Yamamoto's period of "running wild" was over.

A deception plan was set in motion to cover the evacuation of thousands of Japanese soldiers from the island. Air and naval skirmishes would be launched to convince the Americans that another large attack was eminent, and infantrymen would fight rearguard actions as they retreated. Tokyo Express convoys would sail down the Slot, but arrive empty, for instead of landing troops, they would remove those on the island to safety. The Americans would not know the battle was over until the Japanese had vanished.

The coming evacuation, however, did not mean that Yamamoto had lost his fighting spirit, only that new tactics were required. The Japanese were building new air bases on many of the other islands north and northwest of Guadalcanal, all the way up to Rabaul, strategic locations such as Rekata Bay, Munda, Kahili, Ballale, Tonolei, Buin, and Kara. From those bases, Zeros not only could attack to the south, but also would have a web of interlocking defenses. If the Americans tried to advance, they would have to fight through a ring of fire.

Guadalcanal was not the end of the war, but the way the war was going to be fought had changed dramatically. Admiral Ugaki, the chief of staff of the Combined Fleet, picked up his diary and wrote a solemn entry for the final day of the year. "The year 1942 is going to pass tonight," he confided. "How brilliant was the first-stage operation in April! And what miserable setbacks since Midway in June! The invasions of Hawaii, Fiji, Samoa, and New Caledonia, liberation of India, and destruction of the British Far East Fleet have all scattered like dreams."

18

Patrol

Guadalcanal

There had been a mood shift among the American forces, from desperation to a growing confidence, as the relentless Japanese attacks came to an end. Bitter fighting continued in the jungles and the skies, but reinforcements of planes, pilots, supplies, ground crewmen, aviation gasoline, ammunition, and all of the things so vitally needed were showing up in great quantities. The army, marine, and navy pilots who went into New Guinea and Guadalcanal during 1942 were only the pioneers, the sharp leading edge of a swelling wave of talented fliers. Paired with the improved airplanes and cross-trained to fly several different types, they were lethal.

In January, instead of having to concentrate on protecting the airfields for their very survival, the pilots were going hunting in packs. The army fliers concentrated on supporting infantry units clearing the high ground near Henderson Field and shepherding dive-bombers against the Tokyo Express ships that still ventured down the Slot. The long-range P-38s spun off for distant escort missions, flying high cover for bombers attacking the newly built enemy bases that intelligence reports from various sources were identifying along the island chain.

There was a learning curve for all the new troops, both on the ground and in the air. A P-39 on a strafing run accidentally killed eleven American soldiers. An infantry unit set up its machine guns on high ground and went off to have dinner. When they returned, they were mowed down by Japanese soldiers who had walked in and taken over the unguarded automatic weapons. When National Guard kids quit on a charge to capture an enemy position, an infuriated marine officer recognized that their inexperience was coupled with their fears of the consequences to their loved ones back home, and he cried out in despair, "Too many wives! Too many families!"

Just as battle fatigue was not uncommon among the ground soldiers, so some pilots lost their nerve and had to be dispatched to duties elsewhere. But most soldiered on, day after day, moving cautiously through the beautiful but deadly, trackless jungles and flying among towering white cumulus clouds over islands that looked like ink blots on the sea.

"Guadalcanal ain't what it used to be" was the refrain of the old-timers, who remembered hiding behind their planes to evade snipers. The newcomers found it was still dangerous enough. The Japanese troops still on the island fought with anything they could find, not only because of their Bushido never-give-up training, but because few prisoners were being taken. Americans frequently found the mutilated bodies of their fellow soldiers who had been taken captive, and U.S. troops routinely killed Japanese prisoners, and sometimes even went hunting stragglers just to collect souvenirs.

"There have been few Japanese surrendering despite our efforts to propagandize them," Bob Miller wrote in the middle of January. "The reason is our trigger-happy army is shooting every Jap who shows himself despite the General's promise of safety. One came out today with hands raised, crying that he was sick. The major beckoned him to come in and knocked a gun out of the wary Jap's hand. An infantryman standing alongside him calmly blew the defenseless Jap's head off with a shotgun."

While the complexion of the battle on Guadalcanal was being altered, many of the weary pilots of the 67th Fighter Squadron were getting long-overdue leaves, and their morale surged as they discovered the almost impossible-to-imagine pleasures of New Zealand and Australia.

Soft, clean beds. Long, soaking baths. Fresh eggs and bacon for breakfast, milkshakes in the afternoon, and two steaks for dinner. True, American and Australian soldiers brawled in a huge fistfight called the Battle of Brisbane in November, but all that was forgotten in the euphoria of the victories in the islands and the lifting of the Japanese threat to Australia and New Zealand. The Allies toasted each other with an unending supply of beer.

Compared to Guadalcanal, Australia and New Zealand were paradise. Paradise with women. "There were always girls," said one smiling flyboy. "And girls love fighter pilots. We were young, we were always ready for a party, and we had money that had been saved and won in poker games." They would spend whatever was in their pockets and borrow more. Cargo planes that brought the pilots into the rest centers frequently developed mysterious mechanical ailments that kept them on the ground long after they were scheduled to return to their bases.

The army pilots returned to New Caledonia refreshed after their leaves and slept in the safety of a boring rear area. Just being able to sleep all night was a treasured experience. Rumors abounded around the main base at Tontouta that the 67th would be sending the veterans home, and the lean men eagerly awaited the ships or planes that would whisk them back to their families. Instead, different orders came. Seven pilots went straight back to the Canal, and were in combat the day after they landed.

Fighter II

While there might have been a shortage of actual combat fighters available on Guadalcanal at any given moment, the administrative tail of clerks, cooks, and commanders grew steadily. An umbrella organization, the 347th Fighter Group, commanded by Major George McNeese, was formed out of four squadrons—the old 67th, the 70th, the 339th, and the recently arrived 68th, which flew another type of fighter, the P-40, which had a powerful Allison engine. Among the pilots of the 68th was the tall kid who wore the oddball radio call sign of Heathcliff. Lieutenant Ray Hine had reached Guadalcanal.

Other squadrons of various types, from service units to reconnaissance planes to bombers, also were operating with regularity out of Guadalcanal. The XIII Bomber Command ran the bombers, and the fighters were all beneath the umbrella of the XIII Fighter Command, whose commander was Major Henry Viccellio. Although the bosses would spend time on Guadalcanal, the headquarters were far away in New Caledonia, the administrative home of the XIII Air Force.

A peculiar policy that accompanied all of the reorganization deemed that some staff officers were too valuable to engage in combat, immediately earning them the disdain of those who were flying into harm's way.

Major John Mitchell was not among the protected group. He would not keep himself out of the cockpit, for he was a fighter pilot, not a desk jockey, and he imbued the men of his 339th Fighter Squadron with the aggressiveness of those who had come before them.

On the morning of January 5, 1943, Mitchell led a flight of six P-38s out of Fighter II on a bomber escort mission. Twenty-five Zeros jumped them. The Lightnings, outnumbered four to one, tore into the attacking Japanese formation, and Mitchell shot down one Zero. Other members of his flight shot down two more and chalked up three "probables" before the bombers finished their attack and the fighters broke off contact.

The accounting rules for aerial combat victories were simple. A pilot got credit for downing an enemy plane only if there was a witness to the crash, because a wounded pilot might be able to nurse his plane back to safety. A "probable" meant no one could say for certain exactly what had happened to an enemy plane that had been damaged in a fight, although it most likely crashed. Things happen so fast in a dogfight that the eyes play tricks, reports are easily confused, and, as Admiral Yamamoto once noted, fighter pilots tend to exaggerate. Therefore, "no proof, no victory" was a hard-and-fast rule of the pilot fraternity, and it would play a huge role in the events to come.

Three weeks later, Mitchell led another half-dozen P-38s into a thirty-plane horde of Zeros over Guadalcanal and shot down two. Two days after that, he went up alone before dawn and shot down an annoying Washing Machine Charley making a low bombing run on Henderson Field. Normally, the Americans did not go after these aircraft because a growing number of antiaircraft guns around the fields were trying to shoot him down. Mitchell earned a salute from everyone on the island for that night's work, but another Charley showed up the next night.

A few days later, he took a flight of four P-38s up to the Shortland Islands to escort B-17s attacking enemy ships. There he bagged another Zero, again with two more downed by other members of his flight.

His hell-for-leather flying earned him the Distinguished Service Cross. The accompanying citation stated: "He has destroyed more than five enemy airplanes, having shot down a total of eight confirmed, destroyed an undetermined number on the ground and water during strafing strikes at Rekata Bay and Munda Point, and led numerous other missions in addition to those specifically mentioned, in over 150 hours of combat flying as Flight Commander."

It did not mention the many other missions he flew, such as the long over-the-water, bad-weather flight with ten fighters escorting a PBY flying boat searching for a downed pilot on January 19. He kept them searching without letup until they found him, but by then the flight was so low on fuel that another plane had to ditch while the first pilot was being rescued. The second downed pilot was also picked up. Mitchell got an Air Medal for that one, almost as an afterthought.

John Mitchell had become more than a five-victory ace, and his score would continue to climb, but the rewards and medals and rank were unimportant to him. He was a meticulous commander who was determined to inflict maximum damage on the enemy and bring his pilots back alive. He taught them to attack an enemy airplane by pulling in almost close enough to read the other guy's instruments before opening fire. That way it was impossible to miss.

Pilots joining Mitchell's 339th Fighter Squadron usually came in full of bravado, already convinced they were sharpshooters who could go out and get some Zeros. The commander had no time for such foolishness. He made them prove themselves all over again and gain skills by flying alongside more experienced pilots. They would fight when he was personally satisfied they were ready for combat. He liked to bring his planes and pilots home.

Mitchell also held a passion for the squadron's guns, and made his pilots work alongside the ground crews to keep the weapons clean. In combat, everything depended on the guns. "When you jump a Zero, you have him in range for just a few seconds. Hit him squarely, and he'll go down," he warned. "Miss him and you may get your tail shot off."

When the newcomers complained about the single-minded toughness of their squadron commander, the old-timers laughed at them, told them to shut up and do what they were told, then they might live through their Guadalcanal assignment. They pointed out that Mitchell knew what he was talking about. He was, after all, the highest-scoring army ace on Guadalcanal.

Tom Lanphier of the 70th Fighter Squadron was a very popular guy. He seemed to know everyone, joked continually, and welcomed one and all to his tent, where classical music played on the phonograph and books lay in piles. He was always open to conversation, anything from the war to the works of philosophers.

"He was a handsome guy—Mister Personality," said Stan Palmer, the commander of the 68th Fighter Squadron. "A natural leader who, as an army brat, knew his way around the air force."

Palmer, who had no allegiance to the old 70th Fighter Squadron and did not understand the personal links that stretched all the way back to Hamilton Field in San Francisco, noticed that, of all of the fighter pilots, Lanphier stood "number one" with Major Viccellio, the head dog of the XIII Fighter Command.

Tom Lanphier seemed never to stop looking for the angle, something that could separate him from the pack, for he had not abandoned his quest to become famous. One such moment was just about to present itself, deep in the dangerous trails of Guadalcanal. As was often the case with Lanphier, there would be no witnesses to the event.

It was not uncommon for army pilots to be taken to the front lines to give advice on air strikes or to man radios to call in the planes flown by their brother pilots. When they stepped into the jungles that they had only flown above, the sheer beauty of the place astounded them. Huge butterflies, songbirds, gorgeous flowers, and a nervous, tingling peace and quiet overwhelmed them because it contrasted so sharply with the barren, ruined landscape around noisy Henderson Field.

The sense of awe ended at the first sniper shot. Once they were at the front, the savagery of ground warfare made them long for their cockpits. There they at least had some control over their lives. In this dark, green shooting gallery, vines covered old bones and flies feasted on new corpses. One pilot accompanying a patrol remembered the terror of being pinned down next to a marine who was suffering a dysentery attack as gunfire whip-cracked the air around them. As the pilot huddled against a tree for protection, the young marine crouched nearby in pain and fright, crying and crapping while bullets popped the dirt around him.

According to his memoirs, Tom Lanphier took his jungle trek in somewhat different style. General Lawton Collins, the silver-haired commander of the army's 25th Division and an old West Point friend of Lanphier's father, personally dropped by the pilot's tent during January to invite him out on patrol. Collins wanted Lanphier's input on how the army planes could drop navy depth charges, which he wanted to use in an upcoming attack. After a briefing, the lieutenant was invited to dine with him.

A table was placed in Collins's spacious tent, and a clean linen tablecloth appeared, along with crystal, silverware, and a centerpiece of fresh wild flowers. Cocktails were served before a sumptuous meal of hearts of palm salad and steak, and the conversation included polite discourse on poets and music and Shakespeare. Lanphier would write that he wholly subscribed to the general's idea of tolerating whatever was required when in combat, but once off the line, a soldier should "enjoy the moment as a civilized person and, when the viands are at hand, [be] an epicurean human being, leaving the war outside the tent." The haven of elegance existed where, only a few weeks earlier, marines on half rations had been happy to eat Japanese leftovers. Elsewhere on the island, dehydrated potatoes and powdered eggs remained the norm, along with the ubiquitous rectangular tins of Spam, the spiced ham luncheon meat that was being produced by the Hormel company in

Minnesota at the rate of 15 million cans a week and was being shipped to troops of allied nations all over the world.

Collins, two other generals, a half-dozen staff officers, and Tom Lanphier trekked into the jungle the next morning, accompanied by a couple of riflemen. According to his autobiography, although he was in the middle of the group, he became separated from it. Suddenly there was a rustle in the bushes and a very young Japanese soldier, half Lanphier's size, rushed at him armed with a rifle and a bayonet. Lanphier claims that the soldier lunged and stuck him in the left palm and that he fought back, not with his gun, but by strangling the man with his right hand. Lanphier recounts, "I squeezed his slender neck as we both fell to our knees, and he died, struggling." A rifleman from the patrol found Lanphier and led him back to the main column, according to Lanphier's account. No one witnessed the incident, and there are neither records of anyone having seen the corpse nor any mention of medical treatment being administered to Tom Lanphier for his wounded hand.

The patrol continued, and upon reaching the scene of the planned action, Lanphier watched marine aviators do some dive-bombing, and told the general they were not effective. The following day he personally led a flight of six P-39s in to drop depth charges instead of bombs through the trees, then come back and strafe the same area with their machine guns. It was the kind of attack that army pilots had been doing for months. It had been the specialty of the *Jagdstaffel*.

General Collins was so delighted with the show that he awarded Lanphier a Silver Star for gallantry in action. The citation did not mention what would have been a much more courageous act: A wounded Lanphier, using only one hand, had killed an enemy soldier armed with a rifle and bayonet.

Guadalcanal

Every American fighter plane that could get off the ground took off from Henderson Field, Fighter I, and Fighter II on January 21, even if it had no weapons or some instrument in the cockpit was on the fritz. Secretary of the Navy Knox, Admiral Nimitz, Admiral Halsey, and a gaggle of other ranking officers were coming to visit Guadalcanal aboard a single navy PBY flying boat. There must be no opportunity for a Japanese plane to attack it.

Major John Mitchell climbed to a high cover position in his P-38 Lightning and considered the mass of aircraft spread below him, possibly the greatest concentration of fighters the Cactus Air Force had ever put up for any single mission. Veteran army, navy, and marine combat pilots wrapped the lumbering PBY in a cocoon, with all of the pilots under orders to shoot down any intruder—and if your guns don't work, ram your target. The life of any single pilot was of no consequence when weighed against the value of the men aboard that oddly shaped blue airplane.

Mitchell realized that the outcome of the war depended not only upon guns and planes and fighting men, but also upon the leaders in charge. A man in a foxhole could only see a few feet around him, but top admirals and generals and civilian leaders carried knowledge of the entire panorama of the conflict. To lose Knox, Nimitz, or Halsey would be a national disaster.

Secretary Knox, wearing a pith helmet and khakis with no tie, stepped off the plane first when it landed. The white-haired Nimitz followed him, trim and polite. Then down the ladder came Admiral Halsey, looking like a nightclub bouncer. As a convoy of jeeps hauled the official party up to the war, they passed a returning jeep that carried the blanket-covered body of a dead marine. Suddenly, the men running the war were not seeing statistics on a piece of paper, but the dead son of a mother somewhere back home.

They drove closer to the front by following a series of hellish roads that left them all dirty and sweating, then boarded an armored vehicle to get even nearer, to have a good look at what it was like fighting in a jungle. Following the tour, the officials returned to Henderson Field and bedded down after dinner and a brief press conference. Japanese planes flitted overhead throughout the night, scattering bombs and killing several men, although none of the official party was injured.

They all left safely the next morning, again with an umbrella of fighter planes, and everyone on Guadalcanal breathed easier. The visit of the dignitaries was rather routine, but it left an impression on John Mitchell. In less than three months, he would remember all of that protective air power.

Truk

Admiral Yamamoto spent hours in his shipboard cabin copying famous poems, writing with careful brush strokes in his calligraphy book. The poetry seemed to comfort his soul, give meaning to the deaths of so many of his men, and light the path for what he could do next.

He judged Guadalcanal in the context of the overall war. The entire southern edge of Japan's grand advance was crumbling, but Japan still controlled vast reaches of the Pacific Ocean, and there would be many future opportunities for battle.

As if to confirm his cautious outlook, the Allies demonstrated their growing air supremacy on February 1, 1943, when American bombers utterly destroyed a relief convoy of six thousand soldiers heading for New Guinea. While fighters devastated the Zeros sent to protect the ships, the bombers roared in at wave-top level and skipped their bombs off the water into the sides of eight transports and eight escort destroyers. After they cleared the sky of Zeros, the fighters slid in on strafing runs and machine-gunned the Japanese soldiers who had taken to lifeboats or were swimming for their lives. The horrific Battle of the Bismarck Sea put an end to major attempts to reinforce the isolated Japanese garrisons on New Guinea.

Still, Yamamoto stayed calm. Just as in one of his frequent bridge games, he was about to slam his opponents again. Another giant buildup was well underway, even while the careful evacuation of Guadalcanal continued.

Almost every day, echelons of Imperial Japanese Naval Air Force fighters and bombers were arriving from other bases, even from the remaining aircraft carriers, taking position in Rabaul and the surrounding area. Even the army finally was releasing some of its planes and experienced pilots for use in the coming operations.

Allied intelligence officers had noticed the movement of so many planes but misinterpreted it. They had seen the pattern of buildup before and believed the arriving aircraft would work in concert with the accelerated runs of the Tokyo Express, which in the past had brought more infantry troops to Guadalcanal. They concluded that another big fight was looming for the ownership of the island.

The analysts had been deceived by the Japanese. The ships of the Tokyo Express actually were evacuating some thirteen thousand Japanese soldiers. They would live to fight another day, on some other island. By February 5 the Japanese had abandoned Guadalcanal.

BOOK III

Bogeys

19
I/Go

Guadalcanal

Lou Kittel of Castleton, North Dakota, arrived on Guadalcanal with a beard, a dog, and a motorcycle. He and the other fliers of the 12th Fighter Squadron, the "Dirty Dozen," felt as if they had been released from exile after spending a year on Christmas Island. While the war had raged, they had been cooped up on that lonely coral outpost, honing the skills of other pilots; who then were passed on into combat posts. Finally, it was their turn. Kittel had to leave behind the tidy house he had built by hand from cast-off wooden supply crates, and he would have to start making himself comfortable all over again, this time in a war zone.

He and his fellows arrived aboard a cargo plane in March 1943. Major Kittel stepped down to the metal matting of Henderson Field, took a look around his new station, stroked his beard in thought, and concluded once again that he might be there for a while. He cranked up his motorcycle, propped his dog up in front of him, and dashed away to buy some chickens.

Shortland Islands

An American reconnaissance plane spotted a covey of float Zeros, fitted with pontoons instead of wheels, resting in a lagoon in the Shortland Islands, and the planners on Guadalcanal ordered a strike by sixteen army and marine pilots on the morning of March 29.

The night was miserable, and a hard rain steadily strummed on the canvas tents, giving the pilots little time for sleep, since take-off was at 3:30 A.M. Although things had changed on Guadalcanal, the grab-bag way of assembling missions continued. The pilots lived together on the ground and frequently flew together. During the previous month, the 339th had lost six pilots in combat, and more had fallen to sickness, so multiservice, mixed-squadron operations were a necessity. Men from the other army squadrons had been trained to fly the P-38 Lightning, and enough of the twin-engine planes were now around that regulars were assigned to their own aircraft.

The army flight that morning consisted of eight P-38s, and it would be led by Captain Tom Lanphier, who had been promoted earlier in the month, given the higher rank over many other lieutenants on Guadalcanal who had substantially more seniority, more combat time, and more enemy planes to their credit.

On his wing was Rex Barber. Most pilots named their planes after wives and sweethearts, but Barber called his *Diablo*, and the quiet Oregonian flew like the devil himself. Three small red-and-white Japanese flags, one for each enemy plane he had shot down, were painted on the nose.

After reaching altitude, the planes nudged into formation, but when the Corsair of the marine leading the mission malfunctioned, he turned back to the base, and Lanphier assumed command. The flight headed north and soon ran into turbulent air as it entered a belt of storms.

The thick, violent squalls that often moved between Rabaul and Guadalcanal were not mere curtains of raindrops; they were more like earthquakes in the heavens, and many pilots had died trying to fly through them. In these giant thunderheads the American planes were tossed about, the pilots jerked hard against their seat belts, and the visibility dropped to zero. One by one, nine more pilots became separated from the flight and turned their Corsairs and Lightnings back to the safe haven of Guadalcanal.

A story that Lanphier would not have shared with his flying buddies was that his father, when in command of the 1st Pursuit Group in 1925, had been criticized for his "reluctance" to complete a long-distance test flight from Michigan to Miami, partly because heavy weather had forced down some of the planes in his command. His son would not to repeat that mistake; he bulled on through the churning storm. Of the sixteen planes that began the mission, only five P-38s and a single Corsair remained when they reached calmer skies.

Lanphier quickly oriented himself. Shortland was a small island located near the top of the Slot, like a cork in a bottle. Beyond it lay the huge mass of Bougainville Island, and there was enough light from the new dawn to locate the enemy planes at rest on the lagoon. The American pilots spread out, fell into line, and came in at treetop level, pouncing out of the morning sun on the small Japanese base as it was just waking up.

In a single, shattering run, with their machine guns pumping out a 1–1–1 mix of tracers, explosives, and armor-piercing rounds, the shadowy American fighters ripped into the parked Zeros. The bullets would hit short of the planes, digging into the water, and the pilots would use those splashes to walk their gunfire right across their targets. The Japanese planes shuddered with the hits until a gas tank or ammunition tray was struck, then they exploded in bright orange-and-red fireballs that shone on the dark water.

Done with their primary target, the Americans hopped over to another lagoon and found some more Zeros. Eight Japanese planes were destroyed and one was left smoking before the Americans sprinted away through a curtain of antiaircraft fire. Surprise had been so total that all of the Japanese planes were destroyed before any could rise and challenge them.

Lanphier's undamaged flight headed for home, but the pilots spotted what they believed to be a Japanese destroyer only about six miles away and immediately dived on it. The first strafing runs were aimed at knocking out the antiaircraft guns, and the planes stitched the metal armor and pummeled the ship from bow to stern. Ricochet bullets sparkled like bright, sudden lights along the deck. The planes wheeled about and came in again, lower, and this time peppered the ship with bullets and cannon shells until it lay like a seagoing bonfire, wreathed in smoke and heeling over with a sharp list. Sailors could be seen leaping overboard and swimming away.

On his final run, Rex Barber watched the path of the tracer bullets and tapped his controls to shift the snout of *Diablo* around as if it were sniffing new victims. His light touch moved the nose guns to fire at the heart of the ship. Barber, a disciple of John Mitchell's close-in philosophy, came in hard and tight, hosing the bridge and midship area of the flaming vessel with the concentrated firepower of his P-38. Caught up in the action, he misjudged both his speed and distance. "I got too aggressive," he said sheepishly of a lapse that almost cost him his life.

The bulk of the gray ship suddenly loomed immediately in front of him, points of antennae sticking up even higher than his cockpit. It was as if the ship had jumped up from the water, and he could barely look over it. All he saw was *ship* and he was barreling along at a breakneck speed. He brought the steering yoke back into his stomach in an attempt to leap the plane over the growing mass of the superstructure, but the tangle of antennas on the radio mast reached out for him. With a grinding crunch, the steel foremast scythed through the end of *Diablo*'s right wing.

But the plane did not spin out of control into the water. Its two powerful Allison engines pulled the fast-moving plane through the collision, and Barber, much to his surprise, found himself still in the sky. He gingerly tested the controls, one by one, and found he was able to climb and maneuver. "The darn thing flew better after the loss of the wing tip than before," he said.

Diablo landed back at Fighter 1 looking like a wounded duck, and Barber was properly chastised by the ground crew chief, who wanted to know what the lieutenant had done to the plane. Three feet of the right wing was gone, and shards of metal and wiring hung from the ruptured end like tendons from an amputated arm. Barber joked to the irate crew chief, "Cut the other one down to size." *Diablo* was not ready for the boneyard, but it would need some serious work before it could fly again.

All five of the P-38 pilots returned, as did the lone marine Corsair pilot, who ran out of gas as he touched down on Guadalcanal. All were awarded Silver Stars for bravery. Since aircraft destroyed on the ground or the water did not count toward aerial victories, none got credit for any enemy planes. Barber told his crew chief to paint the silhouette of a sinking ship beside the three Japanese flags on the nose of *Diablo*.

The unplanned attack on the ship had been something of a madcap idea, though some headquarters types thought it might be a court-martial offense. The P-38 pilots really didn't care. They saw an opportunity and took it, and whether the target had actually been a destroyer or only a subchaser or a rowboat did not matter. They had still taken an enemy vessel out of the war.

Word spread around the island about the hotshots in the P-38s. Lanphier had taken his flight through a mind-numbing storm, and Barber, the lucky bastard who had once bombed a plane, had now collided with a ship and was still walking around, cool as could be.

Almost sixty thousand American troops now controlled Guadalcanal, but the skies over the Solomon Islands remained dangerous, and Admiral Halsey had to pick someone to take over the Allied air operations there and during the coming push to the north. He chose Marc Mitscher. Less than a year before, he had teamed with Mitscher to slip into the North Pacific aboard the *Enterprise* and *Hornet* and deliver Jimmy Doolittle's unexpected attack on Tokyo. The man knew air, Halsey said, and "was a fighting fool."

Mitscher arrived on Guadalcanal in time to watch a ferocious dogfight right over Henderson Field, during which three Japanese Zeros and four marine Wildcats were shot out of the sky. He moved into a canvas tent and began enduring life in the pouring rain and blistering sun.

Mitscher ignored the personal discomfort. Using the top of his footlocker as a desk, he was soon laying plans to take the fight to the enemy. Of particular interest were the new fields at Munda Point in the New Georgia Islands, on the northwestern edge of the Slot, about two hundred miles from Henderson Field. Another Japanese base had recently been discovered in the same area, on the island of Kolombangara, and both remained operational despite frequent air attacks and ship bombardment.

. . .

Lou Kittel and the 12th Fighter Squadron fit right in with the rest of the crowd in the pilots' mess tent on Guadalcanal. It was noisy and good-humored beneath that canvas awning, where past fights were discussed, friendly insults were hurled, and open hands chased each other to illustrate a dogfight. Pilots came and went, and their names were forgotten quickly, because there were so many.

One morning Kittel walked in and handed the mess cook two eggs, and a few minutes later they came back to him over easy. A pilot who had just arrived said, "Make mine scrambled." The mess sergeant laughed and spooned out a blob of mush. "Why can he have fresh eggs and I can't?" the new guy demanded. The sergeant shrugged, "The major has his own chickens."

The fact that the bearded major, small and lithe, was a tad eccentric disguised his ability in the cockpit. One night he and John Mitchell sat side by side listening to the latest version of Washing Machine Charlie buzz and bomb the airfield as searchlights scissored brightly around the enemy plane and antiaircraft blossoms erupted far below it. Mitchell described how he had shot down one of those, and Kittel allowed as how that seemed to be a good idea. Admiral Mitscher had been complaining about the pesky Japanese night visitor.

So Kittel alerted the antiaircraft guys that he was going up the next night. He took off in his P-38 and circled high and invisible in the moonlit silvery clouds until the coughing Japanese bomber made its usual visit. The antiaircraft fire died away, as arranged, and Kittel tipped into a steep dive, got right on Charlie's tail, and opened fire as everyone below watched. As he held down the triggers, tracers flashed through the night sky, and his cannon and machine guns blew gaping holes in the Japanese plane. It stumbled, as if it had hit a rock, then caught fire and exploded with a rumbling roar. Pieces of the plane scattered and fell like hail. Kittel swept back in over the palm trees and landed to the cheers of the troops.

Truk

Yamamoto needed new aircraft carriers and as many planes as he could get, but instead he got another monster battleship. The *Musashi*, even more splendid than its sister ship, the *Yamato*, finished its maiden voyage from Japan by elegantly cruising into the protected anchorage at Truk. If stood vertically, the ship would have been as tall as the Chrysler Building in New York City, and it weighed three times as much as a large aircraft carrier. Six eighteen-inch guns dominated the foredeck above the needle-nosed bow, and three more of the big cannon were mounted aft. The ship wore belts of armor eighteen inches thick. Yamamoto knew the largest battleship ever built would be useless in modern warfare, which was why he had fought against ever building it in the first place. True to his prediction, the *Musashi*'s big guns would never fire at another ship, and despite the suit of armor, torpedoes and bombs eventually would sink it.

Nevertheless, Yamamoto was piped aboard on the first day of February 1943, and it became the flagship of the Combined Fleet. The *Yamato* would become little more than a floating fuel barge for other ships.

A few weeks later, the admiral received an order from Tokyo that dealt him a rare and important setback in the ongoing argument between the Japanese army and navy. Although he considered New Guinea as much of a lost cause as Guadalcanal had been, the army still held the political reins in Tokyo and demanded that priority be given to protecting what was left of its operations in the south. The generals even dreamed of taking the offensive again in New Guinea.

To do so, the Japanese would first have to regain control of the air at the most distant points of the battlefront, which Yamamoto knew was impossible. The "Army-Navy Central Agreement" of March 25 instructed the C-in-C to clear the skies of enemy planes.

The admiral's staff drew up I-Go (Operation I), which would commit the huge aerial armada that had been carefully built up around the 11th Air Fleet and was carefully dispersed at little bases in the many islands north and west of Guadalcanal. They could reach New Guinea with ease. With little choice, Yamamoto approved the plan, although he knew it would commit his deteriorating naval air force to almost suicidal attacks.

The strain of orchestrating a battle that he did not want to conduct was affecting his health. He was taking vitamin shots to alleviate numbness in the fingers on his right hand. The only soothing news seemed to come from officers who had paid courtesy calls in Tokyo on his beloved mistress, Chiyoko. He sent her a lock of his hair and a poem on Friday, April 2, and in the accompanying letter Yamamoto mentioned, "Tomorrow, I'm going to the front for a short while."

He played the Japanese board game known as *shogi* that day with his senior aide, Commander Yasuji Watanabe, one of his favorite partners. He won two out of three games. As they worked at the board, the black and white marker pebbles defining small strategies, the two old friends talked about the planned trip that would take the admiral from Truk to Rabaul. Great pressure was upon him to make this aerial assault work, and Yamamoto felt he had to move closer to the front for this operation, for his presence would boost the morale of the pilots. However, just as he criticized the honored practice of experienced captains going down with their ships, he wondered about the wisdom of any top commander, including himself, being drawn too close to the front line. "I'm not very keen on going to Rabaul," he told Watanabe.

His chief of staff, Ugaki, noted about the same time that sometimes risk cannot be avoided for a commander, and this was one of those times.

On a clear Saturday morning, the small man who ran the Combined Fleet left the giant battleship, expecting to be gone for about a week. As was his practice, he divided the traveling staff into two flying boats so that the loss of a single plane would not get them all. He flew in one, and Ugaki went in the other. The flight to Rabaul, made with an escort of only three Zero fighters, was uneventful, and the admiral arrived exactly on time. Yamamoto retired that night to a comfortable bed in a hilltop lodge, listening to the roll of thunder, the slash of wind, and the steady rain falling *drip-drip-drip* from the eaves. He may have thought of his family, or of Chiyoko, the only person to whom he would bow other than his emperor. Certainly, he would have fallen asleep very aware that he was moving closer to the sound of the guns.

Fighter II

Gray clouds of dust rose behind everything that moved around the fighter strips and trailed after taxiing planes like dirty sails. Men held helmets over their faces like gas masks when they rode in open vehicles.

Correspondent Dick Tregaskis noted, "You put on clean clothes at nine o'clock and walk down the road, and at 9:30 you look like a chimney sweep."

The same day Yamamoto mailed his final letter to his mistress, Tom Lanphier, Rex Barber, Doug Canning, and other veteran pilots strapped on their P-38s and took off through those clouds of sticky dust. Their patrol found little of interest until they were on the way home, when one spotted a Japanese cargo ship in a cove.

The first Lightnings that came roaring in dropped the spare fuel tanks that hung beneath their wings at just the right moment, and the teardrop-shaped canisters skipped on the water like deadly pebbles and shattered against the side of the ship. As gasoline spewed all over the boat and the surrounding water, two more P-38s flew in close to light it up with their red-hot tracer rounds. The ship erupted in an inferno of flame as the P-38s wove back and forth on strafing runs, the noses of their planes shaking with the recoil of the hammering guns. They pounded the devastated vessel into a burning hulk.

Admiral Mitscher, navy to his boots, liked these young army fliers who seemed to enjoy attacking anything that moved. Halsey felt the same way, and he sent the pilots a case of booze.

But Mitscher's job was to look at a picture that was much bigger than a single, although spectacular, attack on a cargo ship. Enemy air strikes on Guadalcanal had diminished in recent weeks, and the sky was ominously silent except for the buzzing of American aircraft taking off and landing. The guys from Cactus had been flying for days without serious interference; they had blown up barges, strafed troops, bombed ships, run recon missions, and, except for a few dogfights, found little opposition.

Where were the Japanese planes?

20

Message

Rabaul

The massive aerial assault that would hit Guadalcanal on the first day and, after that, change targets and pummel New Guinea, was to begin on Admiral Yamamoto's sixtieth birthday, April 4. Hundreds of fighters and bombers, some of which had been flown in all the way from Japan, were poised for the battle, but a thick front of bad weather moved in and shut down the skies for three days.

Yamamoto was stymied, and his mood was as black as the stormy tropical night that enveloped the hilltop mansion where he had taken up residence. He was looking forward to the end of the operation as much as the start, so he could put his navy pilots to better uses. Raiding places that no longer had strategic value made no sense to him. Also, he felt his physical strength waning, and he was constantly tired. His ankles hurt so badly that he changed shoes several times every day, and the doctor who examined the numbness in his fingers and his swollen joints thought he might be falling victim to the debilitating disease called beriberi, usually brought on by a lack of a B vitamin in the diet. Even the mighty C-in-C could get sick in these hellish islands.

Yamamoto tried to fill the otherwise useless hours prior to the attack by visiting hospitals, listening to staff reports, touring workshops, playing chess and cards, and waiting for the weather to improve. It seemed, as he gazed out over the vastness of Saint George's Channel, where ships moved dimly through rain-swept Simpson Harbor, that things were slipping out of his hands.

On April 6, the rains appeared to be subsiding, and Yamamoto went out to visit several units of combat planes that were leaving for more forward positions. Rabaul was a heavily defended port, with a hundred thousand men assigned to it, and the Japanese had built five airfields there, from Keravat in the west to Cape Gazelle in the east. All were jammed with aircraft.

The wheels of his automobile churned through sticky volcanic ash to deliver him to one of the bases, and he stepped carefully from his car to avoid the mud. Immaculate in a dress white uniform, he mounted the veranda of a small building and exhorted a group of pilots to attend their duties well. "However difficult a time we are having, the enemy also has to be suffering," he said. "Now we must attack his precious carriers with Rabaul's great air strength and cut them down so they cannot escape. Our hopes go with you."

He walked to the edge of the runway and stood stiffly erect, waving his white hat in salute as the aviators took off, their planes skimming through pools of water. But the storms had not truly eased, and the fliers were forced to return a short time later, shamed that their mission was unfulfilled. It made little difference to Yamamoto, for he knew the weather was clearing, and the aerial gate would soon open to Guadalcanal. Before he went to bed that night he could see the stars, and fireflies blinked around the house.

The next day, April 7, a fresh sun rose in a beautifully crystalline morning sky with the splash of bright red rays that was always taken as a good omen by the Japanese. When Yamamoto received his morning report, he was told that the Americans had crowded a task force of thirty-one warships and transports into the killing zone around Guadalcanal. It was a perfect time to launch Day One of I-Go, and strike the island.

Yamamoto knew, however, that no matter how much he might hurt the Americans on that blood-drenched island, there were no Japanese soldiers on the ground to take and hold the airfield. He might destroy machines and kill some men, but he could no longer deny the Americans the strategic advantage offered by Guadalcanal and its busy

airfields. That battle had been lost. This time, he was the obedient officer, doing what he was told. It was a waste.

He again put on his white uniform and descended the hill to watch
some of the squadrons depart. Twin-engine Betty bombers, Val dive-
bombers, and Zeros, all armed to the teeth, clawed from the fields,
formed into Vs and flew away, the concerted roar of their engines filling
the sky. As they passed over island bases such as Buin and Kahili and Ballale, more planes rose to join the formations until more than two hundred Japanese fighters and bombers were powering toward Guadalcanal.

Fighter II

The Americans knew what was coming. Code breakers and reconnaissance missions had been tracking the buildup of Japanese planes in the
north and had expected the assault to start on April 4. When the
weather cleared, they knew the enemy planes would fly, and Guadalcanal went to the rare status of Condition Very Red. Coastwatchers
confirmed the oncoming attack, reporting by radio that wave after wave
of enemy planes was passing overhead. The improved electronic eye of
radar had come to the island, and blips representing approaching aircraft pulsed on the screens.

The ships in Ironbottom Sound scattered to safer waters, crews on
antiaircraft guns checked their ammunition, and Admiral Mitscher
scrambled the fighters.

There was a madhouse of activity as ground crews spun up the engines and pilots ran to their planes, struggled into parachute harnesses,
pulled down the cockpit canopies, and trundled to the runways. The
Japanese were about an hour away and closing fast.

A flight of four P-38 Lightnings lifted from the dusty coral strip, and
Tom Lanphier, Rex Barber, and their frequent flight partners Joe Moore
and Jim McLanahan headed upward to patrol about thirty thousand feet
over Tulagi, across the channel from Guadalcanal. Since his own *Diablo*
was still down with its broken wing, Barber was flying a borrowed plane.

From their position in top cover, the four pilots had a perfect view
of a solid wall of seventy-six eager American fighter planes moving
into position, layered down almost to the dark waters below. The P-38s

were on top, Corsairs were five thousand feet below them, Wildcats circled three thousand feet below that, then the P-40 Warhawks and the P-39 Airacobras patrolled close to the deck.

The Japanese arrived in a swarm, with the Zeros flying close cover for the dive-bombers at thirty thousand feet, unaware that almost every fighter plane on Guadalcanal was waiting for them. American soldiers and marines on the ground and sailors aboard ships craned their necks to watch dogfights as the sky exploded in duels and sudden death. Among the spectators that day was young Lieutenant (j.g.) John F. Kennedy, a future president of the United States, who had reported for duty at the PT boat base on Tulagi only the day before.

Fighters tangled in mortal combat, swirling and diving and writhing and climbing and shooting, then the Japanese dive-bombers pushed over in steep, angled falls toward the airstrips or ships that still were in Ironbottom Sound. Some planes exploded in bright buttons of orange and red, while other crippled aircraft spun ribbons of black smoke in twisting spirals as they fell thousands of feet to the gray water or green jungles below.

Lanphier, Barber, Moore, and McLanahan horsed their P-38s down to attack seven Zeros that were pouncing the Corsairs and Wildcats. Many years later, in his autobiography, Lanphier wrote about the fight. He said the tailing pilot in the first echelon of Zeros never saw him coming and was demolished by his machine guns and cannon fire. As Lanphier pulled sharply around, he found himself head to head with another oncoming Zero, and the only effective tactic was to barrel right in, for pulling up or down would expose his plane to the Japanese guns. They closed at about five hundred miles per hour, and the Zero pulled up first, exposing his belly to the Lightning's circle of gunfire. It exploded as it passed over Lanphier's head. A few minutes later, he blasted a third Zero that was pursuing a P-39 down low.

His flight mates were just as busy with dogfights of their own. Barber shot down two Zeros, and Moore and McLanahan each got one. Although the army flight had taken out seven enemy planes, the day's honors in single combat went to a marine pilot, Jim Swett, who shot down seven by himself.

The Japanese attack ended immediately after the bombers finished their runs, because on any flight from Rabaul to Guadalcanal, a pilot used up most of his fuel just covering the 675 miles that separated the two. Getting there and back left little time to loiter and fight.

Rabaul

The returning Japanese pilots were ecstatic. A cruiser and a destroyer had been sunk! Ten transport ships! Thirty-six American planes were blown from the sky! Only a dozen Japanese planes lost!

Yamamoto knew pilots exaggerated their victories, and this time probably was no exception. He was correct: they had sunk only one American destroyer, a New Zealand corvette, and a U.S. tanker, and had shot down seven marine fighters while losing thirty-nine of their own planes.

Nevertheless, he was satisfied that they had inflicted enough damage to launch the follow-up attacks, but Guadalcanal would no longer be the main target. The next three days would focus on New Guinea, in support of the Japanese infantry garrisons still clinging to a few coastal positions. Bad weather hampered those attacks, too, and although the pilots returned with enthusiastic reports about the planes they had shot down, the ships they had sunk, the troops they had slain, and the airstrips they had destroyed, the actual results were minimal.

Yamamoto went to the air bases each morning and waved his white hat to the departing attackers, and then was driven back up to his lodging on Residency Hill to discuss staff business and play games of *shogi* to while away the hours until the pilots returned for debriefing. As the I-Go mass assaults reached a crescendo, he received a congratulatory message from the emperor, relayed through the naval general staff: "Please convey my satisfaction to the Commander in Chief, Combined Fleet, and tell him to enlarge the war result more than ever." It showed that Yamamoto still had the all-important support of the throne.

On April 13, he decided to make a one-day visit even closer to the front and issued instructions for his staff to plan a trip to the southern bases around the tip of Bougainville. He would personally salute his navy pilots and crews, as well as the army infantrymen who had survived

the horrors of Guadalcanal. The travel date was set for April 18, after
which he would return to his flagship, still anchored at Truk.

Dinners for the admiral and his staff were still lavish but sometimes now included native dishes of tapioca, coconuts, and squash. On
the evening that he made the decision to visit the bases, he learned that
some officers who had served together on the naval academy's training
ship were holding a reunion party. Yamamoto had been one of the officers aboard the ship during that round-the-world cruise, and the C-
in-C arrived at the party unexpectedly, carrying two bottles of scotch,
and spent several nostalgic hours talking about old times, the peaceful
times, when they had roamed the oceans in an old square-rigged sailing ship.

Meanwhile, Yamamoto's meticulous administrative staff officer and
frequent *shogi* partner Yasuji Watanabe set the details for the trip south.
Well aware of his boss's penchant for exact timing, he consulted the
mileages to the bases around Bougainville, established exact speeds for
the planes and boats involved, laid out precise times for meetings with
the soldiers and airmen, lunch, and visits to the sick wards, and carefully
studied the tide tables for a stretch of water the admiral would cross
aboard a ship. Watanabe noted the tide would be flowing against the inspection party on the return trip to Ballale, which would slow the ship,
so he added another five minutes to that leg of the trip. When he was satisfied that everything was timed to the minute, just as Yamamoto required, Watanabe drafted the orders.

TO: COMMANDER, 1ST BASE FLOTILLA
             COMMANDER, 11TH AIR FLOTILLA
             COMMANDER, 26TH AIR FLOTILLA
             COMMANDER, 958TH AIR DETACHMENT
             CHIEF, BALLALE DEFENSE UNIT
FROM: C-IN-C, 8TH FLEET, SOUTH-EASTERN AREA FLEET
INFORMATION: C-IN-C, COMBINED FLEET
C-IN-C, COMBINED FLEET WILL INSPECT RXZ, RXE, AND RXP ON "SETSUA" AS
FOLLOWS:

1. AT 0600 LEAVES RR BY "CHUKO," A LAND-BASED MEDIUM BOMBER (6
    FIGHTERS ESCORTING)
AT 0800 ARRIVES AT RXZ

AT 0840 ARRIVES AT RXE BY SUBCHASER (COMMANDER, 1ST BASE FORCE WILL ARRANGE ONE CHASE IN ADVANCE)

AT 0945 LEAVES RXE BY SAME SUBCHASER

AT 1030 ARRIVES AT RXZ (AT RXZ A "DAIHATSU" WILL BE ON HAND AND AT RXE A "MOTOR-LAUNCH" FOR TRAFFIC)

AT 1100 LEAVES RXZ BY "CHUKO"

AT 1110 ARRIVES RXP

LUNCHEON AT HQ, 1ST BASE FORCE (ATTENDED BY COMMANDANT 26TH AIR SQUADRON AND SENIOR STAFF OFFICERS)

AT 1400 LEAVES RXP BY "CHUKO"

AT 1540 ARRIVES AT RR

2. OUTLINE OF PLAN

AFTER THE VERBAL REPORT ON THEIR PRESENT CONDITIONS BRIEFLY BY EACH UNIT, UNIT MEMBERS WILL BE INSPECTED (1ST B.F. HOSPITAL WILL BE VISITED).

3. THE COMMANDING OFFICER OF EACH UNIT ALONE SHALL WEAR THE NAVAL LANDING PARTY UNIFORM WITH MEDAL RIBBONS.

4. IN CASE OF BAD WEATHER IT WILL BE POSTPONED FOR ONE DAY.

Watanabe took the document to the headquarters of the Eighth Fleet in Rabaul and requested that couriers be dispatched to personally hand-deliver the orders to the various commanders. He was stunned when he learned that it would instead be broadcast by radio. No matter how ironclad a code might be, there was no use taking a chance that the enemy might piece enough of it together to figure out what it said. The communications officers assured him there was no chance of that, for it would go out in a new code that had only gone into effect two weeks earlier, and it could not have been broken. Watanabe insisted that, if it was to be broadcast at all, it had to be transmitted only in the naval code, which he wrongly believed to be more secure.

The message went out to the far-flung commands at five minutes before six o'clock on the evening of April 13, and, indeed, the Americans were listening.

Fighter II

After the big raid on April 7, things quieted down for the American fliers on Guadalcanal as Yamamoto's aerial armada surged instead toward New Guinea. Routine patrols and snooping for ships and barge traffic just did not measure up to the excitement of battling a sky full of Japanese planes. To find worthwhile targets, the P-38s had to fly long and grueling missions farther up the chains of islands and escort long-range bombers on their distant runs.

Finally, however, the pressure against Guadalcanal was eased, and there were more pilots than planes. John Mitchell's 339th Fighter Squadron, including a few pilots on temporary assignment, were sharing the available P-38s with Lou Kittel's bunch from the 12th, which meant everyone had a day off between shifts. Rest leaves became frequent as more pilots qualified to fly the Lightnings, and rested pilots were better pilots.

Mitchell and his crew were coming to the end of their latest six-week assignment at Fighter II and were looking forward to some rest and recreation time in New Zealand and Australia, then some more down time at a rear base before rotating back to Cactus. With such thoughts in their minds, the daily rain, the slurping mud, and the choking dust did not seem as bad.

In April 1943, Mitchell was twenty-seven years old but felt and looked much older. The somewhat chubby face and body had thinned to sharp angles and muscle, and his experience had instilled in him a steely confidence. Exactly eleven years earlier, he had failed to qualify for flight training, and now he was one of the hottest pilots in the Pacific. He flew several types of fighters, was the respected leader of an aggressive troop of P-38 bandits, and the winner of medals for bravery. But he was tired and needed a break.

A fighter squadron commander had to be more than a pilot. His job was to lead men on dangerous missions day and night, rain or shine, out of bumpy airstrips, and into enemy gunfire that sometimes took their lives. If he doubted himself, the men would not follow him, and John Mitchell had matured into the role. When he spoke to someone, his intense brown eyes remained fixed on that person, probing, looking for something intangible that would tell him more than just the words he was hearing, and he never compromised with rookie pilots, who always wanted to do more than they were capable of doing. War was his business. "Stay alert," he would insist. "There are no peaceful skies, safe water or land here."

Mitchell seemed to function best when things were toughest, but the physical strain on pilots was enormous, even on veterans like himself. He had missed a few weeks with malaria, had had a brief stay in Australia, and was looking forward to more of the same. He would leave Guadalcanal for a while but knew he would return to the action. Although the fighting had moved farther north, the war wasn't over: It had only changed addresses. There were many more islands out there.

Every pilot, including ground-bound staff officers, had to record time in the air in order to qualify for their flight pay. But they could not go flying alone in a combat zone, where even a routine mission had the potential for trouble. That meant that some other pilot would have to go along and fly on their wing. Sometimes even three more pilots were assigned, to form a complete flight, so that if they did see something, they would have enough weaponry to hit it. Combat veterans often resented having to fly such missions and thought that letting headquarters types strap on a plane for a quick jaunt around the island smacked of politics because it allowed the desk officers to chalk it up as a combat mission.

One day Major Henry Viccellio, whose star was obviously rising as an administrator, needed to line up such a flight for himself. By April 1943, the major was no longer the daring boss that he had been when he flew dangerous missions with the fledgling 70th Fighter Squadron rather than handing them off to some other pilot. In their training days on Fiji, it was Viccellio who had honed the ability of the lightweight P-39 to drop a heavy bomb. The small plane would actually jump in the air when the bomb was released.

The men who remembered those exploits were no longer in the majority, and some of the newer pilots on Guadalcanal grumbled about how he ran things in the XIII Fighter Command. If he was so good, they asked, why wasn't he up there on the point, leading combat strikes? The day in April that he wanted to go up and get the cockpit time, some of the veterans balked when an operations officer asked them to fly escort. The camaraderie of the desperate early days of Guadalcanal, when lives depended on working together and accepting one another, was breaking down, giving way to the sort of divisions and resentments common to any bureaucratized military structure. One pilot bluntly told the operations officer not to assign him to fly around Guadalcanal with Viccellio because he would be tempted to shoot the major down!

Tom Lanphier was returning down the Slot from a routine flight when his radio began to call his name. He responded, only to be cut off by someone else. After this had happened several times, he and the other pilot started swearing at each other to get off the frequency, that *he* was Lanphier. They soon figured out that Tom was talking to his brother Charlie, who was flying a Corsair with a marine fighter squadron.

Once on the ground at Guadalcanal, the brothers got together and caught up on family stories. Mom was running the exclusive Whittier Hotel in Detroit, brother Jim was working as an actor after diabetes kept him out of the service, and Dad was the air intelligence officer for the army chief of staff. The athletic Tom had always considered Charlie, a Stanford engineering graduate, to be somewhat soft, but now he looked fit and tan and very much a fighter pilot, even if he was a marine. On April 7, when Tom was credited with shooting down three Zeros, Charlie had also bagged one, and the brothers were pleased that their father could keep track of them through the daily reports coming out of Guadalcanal.

21

Jackpot

Pearl Harbor

Many things had changed in the U.S. Navy's turbulent world of communications intelligence during the previous six months. As the war had grown, so had units involved in the spooky art of picking up Japanese radio signals and analyzing that data. At the time of Pearl Harbor, there were 730 people involved in the entire naval radio intelligence community, but by April 1943 that number had tripled. New buildings were under construction, universities were turning out dozens of well-trained linguists, operations and goals had expanded, and the prickly genius Joe Rochefort had lost his battle with Washington and was unceremoniously transferred to command a floating dry dock under construction in Tiburon, California.

The fiery leader of Station Hypo was gone, but many of his disciples remained in key positions, including A. Bryan "Red" Lasswell, a tall and husky marine officer with thick, sandy hair that he combed straight back. Although born in a small town in Illinois, Lasswell spoke the Japanese language with ease, had lived in Japan, and served in radio intelligence in the Philippines and China before arriving in to Pearl Harbor in May 1941. He repeatedly requested a transfer to a combat command, but Rochefort refused to surrender such a talent.

Lasswell and his friend Joe Finnegan swapped twenty-four-hour shifts running the code and translation section at Station Hypo, which had been moved from the Dungeon to more spacious quarters and renamed the Fleet Radio Unit, Pacific, or FRUPAC. On any given shift, staring out from beneath a green eyeshade, Lasswell would review about a hundred messages and choose those that were important enough for further translation. His desk would contain only the piece of code work that occupied him at the moment, and he would totally focus on it to the exclusion of everything else. Lasswell was pulling the watch in the early morning hours of April 14, 1943.

American listening posts had picked up Commander Watanabe's enciphered message from Rabaul, and bulky IBM machines sorted through the five-digit groups, automatically plugging in known elements of the Japanese naval code. The Japanese cipher had been modified with the start of I-Go, but the machines could still hit about 15 percent of the total content. For Lasswell, filling in the blanks usually was an exercise in imagination, but in the critical message that came to his hands that morning, no imagination was needed at all, for he seized immediately on the title: CINC COMBINED FLEET.

The veteran code breakers of Station Hypo attacked the message and reached a preliminary translation, deducing that Admiral Yamamoto was to make an inspection out of Rabaul to several forward bases to the south. At Midway, Yamamoto had been far from the action, and in recent months he had stayed safe aboard his flagship in the anchorage at Truk. When he visited Rabaul, he was surrounded by hundreds of planes and thousands of troops. But now he was going out to the front edge of the conflict.

The message quickly made its way up the chain of command, both in Pearl Harbor and in Washington, where "crippies" also were trying to break out the full text of the message. Everything was there—destinations, exact times of departure and arrival, and even the type of plane in which he would fly and the kind of boat he would use to visit a specific island. For once, the admiral was stepping beyond his safety net, and his precise movements were known in advance. "We've hit the jackpot," Lasswell told one of his linguists. "This is our chance to get Yamamoto," said a watch officer.

Commander Edwin Layton, the Pacific Fleet intelligence officer, walked into Nimitz's office a little after eight o'clock in the morning and handed him the decrypted message. The admiral read it carefully and then studied a wall map to confirm that Yamamoto would indeed be within the extreme range of American fighter aircraft. "Do we try to get him?" Nimitz asked in a steady voice that carried no trace of his Texas upbringing.

The commander and the admiral found themselves in an ironic situation when the fate of Admiral Yamamoto fell into their hands, for they both respected the man. In 1937, Layton had been an assistant naval attaché in Tokyo while Yamamoto was vice minister of the Japanese navy; they had played bridge and watched kabuki theater together. Yamamoto had even invited Layton to a duck-netting party.

Although Nimitz had never met Yamamoto personally, he shared his admiration for the legendary Admiral Togo, who had defeated the Russian fleet. As a twenty-one-year-old ensign, Nimitz had been introduced to Togo at a garden party hosted by the emperor. Some thirty years later, as commander of the cruiser *Augusta*, Nimitz attended Togo's funeral. He organized an honor guard of American sailors, none shorter than six-feet, four-inches tall, to march in the funeral procession. He had something else in common with Yamamoto: Yamamoto had lost two fingers of his left hand, and Nimitz was missing one.

No personal thoughts of more gentle times would be allowed to color the decision thrust upon Nimitz and Layton, for Yamamoto was now their implacable enemy, the man who had launched the sneak attack on Pearl Harbor and had not willingly yielded an inch since then. From Hawaii to the Philippines to Java to Australia to the Solomon Islands, the blood of thousands of American and Allied soldiers, sailors, and airmen had been spilled because of Yamamoto, and here was an opportunity to eliminate him.

Yamamoto was the beating heart of the Japanese navy. In his own country, he was seen as embodying the unwavering Bushido fighting spirit. In the United States, however, he was the hated face of the Japanese war machine. Americans still believed the small admiral arrogantly planned to dictate peace terms in the White House. Killing him would be a horrific setback for Japan, and, for America, payback for Pearl Harbor.

The other side of the ledger held two major items. The first was that an attack might reveal to the Japanese that America had broken their codes. Tokyo would change their codes immediately, and America would lose a huge strategic advantage. Was killing Yamamoto worth that risk? The second point was that many naval intelligence officers were surmising that Yamamoto might be a key to stopping the war. He had long been against fighting America, until just before personally starting the war, and he was a military hero who stood in great favor with the emperor. Yamamoto had always believed Japan could not win the war outright, and if he chose to give up his command and take a position in the War Cabinet, the intelligence analysts believed he might supply a voice of calm and reason around which a peace faction could form within the Japanese government and perhaps bring the fighting to an end.

Layton and Nimitz also discussed the possibility that a successor to Yamamoto might present an even more formidable foe; they concluded that the Japanese navy had no comparable leader of strategic vision, stature, and daring. He was, without a doubt, *the* leader, the man who made that huge fleet work.

"You know, Admiral Nimitz, it would be just as if they shot you down," said Layton. "There isn't anybody to replace you."

Nimitz made his decision. "It's down in Halsey's bailiwick. If there's a way, he'll find it. All right, we'll try it."

Within two hours, Pearl Harbor passed the word to Halsey's headquarters on New Caledonia, where it was already Thursday, April 15. Halsey was away from his office for a meeting with General MacArthur, and the message went to his deputy, Rear Admiral Theodore Wilkinson, who was reluctant to compromise the important secret that the Japanese codes had been broken. After the war Wilkinson told an inquiry committee, "Admiral Nimitz sent his best wishes, told us to go to it, and said he would take the responsibility for the security risk we were running." That was a direct order, and Wilkinson forwarded it to his area commanders. The message arrived with the additional comment, "TALLEYHO X LET'S GET THE BASTARD."

Fighter II

A jeep hurried from one end of Fighter II, where the marines stayed, to the army encampment at the other end, and the driver wheeled toward a cluster of men on the flight line. Captain Tom Lanphier was talking with a couple of pilots in the 70th Fighter Squadron who had just come back from an afternoon mission to the enemy base at Rekata Bay. They had seen an American on the beach up there, who waved as they passed overhead.

In his memoirs, Lanphier described what happened next. A marine jumped from the jeep and told Lanphier that his brother Charlie had been shot down near Rekata Bay, but had been seen climbing into his life raft. The guy on the beach had to be Charlie!

Lanphier grabbed a bottle of good booze to use as a bargaining chip and in the day's fading light hustled to the dock where the PBY flying boats were stationed. He tried to persuade the commanding officer of Patrol Squadron 54 to fly out and rescue his brother. The PBY pilot responded that the mission had already been set, but since the sun was going down, they would have to wait until first thing the next morning. Trying to land a flying boat on enemy waters in the dark was suicide.

The next morning, a small amphibious plane, escorted by Wildcat fighters, went out as scheduled, but turned back because of engine trouble. When Tom Lanphier saw it come home empty, his worry grew. Three hours later, another PBY went out, and this time Tom Lanphier was aboard, sitting in the belly of the plane. Fellow pilots of the 70th voluntarily joined the marine fighter escort going out to retrieve their buddy.

Charlie Lanphier, after an uncomfortable night in the jungle, was waiting on the sandy beach when he spotted the PBY. A Japanese patrol was only five miles away, around a curve and moving toward him. The enemy soldiers broke into a run when they saw the plane touch down some two hundred yards from shore. Charlie, who did not know about the patrol, refused to swim out to the plane because he thought he saw sharks. A raft was tossed overboard, and a PBY crewman and Tom Lanphier paddled in to shore, racing the enemy patrol. Charlie climbed aboard and grumpily asked his smiling brother what took him so long.

They made it back to the PBY, which took off in a hail of gunfire from the Japanese soldiers.

Rabaul

That same day, Friday, April 16, Yamamoto declared I-Go a success. The crafty admiral had once again surprised his enemies with unorthodox, daring tactics and, according to his pilots, achieved a great victory. He may have celebrated the operation in public, but privately Yamamoto considered his losses appalling. Success and defeat sometimes looked the same, and Yamamoto knew that winning individual battles and conducting surprise raids could not, by themselves, win wars.

Twelve percent of the 286 carrier planes involved in I-Go were gone, 18 percent of the 81 land-based Betty bombers had been shot down, and of the 81 dive-bombers, a staggering 26 percent had been lost. And for what? The risky operation had kept some momentary pressure on the enemy, but to continue the carnage would exhaust the carrier force to the point of ineffectiveness. Attrition was a serious problem, and his pilots were dying for reasons that were hard to discern.

When reconnaissance planes on Friday morning found no worthwhile targets along the coast of New Guinea, Yamamoto closed the operation down and sent the carrier planes back to their ships to save them from useless slaughter, for they would be needed in future fights.

He had grown weary of Rabaul and looked forward to getting back to his flagship in a few days. A staff conference was scheduled on Saturday to weigh the next moves, and on Sunday he would make his brief trip to the forward bases in a dramatic personal demonstration of his support for his men.

Guadalcanal

In his rough headquarters, Admiral Mitscher called a secret meeting of his senior staff, which included only naval and marine officers. No army representatives were present.

For the past two days, the intercepted message outlining Yamamoto's trip had been an all-navy show, going from the code breakers to Nimitz to Halsey and then out to Mitscher, who was in command of all the air assets in the Solomon Islands. No records have survived to fully track the path of the message in Washington, although some participants claim Navy Secretary Knox consulted with other authorities, possibly even President Roosevelt, and sent an order on his own to carry out the attack. Nimitz, however, made the tactical decision.

In his wood-sided tent, Mitscher's staff dissected the message, scoured maps, and examined options. According to the code breakers, Yamamoto was to land on Ballale Island, not far from the eastern tip of Bougainville, and after an inspection there, he would board a subchaser and return to Buin. Since the private meeting of Mitscher's staff had a decidedly navy slant, they naturally leaned toward hitting Yamamoto while he was on the subchaser, between the bases.

Then they considered the true determining factor of the mission, the distance between Guadalcanal and the target about four hundred and fifty miles away. They went through the inventory of navy and marine planes on Cactus and concluded that none, not even the formidable F4U Corsairs, were suitable. The only birds on Guadalcanal that could be modified with extra fuel tanks to reach the probable attack area and have a chance of making it back home were the P-38s, and they belonged to the U.S. Army.

That did not please some of those present, who had complained openly that the P-38 pilots were not aggressive enough. Before, when the army pilots had flown P-400s and P-39s in close support of the ground troops, and were easy meat for attacking Zeros, they were not seen as true rivals by the other services. Now the superior P-38s could dogfight as well as any Wildcat or Corsair, and they were stealing some of the thunder of the navy and marine squadrons. Competitive grumbling was natural.

As the 339th and 12th Fighter Squadrons spent more time in action with the new aircraft, they had built reputations that could not be ignored. Marine Major John Condon, the operations officer for the Fighter Command headquarters, and one of the most severe critics of the early P-38 pilots, finally admitted the Lightnings and the men who flew them were among the best on the island. Nevertheless, a mild sense of jealousy seemed to have taken hold around Fighter II, and the decision to use P-38s was made, according to one army pilot, "much to the navy's disappointment."

Mitscher was not among the skeptics. He believed the army pilots who would go after Yamamoto were made of the same stuff as another army pilot he had worked with only a year ago, Jimmy Doolittle.

To lead this mission, they chose John Mitchell, commander of the 339th Fighter Squadron. The job might have fallen to Lou Kittel, the CO of the 12th, but he had only been on the island a few weeks, while Mitchell had been in and out of Guadalcanal for almost six months! He knew the surrounding islands and the enemy, was the army's leading ace on Canal, and was absolutely relentless in carrying out an assignment.

Four other P-38 pilots in particular had impressed Mitscher, for they had been shooting up ships and Zeros alike, not only over Guadalcanal, but also around southern Bougainville, the area of the coming strike. He wanted Captain Tom Lanphier and his flight of Lieutenants Rex Barber, Jim McLanahan, and Joe Moore in on this one. The admiral liked the sort of nerve displayed when Barber left part of his wing stuck in a ship during a low-level attack. Mitscher personally decided this foursome would constitute the "killer flight" that would actually hit Yamamoto. The other P-38s would fly as protection for them in what had all the earmarks of a very dangerous mission.

Before closing the meeting, Mitscher emphasized the need for utmost secrecy. Nothing must tip off Tokyo that its innermost military secrets were being read by the allies.

Rabaul

Yamamoto was in a good mood as his top commanders gathered for the Saturday staff conference. The massed aerial strikes were complete, and the carriers were on their way back to Japan to refit and train replacement pilots. When they were ready, he would bring them back and again strike the Americans where he could hurt them the most. He would have planes operating from land bases, and his carriers would sail, well protected, in waters that he thoroughly controlled. The Americans would pay dearly for any future advance.

Some of Yamamoto's advisers had a hard time paying attention at the conference. They were extremely concerned about Yamamoto's upcoming visit to those frontline units, and the idea that their beloved leader would expose himself to danger appalled them. In their eyes he was irreplaceable. Men fought for Yamamoto because they believed in him. Although small in size, he was a giant in uniform. If their charismatic leader was lost, the entire course of the war would be tilted.

There was spirited discussion about how many fighter planes should fly along to protect him. Some insisted that at least twenty Zeros should accompany Yamamoto. A compromise was reached, and only six Zeros of the 204th Naval Air Squadron on Rabaul were assigned to escort him. The admiral in charge of the Third Fleet argued that six was not enough and offered to furnish as many planes from his carriers as Yamamoto might want.

The general commanding the 18th Area Army told Yamamoto of a close call of his own. He had recently made a similar inspection flight, flying out of Buin to New Guinea, and run into a large formation of American fighters, but his plane had escaped into storm clouds. Yamamoto might have a similar encounter if he ventured closer to the front line. The admiral congratulated him on his narrow escape and praised the skill of the pilot but shrugged off the warning. He was confident of Japanese strength throughout the area, and since Japanese troops occupied almost every island north of Guadalcanal, all they had to do was look up to spot any American planes coming up the Slot. There would be plenty of warning of the Americans' course, speed, and altitude, and defending Zeros could be in the air long before the enemy arrived. Besides, while occasional high-flying bombers had come this far north, American fighters—the only planes that would have a chance against the Zero escort—had not.

Rear Admiral Takoji Joshima, the naval commander in the Shortland Islands, was even more emphatically against the trip. He felt that sending the admiral's schedule out over the radio, even encoded, was extremely foolish, and he flew to Rabaul to personally plead with his chief not to go. Yamamoto brushed off all warnings. He was determined to show his men that he would stand beside them, even in the danger zone.

"I've let them know, and they have got things ready," he said. "I'll leave tomorrow morning and be back by dark."

22

The Opium Den

Guadalcanal

Saturday, April 17, sped by as final preparations for the attack were made. The army pilots who would lead the flight were summoned to the admiral's tent with less than twenty-four hours remaining before they would have to take off on the Yamamoto intercept.

There were eighteen P-38s on the island, and they were maintained by Lou Kittel's 12th Fighter Squadron, which flew them on alternate days with John Mitchell's 339th.

Newly promoted Lieutenant Colonel Viccellio, who had been named head of the 347th Fighter Group, personally delivered the word to Mitchell. Colonel Aaron Tyer of the 18th Fighter Group alerted Kittel. Both squadron commanders headed for the navy headquarters tent known as the "Opium Den" because of the thick layer of cigarette smoke that hovered so thickly inside. During the short drive over from Fighter II, Mitchell spotted Tom Lanphier, who was still assigned to the 70th, and brought him along.

The pilots had not yet even been given their assignment, and it was already a typical Cactus Air Force mix-and-match affair.

When Mitchell, Kittel, and Lanphier entered the tent, they were among the lowest-ranking officers of the approximately thirty men there, and as army officers, they felt almost like intruders in the navy-marine gathering. The hand of a marine major trembled as he gave Mitchell a message that outlined the job.

The name Yamamoto didn't register immediately on Mitchell until Lanphier murmured, "Pearl Harbor." Mitchell now understood why the marine officer was nervous. So was he.

Lanphier knew from the moment he read the name that this mission would be important to him. He had been making a huge impression as a combat pilot, and suddenly the opportunity of his military career was being placed before him. With his Stanford education, he would have known the Latin term for such fleeting moments—*Carpe diem!*, Seize the day!

It seemed that everyone in the tent was staring at the three scruffy army officers: the bearded Kittel, the serious Mitchell, and the eager Lanphier. This would be biggest mission any of them had ever flown, for if they knocked Yamamoto out of the war, it would be both a stunning military victory for the Americans and a horrendous setback for the Japanese. They were being assigned to a mission of ultimate revenge, to settle accounts for all of the maiming, misery, and blood that had been spilled in the South Pacific.

To keep secret the origin of the message, the pilots were told the information had come from Australian coastwatchers. They did not raise the obvious question how a coastwatcher hiding in the bushes had been able to furnish the exact route, timetable, and other details of a flight that had not taken off yet.

The briefing then turned into a lecture, with the army fliers crowded out of the conversation. Planners had finished their preliminary work and decided to make the attack while Yamamoto was aboard a subchaser. They distributed strip maps that noted the directions for speeds and compass headings. Here's the plan, the army pilots were curtly told. Your job is to fly up there, sink that boat, and kill the admiral.

It was all too navy for Mitchell. They wanted him to be a leader in name only. The navy, which was not going to fly the historic mission, still wanted to control it.

The briefer went too far when he said that on the final leg of the flight to make the interception, the pilots would encounter a small to moderate wind off the port quarter. *Port quarter?* "What the hell does that mean?" snapped Mitchell.

With that one sharp question Mitchell let everyone in the tent know that he was going to lead this mission. After all, it would be his ass on the line up there, along with the butts of the other army pilots. He would not treat this like some take-it-or-leave-it order from a bunch of guys who had no idea what it was like to fly a P-38 in combat. He had questions they had not even thought about.

Mitchell immediately discarded the idea of attacking a subchaser crossing an open channel. "I don't know one boat from another, and even if we sink the boat, he could jump in the water in a life vest and survive. What if there are several boats? Which one would he be on?" He looked at all the men who outranked him and did not blink. "We're fighter pilots. We should take him in the air."

The discussion went on and on, growing hotter and louder, with neither side giving up. The navy insisted that sinking the subchaser was the best bet because Yamamoto would be isolated on a ship. Anyway, hadn't Lanphier's bunch run exactly this sort of attack on Japanese vessels?

All boats look alike to us, the pilots replied, and you don't even know if the man can swim. Other ships probably would be around to launch rescue boats, and sailors would certainly sacrifice their own lives to save the commander in chief from a sinking ship.

Then they argued that the attack would not be taking place without enemy opposition. In addition to the six-plane escort, a mob of other Zeros would probably be in the air from every strip in the area to protect their leader, just as the Americans scrambled every available fighter on Guadalcanal just two months ago to escort Secretary Knox and Admirals Nimitz and Halsey. Mitchell estimated that his P-38s might be outnumbered about five-to-one. Antiaircraft guns would be blasting away at them from every ship and shore base in the area.

Fuel would be another huge problem. The P-38s would need special auxiliary fuel tanks in order to make such a long-range interception. The planners said that while none of the right size had been found on Guadalcanal, an emergency request would be sent to 5th Air Force headquarters on New Guinea to ferry up some of the larger tanks as soon as possible. Mitchell said that even with the bigger tanks the Lightnings would only have enough time at the intercept point for a couple of passes before being forced to leave and make the long flight back to Guadalcanal.

Finally, Mitscher intervened. There wasn't enough time for this debate. "Well, since Mitchell has to make the interception, I think it should be done his way," the rugged admiral told everyone in the tent. It was an unstated order for everyone else to shut up. He turned to Mitchell. "Where do you want to do it?"

"In the air, sir," Mitchell replied.

"You got it," the admiral said. As usual, his decision came without emotion, and with a solemn finality.

Rabaul

Late that afternoon, final arrangements were being made for Yamamoto's trip. As always, he would not allow his entire staff to fly aboard a single plane because of the risk that they all could be lost at the same time. Therefore, a pair of brand-new twin-engine, medium-range Betty bombers of the 705th Naval Air Squadron were carefully prepared. Bomber number 323, in which Admiral Yamamoto and three members of his staff would fly, would be piloted by Flight Warrant Officer Takeo Katani with an additional aircrew of six. Admiral Ukagi and the other four staff members would be aboard bomber number 326, with Flight Petty Officer Hiroshi Hayashi as the pilot and also an aircrew of six.

For the important fighter escort mission, six experienced combat veterans were picked at Rabaul, and they would fly in triangle formations, two groups of three planes each.

The first flight would be led by Lieutenant (j.g.) Takeshi Morizaki, who also would be in overall command of the escort. Flying on his wings would be Flight Petty Officer First Class Toyomitsu Tsujinoue and Assistant Flight Petty Officer Shoichi Sugita.

Chief Petty Officer Yoshimi Hidaka would lead the second flight, which would include Petty Officer Second Class Yasuji Okazaki on one wing and Assistant Flight Petty Officer Kenji Yanagiya on the other. They were old friends and had graduated from the same flight school and survived numerous combat missions.

Their evening briefing was short. That left Kenji Yanagiya a bit uncomfortable. He was honored to fly guard for Admiral Yamamoto, but he wondered why more Zeros had not been assigned to this mission.

After all, they were covering no ordinary general or admiral but Yamamoto himself! But the briefer said nothing about American planes posing any threat, so Yanagiya simply decided that "Tomorrow we will protect him."

They would take off at six o'clock in the morning, and the trip would last an hour and forty-five minutes, from Rabaul to the coastal town of Buin on the eastern coast of Bougainville Island, a jump that the Zero fighters and the Betty bombers could make easily. None of the fighters would carry a radio. Not only were these static-producing devices virtually useless for communications, but removing them lightened the already nimble Zeros even more. Pilots were known to even saw off the wooden radio antenna to gain an extra knot of airspeed.

Kenji Yanagiya had been in combat for eight months, was not afraid to fight, and had no doubts about the other flyers assigned to the mission. One of them was among the best fighter pilots Japan had. Shoichi Sugita was considered a wild man in the sky, a *gekitsui-o*—a "Shoot-Down King." "Whenever I see an enemy plane, I go after him, no matter what," Sugita claimed, and he repeatedly proved his words. He had been barely nineteen years old when he brought down his first enemy plane, an American B-17 bomber. Somehow Sugita later survived the Battle of Midway, and he never slowed down. Over the next three years, Sugita would stack up more than seventy confirmed aerial victories and share in another forty before he was shot down and killed over Japan.

Yanagiya felt better knowing that Sugita would be along on Sunday morning. Certainly, if Yamamoto needed a special guardian spirit, the muscular Sugita would be there. After all, both had been born into poor families in the harsh land of Niigata Prefecture, and Yamamoto always liked the soldiers from home.

Guadalcanal

Darkness was already falling when Mitchell returned to his 339th operations tent on Fighter II, put a match to a lantern, and in its dim glow got down to work. Everything that had been said by the navy and marines was only prelude, for it was up to Mitchell to make the mission work, which meant he would approve every detail. The planners were good men, conscientious in their jobs, but most were not combat pilots, and none knew know how to fly a P-38. Figuring out direction headings was one thing, but calculating such vital matters as the appropriate fuel mixtures so the engines ran at maximum efficiency and factoring in the quirks of Lightnings was another. Just staying on course would be a problem, and he had requested that a big navy compass, the kind they used on ships, be mounted in his plane. As he studied the course drawn up by the planners, he decided it was faulty. It would leave him about fifty miles away from where he needed to be. Mitchell put their maps aside and started from scratch.

Somehow he would have to find a dot in the air. Nowadays, sophisticated on-board radar systems can detect targets many miles away, but there was no radar of any sort mounted in fighter planes early in World War II. Finding enemy planes meant actually seeing them, and pilots spent much of their flight time swiveling their heads around and craning their necks to look above them in an everlasting search of the skies. He would take his flight to the point where they would have the best chance of finding Yamamoto, but then it would be up to the men flying the mission to actually eyeball the Japanese bombers and fighters, which at best would appear as dark pinpoints against the blue sky. The attack flight would have to be at just the right altitude, in the right place, and at exactly the right time. One minute or one mile off and the P-38s might never even see Yamamoto's plane.

In the dull glow of the lantern and narrow beams of flashlights, Mitchell began nailing down the daunting mathematics of the plan.

The assumption was that Yamamoto's plane would fly as straight as possible across the three hundred and fifteen miles from Rabaul to Ballale Island. That might be so, but Mitchell could not fly equally straight from Guadalcanal, for to do so would take his crew across the beadlike string of islands that lay out to the northwest—the Russells, Vangunu, New Georgia, Kolombangara, Vella Lavella, and the Shortlands. The Japanese held most of them, and although their radar was unsophisticated, it might be good enough to pick up the attack flight. If radar did not see them, then soldiers might, and either way the Americans would

lose any chance of surprise. They could not take a direct route. Therefore, a long, looping course over open water would be needed. Once
they passed off the coast of Guadalcanal, they would not see land again
until they came up on Empress Augusta Bay at Bougainville. There
would be no landmarks at all out there by which Mitchell might steer.
He would have to fly by clock, altimeter, airspeed indicator, and compass readings alone.

Radio silence would be absolute, also to prevent alerting the Japanese, so the pilots would have to fight the boredom of a long ride and keep
within sight of at least one other plane. Mitchell would be in front, and
everyone else would play follow-the-leader. Getting separated over the
open ocean, becoming disoriented in a place where everything looked
alike, probably would be fatal.

They also had to hug the water for the entire trip up, for the higher
they rose, the easier they could be seen from a distance, and the easier for
the crude Japanese radar located on the islands to find them. Mitchell
decided to fly more than four hundred miles at an altitude of no more
than fifty feet above the waves. Only pilots with tremendous experience
could manage that.

Then he had to figure out relative speeds of the approaching forces.
He had no idea how fast the bomber carrying Yamamoto would be flying. "Knowing our chances were perhaps one in a million, I decided to
set his speed at 180 miles per hour. I decided to intercept him about forty
miles before he reached his destination," Mitchell said. That would catch
the bomber just as it slowed down to settle into a landing approach.

He settled on a flight plan that would have five distinct legs. The first
four would be over water, controlled by time and speed, and take them to
the intercept point over Empress Augusta Bay. The fifth leg would serve
as a backup plan in case they did not find Yamamoto. It would cross over
Bougainville and come down the north coast of that big island to see if
the admiral's plane was coming in by that route, and possibly attacking
some airfield or other targets if they could not find him. He did not in-
tend to bring all of those bullets back home.

While he worked, other officers came over from the naval headquarters tent to help, carrying slide rules and sharp pencils, and
everyone eventually agreed that it would take two and a half hours to
cover the four hundred and thirty-five miles to the anticipated area of

interception. Getting home should be no problem. Although the flight probably would be scattered all over the sky by then, they could pick their way back to Guadalcanal simply by following the island chain. There would be no need for secrecy at that point.

"Mitchell laid out the course, speeds, gas mixture settings, and finger-to-the-wind estimates of what the weather elements would be the next day," Lou Kittel would recall many years later, still impressed by the feat. "All the credit for the planning should stop with Mitchell."

Meanwhile, word had begun to seep out of the tight circle of officers who had been in the Opium Den that a big mission was being laid on. The secret was being opened to a wider circle. As Mitchell and the other planners worked, one pilot after another stuck his head into the tent to throw his name into the pot. It seemed that every one of the approximately forty pilots available to fly P-38s, even those who were sick, wanted to be in on the action. Mitchell said he would let everyone know the next morning.

He decided to use all eighteen of the available P-38s on the raid. Four would make up the team that would attack Yamamoto's bomber. The rest would be led by Mitchell into a high cover position to protect the strike unit from marauding Zeros. He expected a lot of enemy planes to be waiting for them.

Mitchell and Kittel agreed that the 12th Fighter Squadron, which was flying the same planes as the 339th on alternate days, deserved half of the mission slots. Each would furnish eight pilots, and Mitchell would appoint two spares, in case they lost anybody along the way. Some of the pilots still belonged officially to other units, but were temporarily attached to the pair of P-38 squadrons.

Mitchell would lead the entire flight, and, as always, he put steady Jack Jacobson on his wing. Doug Canning, so experienced that he normally led every mission he flew, would lead an element of two planes on this one, and his wingman would be his frequent partner, the athletic Del Goerke. On the other side of the formation would ride the killer flight of Tom Lanphier, Rex Barber, Joe Moore, and Jim McLanahan—"Four of the best men we had," Mitchell said. All four members of the killer flight had been due to leave Guadalcanal the next day for a rest period but were held over especially for the attack.

Kittel had chosen himself and seven other pilots from the Dirty

Dozen squadron with equal care. He wanted only men who he knew possessed the courage to engage the enemy, even when outnumbered, and could be trusted to stick to the attack plan. Friendship could play no part in his decision. It was what you had done, not who you were, that counted, because he wanted only experienced shooters on this mission. Chances were good that some of them wouldn't be coming home.

He picked Gordon Whittaker to be his wingman. Everett Anglin, a man of few words, would pair with the equally quiet Bill Smith. The smartest twosome would be the scholarly Roger Ames and tall Larry Graebner, who after the war would earn a Ph.D. and become a university professor. At the rear would be Louisiana's Albert "Huey" Long, the oldest pilot in the 12th and self-appointed father of the group. Flying on his wing would be Missouri-born Eldon Stratton, who had several hundred hours of flying time in P-38s.

Flying as spares were two more veterans, Besby Holmes in the lead and Ray Hine as his wingman. Hine had never taken a P-38 out on a mission, but he was a tough kid with months of combat experience with the 68th Fighter Squadron.

All were nervy, first-class shooters with a wealth of combat experience. Most of Mitchell's team dated back to the earliest days at Hamilton Field, and Kittel had known his Dirty Dozen boys all the way through those long, unreal months on little Christmas Island. Most had flown together so often that they recognized each other's voices on the radio.

Mitchell made out the full roster, wrote the names on a blackboard, and put a cloth over it, then sent out word to the pilots to be up at five o'clock the next morning, get breakfast, and come to a briefing at six o'clock sharp. Don't be late, they were told. Everything depends on time. Then John Mitchell rolled into his own cot.

Soft big-band music washed through the area from Doug Canning's phonograph, and Mitchell fell asleep that night praying that his work was accurate and that his decisions had been the right ones, but realizing that the chance of success was slim. They would be deep in enemy territory, and he envisioned a hellacious bunch of Zeros waiting for them. He was betting the lives of himself and his boys on his cobbled-together plan.

· · ·

Out on the flight line, the humid night snapped with lightning, thunder grumbled, and the rain came pelting down. Several B-24s from Port Moresby had landed at Henderson Field, and from their holds came large teardrop-shaped fuel tanks that were to be hooked to the P-38s. Trucks hauled the tanks over to Fighter II, where ground crews and mechanics were waiting. Raucous noise rose from the revetments as each Lightning was hurriedly modified to hold one big 310-gallon tank beneath one wing and the usual 165-gallon tank beneath the other. The strong P-38 would have no problem handling the imbalance of weights.

Other mechanics crawled into the cockpit of Mitchell's plane, *Mitch's Squitch,* and installed a large, accurate ship's compass for the mission leader. He would depend upon it to get him where he needed to go.

Most of the crews did not know exactly what was happening, other than that it was something big. The instructions were only to have all of the planes ready to go, and they labored through the stormy night to patch every dent, plug every hole, fix every circuit, fill the ammo trays, and test absolutely everything that a P-38 had.

But there was no hiding the intense interest in their work. Even the top-ranking officers on Guadalcanal and pilots drifted out to the planes to see how the work was coming. Slowly, startling information seeped around that the target today would be none other than Admiral Yamamoto. *The bastard who bombed Pearl Harbor!*

Like a genie that could not be put back into the bottle, the word was out, and the work of the code breakers—one of the biggest secrets of the war—was at risk.

23

At All Costs

Fighter II

John Mitchell was up at 4:30 A.M. on Palm Sunday, April 18, finalizing his plan to stalk and kill a man. Religious holidays were not observed where he worked. He suited up, had some breakfast, choked down an antimalarial tablet, and walked over to the operations tent to give his briefing.

Instead of just the P-38 fighter pilots, about a hundred men had gathered in the predawn gloom. There was a different feel to this day, something almost electric, and a quiet sense of excitement had drawn them to the hillside tents to hear what was going on.

Mitchell swept back the curtain that covered the mission board and announced the names of those who would fly that morning. Looking at them, he emphasized this was a volunteer-only mission. Anyone not wanting to go would be replaced, no questions asked. No true fighter pilot would back down from such a challenge, particularly in front of his brothers. The only responses were grumbling complaints from those who were not picked.

Mitchell kept his instructions short and to the point. Take-off, he said, would be at exactly 7:10 A.M., about an hour away, and the crews were putting the final touches to the planes. Fuel was topped off, ammunition was loaded, and the steel buckles on the drop tanks they were carrying instead of bombs were double-checked to be sure they would release on command. Strip maps were passed out to the pilots.

The target today, Mitchell confirmed, would be the top man in the Imperial Japanese Navy, Admiral Isoroku Yamamoto, the guy who planned the attack on Pearl Harbor. The men around the tent exchanged looks: *The rumors were true!* Mitchell continued, saying the admiral would be flying down to Ballale, an island just off of Bougainville, in a Betty. The P-38s would intercept the flight and shoot him down.

There could be a hell of a fight. A large number of Zeros, maybe as many as a hundred, could be expected to try to stop them. While Mitchell would take most of the Lightnings up high to provide a covering shield for the attack, the four-plane killer flight would hit the admiral's bomber, then everybody would highball out of there.

Silence fell on the crowd, because, as one pilot remembered, there wasn't a hell of a lot left to talk about. The obvious importance of the mission weighed upon them.

Mitchell talked them through the path marked on the narrow maps that would be strapped to small boards on their left thighs. After takeoff, the planes would make one circuit of the field to gather everyone in formation and then strike out on the first leg of the long trip.

Their flight would go straight to exact points, but far out to the west over the Coral Sea, then angle back three times before reaching the interception point over Empress Augusta Bay on the southeastern coast of Bougainville. The entire trip up would be made in radio silence, and the Lightnings would hug the water to stay out of sight.

The course for the first leg would take them west on a heading of 265 degrees for exactly fifty-five minutes at an airspeed of 210 miles per hour. That would take them precisely 183 miles to a point between the sun and the sea with no land in sight. Just follow me, Mitchell said, and his southern drawl made it sound easy.

The pilots studied the course. Just getting there was going to be a problem. Staying awake out over the water for so long, flying low, being trapped in the cockpit and broiled by the sun, would be grueling, and dozens of other hazards ran through their minds. A lot of things could go wrong, and, in fact, something already had: They were heading to the wrong place.

The American code breakers had misread part of Japanese message and believed Yamamoto was flying all the way from Rabaul to Ballale, an island off the southeastern tip of the big island of Bougainville. In fact, the admiral's plane was to land at the airfield at Buin, on the edge of Bougainville itself. Considering the difficulties of translation, it was an understandable error, but all of the planning for the attack was thereafter based upon that incorrect assumption. The only thing that saved the mission was that, from the air, it did not make much difference at which of the bases Yamamoto was supposed to land. They were close together and in a straight line along the main flight path. As long as Yamamoto took off on time, the interception could still work.

Rabaul

After a quiet dinner with aides following the long conferences on Saturday, Yamamoto slept well in the spacious home that had once belonged to the governor before World War I, when the island was a German possession. It sat atop Residency Hill, a thousand feet above the shore, and was cooled by the ocean breezes.

Dawn broke bright and mild. Yamamoto dressed with some care because a photographer was scheduled to record his appearance. On this day he did not put on the usual, perfectly clean white dress uniform, because it would be very conspicuous as he toured near the front. Aides had convinced him that he should wear a new dark-green field uniform. Making last-minute adjustments, he stuck a handkerchief into one pocket, some folded toilet paper into another, and his diary containing poems he had copied from the works of the Emperor Meiji into a breast pocket. He would travel light on this out-and-back trip that would return him to Residency Hill by nightfall.

Then he pulled on a pair of white gloves, with the two empty fingers on the left hand tied back by string, and picked up a long, heavy samurai sword that had been a gift from his deceased elder brother.

The man in the green uniform and black boots who emerged from the residence that morning hardly looked like the commander in chief of the Combined Fleet. He looked like a determined soldier, ready for a fight.

The photographer failed to show up for some unknown reason,

and Yamamoto left. A cameraman might miss an appointment, but not the admiral. His car was driven down the hill, descending into the thick green forests until it finally broke out onto the flat coastal roads that traced through black volcanic ash. Other automobiles bearing members of his staff followed. Two of the officers were quite disturbed that they had not learned of the change in uniform requirements and arrived wearing the usual whites.

Two Betty bombers that had flown to the east airfield from another strip seven miles away were waiting. As Yamamoto stepped from his car and straightened his uniform, one of the pilots, Hiroshi Hayashi, was startled by the diminutive stature of his leader. "Why the C-in-C is only half my size!" he thought.

The admiral was greeted by a gathering of ranking officers, and, after mutual bows, he handed a special gift to the newly appointed commander of the Eighth Fleet, two scrolls of his copied Meiji poetry. Then Yamamoto climbed aboard the bomber, which had the number 323 painted on its tail, and settled into a seat on the flight deck right behind the pilots. The chief surgeon of the Combined Fleet, a naval air force staff officer, and Yamamoto's secretary found places farther back in the plane.

Vice Admiral Ugaki stepped into the second bomber, number 326, and was joined by the fleet paymaster, the chief meteorologist, the staff communications officer, and another air staff officer.

The engines roared to life, and the two bombers hurried down the empty runway and lifted easily into the air. Behind them came the six Zero fighters, churning up a cloud of dust. As they climbed for altitude, the escort planes broke into two groups of three and slid into position on the flanks of the lead bomber.

The officers who had come to see Yamamoto off waved until all the planes were airborne. The admiral, they noted, was exactly on schedule.

Fighter II

John Mitchell was also right on time. He toured the flight line for a last check of the planes, climbed to the wing of his P-38, and stood for a moment in the early morning chill to get into his parachute. Then he climbed into the cockpit, adjusted his throat mike, and touched the small escape pouch that contained some English pounds sterling, a small morphine needle, a handheld compass, and some sulfa powder. He was about to make the flight of his life, and the familiar movements and the sturdiness of the plane soothed his nerves. Everything seemed normal. Maybe this would be just like any other mission.

All along the flight line, cockpits closed, the crews stood away, and thirty-six Allison engines shattered the morning stillness as the P-38s came to life and rolled heavily toward their take-off positions on the metaled runway. Mitchell, with Jack Jacobson on his wing, lifted off at precisely ten minutes after seven, as planned. Doug Canning and Del Goerke sped out right behind them.

Men on the ground stood around in groups to wave and cheer them on, even the envious marine and navy pilots. Since the mission had been revealed, the information had spread like wildfire around the moon- scape of Henderson Field and the two fighter strips. The P-38s were go- ing after the man who personified the Pacific war to Americans and had been hammering Guadalcanal, killing hundreds of Americans, for months. American cartoonists depicted Yamamoto as little more than a monkey wearing a fancy uniform playing with ships, but to the U.S. fighting man, Yamamoto was an omnipresent, deadly colossus; he impacted every facet of their lives and killed with a snap of his fin- gers and without a second thought. Everyone on the Fighter II strip who watched the twin-engine "fork-tailed devils" lift noisily into the brightening sky remembered lost friends and believed that Yamamoto needed to die. The guys in the P-38s would avenge the ghosts of Pearl Harbor today.

As the first four planes climbed away, Tom Lanphier brought the killer flight to the starting point. He wore the good-luck sweater knit- ted for him by his fiancée, Phyllis Fraser, whose nickname, *Phoebe*, was painted on one side of his plane, while on the other side was *Man-o'- War*, the name borne by the pursuit plane flown by his father in an ear- lier war. At his wingtip was Rex Barber, revving up the *Miss Virginia*, which would be his ride again, since *Diablo* was still being repaired. Even before Lanphier and Barber were wheels-up, Jim McLanahan and Joe Moore released their brakes, opened the throttles, and headed down the strip. McLanahan was moving fast when a tire hooked a ragged piece of runway matting and blew apart. The plane rumbled out of control and off the runway before coming to a halt. As he shut down the engines and cursed his bad luck, McLanahan watched the other Lightnings dash past him and reach into the sky, two by two.

The killer flight had lost one of its handpicked shooters.

Admiral Mitscher, seated in a jeep, saluted the big P-38s as they left, the roar of their engines punishing his ears and the prop blast washing over him. Exactly a year earlier, on April 18, 1942, he had experienced a similar moment—almost pushing the planes aloft through his own formidable willpower—when he watched Doolittle's bombers lurch from the deck of his aircraft carrier and head for Tokyo.

The P-38s gathered into formation during a single long, slow circuit of Henderson Field and headed west in a gradual descent toward the water. Each pilot tested the tank selector valves, one at a time, to be certain that fuel could be drawn from the external tanks into the engine. When Joe Moore turned one switch, an engine quit. The tank was not feeding in the fuel, which meant Moore also would not be going after Yamamoto. He couldn't make the trip just on internal fuel, so he switched back to another tank and the engine coughed back to life. He had no choice but to signal Lanphier that he was turning back. He banked away toward Guadalcanal.

The mission was only two minutes old and already Mitchell was down to sixteen P-38s, and half of the killer flight was gone. Using hand gestures, Mitchell shifted Besby Holmes and Ray Hine over to the remaining shooters. Holmes and Hine barely knew Lanphier and Barber, who had flown together for months. Instead of being a single cohesive team, they were almost strangers.

Bougainville

The Japanese formation of two bombers and six Zeros hummed along at a steady altitude of only 6,500 feet. From Rabaul, they had flown east for a few minutes, then banked southeast, crossed the Saint George Channel and went over the lighthouse at the edge of neighboring New Ireland. Then, flying in a straight line, they crossed the water again and found the long coastline of the violin-shaped island of Bougainville.

Twenty-four minutes after take-off, the major Japanese base at Buka passed on their left.

Fighter pilot Kenji Yanagiya gazed beyond the canopy of his Zero toward the distant horizon. Only a few intermittent cumulus clouds dotted the blue sky, although far out to sea some dark thunderheads were forming to bring in the daily rain. For now, however, visibility was better than average, giving the Zeros an advantage in spotting any enemy planes long before they could become a threat. An attack, if any took place, would most likely come from the east, out of the bright morning sun, and from on high, for Americans liked to plunge down through Japanese planes on a single pass and then flee.

When not scanning the skies, Yanagiya would occasionally check on the twin-engine bombers. With a wingspan of almost eighty-two feet, and about sixty-five feet in length, they were cumbersome beasts, but they had an incredible range of almost two thousand miles when carrying a full bomb load. They seemed powerful enough and bristled with machine guns for defense, but the big planes were mostly flying fuel tanks. They were gaining a terrible reputation among pilots for turning into torches when hit by enemy fire. Yanagiya preferred his Zero anytime.

The Coral Sea

Once John Mitchell's flight was down to about fifty feet above the waves, he gave his rudders a kick and let the Lightning fishtail in the air, the signal for the planes to spread out. He did not want any accidents or bumped wings during the long flight just because they were flying in a clump. When the pilots fanned out to their new positions, Mitchell himself could only see a few of them, but as long as everyone stayed in sight of his wingman, and as long as they did not hit bad weather, all would be well.

He concentrated on his navy compass and his watch as he flew on in radio silence, fighting boredom mile after mile and minute after minute, without a single checkpoint to verify his position. The responsibility of this mission weighed on him like an anchor, but the order was to bring down Yamamoto, no matter what, and that is what he would do.

He checked his watch and the compass again, the only tools he had for the intricate navigational problem. Navigation had always been his strong suit. From his earliest days as an aviation cadet, when his flying abilities were abysmal, he had always been able to find his way around the sky as if he were following a signposted road. Today, out over the water, if he went off course, they would all go off course. The big navy compass became his most important instrument.

After 55 minutes, Mitchell turned to 290 degrees for twenty-seven minutes to cover another eighty-eight miles, and the other P-38s tilted over and mirrored his move.

As time passed, Mitchell fought the torpor that tried to engulf his senses, the lack of sleep pulling at his eyelids. Every wave looked just like the one before it and the one after it, and Mitchell considered the odds of a successful intercept to be about a million to one. Even if he had made a personal appointment with Yamamoto to meet at the designated invisible point in the sky, chances were slim they could make it happen.

The morning sun beat down mercilessly on the American pilots flying only a few degrees above the equator, and with no cooling systems in the cockpits, they had to endure the heat. They could not get up and stretch, and flying such a long mission was like sitting in a bathtub for hours on end. Thoughts wandered to girlfriends or food or bits of song, and several dwelled on the warnings they had received during the morning briefing. This could very well be a one-way trip.

Larry Graebner checked his altitude again, checked his wingman, checked his fuel, and remembered that Mitchell had said not once, but twice, that they were to get Yamamoto at all costs. "The damned admiral is worth a whole squadron of us," he thought.

Near the front of the pack, Doug Canning considered the blunt words of a marine officer who had approached him at the morning briefing and put it to him very pointedly: Don't come back until Yamamoto is dead.

Every man battled to stay alert and not be lulled into staring at the water, which plays tricks on even fresh pilots by ruining depth perception. A pilot could fly straight into it before he realized anything was wrong. The danger was even more acute over water with no whitecaps, only a smooth, mirrorlike surface. To Mitchell's horror, he saw one plane drop so low that the tip of a propeller blade ticked the water and a curtain of spray covered the cockpit. The pilot somehow wrestled his way up and back into formation.

To the pilots being down so low felt like being at the center of a saucer, with the horizon actually seeming to be above them before vanishing over the curve of the earth. Still the flight drudged on. Del Goerke found that he was not frightened at all, just excited, glad to be coming to the end of the over-water part of the mission. Land had to be out there somewhere. He hoped Mitch's arithmetic was accurate.

Now they were coming out of the third leg, during which they had flown for thirty-eight minutes at 305 degrees for 125 miles. It had been prime viewing for sea creatures, with the brisk shadows of their planes crossing the slim shapes of big sharks, a pod of whales, and a huge manta ray weighing maybe a ton. The prop blast of their planes created little feathery wakes in the moving sea as they sped along.

At 9:45 A.M. Mitchell checked his time and direction once again. He made the final turn, a sharply angled change to 020 degrees for the sixteen-mile dash that would take them in over Empress Augusta Bay.

His flight had completed an incredible journey of 494 miles, close to the water and without a checkpoint—the longest fighter intercept in history. Now it was time for action. He rocked his wings and everyone woke up, test-fired their guns, and slid back into close formation for the final approach. Mitchell glanced at his watch. One minute ahead of schedule.

They were only a minute early, but a minute might make all the difference on this mission. The Lightnings were still low, tearing through a light haze. Not only did the sky seem totally empty, but Mitchell couldn't see any land! He held course, but was beginning to feel the thump of butterflies in his stomach. Where was Bougainville? He couldn't figure it out.

They broke through the mist, and green mountains spread out abruptly before them. They were still flying at only about fifty feet, so close to the water they could see the spray from waves breaking in the bay. They were exactly where they needed to be. They began climbing to ten thousand feet, where they would wait in ambush. All that was needed now was the arrival of Yamamoto, but Mitchell saw only empty sky for miles around.

The radio crackled in his ears, loud after the several hours of silence. Doug Canning spoke, his voice as calm as if he were making a
casual greeting back home in Nebraska.

"Bogeys," he said. "Eleven o'clock high."

Bougainville

The pilot of the second Betty was happy to be nearing their destination, because his plane was acting funny. Apparently a screw had come
loose on an antenna, and the external post was vibrating. He could
feel it in the steering yoke. He cut his speed, and the lead Betty pulled
slightly ahead. The distance did not make much difference, because they
were cruising easily, having come down to 4,500 feet, and were almost
to the destination, the air base at Buin. Mechanics could make repairs
before the return flight.

The airfield was ready, for the commander had his people work
throughout the night to clean the runway, sprinkling it with water to
hold down the dust. As the time of arrival drew near, the officers and
men put on clean uniforms and formed up along the edges of the strip,
to stand at attention for the arrival of the C-in-C.

In the rear of the second bomber, Ugaki had spent most of the trip
dozing, lulled by the drone of the engines. Awakened when the plane's
crew chief handed him a note that said they were ten minutes from
landing, he began to prepare for the workday ahead. A look at his
watch confirmed the flight was arriving on time. He saw Yamamoto's
bomber not far in front of them.

The escort Zero pilots had scanned the skies with a growing sense of
relief. There were no planes coming out of the sun to the east of them,
nothing up top represented a threat, and they were almost within sight
of the Buin airfield. Everyone would be on the ground in a few minutes.

Suddenly, the lead fighter in the second group of Zeros spotted a
flight of enemy planes rising up from *below*, virtually invisible against
the deep-green jungle canopy. American fighters always favored diving
attacks from above, which was why Zero pilots constantly scanned upward from the horizon. American fighter planes *never* attacked from
below!

The shock lasted for one incredible moment, then Hayashi realized he had to act immediately. With no radio on board, he could not verbally warn the bombers, so he nosed over into a steep dive and waggled his wings to alert them as he dived into his attack on the approaching P-38s. His two wingmen, trailing on either side, followed without hesitation.

The Americans had appeared out of nowhere and were heading straight for Admiral Yamamoto's plane. The Japanese fighters angled down to cut them off.

24

The Fight

Bougainville

As soon as Canning announced the planes, Mitchell spotted them. He estimated they were about five miles away, and at a ninety-degree angle from his path. Although uncertain that this was indeed the Yamamoto flight, because there were two bombers instead of the one that had been predicted, Mitchell turned his flight of P-38s onto a parallel course. Then he began to climb. As he did so, he counted six Zeros flying about one thousand feet above the bombers. He decided that he had the right target.

"Skin off your tanks," he ordered, and his pilots pulled the handles that sent the big silvery auxiliary fuel tanks tumbling away. Unleashed from the extra weight, the P-38 Lightnings lunged forward and upward, and were almost level with the bombers within moments. Mitchell was tempted to go after the big planes himself, because while the four planes in the killer flight certainly could handle a single Betty, they were now going to have to bring down two of them. Mitchell knew that he and his wingman might be able to add some extra firepower, but he decided to stick with the plan.

The eleven planes he was leading climbed to reach a higher altitude in order to provide cover for the killer flight, because chances were very good that a horde of Zeros could be on the way. The Japanese had about seventy-five planes on the Kahili airstrip, also near the southern tip of Bougainville, and Mitchell anticipated at least half would rise to escort Yamamoto into the base. "Old John is going to have himself a turkey shoot," he thought, hoping to bag at least two or three Japanese fighters before the morning was done. The P-38s in his covering flight needed to reach twenty thousand feet to establish an altitude advantage, so the pilots opened their throttles and were pressed hard against their seats as they "went for angels." From up high, they would be able to use the preferred and proven American tactic in fighting a Zero, which was to dive down on him, with guns firing, in an initial pass before the enemy pilot could react.

Mitchell trusted that the four guys in the killer flight, all of whom were veteran combat pilots, could fight through the six escort Zeros and bring down the bombers. The job of the remaining P-38s was to wall them off from the expected counterattack by dozens of Zeros, although none had yet been spotted.

Mitchell radioed Lanphier, "All right, Tom. Go get 'im. He's your meat."

When Besby Holmes heard the order to shed his external fuel tanks, he yanked the handle and nothing happened. He pulled on it harder, again and again, but the outside tanks stuck like glue beneath his plane. He called out, "Hold it a second, Tom. I can't drop my tanks. I'll tear them off."

Holmes spun back to the west, and went down into a violent power dive, corkscrewing his plane. "I put my nose down at 350 miles per hour, pulling such high G's [multiples of the force of gravity] that I almost blacked out, then I kicked the rudder. No external stores will stay on an airplane at those forces," he said. The stubborn auxiliary tanks finally ripped away.

At the speeds they were moving, he soon lost sight of the others, except for Hine, who had followed the ironclad rule of a wingman and stayed with his leader, despite the slewing, jerking, diving maneuvers.

But this was not a normal mission on which normal procedures were to be followed, for their firm instructions were to get Yamamoto, no matter what the cost. "We were ready to do anything, even if that meant ramming him," Mitchell said. "Those were the orders."

By dropping from the formation to rid his plane of the fuel tanks, Holmes also pulled Hine away from the attack, and thus cut the strength of the killer flight by 50 percent.

That left only two P-38s—Lanphier in the lead, with Barber off his right wing—going after the two bombers, with no way to tell which Betty contained the admiral, and three of the escorting Zeros fully alert and coming at them.

The Bettys had begun their gradual descent for landing when the Americans were spotted, and the pilot of the lead bomber steepened his dive toward the haven of the airstrip, picking up extra speed as he nosed over and slammed his throttles to full power. The second bomber followed. Admiral Ugaki looked out of the window and saw the green jungle canopy coming up fast.

The P-38s had closed to within a mile by the time the first three Zeros reached them. Lanphier had watched silver belly tanks flutter away from the escort fighters, which had also carried extra fuel, then saw them rocketing toward Barber and himself in a race that the Zeros were sure to win. There was no way to reach those fleeing bombers before the enemy fighters would bounce them. The other three Zeros also were closing in.

History is measured in fractions of moments, and when the fighting erupted in savage, sudden fury in the sky above the southern tip of Bougainville Island on April 18, a controversy was born that would last beyond the twentieth century. Each pilot would recall the fight from a different angle and would remember it the way he saw it unfold. But the recollections were conflicting and confusing when matched against one another and against facts that would emerge years later, and those differences would become significant.

According to Lanphier, he assumed the Zeros would shoot down both himself and Barber, or even ram their planes, to protect the Bettys, so he pulled up to meet the lead Zero head-on. Tactically, it was the correct maneuver, for it allowed a Lightning pilot to fire effectively with all of his machine guns and cannon. Their closing speed was hundreds of miles an hour, and both were throwing bullets. He remembered that the Zero gave way first and slipped beneath him, on fire, with its left wing twisted. By then Lanphier was dashing higher, and flew right between the Zero's two wingmen.

His split-second decision, which many believe blocked the first wave of attacking Zeros, again reduced the strength of the killer flight by half. Now there was a single P-38 left to bring down two bombers. And they were running for their lives, with the fighter escorts swarming to protect them.

Mitchell, looking down at the action from his own rising P-38, was furious. The careful plan was falling apart before his eyes. He called out for Lanphier to forget the attacking fighter planes. The target was Yamamoto! "Get the bombers," Mitchell said. "Damn it all, the bombers!" That message apparently was not heard.

Meanwhile, the P-38s in Mitchell's cover flight were already miles from the action and going even farther and higher as fast as they could. Their job was not to shoot down the bombers but to prevent the killer flight from being jumped by any Zeros from the land bases.

For Mitchell, there was an inviolable rule for the pilots of his 339th Fighter Squadron: "Formation flying is vital."

"We fought the Japs all over Guadalcanal and the Solomons for months, and I can't remember a time when we weren't badly outnumbered. You can meet that kind of opposition in one way only, by sticking together. You must stay together, at least in pairs," he said.

Just as Ray Hine had stayed on the wing of Besby Holmes, Rex Barber ordinarily would have stayed with his leader, Tom Lanphier. By not doing so, he hung Lanphier out to take on three Zeros by himself. He also turned his own unguarded tail to the enemy planes. But if he had made any other decision, there would have been no one at all left to hit the bombers.

Barber and Lanphier had been approaching the Bettys from a ninety-degree angle, with the big planes moving in front of them from left to right. Then the escort fighters came in hard, Lanphier was gone, and the bomber pilots dived for the treetops.

Barber would recall that he was closing in on the bombers too fast as he overtook them. He had to slow down to get behind them, although by reducing his speed, he knew he would be a perfect target for an attacking Zero. He did it anyway. "My primary job, as I saw it, was to get that bomber," he said.

Barber banked sharply right to swing in behind his targets, and his left wing and engine tilted upward, momentarily blocking the bombers from his view.

Hiroshi Hayashi, at the controls of the second bomber, had maintained a loose formation with the lead Betty. Later he said that he was unaware of what was really going on until he saw the flash of red tracer bullets. Looking up through the top of his cockpit, Hayashi saw Barber's P-38 almost sitting on him, and the Japanese pilot bent away to a new course.

Barber said he did not know he had almost collided with Hayashi, below him, because when he rolled back level, he saw only one bomber. He was slightly to the left and fifty yards behind it, and even with his throttles back, he was quickly overtaking the Betty.

Barber held that he nosed in until he was only a plane's length away from his target and able to look into the position of the bomber's rear gunner, wondering when that 20-mm cannon would start shooting at him. It never did. Instead, Barber said he pulled his own triggers, and the P-38 spat a line of bullets and cannon shells over the fuselage of the bomber and into the right engine. As the smell of gunpowder filled his cockpit, bits of the bomber's engine cowling spun away. Barber slid in directly behind the Betty and walked the line of fire into the vertical fin. Pieces of the rudder came off. Barber saw the plane shake. He put another long burst into the right engine, then raked his fire across to the root of the wing against the fuselage, across the body of the plane and into the left engine. The bomber shuddered with each bullet that hit it now, and a plume of heavy, black smoke spewed out as it staggered downward, with only about five hundred feet of altitude left. Still riding the tail of the burning aircraft, Barber said he nearly ran into the

Japanese plane's right wingtip when the Betty heeled over and seemed almost to stop in midair. Barber thought the pilot may have been hit and reflexively jerked back on the controls in his final moment.

The P-38 dashed away from the stricken plane that was falling fast. Barber said he never saw it crash; he never saw that Betty again at all. He had other problems to think about, because several Zeros were on him and firing in fury. He had no idea where the other P-38s were, and as far as he knew, he was the only American still in the sky. The *Miss Virginia* was peppered with 7.7-mm machine-gun bullets, as he dodged and twisted to escape, trying to make himself small behind the armor plate that covered the back of his seat.

Hiroshi Hayashi had turned the second bomber sharply toward open water to escape his attackers when he noticed that the lead Betty was on fire. Zero pilot Kenji Yanagiya also watched Yamamoto's plane trailing a stream of black smoke and saw it fall into the jungle, still burning. Ugaki, whose own life was in jeopardy, was helpless as he, too, watched the plane that carried the commander in chief burn and fall.

After plowing through the three Zeros, Tom Lanphier recalled, he also was alone, still arrowing up into the blue sky. He flipped his P-38 onto its back and, hanging upside down in his straps, looked around. In the distance, he said, he could see Rex Barber way off to the right, being chased by some Zeros, and the two enemy fighters that Lanphier had passed between were circling around for another run. Against the jungle below, he spied a darting shadow. It was one of the bombers. "The [Betty] pilot must have executed a perfect circle in his evasive dive and flattened out of it, once again on his original course," Lanphier said.

In Lanphier's scenario, it was as if he and the Japanese bomber pilot were at some macabre carnival, with Lanphier going up-and-over on a Ferris wheel while the Betty spun on a merry-go-round. In a matter of seconds he had made a complete roll while the bomber apparently had flown around in a flat circle. Both planes were back in the patch of sky where they had started.

Lanphier said he cut back on the speed, dropped his flaps, and made a controlled skid to slow down as he dropped into the attack. In his auto-biographical account, Lanphier described approaching the Betty from a near perfect right angle. He saw the pesky Zeros coming again and guessed everybody was going to arrive in the same place about the same time. He had time for only one shot. He fired a long, steady burst of his machine guns at the extraordinary deflection angle of some seventy de-grees beyond the target in the bomber's estimated line of flight. The bul-lets ripped into the right wing, and the engine burst into flame, then the wing caught fire, too. He said that, despite the damage, the rear gunner in the Betty was pumping a steady stream of bullets at him.

Lanphier remembered being very close to the plane when the bomber's right wing tore away and the plane slammed into the jungle. He had slowed down so much to attack that the Zeros were back on him and, with only a few feet of altitude, he had little room to maneuver.

He called for help as he dodged into gullies and wove close to the treetops. Flying down so low would prevent the attackers from making easy, steep dives to attack him. They needed room to pull up.

John Mitchell and his wingman, Jack Jacobson, had passed through eighteen thousand feet and were still leading the other Lightnings up in a steep climb for more altitude when they heard the cry for help over their headsets. Looking down, they saw a P-38 in trouble, and the blink of guns of a pursuing Japanese fighter. Mitchell and Jacobson had flown together for so long that no words were needed. They rolled over and dived in perfect tandem. The rest of the cover flight kept go-ing, the pilots sticking to their orders and looking for a pack of enemy fighters that had not shown up. Surely, they thought, with all of the air-fields around Bougainville, there had to be more than just *six* Zeros protecting Yamamoto.

Mitchell and Jacobson swept down on the attacking Zero, closing in straight above Tom Lanphier's head and shooting as they came. They said that as their bullets reached out for the enemy plane, it winged over and escaped.

That was enough to spring Lanphier free. As he dashed away, thinking that he was putting distance between himself and trouble, he flew through a thick cloud of dust. When he looked down, he was shocked to discover that he was passing over the left edge of the Kahili air base, and that Japanese fighters were scrambling to take off. He pulled up the nose of his P-38 and started the kind of high-speed climb that no pursuer could match, but as he roared over a harbor, ack-ack guns popped away. He soared for safety.

Most of the P-38s in the high cover flight had reached their desired altitude only to find nothing but sky. When they had heard excited calls from the killer flight, they had braced for the anticipated rush of enemy planes, but now as they looked around, the heavens were empty. The action involving the bomber had been left far behind and far below them, down near the trees. Once the nervous guardians reached their assigned altitude, thousands of feet above where the action was hot, they had nobody to fight.

The passing seconds seemed like hours to Barber. He recalled hunching down as low as he could get in his armor-plated seat while Japanese bullets hammered against it with loud metal-on-metal smacks. "The Zeros had found my range and I was taking hits all over the plane," he said. *Miss Virginia* was receiving terrific punishment, but somehow still answered the controls as he skewed about the sky in a violent, low-level dance with three aggressive Zero pilots. He hugged the treetops, jammed his throttles full, and hurtled toward the coast, relying on the speed of his two big engines to pull away from the stubborn Japanese.

More controversy was born when the P-38s found the fleeing, dodging second bomber.

After shaking his fuel tanks, Besby Holmes and Ray Hine witnessed the strange sight of a bomber being chased by a P-38 that was itself being chased by three Zeros. Back in the fight, they dived in to join the parade and sped into the unsuspecting Japanese planes.

Holmes said he gave one Zero a long burst and blew it apart in a sheet of flame. He automatically flinched as he went through the debris, and then opened up on another Zero that fell, burning, into the sea.

Hine shot down the remaining Zero as the two P-38s flashed along at an airspeed of about 425 miles per hour. Holmes zoomed directly over Barber's plane and closed in on the Betty bomber that was hugging the water, with the tail gunner shooting up at him. A short burst from Holmes was off-target, a second splashed behind the bomber, and the third burst he adjusted to put machine-gun bullets and cannon fire into the target. He held his trigger down firmly and pounded the Betty as his P-38 bucked with the recoil of the guns.

He pulled even nearer and fired into the right wing and engine, which began to burn, but the bomber still refused to fall! "Go down! Go down or blow up, dammit!" Holmes yelled. "What do I have to do to make you go down?"

As he remembered it, Holmes believed he had hit the Betty with enough bullets to knock down a dozen planes, but he continued shooting until there was a puff of smoke and a flash of orange flame. His concentration had gotten him too close and he was moving too fast. To try to fly over the bomber would risk a collision with the large tail, so he rammed the controls forward so hard that negative G forces briefly lifted him off the seat as he flew *under* the falling plane. Holmes was aware of the shadow of the bomber over him, then he was out and free, hauling back on his controls. He was pulling up for another pass when he saw the bomber hit the water and explode and watched Rex Barber barrel across the wreckage with his own guns blazing.

According to Barber, it happened differently.

His P-38 had already evaded the chasing Zeros by the time he crossed the coast. There he saw Holmes and Hine circling and the second bomber flying south, parallel to the shore, so low that the blast from the propellers created a wake on the surface. The plane was only about ten feet above the water, almost as if it were a cruising boat.

Barber watched his two fellow killer flight pilots dive on the bomber, with Holmes closing very fast and walking his gunfire from far behind the Betty and through the right engine, which emitted a puff of smoke. Hine's bullets stitched the water ahead of the bomber, then both P-38s flew over it and continued south. Somehow, the Betty was still in the air, but was leaving a streak of dirty smoke as it ran away.

Over the next three minutes, Barber slowly pulled to within twenty feet of the bomber. He opened fire, and the big Japanese plane blew apart with a tremendous detonation. Barber was too close to dodge away and flew right into the exploding debris. A large piece sliced into his wing, another banged against the bottom of the cockpit, and bits of shrapnel needled into the skin of the *Miss Virginia* and heavily damaged it.

By the way the bomber crashed, it seemed to Barber that Holmes must have severely damaged the right wing fuel tank and then his own bullets sparked off the fumes. The bomber carrying Admiral Ugaki went into the water.

The entire fight had lasted no more than ten minutes from the moment Doug Canning called his warning until John Mitchell, believing the mission to have been successful, spoke on the radio: "Let's get the hell out of here."

25

The Curse

Admiral Isoroku Yamamoto, who had been larger than life, was to prove larger than death as well. As the killer flight dashed away, it was almost as if the C-in-C reached up from the jungle with his samurai sword and struck at each of the four pilots.

Tom Lanphier would be consumed by an inferno of self-generated publicity. Rex Barber would shun the spotlight but would be wrapped in stinging controversy until the end of his days. Besby Holmes would see his career wrecked for challenging the official version of the mission. Ray Hine would not make it back to Guadalcanal alive, and his remains would never be found.

All four were heroes that day, men who proved they were willing to lay down their lives for one another, but the tight fabric of their brotherhood was torn beyond repair by the curse of Admiral Yamamoto. It did not stop there, for in the ensuing scramble the United States Army Air Force and its successor, the United States Air Force, soiled its honor to protect a false image of what happened above Bougainville on April 18, 1943.

The Lightning pilots who had flown high cover returned to Guadalcanal without mishap. They had made the long and arduous flight, but except for hearing static-filled radio calls involving the killer flight, few had seen any of the action, which had happened some three miles below them, right above the trees and the water. For most, it had just been one long trip.

Major John Mitchell had expected a turkey shoot, but except for the one pass at the Zero chasing Lanphier, he came up dry. The best shooter in the outfit was going home without a bomber or a Zero.

He had seen a column of smoke rising from the jungle, but the unexpected appearance of the second bomber had caused him concern. Did they get the right one? Did they get both of the Bettys? Was Yamamoto really dead? He thought so, but there was no way to be absolutely certain, and he regretted not having led the killer flight himself.

When he glanced down for a final look from his altitude of fifteen thousand feet, Mitchell caught a glimpse of a faraway P-38, down near the treetops, trailing oily smoke from its left engine, with a Zero on its tail. When he dropped in to attack, the enemy plane fled, but he had lost sight of the wounded Lightning. Mitchell would later believe that it had been the aircraft piloted by Ray Hine.

Hine, Barber, and Holmes had to fight their way out of the area. Several Zeros were on them, and Barber said he saw Holmes roll over on one of them and shoot it down. Then Barber outmaneuvered another Japanese fighter and blew it up with a short burst of gunfire. Both Zeros went into the clear water, splashing into a roiling cauldron of bubbles and froth.

Holmes said that about that same time, he was in a high-altitude climb, chasing still another Zero. But the right engine of his P-38 began to sputter, and Holmes knew that if he lost power, the enemy pilot would blast him out of the sky. All he could do was to continue firing his guns as long as possible, and he managed to hit the Japanese plane. The Zero spun out of control, and Holmes leveled out his Lightning. Barber and Hine were nowhere to be seen, so Besby Holmes headed back alone, counting his personal score for the day as one bomber and three Zeros.

His instruments showed that he did not have enough fuel to make it home.

. . .

Kenji Yanagiya, flying one of the escort Zeros, had broken off from the dogfights to spread the warning to the base at Buin. He roared down, made a tight turn and fired his machine guns to get the attention of those on the ground, then zoomed away again to look for the Americans. He said he found a P-38 flying by itself at about nine thousand feet and opened fire until he saw smoke trailing from its wing.

Shoichi Sugita, the young Shoot-Down King, also reported attacking a plane and seeing it emit a plume of black smoke. He identified it as the P-38 flying beside the one that had not dropped its belly tanks. Since Holmes was the pilot who encountered problems shedding his tanks, Sugita was referring to the wingman Hine.

Lieutenant Ray Hine had been the least experienced pilot on the mission, not because of a lack of combat time, but because he had not flown a P-38 since qualifying in one at the end of 1942. He remained with his original 68th Fighter Squadron, which flew P-40s, so the Yamamoto flight was his first and only combat mission in a Lightning. Although he shared a tent with Jacobson, Hine was from another squadron, and somewhat of a mystery to the others. His comrades hoped that he had bailed out and been picked up by friendly island natives, but when time passed without any word, the grim task of gathering the personal effects from his empty bunk and footlocker fell to Jacobson. Once they had laughed about enjoyable times in Australia during rest leaves, but after Hine disappeared, it was as if he had never been there. Someone else took the bunk, and the war continued.

What happened to him was never accurately determined.

To dodge the P-38 attacks, the pilot of the second Betty had brought the bomber down until the propellers almost dug holes in the ocean. When he lost control, a violent explosion ripped off the right wing, and the plane punched into the sea and sank.

The last moments inside the bomber were a hell of confusion and blood for Matome Ugaki. Seated on the flight deck right behind the pilots, he had actually watched a P-38 roll in to attack them with its nose guns twinkling flames. The bomber vibrated as bullets drummed into it, and the admiral held on tight as men around him fell dead.

Then came the crash. Ugaki was thrown from his seat, unconscious. He awoke, choking and stunned, as cold water flushed into the broken fuselage. The admiral thought he was dying, but somehow popped to the surface of the water. Fire burned brightly near the plane. A rescue boat picked up Ugaki, the bomber pilot Hayashi, and the fleet's chief paymaster, Rear Admiral Motoharu Kitamura. They were rushed to shore for treatment.

Doug Canning was the last American out of the area. He had spotted a Zero, turned his plane sharply to the left, went into a screaming dive, and looped up right behind the surprised Japanese pilot. "I had him bore-sighted; he was dead," Canning said.

But just when he was ready to shoot, a thick mist covered the inside of his canopy and Canning found himself flying blind, as if he had been wrapped in a cloud. He had no idea where the Zero was, and only the most general idea of his own location. If the enemy plane got behind him, it would be Canning who would die.

Using his handkerchief, he frantically scrubbed away the condensation, and when he regained his view, the Japanese plane was gone. Canning poured on the throttle and went into a hard climb to twenty thousand feet, looking back to see the "exploding beehive" of Kahili beneath him. Zero fighters were roaring off the runway in a whipping cloud of dust. It was definitely time to leave.

A telegram arrived at the Buin air base. The staff at Rabaul was curious about the silence from the always-punctual Yamamoto. The admiral's flight had left on time at six o'clock and was scheduled to land no later than eight o'clock, but the usual routine confirmation message that he had arrived safely had not come across. After waiting until forty-nine minutes after the hour, they asked:

HAS C-IN-C PLANE ARRIVED?

There had been no communication with Buin from the other fighter bases, such as busy Kahili, and Yanagiya's earlier gun-firing warning pass had been ignored. The base commandant replied that the Yamamoto flight had not yet landed.

Despite the firm beliefs of the American pilots that they had shot down several Zeros, all six of the escort fighters survived. One made an emergency landing on Shortland Island, but the other five came in one by one to the coral strip on Buin. Men were still standing at attention in their dress uniforms along the immaculate runway, waiting for Yamamoto. The commander of the escort fighter unit, Lieutenant Takeshi Morizaki, immediately reported the disaster, and the Japanese finally realized what had happened.

Yanagiya was the last to land. He was not interviewed, although he wanted to talk. He believed the Japanese code had been broken because the large group of the twin-engine Lightnings had appeared out of nowhere and had gone directly for the two bombers. The Americans must have known in advance exactly who they were after.

When he landed at Buin and saw the elaborate preparations that had been made for Yamamoto's arrival, the pilot realized there must have been a lot of advance message traffic. "They knew who was flying in the plane," he said. "It was deliberate. It was not an accident." But he was just a fighter pilot who had failed to protect the commander in chief of the Combined Fleet, and no one was interested in his opinion.

Three hours after they landed, the Zero pilots were ordered to return to Rabaul. Each was psychologically shattered by their failure, and all were ready to commit ritual suicide.

Some thirty minutes after he began his return trip, Doug Canning found Besby Holmes limping through the sky. Holmes was never so relieved to see a fellow pilot in his life. He was almost out of fuel and the engines were running so rough that even reading the instrument panel was impossible because of the plane's vibration. "I've got trouble, Doug. Not enough gas to get back to the Canal."

Canning edged in so that he could look through his right propeller to see the right propeller of Holmes, and then adjusted his own engine until they matched speeds in order to get an accurate RPM reading.

That allowed Holmes to calculate a minimal, fuel-saving speed "to keep the old bird in the sky." Canning settled in and rode beside him for an hour, ready to pinpoint the place if Holmes crash-landed. A large clutch of Zeros passed in the distance but did not spot them.

Holmes was almost flying on fumes when the two Americans sighted the Russell Islands, just northwest of Guadalcanal. The Japanese had recently abandoned the islands, and American engineers were laying out a new airstrip there. Canning pushed his throttles open wider and flew ahead to warn the workers to clear the runway so Holmes could land.

He buzzed by on a low pass, but the construction crews just waved happily to him. Canning climbed back up to make another pass. This time he would get their attention with a maneuver so dangerous that it was prohibited, but he had to get those road graders and bulldozers off the runway if Holmes was to land. He pulled off a "widowmaker," in which he banked around sharply, chopped his throttles, and lowered his flaps and wheels, with one wing pointed at the ground. The workers got the message, because it looked like the plane was going to fall right on top of them. They scattered like ants.

Canning snapped out of the way, and Holmes, switching from one fuel tank to another to drain the last drops of gas, touched down on the short, incomplete runway, stood on his brakes, and dodged a huge boulder before coming to a stop. He turned the power off, climbed out of the cockpit, and was sitting on the wing when a marine lieutenant charged up to chew him out. Instead, after one look at the haggard pilot, the lieutenant had marines bring Holmes some water and help him stagger away. His plane had only four gallons of gas and four .50 caliber bullets left.

Rabaul

Telegram number 181108, from the commandant of the 6th Air Force, landed on the desk of the commandant of the 11th Air Fleet in Rabaul carrying the extraordinary heading of "Highest Priority, Confidential." It was transmitted in the top secret Ro-3 code.

1. Two Rikko carrying C-in-C, Combined Fleet, and his party engaged in aerial combat with over 10 P-38s at about 0740. Second plane was forced down into the sea off Moira Point. Chief of Staff, Chief Paymaster (both wounded), one pilot rescued. First plane in flames seemed to have plunged at a slight angle into the jungle about 11 miles west of RXP. Searching underway.

2. Two direct-escorting planes shot down six hostile planes (of which three planes were forced landing; certain). No damage to our side.

The confusion about who shot down what had infected both the Japanese and the Americans, and there would never be a satisfactory accounting. It reflected a truth of combat: Just because someone said he shot down a plane, even if someone else observed it, did not necessarily mean that it happened.

Guadalcanal

The crews who kept the planes flying had lashed up a powerful radio receiver near the Fighter II runway so they could listen to their pilots during missions. Many men had gathered around it that Sunday morning, or stopped by while working, to hear what was happening to the guys on the Yamamoto mission. For the first hours there was only empty static, since the flight to Bougainville was made in total radio silence.

Then the fight erupted and they heard excited snatches of conversation, pilots talking over one another, but little could be understood. So they waited.

As the P-38s returned, the radio crackled and a jubilant Tom Lanphier burst onto the air, his words sharp and clear. He announced to the ground-control station known as RECON, "That son of a bitch will not be dictating any peace terms in the White House."

The place went nuts. The infamous and incorrect story that Yamamoto wanted to march down Pennsylvania Avenue and force the president to accept Japanese terms had become a legend in the Pacific, and Americans hated him for it. That radio call meant they had done it! They had bagged Yamamoto! Men cheered and slapped each other on the back.

As if in confirmation, the first returning P-38s put on an impromptu air show, buzzing the field with celebratory barrel rolls and some heart-thumping "widowmaker" landings. "They tore the place up," said one sergeant.

The pilots had flown the entire mission in quiet solitude until the air battle began, but radio discipline had kept chatter to a minimum, and cross talk was minimal on the way home. Lanphier's radio call ended that total secrecy, and many officers were taken aback by his breaking radio silence. If the Japanese were listening, the comment could indicate that the Americans knew who their target was. That would mean the coded message about his visit had been broken.

"*Oh, my God,*" thought Lieutenant Larry Graebner, who was coming in somewhere behind Lanphier. "*What are you doing?*"

Their orders were that the secret was not to leave the island, but Lanphier's call violated that rule. He was the only one to do so. Although some other pilots were happy enough to do aerobatics, they did not broadcast anything about the mission over the open airwaves.

Lanphier flared into an easy landing on Fighter II, and his left engine died from lack of fuel as he rolled to a stop. Two bullets had punctured his plane. From the moment he opened his cockpit, the happy Tom Lanphier assumed the role of a conqueror.

The first pilots to land were welcomed by cheering groups of men, and several watched in amazement as Lanphier came down the runway standing in the back of a Jeep, shouting, "I got him! I got that son of a bitch! I got Yamamoto!"

By the time they reached the headquarters tent, the die had been cast. Lanphier had staked his claim, although no one had seen him shoot down anything.

A party atmosphere reigned as the returning pilots dribbled in one by one to be welcomed by enthusiastic commanders. General "Lightning

Joe" Collins sent over some steaks, Lieutenant Colonel Viccellio gave the fliers a rare treat of fresh milk, and Admiral Mitscher chipped in a case of bourbon. Everyone was talking at the same time, amid whoops of joy.

In the crowd were officers whose job it was to figure out what had happened: Marine Lieutenant Colonel Ed Pugh, the officer in charge of Fighter Command on Guadalcanal; his number-two man, marine Major John P. Condon, the Fighter Command operations officer; navy Lieutenant Joe McGuigan, the air combat intelligence officer; and army Captain Bill Morrison, another intelligence officer.

But debriefings after missions were never a high priority on Guadalcanal. "It wasn't a formal thing at all," said Condon. Pilots would tell what they thought happened, and the information was telephoned or sent over to Mitscher's headquarters to be included in an overall summary. Some missions were never debriefed at all.

This, however, was far from being an ordinary mission, and every scrap of information had potential historic importance. Incredibly, the Sunday afternoon session was more of a postgame celebration of excited athletes caught up in a big victory than a sober reflection on what actually took place. Even those who participated in it would say there was no official debriefing and that nothing was immediately typed up for the files. When questioned about the meeting years later, Condon snapped, "We didn't have court reporters."

"We had no one who could conduct debriefings in those days. We were uneducated then," said Mitchell, who would forever insist that he was never debriefed after the Yamamoto mission. "We only knew what we had been through and accepted each other's version of what happened."

When Rex Barber climbed from his plane, the ground crew was amazed. The *Miss Virginia* was shot to pieces. There were fifty-two bullet holes in the rear, and the intercooler in the leading edge of his left wing was severed, which had drastically reduced the power of one engine. A large chunk of the exploding bomber struck the underside of the pilot's gondola, gouging a long dent just below Barber's feet. Seven bullets chewed out parts of his propellers, ragged fragments from the exploding bomber stuck out like porcupine quills, and the fuselage was streaked with paint from other pieces of shrapnel. Altogether, there were 104 holes. Once again, Barber had brought back an airplane that should have fallen out of the sky.

Now he sat at a table in the loud headquarters' tent, irked at listening to Tom Lanphier boast, "I got Yamamoto! I got Yamamoto!"

Barber didn't understand. He had flown out on Lanphier's wing, had seen Tom peel away from the bomber chase and fly up into the oncoming Zeros, and that was the last he had seen of Tom until they landed on Guadalcanal. Barber knew he had shot up both of the Bettys. He had last seen the first one on fire, rolling sharply to its left, with its right wingtip straight up as he passed it, just above the treeline. When he looked back, he saw the Zeros chasing him and a plume of smoke rising from the jungle. Then he had had attacked the second Betty just above the water, and it exploded right in front of him before the remainder fell into the water. In truth, he did not know if Yamamoto was aboard either one of them.

Barber wasn't questioning that Lanphier might have shot down a bomber, for aerial battles are confusing things. But it was too early to assign victories, for the rest of the pilots were still straggling in, and two members of the killer flight, Besby Holmes and Ray Hine, weren't even back yet! Barber had seen both of those men tangling with a bomber, but not Lanphier. So how could Lanphier stand there and flatly claim that he killed the Japanese admiral when none of the Americans, including Lanphier, knew in which bomber, if either, the admiral had been riding? He was used to Tom's bragging, but this was absurd.

"How in the hell do you know you got Yamamoto?" Barber asked. The sharp rebuke, coming from the usually placid Barber, stung Lanphier. One gunfighter was challenging another, in the middle of a crowd.

"You're a damned liar! You're a damned liar!" Lanphier barked back at his longtime friend.

"But I haven't made a statement," Barber responded. "I just asked a question." Rather than argue further, he walked out of the tent.

"No one on God's green earth knew who had shot down which bomber, much less who had shot down Yamamoto," John Mitchell declared later. Even Lanphier would write in his autobiography after many years had passed that he knew only that one bomber had splashed into the sea and that he had shot down one in the jungle. He belatedly admitted that he did not know which plane carried Yamamoto. All he knew was that "Yamamoto had gone down."

Near the end of the session, Mitscher brought over the case of whiskey, shook hands all around, and personally clasped Lanphier in a big bear hug. Everyone on Guadalcanal knew the top man in Japan's Combined Fleet had been shot down, and word was that Tom Lanphier did it.

Later that evening, Paul Bechtel, a pilot with the Dirty Dozen, noticed Lanphier seated at a table, working at a typewriter. Bechtel later would recall assuming that Lanphier, the former newspaper reporter who could make a typewriter sing, was writing a mission report.

BOOK IV

Faded Glory

26

The Report

Bougainville

The report that Admiral Yamamoto had crashed somewhere in the jungle threw Japanese authorities into a confusion that caused delays in getting search parties organized. Area forces were ordered to begin an immediate rescue mission, and half the planes of the 204th Flying Corps were sent in to strengthen the already substantial contingent of fighters on nearby bases, both to cover and assist in the search operations. Because of the sensitive nature of the job, the commanders decided not to use native guides, although they knew the jungles much better than the Japanese.

Then came the hard part, drafting a "highest priority" message to the naval general staff in Tokyo. These were given the code name of "Ko Reports," and the first one stated that Yamamoto's plane was last seen plunging at a slight angle and on fire into the jungle.

The crew of a search plane soon spotted the wreckage of the bomber about ten miles from Moila Point but could see no one moving. Three platoons of the navy's Sixth Sasebo Special Landing Party and two army platoons began hacking through the thick jungle to reach the site. But no matter how hard the sweaty, desperate searchers swung their machetes, the vines and undergrowth seemed a solid wall of tangled green. Muck pulled at their boots with every step, insects swarmed, and the smell of rot nearly overwhelmed their senses. They started at eleven o'clock in the morning and, overtaken by exhaustion, halted for the night still three miles from the crash site.

Meanwhile, doctors at the First Base Force Hospital on Bougainville worked on the survivors of the second bomber. Admiral Ugaki had a compound fracture of his arm, wounds on the right biceps, and was bleeding profusely from both lower thighs and his right eye. The fleet paymaster had multiple head wounds and a damaged right kneecap. The pilot sustained only minor injuries.

Fighter II

Besby Holmes arrived back on Guadalcanal with stories to tell. He had made the long flight to Bougainville, shot down a bomber and three Zeros, twice saved Rex Barber's tail, made a miraculous landing in the Russell Islands, had a PT boat fetch cans of gas so he could take off again, and now here he was back at Fighter II, sweaty and tired but overjoyed and ready to talk about the most exciting day of his life.

Nobody cared. By the time he arrived, three hours after everyone else, the excitement was over. There was no one there to greet him except his ground crew, and he had to hunt up the other pilots.

The more he learned of what happened before he got back to the base, the angrier Holmes became. The victories had already been distributed—a bomber to Lanphier and two bombers to Barber, with Lanphier claiming the Yamamoto kill. Holmes felt cheated. His actions, and those of his wingman, Ray Hine, had not been included. Where was Hine, anyway? Ray was an eyewitness who would back him up. How could these decisions have been made without first talking to half of the pilots in the killer flight? "I was mad as hell," Holmes said, and he argued with Lanphier, Barber, and Viccellio.

The developing after-action report was altered to allow him a share in the credit by giving him a Zero and a Betty, in effect taking one away from Barber. But both formulas, no matter how the victories were shared, meant that there would have had to be *three* Bettys up there! That compromise quieted Holmes somewhat, but the mistake would persist for many years. Everyone had seen two bombers, not three, so an assumption was made that the third Betty wasn't part of the Yamamoto flight, just some plane on a test hop that happened to blunder into the fight.

New Caledonia

A coded message was transmitted from Guadalcanal on the afternoon of April 18, from Admiral Mitscher to Admiral Halsey, with a copy to Admiral Nimitz in Pearl Harbor:

> P 38's LED BY MAJOR J. WILLIAM MITCHEL (SIC) USAAF VISITED KAHILI AREA. ABOUT 0930L 18 SHOT DOWN TWO BOMBERS ESCORTED BY 6 ZEROS FLYING CLOSE FORMATION. 1 OTHER BOMBER SHOT DOWN BELIEVED ON TEST FLIGHT. 3 ZEROS ADDED TO THE SCORE SUMS TOTAL 6. 1 P 38 FAILED RETURN. APRIL 18 SEEMS TO BE OUR DAY.

It made no mention of Yamamoto, thus keeping the code secret secure, although the last sentence was a personal reminder from Mitscher to Halsey that it was the first anniversary of the day they launched the Doolittle raiders toward Tokyo. Had Japanese analysts in the sprawling radio intelligence collection center at Owada picked up that message and deemed it important enough for their attention, they might have deduced that something had happened in the Kahili area that was more than a few P-38s fighting with Zeros and bombers.

Bill Halsey was obviously pleased with the news but couldn't resist being the crusty cynic. When members of his staff began to whoop and celebrate, the admiral grumbled, "What's so good about it? I'd hoped to lead that scoundrel up Pennsylvania Avenue in chains, with the rest of you kicking him where it would do the most good."

He flashed a message back to Guadalcanal:

> CONGRATULATIONS TO YOU AND MAJOR MITCHELL AND HIS HUNTERS. SOUNDS AS THOUGH ONE OF THE DUCKS IN THEIR BAG WAS A PEACOCK.

That was another breach of security, since at that point, no one was supposed to be talking about who was aboard those planes. Even the people at headquarters couldn't keep their mouths shut, but fortunately the Japanese were not paying attention.

Fighter II

A four-page document describing the mission and dated April 18 would soon be forwarded to higher headquarters. It was supposed to have been created by "Army Intelligence," was signed with the handwritten last names of Morrison and McGuigan, and carried the imprimatur of the XIII Fighter Command. Most mission reports were little more than shorthand, fill-in-the-blank forms that contained a minimum of bare facts and no embellishment. With so many missions being flown each day, the enormous volume of paperwork had to be kept simple for the sergeants and corporals and privates who typed it up for the files. The Yamamoto report, which was to become the official Air Force bible on the incident, resembled a novel, and it tilted history.

Sergeant Brooklyn Harris was the clerk for the 339th Fighter Squadron, and as such he handled all classified and secret documents, including combat reports, concerning the squadron's pilots. The typewriter that clacked out the Yamamoto mission report did not have Brooklyn Harris at the keyboard. He never saw the document, the heart of which stated:

> 7. The Action:
> From the take-off at Cactus, the flight went 410 miles over the circuitous all-water route, flying all the way at an altitude of 10 to 30 feet above the water. The course had been figured and timed so that the interception most probably would take place upon the approach of the P-38's to the Southwestern coast of Bougainville at the designated time of 0935. As this point was reached *the Enemy was sighted.*
> It was almost as if the affair had been pre-arranged with the mutual consent of friend and foe.
> The picture was this: The Lightnings were at 30 feet, heading in toward the coast, and just about to begin to get their altitude for the

presumed attack. The enemy was sighted, in a "V," about 3 miles distant proceeding down the Southern coastline toward Kahili. The two bombers were together, flying at 4500 feet, with two sections—3 Zeros each—1500 feet above them and slightly to the rear. As the enemy force, apparently unaware of the opposition, pursued his course, Mitchell led his covering group in their climb for altitude, ultimately reaching 15–18000 feet, from which point they stood their protecting vigil. Lanphier led his force parallel to the course of the enemy, flying in toward them a bit, and indicating 200 MPH, in his 35° climb. The P-38s actually climbed at 2200 feet per minute. When level with the bombers, and about 2 miles away, Lanphier and Barber dropped their belly tanks and swung in to the attack at 280 MPH indicated. Holmes had difficulty in releasing his tank, and Hine remained with him until he could do so.

When Lanphier and Barber were within one mile of contact, their attack was observed by the enemy. The bombers nosed down, one started a 360° turn dive, the other going out and away toward the shoreline; the Zeros dropped their belly tanks and three peeled down, in a string, to intercept Lanphier. When he saw that he could not reach the bomber he turned up and into the Zeros, exploding the first, and firing into the others as they passed. By this time he had reached 6000 feet, so he nosed over; and went down to the tree tops after his escaping objective. He came into it broadside—fired his bursts—a wing flew off and the plane went flaming to earth.

The Zeros were now pursuing him and had the benefit of altitude. His mission accomplished, he hedgehopped the treetops and made desperate maneuvers to escape. He kicked rudders, slipped and skidded, tracers were flying past his plane—but he finally outran them. In all the action he had received two 7.7's in his horizontal stabilizer.

Barber had gone in with Lanphier on the initial attack. He went for one of the bombers, but its maneuvers caused him to overshoot a little. He whipped back, however, and although pursued by Zeros, caught the bomber and destroyed it. When he fired, the tail section fell off, the bomber turned over on its back and plummeted to earth.

By this time, Holmes had been able to drop his tank and with Hine, who had stayed in formation with him, came in to ward off the Zeros who were pursuing Barber. A dogfight ensued, many shots were exchanged, but results were not observed. The flight was on its way out of the combat area (in the neighborhood of enemy bases at Kahili, Ballale, and Shortland-Faisi) when Holmes noticed a stray bomber near Moila Point flying low over the water. He dove on it, his bursts getting it smoking in the left engine; Hine also shot at it and Barber polished it off with a burst in the fuselage. The bomber exploded "right in my face"; a piece of the plane flew off, but through his left wing and knocked out his left inner cooler and other chunks left paint streaks on his wing—so close was his attack driven home.

Holmes, Hine, and Barber then turned up for home, their mission—to destroy the bombers—a complete success. However, Zeros were coming in on Barber's tail and Holmes whipped up and around and shot one down in flames. Another attempt to draw away ended in another dogfight during which Barber exploded a further Zero. During these minutes, Hine's left engine started to smoke and he was last seen losing altitude south of Shortland Island. It is believed that Hine also accounted for a Zero as a total of three enemy fighters were seen to fall into the sea during this part of the combat.

Barber and Holmes were forced to use extreme evasive measures in order to successfully escape from the enemy hotbed and their course out, as was Lanphier's, was further complicated by a huge cloud of dust fanning out from a swarm of planes taking off from Kahili airfield. Holmes eventually ran out of gas and made a successful emergency landing at the Russell Islands, from which he later brought his plane safely home to base. The damage to the cooling system of Barber's left motor prevented him from pulling more than 30 inches of mercury at low levels and 25 inches at 4/5000 feet but despite this limitation to his speed and rate of climb he also brought his plane safely home to base.

8. Comment:

The success of this extraordinary mission—a 425 miles [sic] interception by land planes largely over water—was due in large measure to the leadership of Major Mitchell. On the eve of the flight, the mission was thoroughly explained to each pilot—there were no generalities. Each minute detail was discussed, with nothing taken for granted; take-off procedure, flight altitude, exactly when and how to drop belly tanks, radio silence, the tremendous importance of precise timing and position of covering elements, until Major Mitchell was sure that each of his pilots knew both his part and that of each other pilot from take-off to return.

The results bear witness to the thoroughness of this briefing. Radio silence was absolute until Canning's quiet "Eleven o'clock" announced contact with the enemy. The time resulting from Major Mitchell's close control of the flight's speed and the unwavering formation maintained was so exact that the enemy was met on the minute, where a few minutes' delay would have meant complete failure. The covering flight covered the combat action—as it should have—and when help was called for by the attacking element, Major Mitchell immediately diverted the pre-arranged section and the balance remained on station. This discipline—intelligent discipline—was throughout the mission flawless, not one of the twelve covering planes yielded to the temptation to peel off and mix it with the enemy.

Once again the following fundamental principles of modern, organized air attack—the first instructions which new pilots receive from Col. Viccellio—have proven their soundness: "When you are on a mission, whether leading a flight or flying a wing, know exactly what your mission is, where you are going, and how to get back—and be on time."

The document stopped short of actually assigning credit for the Yamamoto kill, but it precisely echoed Lanphier's view that he had bagged the lead bomber. In later years, Lanphier, the former newspaper reporter and master storyteller who was adept at both shorthand and typing, vehemently denied authorship, but a number of interesting coincidences surfaced.

- The report said the mission ended at 1140. Tom Lanphier wrote in his autobiography that his plane rolled to a stop at exactly that minute. Others had arrived earlier, and others, including mission leader John Mitchell, arrived later.
- Lanphier's name was listed first among the pilots involved, and not that of Mitchell, the ranking officer and mission commander.
- It mentioned that Lanphier's plane had two bullet holes, but

although it said that Barber's aircraft sustained some damage, it did not mention that it carried 104 holes.

• The last paragraph had nothing at all to do with the flight, but was arbitrary praise for Lanphier's good friend and tent mate, Henry Viccellio.

• Finally, Barber said that Lanphier told him the morning after the mission, "Don't worry about it, Rex. I went over to the Ops Tent . . . and wrote the report." Lanphier later denied making such a statement, although Barber would recall that it was said not once, but several times, in the coming weeks, and not only to him.

The marines were in charge of all air activity on Guadalcanal, but even John Condon, the fighter command's operations officer, would dodge ownership of the statement. He was among those in the headquarters tent during the boisterous celebration for the returning pilots, but would tell an interviewer the document did not originate from within the fighter command. Instead, it "came over from Fighter II as an air corps debriefing output." There was no separate debriefing of the pilots by air force officers. John Mitchell did not read it before it was transmitted to higher headquarters, and Rex Barber did not even *see* the report until the 1950s. Condon said he did not know who wrote it.

A bell cannot be unrung once it is sounded, and for decades to come, all future challenges to the question of "Who really shot down Yamamoto?" would terminate at that single flawed and inaccurate "official" version.

Author Burke Davis reported in his book *Get Yamamoto* that an air force officer who later reviewed the document said, "The report is enough to make one weep. It reads like a fiction tale and the facts appear to be entwined like Medusa's locks."

That night, dozens of U.S. soldiers and airmen were watching a black-and-white movie being shown on the outside wall of a makeshift church on Guadalcanal. During a change of reels, an officer stepped to the front and announced to all that Admiral Yamamoto, the commander in chief of Japan's Combined Fleet, had been shot down that day by army pilots from Guadalcanal. And as if he wanted to be sure that everyone on the island knew about the mission, he said there would be a special awards ceremony on Fighter II tomorrow.

Tom Lanphier took a bottle of booze over to the nearby camp of the marine pilots and celebrated with his brother Charlie.

Fiji

Correspondent Bob Miller of the United Press, back at work after two weeks in the hospital for malaria and catarrhal jaundice, soon heard the big news that Yamamoto had been downed. During the past year, Miller had roamed the entire Pacific Theater and was almost adopted by the Marine Corps for his work under fire on Guadalcanal. The gregarious reporter had made friends with sergeants and generals, aides and admirals, nurses and diplomats, and carefully cultivated excellent sources within the naval intelligence community. He went to talk with them off the record, and was surprised at how many of the intel people were outraged by the death of Yamamoto.

In his memoirs, written after the war, Miller recalled that instead of a unanimous decision to carry out the mission, some officers in "navy intelligence had argued in vain" against it. "They said that the Japanese would deduce from the attack on Yamamoto's plane that their codes had been broken and would act quickly to change them. That, they argued, would be a military intelligence disaster far outweighing any possible gains accruing from the admiral's death."

There was also a faction that desperately wanted Isoroku Yamamoto to *live*, not die. Miller's sources explained that the War Cabinet in Tokyo, headed by Premier Tojo and his powerful army supporters, would never admit the war was lost. Yamamoto was the only person who stood any chance of challenging them. Not only did the admiral have a close and personal relationship with Emperor Hirohito, he was an acknowledged naval hero and was idolized by the common man. His dominant personality, his engaging personality, and his loyalty to his men inspired people to follow him, and military victories had only increased his stature. The intelligence sources argued that Yamamoto might someday have been able to lead Japan away from the war with America that he had started but never truly wanted.

Yamamoto, weary from the tough months of fighting, had recognized that after Midway and Guadalcanal the momentum of the war had shifted in America's favor and that the end was as inevitable as he had always believed. The admiral was enough of a samurai to perhaps accept a cabinet position, in which he would have made a huge difference in the balance of power. "Because of the respect and admiration with which he was held by both the Palace and the populace, Yamamoto was the one man with enough clout to force the bitter pill of defeat down the throats of the Japanese," Miller's sources said.

Bob Miller was sitting on a news story of a lifetime and could do nothing with it. His sources swore him to secrecy, and Miller knew the censors would never approve a story that not only reported Admiral Yamamoto had been killed, but that he had died because the code had been broken, and the whole thing was not really a victory at all but a gigantic mistake.

"This macho-military blunder, motivated solely by pique, eliminated the one Japanese who might have shortened the Pacific war," Miller believed.

27

Picture Day

Bougainville

Yamamoto's friend, chess partner, and senior aide, Yasuji Watanabe, moved to take charge of the situation but could not immediately get out of Rabaul because of bad weather. The following morning, Monday, April 19, he flew to Buin, along with three aides, and went directly from the plane to the hospital, where the badly wounded chief of staff, in tears, begged him to hurry to the crash site.

"To us, Admiral Yamamoto was virtually a god," Ugaki confided in his diary, as he lay hospitalized for several months, swooning into a deep depression because he felt responsible for the death of the C-in-C. Thoughts of suicide haunted him. Although Ugaki recovered and continued to serve, eventually taking command of one of the fleets, he died on the final day of the war, flying as a common pilot on the last kamikaze death mission. On that flight he carried a small sword that had been presented to him by Yamamoto. Ugaki's diary lived on and became one of the most introspective literary works of the war.

Commander Watanabe ordered a seaplane to fly him over the wreckage in the jungle, but he could see no life below. Little rubber balls were dropped, containing messages for anyone reading them to show themselves by waving their arms. Nothing. Watanabe landed near a ship and took a group of sailors into the hot, dank jungle, slashing a path until darkness forced them to quit.

The naval unit that had set out from Buin the previous day awoke before daylight and resumed working its way forward, but by the time darkness fell for the second time, they still had not found the plane.

An army construction unit led by a young second lieutenant finally discovered the crash site. While the group was working some eighteen miles west of Buin on Sunday morning, they had watched American and Japanese fighters clash in a dogfight above them, and when a trail of smoke rose above the trees, they cheered, believing a P-38 had been shot down. The lieutenant was later told that a plane carrying "top navy brass" had crashed and that he was to find it immediately. He organized a search party and entered the jungle, carefully marking their trail by notching trees, but he, too, failed on the first try and returned to camp. On Monday, the lieutenant's troops were back in the jungle and saw Watanabe's plane circle overhead and drop the rubber balls. They waved a Rising Sun flag in response, but were not seen.

The sun was low in the sky and shadows reached out from the dense forest when the soldiers smelled aviation fuel. They followed their noses until they chopped their way into a clearing that had been smashed in the thick trees by a fallen twin-engine airplane. Broken corpses lay about.

Tokyo

The Imperial Navy's General Staff was disturbed. That Admiral Yamamoto was missing, and had last been seen aboard a bomber that was shot down in flames, was an enormous tragedy, but the appropriate authorities were already dealing with it.

However, there was something else, of equal importance. It seemed that the Americans might have learned the admiral's flight plan by breaking the naval code. If so, it would have to be changed immediately, which meant couriers would have to take new code material to every base on every island and to every ship. But first they had to determine the damage, if any. Top secret telegrams were dispatched to the chief of staff of the South Eastern Fleet and to the commander of the First Communications Corps.

IT IS SUSPECTED THAT ENEMY IS AWARE OF OUR PLANS CONCERNING KO RE-
PORT NO. 1 OF COMMANDER IN CHIEF, SOUTH EASTERN FLEET.

IN CASE OF TELEGRAM CONCERNING THIS ACTIVITY, ASIDE FROM COMBINED
FLEET SECRET TELEGRAM NO. 161107, HAVE SAME FORWARDED.

INVESTIGATE CAUSE OF ABOVE THOROUGHLY WHETHER DUE TO DECODING
OF OUR CODE, ACTIVITY OF SPIES OR OTHERS AND REPORT OF SAME AS SOON
AS POSSIBLE.

The telegram to which they referred, 161107, transmitted on April 16, was a routine informational message from Yamamoto to the navy minister and the chief of the Naval General Staff. It gave an overview of the second stage of I-Go and announced in the last paragraph that the C-in-C of the Combined Fleet planned to return to his flagship in Rabaul after making an inspection trip to the Shortland Island area on April 18.

Was it possible that the Americans had built an ambush around the information?

Fighter II

At daybreak on April 19, a flight of eight P-38s zoomed away from Guadalcanal, headed for Kahili on an urgent mission. The pilots were different, but some of the P-38s had made the trip the previous day. Mitchell's flight had gone out low over the ocean to arrive at Bougainville undetected, but the Monday flight was to do just the opposite and be as obvious as possible.

The American commanders were having second thoughts about the code. The Japanese might well wonder *why* a bunch of U.S. Army Air Force fighters *just happened* to show up where they weren't supposed to be. For the next several days, decoy flights were assigned to fly on a direct course to the area. They would give the Japanese plenty of opportunities to spot them, then make a single dash toward the enemy base at Kahili and fly home.

Even as the fliers made this belated effort to camouflage the Yamamoto mission as a routine patrol, any hope of preserving the secret was dashed on Guadalcanal.

About the time the Lightnings took off on Monday morning, the tired and woozy pilots who had flown it were waking up and shaking off hangovers to prepare for the day's activities. They had partied into the night, fueled by Mitscher's case of whiskey.

Passenger planes from New Caledonia landed at Henderson Field and disgorged high-ranking officers from headquarters, plus a contingent of news correspondents, photographers, and newsreel cameramen. The pilots were told to spruce up. They were going to have their pictures taken.

The fifteen surviving pilots were carefully posed in front of a parked P-38, number 125, Rex Barber's *Diablo*, and told to stand at attention. An actual military formation and adherence to nit-picking formality were foreign concepts on Guadalcanal, where only a few months earlier Japanese snipers tried to kill anybody who even looked like an officer. It was not easy for those who had been on the island a while to stand still in a group.

Colonels and generals, captains and admirals lined up facing the pilots as photographers buzzed about like bees. After the formal photographs, they snapped pictures of the pilots in groups and as individuals. They gathered Tom Lanphier, Besby Holmes, and Rex Barber, who were hardly speaking to each other, together for a single group shot. The three forced a bit of congeniality. Crowds of soldiers and marines watched the spectacle unfold, and news reporters mingled freely among the pilots, planners, and headquarters types to find out what happened. No one had said a word about not talking about the flight, and the story was told over and over. It would be up to the censors to decide what, if any, information could be published or broadcast. Only the most general sort of information—with no specific names or mention of the code or the fact that Yamamoto was the target—would be allowed in any news story. The reporters and photographers were there to gather history, not report the news.

Lanphier would remember the astonishing session as proof that everyone on Guadalcanal knew where they had gone and what they had done.

That same day, papers were drawn up by the Marine Air Wing to bestow awards on the U.S. Army pilots. Congressional Medals of Honor, the nation's highest decoration for bravery, were recommended for Major John Mitchell, Captain Tom Lanphier, and First Lieutenants Rex Barber and Besby Holmes. Everyone else on the flight was to get the coveted Navy Cross.

Bougainville

The small group of Japanese soldiers who found the wreckage did not know who had been aboard the plane. All they had been told was that some top naval brass were involved, and the lieutenant in charge searched for identification on the victims, some of whom were burned so badly that only their names, written on ink on their boots, indicated who they had been.

He had found one body in a condition quite different from the others. It was still strapped into an airplane seat that was beside a tree just beyond the burned area outside of the plane. The dead man's back was toward the wreckage, and his head was tilted forward, as if he were taking a nap. He seemed vaguely familiar to the lieutenant who went through his pockets and checked for mortal wounds.

There was a small hole in the lower jaw, with the exit at his temple. Another small hole penetrated the left shoulder blade, went upward and to the right, but did not come out.

Honor ribbons blossomed on the chest of the green uniform, and the right hand rested upon a long sword, which was grasped by the left hand. Two fingers of the left glove were tied back, and the startled lieutenant recognized the famous disfiguring characteristic and the closely cropped hair. For confirmation, a diary taken from a breast pocket contained the name. This was the body of Admiral Yamamoto.

The lieutenant had his men build a temporary shelter into which they moved the bodies, covered them with banyan leaves, and, as a gesture of respect, placed cups of water beside them. They recovered all ten bodies, including the corpses from inside the plane that had been horribly burned.

An older man in an unbuttoned white uniform, Chief Fleet Surgeon Rokuro Takata, had been found on his back, arms and legs wide apart, only three feet from Yamamoto, with no visible injuries. Warrant Officer Takeo Kotani, the pilot, was discovered about five hundred meters from the plane. Maggots had not yet invaded the body of Yamamoto, a remarkable development for a corpse that had been exposed in the hot and humid jungle.

The soldiers left the bodies in the shelter and were trekking back toward their base at the village of Aku, until they bumped into the naval landing unit search party. They made camp together and would return to the crash site in the morning. The third group of searchers, led by the frantic Watanabe, Yamamoto's friend, remained stymied by the jungle, which seemed to be eating them alive. As the Combined Fleet's senior staff officer, Watanabe was used to clean uniforms, comfortable cabins, and good food, not jungle filth and mosquitoes the size of birds. He was already coming down with the early symptoms of dengue fever.

The following day, April 20, the Sasebo Sixth Special Landing Force, guided by the soldiers, arrived at the scene.

After conducting their own examination, the naval unit made a sketch that showed the plane had broken apart just forward of the "red ball" insignia painted near the midway point of the fuselage. The front section had been badly burned, and both engines were facing the rear, still attached to the wings, as if they had cartwheeled. It contrasted with a sketch made by the army that showed both engines facing forward, and almost a clean break in the fuselage. Neither sketch indicated that the wing had broken off.

In 1972 and again in 1977, Dr. Charles Darby of New Zealand visited and photographed the wreckage. His pictures showed the left wing had been torn off by impact with the trees and had come to rest some distance behind the plane. The leading edge of the right wing was damaged from clipping the top of a tree and lay immediately adjacent to the fuselage. Both engines were thrown forward, the propeller blades bent and broken by impact, but neither was consumed by the fire that destroyed the forward section of the fuselage. The discrepancies in the descriptions of how the plane came down would become important in later debates.

The naval unit loaded the victims onto stretchers and began the long walk out of the jungle, intercepting Watanabe's approaching group in the early afternoon, as a fierce sun beat down. Watanabe identified Yamamoto and issued stern orders that no one would talk about what they had found.

A top secret message, "Ko Report No. 4," was flashed to higher headquarters.

NONE ALIVE ABOARD PLANE A. CORPSES ARE BEING PICKED UP.

It was official. Yamamoto was dead, but few people actually knew it. Neither the Combined Fleet nor the army was to be informed until Tokyo decided what to do next. Watanabe awaited anxiously, all the while growing more ill.

So great was the loss of the revered military leader that everyone was stunned and, it seems, momentarily paralyzed. A new commander in chief for the Combined Fleet had to be named as quickly as possible, and the name of Admiral Mineichi Koga, currently the commander of the Second Fleet, was put into consideration. But the news of Yamamoto's demise was of such great import that even Koga was not to be told immediately of the incident. For the moment, the mighty Combined Fleet was in the hands of a staff officer, Watanabe, who was not even an admiral, and about to keel over from fever.

New Caledonia

Some fifty new P-38s were being prepared at the big air base that had been created on the west coast of New Caledonia at Oua Tom (pronounced "wah tom"), and the blue sky was filled with Lightnings running practice flights over the water. It was the rear base for the 339th Fighter Squadron and a rest area for those who had been serving on Guadalcanal. The pilots rotated after twenty-five combat missions, and the enlisted men swapped places every three months.

The strength of the United States was well demonstrated at that one busy base, and now there were many like it in a chain stretching all the way back to the mainland. Lockheed was turning out so many P-38s that there wasn't enough room for them all inside the hangars in Burbank, California, and final assembly was being done outdoors. Many of the fresh generation of pilots just coming over were already experienced fliers who had had long love affairs with airplanes even before they got into the army's Civilian Pilot Training Program. The army had so many candidates in the pipeline that many were being diverted into other specialities, such as gunnery or navigation.

At Oua Tom, the new pilots came into the 339th already knowing how to fly other types of fighters, and were expected to figure out the P-38 in a sink-or-swim method. George Chandler, a gentle Kansas boy who would soon become a fighter ace, recalled, "A guy would jump on the wing and say, 'Now here's how you start the sonofabitch.' He helped you get the engines running, then slid off the wing, and off you went. It was a little intimidating."

But as talented as the new pilots might be, they had stars in their eyes when a C-47 Gooneybird waddled down to land on Oua Tom. The hatch opened and John Mitchell, Tom Lanphier, and Rex Barber climbed out. *The guys who bagged Yamamoto!* The successful ambush was as widely known on New Caledonia as on Guadalcanal, for men had rotated in and out every day. "Everybody was talking about it," Chandler said. "It was common knowledge."

Mitchell was soon plunged into a sea of paperwork as he prepared to hand over the squadron to a new commander. Lanphier and Barber, however, were just dropping by to get scrubbed up and checked out by doctors before heading down to New Zealand on a well-deserved rest leave. At Oua Tom, they were treated like celebrities, and any bitterness between them vanished. Getting off the Canal was enough to lift anyone's spirits.

To pilots who had never fired their guns in combat, these guys were heroes. Lanphier and Barber, with nothing to kill but time, enjoyed sharing their knowledge of how to fight the Japanese. Better to learn from the veterans than learn the hard way, and since they were all attached to the same squadron, friends were made quickly.

Later, after arriving in New Zealand, the two star pilots were on an emerald golf course with Brigadier General Dean C. "Doc" Strother, the respected operations officer of the XIII Fighter Command on a bright afternoon. They spoke about the mission, and Barber asked if enough information had been gathered to send a report to headquarters. Lanphier replied that it had been taken care of: He had written not only the official report, but also the recommendations for the Medals of Honor. Barber and Strother both remembered his words.

That was not the biggest surprise of the day. A stranger walked up and introduced himself as J. Norman Lodge of the Associated Press. "Sarge" Lodge was the widely known senior AP correspondent in the Pacific, and had close contacts within Admiral Halsey's headquarters.

The reporter had caught a flight from New Caledonia down to Auckland on May 1 specifically in search of more information about the Yamamoto mission, obviously knowing exactly where to look and whom to question. When he met the three military officers for drinks after their round of golf, Lodge said he was already aware of most of the details of the death of the admiral and asked them to clarify and verify some points.

Neither pilot was hesitant about talking to the newsman. After all, everybody seemed to know what had happened. Headquarters had orchestrated the media frenzy, the reporter had been told where to find them, and Lodge was barred by censorship rules from writing anything specific about the mission. Besides, a general was sitting at the table with them. Moreover, Strother took the precaution of refusing to grant Lodge permission to publish the information. "This mission is not a story," he said. With such safeguards in place and the belief there was no secret to protect anyway, they felt safe in telling the newsman what happened.

On May 11, Lodge wrote the story anyway.

Bougainville

A bullet did not kill Admiral Yamamoto. His mortal wounds probably were the result of flying shrapnel or bullet fragments. The P-38 machine guns were firing .50-caliber bullets, and they would not have made nice little holes if they had hit him. The powder-filled cartridges are almost six inches long and as round as a man's thumb, and the heads of the bullets are thick and pointed, jacketed in brass and about two inches long. Fifty-caliber bullets do not wound people so much as blow them apart, and cannon fire would have done even worse damage.

In later years, there would be speculation that Chief Fleet Surgeon Takata had lived long enough to help arrange Yamamoto in the airplane seat, perhaps in an attempt to keep the admiral's dignity intact even after death. No one will ever know for sure, but a doctor who performed the autopsy believed the grievous head wound would have killed the admiral instantly. The fact that Yamamoto's watch stopped when the plane hit the ground at 7:45 indicated the violence of the impact, which also could have been instantly fatal.

The bodies were hauled to the base at Buin on April 20 and placed in wooden coffins.

While preparations were being made that evening for cremation, Japanese radio listening posts that monitored commercial American stations picked up a routine broadcast of war news from San Francisco. The announcer read an item that U.S. army fighters had engaged Japanese planes in the northern Solomon Islands and shot down two bombers and two fighters. One American was downed.

Individual cremations were carried out on April 21, with Yamamoto's body kept separate from the others. Watanabe later climbed into the earthen pit and picked up bone fragments with a pair of chopsticks. Ashes and bone were placed in a container lined with papaya leaves, and two papaya trees were planted on the spot where Yamamoto was cremated.

The devastated and very ill Watanabe took the remains back to Rabaul, where a small, private wake was held. Then his box of ashes was flown back to Truk, taken aboard the new flagship *Musashi* and reverently placed in the cabin of the commander in chief. That done, Watanabe allowed himself to collapse.

The same day, Tokyo dispatched a coded message to the commanders of the Combined Fleet, the Southeastern Area Fleet, the Southwestern Area Fleet, and the Second, Third, Fourth, Fifth, Sixth, and Eighth Fleets.

KOGA APPOINTED BY HIS MAJESTY C-IN-C, COMBINED FLEET ON 21 APRIL. FURTHER, THIS MATTER IS BEING KEPT TOP SECRET EVEN WITHIN NAVY BESIDE COMBINED FLEET TO SAY NOTHING OF OUTSIDE THE NAVY UNTIL SPECIAL FURTHER ORDERS.

Admiral Mineichi Koga, the conservative, logical, capable commander of the Second Fleet, reluctantly assumed the reins of the Combined Fleet. "There was only one Yamamoto and no one can replace him," Koga observed.

Koga's command of the Combined Fleet was brief. He possessed neither the political power nor the vision of Yamamoto, but he was a thorough believer in the doctrine of fighting a decisive battle with the enemy, although he had inherited a naval war he could not win. He faced an aroused and angry U.S. Navy that had survived all of Yamamoto's onslaughts and was growing to a strength never before seen on the world's oceans. Koga would die in March 1944 when the plane he was on disappeared in a storm.

Four days after Sarge Lodge filed his story from New Zealand about the shoot-down, the *Musashi* pulled out of Truk to make a somber two-week voyage to Japan, taking the remains of Isoroku Yamamoto home.

After the recovery of the body and the transition of command, the Japanese officials still had a serious problem. The loss of Admiral Yamamoto was going to be a bitter pill, and the news of his death would have to be handled carefully, for it threatened the morale of the entire country. The War Cabinet did not want panic at home, for it needed all of the support it could get. The propaganda of eternal victories was ringing hollow. They decided to keep the death of Japan's most famous admiral a secret from the general population.

28

Traitors

New Caledonia

Tom Lanphier's version of events carried the day, according to the weekly summary prepared for Admirals Halsey, Nimitz, and King on April 24 by Admiral Aubrey Fitch, the commander of air operations for the entire South Pacific:

THIS IS ULTRA.

HIGHLIGHTS OF REPORT MAILED ON BUIN ACTION OF 18TH. 12 P-38S WERE COVER FOR 4 P-38S WHICH ALL ATTACKING. 33 MILES NORTHWEST KAHILI AIRFIELD SIGHTED 2 BOMBERS TOGETHER AT 4600 FEET. 6 ZEROS 1,500-2,000 FEET ABOVE SLIGHTLY TO REAR. BOMBERS PARTED AND DIVED WHILE ZEROS STRUCK AT P-38S. 1 ENEMY BOMBER WAS ATTACKED JUST ABOVE TREE TOPS, WING FLEW OFF AND BOMBER WENT FLAMING TO EARTH. SECOND BOMBER QUOTE TAIL SECTION FLEW OFF BOMBER, TURNED ON ITS BACK AND PLUMMETED TO EARTH. A THIRD BOMBER ENCOUNTERED WHEN P-38S WITHDRAWING EXPLODED IN AIR.

The summary did not mention Lanphier by name, but by placing his claim of victory first, it tacitly accepted that he shot down the lead bomber. Even if American code breakers had figured out which plane

Yamamoto was on, the implication was that Lanphier had shot down the admiral because he was credited with the first bomber. It also maintained the fiction that three bombers had been destroyed.

Halsey sent the basic combat report from Guadalcanal along to Nimitz at Pearl Harbor, who passed it up the chain of command to Admiral King in Washington. Nimitz then sent a sharp reminder back to Halsey. The operation was on such "a particularly high plane of security" that "no publicity of any kind should be given this action," Nimitz stated. Nevertheless, he recommended appropriate awards for the pilots.

The awards, when they finally came, were much less than expected, and they carried a high price in bitter controversy. John Mitchell was about to learn the hard lesson that had already been imparted to the likes of Joe Rochefort and D. D. Brannon: When generals and admirals get angry, they can also get irrational and unreasonable. The other lesson was the old military axiom that, in the rank-caste system, "Shit flows downhill."

Truk

When Yamamoto's safe was emptied aboard the *Musashi*, a poem was discovered that he had written some six months earlier, just as the bloody battle for Guadalcanal was taking shape. It was a grim and introspective piece that showed the admiral was prepared to expend his own blood, and that of his nation, against the Americans. As it appears in Agawa's biography, *The Reluctant Admiral,* the poem reads:

> Since the war began, tens of thousands of officers and men of matchless loyalty and courage have done battle at the risk of their lives, and have died to become guardian gods of our land.
>
> Ah, how can I ever enter the imperial presence again? With what words can I possibly report to the parents and brothers of my dead comrades?
>
> The body is frail, yet with a firm mind with unshakable resolve I will drive deep into the enemy's positions and let him see the blood of a Japanese man.

Wait but a while, young men!—one last battle, fought gallantly to the death, and I will be joining you!

New Caledonia

U.S. Navy censors could not believe the story submitted by Sarge Lodge of the Associated Press. It not only described a mission that was supposed to be top secret, but there were startling similarities between the reporter's story and the official mission report, which few people had even seen. The story, primarily attributed to Lanphier, mirrored the language of the classified document. It was possible that Lodge obtained a copy of the mission report, but the quotes were from Lanphier, who never denied the interview. The censors stopped Lodge's story in its tracks, but although it was never printed, it created an uproar.

At the time, news stories cleared by the censors would be sent by commercial telegraph across the Pacific, and the charges, levied on a word basis, were costly. To save money, the wire services routinely used codebooks of their own to cut down on the number of words. Editors in the United States would rewrite the transmission in clear English. But even in journalistic shorthand, the story submitted by Lodge and the Mission Report seemed to come from the same mouth.

MISSION REPORT	AP STORY
"flying all the way at an altitude of 10 to 30 feet above the water . . ."	"Quote we flew entire distance about ten to thirty feet above water unquote Lanphier said."
"he had reached 6,000 feet, so he nosed over, and went down to the treetops."	"reaching 6000 feet eye [sic] nosed over and caught bomber at treetop height."
"a wing flew off and the plane went flaming to earth."	"wing bomber flew off burst into flames fell into trees"
"He hedgehopped over the tree tops and made desperate	"so hedgehopped over trees kicking rudders slipping skidding with

MISSION REPORT (*contd.*)	AP STORY (*contd.*)
maneuvers to escape. He kicked rudders, slipped and skidded, tracers flying past his plane."	tracers flying all angles past my plane."
"he finally outran them. In all this action he had received two 7.7's in his horizontal stabilizer."	"eye [*sic*] finally outran them but caught two seven point seven slugs in horizontal stabilizer."

Admiral Nimitz had ordered Admiral Halsey to make absolutely certain that no publicity was given to the mission, but his warning had come much too late.

The Americans had entered the mission almost with a jocular attitude, including the radio order from Halsey's headquarters of "Talleyho! Let's get the bastard." Then the official exchange of information on April 18 contained references to a lucky day, a bagged bird that might be a peacock. Halsey might be able to bottle up this singular report from the Associated Press correspondent, but he could do nothing about the numerous violations of secrecy that had shepherded the entire mission.

The Lodge story dripped with clues that the Japanese code had been broken. It even revealed that the Americans had been tracking Yamamoto's movements for five days!

It had only begun to dawn on many of those involved that risking the code to bag Yamamoto might have been very unwise. If the Japanese discovered the truth, the feat might backfire and extend the war for months. British behavior in a similar situation offered a stark contrast. Code breakers in England learned in advance that the Germans planned to bomb Coventry in November 1940, but Winston Churchill did not warn the population to flee. He sacrificed an entire city to prevent Berlin from learning that their codes had been broken.

Halsey forwarded the story, which was off limits to civilians, on to fleet headquarters in Pearl Harbor, where Nimitz was catching heat from King over the incident. Nimitz, abnegating his promise to take responsibility for the decision to attack, brusquely landed on his favorite fighting admiral, Bill Halsey.

"Secure and seal" the story in a safe, Nimitz ordered: Get all copies and all notes, and warn Lodge and anyone else knowing about the mission to "maintain complete silence." Halsey was not urged, but *told*, to personally supervise an investigation and discipline those responsible for the security breach. "This shows widespread and flagrant disregard of security ultra information," Nimitz said.

Halsey was used to hurrahs, not stern rebukes, and suddenly he found himself on an unsteady deck. There was no way he was going to be blamed for this breach of security, although messages from his headquarters had contributed to the problem.

The top admirals in the Pacific went looking for scapegoats.

Investigators fanned out everywhere. There was still a war going on, but vital manpower was assigned and hours expended trying to get to the bottom of the secrecy breach.

Every one of the seventy-six pilots who had been on the island at the time, whether or not they flew the mission, was to be questioned, although some made themselves hard to find. One of those was marine pilot Greg "Pappy" Boyington of the famed Black Sheep Squadron, who spent part of his rest leave in Australia dodging U.S. Naval Intelligence types. They "kept looking us up and asking all natures of questions [about the Yamamoto mission]. Everyone from Guadalcanal was suspected," said Boyington. The forty men who had been in on the mission briefing were questioned in detail. Officers with stars on their shoulders and mechanics with stripes on their sleeves were interviewed. Doc Strother, who had been present at the golf course interview and actually warned the reporter not to write a story, submitted a brief, official statement, denying any wrongdoing. On the home front, the FBI got involved.

Halsey, however, did not wait for the results of the investigation. He had already decided on the culprits. He summoned the golfing threesome Strother, Lanphier, and Barber to his office in New Caledonia. On an oak table lay the recommendations for the Medals of Honor, which contained stirring phrases like "high courage," "beyond the call of duty," and "superlative gallantry and intrepidity in action" and calling the mission a "masterpiece."

The recommendations had come from Mitscher, on Guadalcanal, who had personally overseen the complex operation. To the fulminating

Halsey, the paper was worthless garbage. He did not even return the salutes of the three men when they entered his office, but just stared so hard that the men almost quaked.

He unleashed a tirade of profanity that was possibly unparalleled in even Halsey's ballistic repertoire. "He accused us of everything he could think of, from being traitors to our country to being so stupid that we had no right to wear the American uniform," Barber said. The admiral paced about with short, jerky strides, yelling and waving his fists the whole time.

"He said we were horrible examples of pilots of the army air force, that we should be court-martialed, reduced to privates, and jailed for talking to Lodge about the Yamamoto mission." It had been a while since anyone had spoken like that to Doc Strother, a one-star general.

Then Halsey fanned through the recommendations for the nation's highest award for gallantry. "As far as I'm concerned, none of you deserve even the Air Medal for what you did! You ought to face a court-martial, but because of the importance of the mission, I'm reducing these citations to the Navy Cross."

He dismissed them abruptly, again not returning the salutes, and the three officers slunk out of the room. "We had been tried and judged guilty," Barber said.

Halsey's diatribe dishonored the sacrifice of Ray Hine and undeservingly besmirched the reputation of John Mitchell, who had never spoken to any unauthorized person about the mission, and wasn't even in New Zealand when Lodge found the pilots. The admiral's decision, however, would remain unchanged.

Tokyo

Japan, a land of earthquakes, was shaken to its very foundations at three o'clock in the afternoon on May 21 when a radio announcer, choked with emotion, read a brief communiqué from the Imperial Headquarters: "In April of this year, Admiral Yamamoto Isoroku, commander in chief of the combined fleet, met a gallant death on board his plane in an encounter with the enemy in the course of directing overall operations at the front line."

The *Musashi* had completed its solemn voyage to Japan that day, the big battleship acting as a giant seagoing hearse. It anchored in Tokyo Bay, and two days later the ship's company stood at attention along the rail when the ashes were transferred to a smaller ship and taken ashore at the port of Yokosuka.

The admiral's family had been informed of his death before the battleship arrived, but the love of his life, the geisha Chiyoko, was off watching a sumo tournament at the time and did not get the news until later. She is said to have almost fainted when the telephone call came through.

The faithful Watanabe personally carried the white box aboard a special train into Tokyo, escorted by Yamamoto's eldest son, Yoshimasa, a high school student. The slow train took the admiral's ashes to Tokyo, where members of the royal family, military leaders, and other members of the Yamamoto family were waiting. Just as he had once paraded grandly from the station to the palace, his remains now were accompanied past the palace to the Navy Club in Shiba and placed on an altar.

There was a nationwide outpouring of grief, and the emperor bestowed honor after honor upon Yamamoto. He was promoted to the rank of fleet admiral and given the Grand Order of the Chrysanthemum, First Class, the highest military honor in Japan. He was to be interred in a state funeral, a recognition of service so exalted that only eleven other Japanese—including Yamamoto's own hero, Admiral Heihachiro Togo—had ever received one. It would cost $23,000 and be planned by a special government committee.

But the details of his death remained murky, and rumors spread that Yamamoto had committed suicide. The Domei News Agency chose this time to broadcast a report honoring the death of a naval captain who had taken his own life after his ship was sunk. The news agency said, "The same spirit is demonstrated again by the death in action of Fleet Admiral Isoroku Yamamoto. Yamamoto told his family when he left for the front: 'Do not consider me your father anymore, for I have given my body and soul to the country. It will be my supreme glory to die for my country.'"

Actually, his wife and children had spent precious little time with him. His widow, Reiko, had remained deep in the shadows of Yamamoto's fame for years, often ignored by or ignoring her husband, but she was now called upon to revere and uphold his memory. And the children were virtual strangers to the hero; he had seldom been home. "We barely know anything about father," Yoshimasa said, summing up the feelings of his sisters Sumiko, in girls' high school, and Masako, in girls' science college, and fifth-grader Tadao.

Thousands of common people filed past the special altar at the Navy Club. Unnoticed in the throng was Chiyoko, who could not intrude into the private mourning of the true family. Watanabe paid a quiet visit to her home in Kamiya-cho to commiserate in her grief.

In the United States, that afternoon of May 21 was a time of good news. The White House press corps asked President Roosevelt to comment on the Tokyo radio report that Admiral Yamamoto had been killed. The president had been thoroughly briefed, but panned in mock surprise, "Is he dead? Gosh!" The reporters broke into laughter, and Roosevelt joined in. His comment carefully sidestepped any mention of the codes being involved.

The extent of Roosevelt's knowledge about the Yamamoto mission before it was authorized has never been determined. Washington knew about the plans, and it is likely that Navy Secretary Knox was fully informed, but FDR was at the time making a goodwill train trip to Monterrey, Mexico, the first visit ever to that country by a sitting American president. In that era before instant and secure communications became routine, when the president was on the road, he received most important and secret business by special courier from Washington. A historian later turned up a message that was received during the train's trip back to Warm Springs, Georgia, where the president enjoyed soaking his crippled legs in hot, medicinal pools of water. That information acknowledged that two Betty bombers had been shot down over Bougainville the previous day. FDR would have known that Yamamoto was dead for a month before pretending to be surprised by the question.

No tears were shed in America for Yamamoto, for, as the *New York Times* would state, "He was regarded as perhaps the boldest, most imaginative and—where the United States was concerned—the most unscrupulous of the Japanese offensive fighters. He hated the United States."

Whether or not that last sentence was true, the United States hated him. From Maine to California, Americans were glad he was dead. The fact that he was shot down by American pilots was considered payback for Pearl Harbor.

New Caledonia

Halsey's blood pressure fell momentarily on May 30, when an official report from Mitscher on Guadalcanal informed him that no information about the source of the original secret message had been disclosed at the pilots' briefings, although the Yamamoto name had been mentioned to stress the importance of the mission.

Thereafter, Mitscher said, the only remark even distantly related to mentioning Yamamoto in the open took place when Lanphier spoke on his airplane radio that "that son of a bitch won't be dictating peace in the White House."

The report from Guadalcanal flatly stated that no evidence was discovered "to indicate it was passed to newspapermen directly or indirectly." Nothing was said about the media circus that was organized on Guadalcanal right after the mission.

The day after the official report was filed, *Time* magazine hit the stands in the United States. It included a story about the death of Yamamoto and, a few pages later, a detailed story about a fighter mission, accompanied by a U.S. Army Air Forces photograph of a shirtless, smiling Tom Lanphier.

The prominent article about the admiral was accompanied by an artist's sketch that depicted Yamamoto looking like a furious monkey in a uniform awash with decorations. "When the name of the man who killed Admiral Yamamoto is released, the U.S. will have a new hero," it continued. "The only better news would be a bullet through Hitler."

In case a reader still missed the point, the story appeared above a photo of the battleship *Oklahoma* being raised from the harbor muck in Hawaii.

The censor had cleared that information for use, and it had approved the information included in a second story in the same issue. Combined, the two items neatly sidestepped the entire censorship exercise, and all but said Tom Lanphier killed Yamamoto.

The other story was headlined "Heroes" and described a fighter plane mission that only slightly veiled that it was about the Yamamoto mission. The daring attack was led by "the squadron commander, lean, black-eyed Captain Thomas G. Lanphier." It reported that three Japanese bombers were shot down, one by Lanphier and two by Rex Barber. Besby Holmes, Ray Hine, and John Mitchell were not mentioned. "The squadron whisked back to its Solomons base, wondered if it had nailed some Jap bigwig in the bombers."

It further reported that Lanphier's brother Charles was flying with the marines on Guadalcanal and that their father was a West Pointer and World War I pilot who currently was on duty with the General Staff in Washington.

If the Japanese were truly suspicious about the safety of their code, all they had to do now was buy a copy of *Time* magazine. But they didn't.

29

The Perfect Hero

He was thus crowned. Tom Lanphier, the brilliant pilot with seventy missions and 175 combat hours, an ace in the air and a pal to the guys in the squadron, had shot down Admiral Yamamoto. Tom Lanphier, the politically ambitious, media-friendly, and well-connected son of a ranking officer on the general staff, had shot down Admiral Yamamoto. Tom Lanphier, the killer flight leader who broke away from the chase, violated radio silence, stood in a jeep to cheer his self-proclaimed victory, wrote the after-action report, and talked openly to a reporter about the secret mission, had shot down Admiral Yamamoto.

He was the perfect hero, handsome and suave and undoubtedly brave, with influential family friends reaching from Australia to Washington. When General Douglas MacArthur read reports that Tom Lanphier had brought down the admiral's bomber, he thought it meant that Tom Lanphier Sr. had somehow gotten back into the shooting war. "He's much too old to be doing that sort of thing," the general mused.

Lanphier junior had finally matched, and even surpassed, his father's military exploits. "The circle had closed, and I was carrying on," he wrote in his life story.

According to Lanphier, the first he knew of being officially credited with the shootdown of the lead bomber was when Admiral Halsey said so, but he could not cite the source of the admiral's conclusion. Most likely it came from the combat report. Lanphier said Halsey "apparently" learned from later radio intercepts that Yamamoto was on the lead plane, and therefore, since Lanphier had shot down that plane, Lanphier must have shot down Yamamoto. The logic was good enough for the army air force.

"It *had* to be Tom," a Guadalcanal pilot remarked. "It could not be just any hero, it had to be this particular hero."

Everybody always knew Tom Lanphier was going places, and credit for the Yamamoto kill would provide fuel for his military and future civilian careers, while simultaneously giving the air force a hero who was a member of its inner circles. His father was a "ring-knocker" from the U.S. Military Academy and therefore part of what was called the WPPA (West Point Protective Assocation). It was to be a mutually supportive relationship.

The Aleutian Islands

Part of Yamamoto's plan to capture Midway the previous year had included a diversionary attack on the Aleutians, an icy necklace of islands that reaches from the Alaskan mainland toward the Soviet Union's Kamchatka Peninsula more than a thousand miles away. The Americans refused the bait and ravaged Yamamoto's carrier force at Midway, but the Japanese captured two of the westernmost islands of the chain, Attu and Kiska.

In May 1943, the time had come for the United States to take them back, and an invasion force led by three battleships launched the fight near the top of the world with tundra-shaking bombardments. Far from the heat of the South Pacific, the frozen soldiers of Attu killed each other in great numbers during more than two weeks of hand-to-hand fighting. Preferring suicide charges to surrender, the Japanese force of twenty-five hundred men was virtually wiped out, and the Americans lost a thousand dead.

Kiska was bypassed and had to wait several months to be invaded. When American and Canadian troops finally came ashore, the place was empty.

When word of Attu's plight reached Admiral Mineichi Koga, the new commander in chief of the Combined Fleet sent his ships pounding north to the rescue, but he pulled them back when it became clear that his main naval forces should not abandon the South Pacific. A frozen island like Attu was not worth the effort.

Admiral Koga had more pressing matters. Not only were the Aleutians destined to fall, with or without his help, but Americans were bombing the island of Tarawa in the Gilberts, and Nauru, another island some four hundred miles to the west. U.S. Marines had landed on a tiny place called Funafuti in the Ellice group, some twelve hundred miles east of Guadalcanal. The Solomons and New Guinea were still active battle areas, and Rabaul itself was being threatened. Koga could not run out to defend every single island in the Pacific Ocean, and he knew things were only going to get worse.

"Yamamoto died at exactly the right time," he told an aide.

Guadalcanal

The changes brought by the demise of Yamamoto were clearly visible on the Canal. Things had quieted so much that the 339th Fighter Squadron, after its historic mission, had no more encounters at all with Japanese planes for the rest of April and all of May.

Mitchell handed the squadron over to a new commander on May 21, and Lanphier and several other pilots were officially transferred into the 339th from the 70th Fighter Squadron. These were just paperwork changes to prepare for the future, when the squadron would take part in the attacks on the Northern Solomons.

It was time for the men of the Yamamoto mission to move on. Following the eruption by Halsey aboard his flagship in New Caledonia, the other mission pilots had been bawled out by Lieutenant General Millard F. Harmon, the commander of the 13th Air Force. It was a half-hearted scolding, for Harmon personally considered the flight to have been a masterpiece and thought the navy was overreacting, trying to close the bureaucratic barn door long after the secrecy horse had escaped. He was displeased that Halsey knocked down the recommended decorations.

Harmon, convinced that the pilots had obeyed the briefing orders not to disclose any secret information, asked them what they wanted.

After serving in the Pacific for the past fifteen to seventeen months, with a lot of combat time, the answer was easy. They didn't really care about medals. Doug Canning, with three tours and sixty-five combat missions on Guadalcanal, spoke for most of them: "We told him we wanted to go home." The general slapped the table and said they were on their way, and when they arrived on American soil, they would be promoted one grade in rank. Just keep your mouths shut, he warned, or you will be court-martialed.

Meanwhile, reports were coming into New Caledonia from the big investigation, and they all said the same thing: The mission to ambush Yamamoto "was common gossip" on Guadalcanal, and with hundreds of men rotating on and off the island, it would have been impossible to keep it bottled up. "The mission in question was discussed quite openly," stated Major General Nathan F. Twining. Even as the final reports were being gathered, Army General Alexander "Sandy" Patch, just back in the United States from Guadalcanal, was discussing the mission before the Washington Press Club.

The only change in procedures came when Admiral Fitch also acknowledged the action had become "generally known throughout the greater part of the South Pacific area." His solution was to blame the press. An order was sent out that military press relations officers should henceforth accompany news reporters and provide "strict supervision" of their movements. That left the military authorities with the comfortable idea that the press was the villain in the episode, and not themselves.

The Japanese also gave up chasing the possibility of a code break. As the travel itinerary of Yamamoto had been steadily forwarded to ever smaller units in the outlying areas, it had been changed into codes that were easier to read. By the time all of the Japanese officers who needed to see the information had received it, Allied radio interception stations in Australia were almost able to read it without consulting their codebooks, and their ideas verified what Washington and Pearl Harbor had pieced together.

The flaw was not within the ciphers, but in the arrogant and in-credibly naïve Japanese belief that Western minds could not possibly understand the intricacies of their complex language, particularly when it was wrapped in dense codes. Despite all of the clues, hubris had over-taken them, and they were unwilling to accept the logical truth that their code was worthless. That allowed the U.S. fleet radio units to suc-cessfully continue eavesdropping and gathering vital strategic infor-mation. They gathered such detailed data on Japanese ship movements that American submarines would eventually be dispatched daily to precise locations, there to lie in wait until a specific enemy ship showed up at an exact time and be blown out of the water.

Tokyo

On June 5, the same day and the same month that Admiral Togo had been buried nine years earlier, Fleet Admiral Yamamoto's remains were honored in an elaborate state funeral.

At the Navy Club, the ashes were divided into two urns and placed in a coffin draped in white, which sailors carried to a black gun car-riage just behind a navy band that led the funeral cortege. Later, a spe-cial dirge, "The Funeral March for Fallen Japanese," would be written in his honor, but for this parade the band played Chopin.

Reiko, his widow, attended, wearing full and elaborate court dress, but the path to the cemetery was laid out so as to pass the home of Chiyoko, his mistress. To the Japanese, that did not seem odd at all.

A throng estimated as high as three million people lined the march route to Hibiya Park, where the official ceremony was held. Prime Minister Tojo and representatives of the royal family led approximately fifteen hundred mourners, and Italy's dictator Mussolini had his em-bassy send roses. Commander Watanabe reverently carried the new sword that had been presented by the emperor to denote Yamamoto's final rank. One of the urns, and the sword, were placed upon an altar with black-and-white striped curtains, riflemen fired a military salute, and for the rest of the week, hundreds of thousands of ordinary Japan-ese citizens came to pay their respects. Later, that urn was moved and interred beside that of Admiral Togo in the Tama Cemetery.

The second urn was returned to Yamamoto's hometown of Nagaoka, near the Sea of Japan. In a cemetery at a Buddhist temple, it was buried beside the man who had adopted him and given Yamamoto his famous name. The admiral's austere gravestone, which cost only seventy sen, was an inch shorter than that of his adoptive father.

The United States

The American pilots of the Yamamoto mission returned home in single reassignments. The war wasn't over, but scuttlebutt was that they would never be allowed to fly against the Japanese again, for what they knew about the mission was too important. That was incorrect, for many continued to fly on Guadalcanal, and others would fight the Japanese elsewhere.

One of the Dirty Dozen pilots, Roger Ames, flew twenty-one more missions out of Cactus before rotating back to the United States. While having a meal in San Francisco, a waitress told him about the Yamamoto mission.

Besby Holmes remained the wild card. He had been in the killer flight, but his part in the mission was virtually ignored from the very start. Despite being awarded credit for aerial victories, Holmes believed he had intentionally been pushed into the background, and being left out grated on him. He had plenty of criticism for both Tom Lanphier and Rex Barber, but without a forum, he was bound by the demands of secrecy. There was nothing he could do but seethe.

Rex Barber spent a thirty-day rest leave at his home in Culver, Oregon, which seemed like another planet after the long months in the Pacific. He quietly fit back into the farming community, for it would have been unseemly to do otherwise. People, even heroes, did not take on airs around Culver. When the month was up, he put his uniform on again and went across the country to Westover Field in Massachusetts, where he was to train new pilots how to bomb and shoot.

Several veteran pilots from Cactus, including a few from the Yamamoto mission, were also at Westover and quickly determined that the lessons being taught to the new guys would never stand up in combat. The squadron commander refused to listen. "We got a little disgusted," Barber said, and the combat veterans started looking for other ways to spend their time.

A sergeant walked into their hangar one day carrying something that looked like a coil of rope and asked what it was. Barber and another guy from Guadalcanal recognized the roll of explosive primer cord and decided to help get rid of it. They stretched it out in a shallow trench between two hangars, attached a blasting cap and set it off with a ferocious detonation that blew out all of the hangar windows and almost ripped their clothes off. "They were pretty mad about that," Barber said. The apoplectic squadron commander considered standing Barber up for a court martial.

A few days later, an officer arrived, carrying an air force headquarters directive to equip and staff something called the Chinese Air Wing. He could take any pilot he wanted, from any squadron, for an assignment training Chinese pilots. All of the Guadalcanal guys volunteered on the spot. Combat was better than Westover, and the squadron commander was delighted at the opportunity to rid himself of the veterans. "Where's the paper? I'll sign these boys out of here as fast as I can," he said.

Barber was soon on a train to Norfolk, Virginia, then aboard a boat to North Africa, with orders that took him all the way to Karachi, which was then part of British India, but is now in Pakistan. He was back in the war, but far from the centers of power.

While he was gone, history would be shaped without him.

As the first day of June 1943 dawned sunny in California, John Mitchell and Tom Lanphier landed back at Hamilton Field outside of San Francisco, their starting point in World War II. A telephone call from Hap Arnold in Washington was awaiting Lanphier. Ordinarily, junior officers tended to be wary when in contact with Arnold, but Lanphier was no ordinary officer. The general was an old friend and called him "Tommy."

Arnold ordered him back to Washington as soon as possible. In his autobiography, Lanphier remembered the top man in the air force saying that Lanphier had Admiral King and other members of the navy brass "frothing at the mouth" because of his "blabbering" about the Yamamoto flight. According to Lanphier's account of the conversation, Arnold told him that Halsey had not yet admitted to King that the Yamamoto mission had been one of the worst-kept secrets of the war.

Lanphier was the one pilot who was rightly in hot water, but he had a four-star angel and a bunch of lesser lights protecting him. Before they left San Francisco, Mitchell and Lanphier were handed their Navy Cross decorations and oblique citations that did not mention the Japanese admiral.

John Mitchell was to deliver a personal letter to Hap Arnold from Lieutenant General Harmon, who believed the air force should pick up the ball and award their pilots Medals of Honor despite the navy's rejection. Not only was that letter in his pocket, but so was a glowing report from Harmon about how well Mitchell had led the mission, which had always been considered a million-to-one shot.

Upon arriving in Washington, Mitchell reported to the office of Admiral King. After cooling his heels for a while, Mitchell was interviewed by a three-star admiral who gravely informed him that King was quite upset about the information leak. Mitchell smelled an attempt to find a whipping boy for the episode and requested the opportunity to tell his side of the story, since he had not told any unauthorized person anything. King would not see him, and Mitchell instead was left to talk to a stenographer. He outlined the lack of security for the naval code all over the Pacific and how Tom Lanphier had broken radio silence.

After that, Mitchell never heard anything more officially from the navy. He and Lanphier were sent on separate tours to sell war bonds and visit training bases across the country, where they showed off the versatility of the P-38s.

Eventually, Mitchell was assigned to the 412th Fighter Group, which was being assembled at a crude base in a particularly desolate chunk of scrubby California desert. As he came down the stairs of the main administration building at the base, where he had received his new orders, he almost bumped into Jack Jacobson. His old wingman had just been reassigned after rebelling loud and long after being parked in Kansas as commander of a bomber maintenance squadron. The two old friends wrapped each other in bear hugs, and Mitchell asked Jacobson if he wanted to come along to this new assignment, which looked like "some kind of Buck Rogers outfit." Jacobson responded, "Where do I sign?"

They were among the first pilots to work at the Muroc Flight Test Base, where the air force would develop its hottest and newest fighters as it moved into, and beyond, jets.

Mitchell was grateful to be out in the desert, flying slick airplanes far away from the gnawing controversy that had clouded the Yamamoto shoot-down. He had always considered it a successful team effort, believed everyone should just accept it as that, and deeply resented the navy's implication that he and his men had done anything wrong.

He still could not say exactly who had shot down which bomber on the flight, and he really didn't give a damn.

30

Tex and Rex

Bougainville

Five U.S. Marine Corps F4U Corsairs of the VMF-214 squadron took off on the morning of August 27, 1943, to raid the Japanese air base at Kahili, near the spot where Yamamoto had been shot down. One of the pilots was Second Lieutenant Charles Lanphier, back for his second combat tour and flying out of the forward bases in the Russell Islands.

Before they reached the field on Bougainville Island, the marine pilots ran into one of the terrible storms that regularly swept the area, and Lanphier did not come out on the other side of the muck. The others completed the strafing run on the target and destroyed most of the Japanese planes parked there, then flew back to the Russells and reported one of their own was missing.

This time the Japanese captured Lanphier and put him in a prison camp at Rabaul, where the daily diet was usually rice and water. Malnutrition led to illness, and there was no medicine. Charlie Lanphier lasted nine months, then died. After the war, his body was moved to the Arlington National Cemetery.

Tom Lanphier would write that one of the last things Charlie told a fellow prisoner was that his brother had shot down Admiral Yamamoto.

London

Tom Lanphier interrupted his trip from California to Washington with a stopover in Boise, Idaho, to marry his girlfriend, Phyllis Johnson Fraser, whose family had deep roots in the area. A friend of the bride opened his department store on a Sunday morning so the wedding participants could buy what they needed for the hurried ceremonies.

By the time Lanphier reached Washington, General Arnold had smoothed the ruffled feathers of Admiral King about the security breach, but Lanphier was ordered not to say anything further about the mission until the war was over. Hap Arnold had climbed onto the Lanphier bandwagon, bringing with him the formidable clout of the air force public relations machine. That all but set the claim in stone.

Lanphier was promoted to major and toured training bases to showcase the abilities of the P-38, then was assigned as operations officer of the 72nd Fighter Wing at Colorado Springs, Colorado. Along the way, the suave and charming officer collected ever more friends in high places, such as Henry Ford, who had been his father's boss in Detroit during Lanphier senior's civilian career, and Hollywood stars like Clark Gable and Jack Benny. He taught air force bomber pilot Jimmy Stewart, also an actor, how to fly the Lightning.

Once on duty in Colorado Springs, Lanphier talked his way into a two-week assignment in London to study the tactics being used by fighter pilots in the European theater. It was the middle of May 1944, a month before the first American soldier would set foot in France on D Day.

He flew with several fighter groups, made some bombing runs in France, and helped escort a thousand-bomber attack on Berlin. Twenty-seven bombers were shot down that day, a total of 270 crewmen lost, and Lanphier marveled at how they could ride those slow, long-range machines day after day to almost certain doom.

Nothing could make one forget the horrors of war like a night out in London, and Lanphier cut a swath few could equal in such a short time. He stayed at the plush Savoy Hotel as the guest of Pulitzer Prize–winning playwright Robert E. Sherwood, who officially was the head of the Office of War Information in Europe, but clandestinely worked for the spy agency known as the Office of Strategic Services, many of whose members later joined the Central Intelligence Agency. The young pilot hobnobbed with great actors such as Alfred Lunt and Lynn Fontaine, writers and photographers like Ernest Hemingway and Frank Capra, and war leaders such as another of his father's old friends, William "Wild Bill" Donovan, the head of the OSS. He even met Winston Churchill.

Tom Lanphier left London on June 4, two days before the invasion.

China

Rex Barber's career was going in a much different, and much more violent, direction, for he was joining the 449th Fighter Squadron, a group of don't-give-a-damn aerial buccaneers who were always outnumbered, always outgunned, and flew as much on guts as on gasoline. He felt perfectly at home.

They were the heirs of the legendary American Volunteer Group (AVG), which itself had evolved from a private group created before the war to train an air force for National Chinese General Chiang Kai-shek. In 1941, the unit became part of the Chinese Air Force, with the assignment of protecting the land supply route, called the Burma Road. The colorful commander of the AVG, General Claire Chennault, put together a motley collection of P-40 pursuit planes flown by adventuresome pilots who were uncomfortable in a strict military environment. They painted the hungry, open red mouth of a tiger shark, outlined by big white teeth, on the nose of the planes, a symbol that changed into the ferocious face of a Bengal Tiger, and the AVG unit became known as the Flying Tigers. On Christmas Day, 1941, after Pearl Harbor and the Philippines were ravaged, the Japanese struck at Burma's major seaport, Rangoon. Instead of gaining surprise, the attackers were jumped by Flying Tigers and Royal Air Force fighters that knocked down nine Japanese pursuit planes and fourteen bombers.

The AVG, with only seventy-nine planes and eighty-two pilots, carved a niche in history with their stubborn exploits against heavy odds. As the war progressed, they gradually lost their singular identity when they were rolled into bigger organizations, but a number of the Tiger veterans still prowled the China skies and were as piratical a bunch as ever strapped on a fighter plane.

One was David Lee Hill, an absolutely fearless skyfighter whom everyone called "Tex." Once, while flying a P-40, Hill found a Japanese strafing an American base and roared in straight against the oncoming Zero, both planes firing every gun they had. Hill shot down the Zero, which crashed and burned on the field, and when Tex landed his plane and walked over to the burning wreckage, he was the very picture of a Wild West gunslinger. The holster of his army .45 slapped against his thigh, his square jaw was set in righteous anger, and his blond hair blew in the wind. It was the second Japanese plane he had shot down that day, and the largest piece of the Japanese pilot, the decapitated head, had rolled away from the smoking debris. "All right, you son of a bitch, if that's the way you want to fight, it's all right with me," he said, and kicked the head back into the flames. He stalked away and had a cup of tea before taking off again.

The latest incarnation of the Flying Tigers was the Chinese-American Composite Wing, which was to be the nucleus of a postwar air force for the Nationalist Chinese. American and Chinese pilots and ground crews worked together on a one-to-one ratio to learn how to operate as a team, but experienced men were hard to find because the war was raging white-hot around the world.

When General Chennault discovered that a pilot of the caliber of Rex Barber had come under his command, he put him into the 449th Fighter Squadron to get him directly into the fighting. It was the only squadron of P-38s in China, and Rex was made second in command. A few steps up the command ladder was Tex Hill, who considered the 449th to be a hard-luck squadron that was on the cutting edge of the fighting, and a unit that needed all the experienced pilots it could get. "I rounded up every damned eight ball I could find to put in that squadron," said Hill. "Even found a guy from the Battle of Britain. Rex got along great with them all."

.   .   .

After the Japanese eventually captured the Burma Road, they controlled the land routes in the area and regularly overran small air bases. The squadron faced many problems, including a lack of fuel for their planes. With the road closed, gasoline had to be hauled in, barrel by barrel, aboard cargo planes that flew over "the Hump," a towering chain of fourteen-thousand-foot mountains between India and Szechuan Province. No P-38 in the squadron was allowed to fly a mission until there was enough gas at the base to refuel it as soon as it returned. It had to be able to scramble into the sky immediately, for otherwise Japanese planes might destroy them on the ground. Planes were hard to replace.

The result was a lack of flying time. From the first of January until April 18, 1944, Barber flew almost every combat mission run by the squadron, but that was only twenty-one in all. In roughly the same amount of time on Guadalcanal, he had flown 110 missions. New pilots sat around doing little and unable to train.

When Barber learned a couple of B-25 bombers were about to fly along the Yangtze River and shoot up whatever might be found on the serpentine waterway, he arranged an escort of eight P-38s and included three rookie pilots in the flight. The bombers strayed too close to a Japanese base in Hunan Province, and when a flock of Zeros came at them, the bombers fled. The P-38s swooped down to cover the retreat of the big planes. One inexperienced pilot lagged behind, on a course that made him a sitting duck for pursuing planes. Two Zeros had pounced on the straggler. "He was flying straight and level, scared to death," Barber said. "I hollered at him to hit the deck and we'd cover him, but he was apparently paralyzed and didn't know what to do."

The boy was still aloft after the first slashing pass by the Zeros, and when they banked around for another try, Barber thought the kid was doomed. He told everyone else to go home and broke off from the rest of the flight to rescue the young pilot. He was mad at the kid for not obeying instructions, he was mad at the Japanese for attacking, and he was making a mistake.

"This is something you never do in combat, get mad. You've got to keep your head about you," he said. Barber forced the Zeros to break off their attack, but he was still so angry that he chased them. One managed to swing behind his plane, and the Zero slammed the P-38 with a hurricane of machine-gun fire. Barber's right engine caught fire, but fortunately the Zeros did not press the advantage.

"They had me burning pretty good," he said. Knowing he would have to bail out, he began looking for a safe place to jump. Below, he made out the familiar outline of Tungting Lake, near the village of Yueyang, and the thin line of a railroad and a fence. On the other side of the fence was a Japanese army encampment. Barber popped off the canopy at about seven hundred feet, got his feet onto the seat, and pushed out as hard as he could, jumping clear of the plane. But the powerful blast of wind jerked him around like a puppet. His right ankle smashed the fuselage of the plane, and his right arm slammed hard against the tail. He never remembered pulling the ripcord, but the parachute opened, and he drifted to earth with a badly broken arm and badly injured ankle.

The man who knew everything there was to know about the Yamamoto mission was falling into Japanese-held territory deep in China, far from any friendly lines. He touched down so close to the Japanese camp on the far side of the lake that he could see soldiers lining the fence, staring back at him.

A few days later, his family was notified that Rex Barber had been lost in combat.

Barber was saved by a couple of Chinese kids, no more than twelve years old, who ran up and gathered his billowing parachute like they knew what they were doing. With one boy supporting him on each side, he hobbled up a trail as a Japanese patrol set out from the camp to find him. The boys carefully stashed the American pilot in a ravine and covered him with thick brush, smoothed out the surrounding area with sticks, and motioned with their hands for him to remain quiet, then hurried away.

The Japanese patrol arrived moments later, calling out to one another, so close that one dropped a cigarette beside the bushes that shielded Barber. He held his breath, despite the pain in his arm and leg, until the soldiers moved off to examine the crashed airplane.

When it was safe, the boys returned with some guerrilla fighters from a nearby village that was separated from the Japanese camp by only the railroad and the fence. The Japanese seldom bothered the village, for they were primarily interested in protecting their lines of communication, and they did not control the vast, empty countryside of China. The guerrillas loaded Barber onto a wooden door, which they carried like a stretcher, and took him to a rough shelter. His run of good luck continued, for two seventeen-year-old boys, twins, appeared and spoke to him in perfect English, with clipped British accents. They had been born and raised in the home of the Englishman who ran the power company in Shanghai.

The boys told him a doctor was coming, a Chinese doctor, not a Western medical man. "Please don't embarrass him," they said.

A small man with a wisp of a goatee on his chin and a long braided queue down his back ducked into the house and carefully examined the damaged arm, which was black from the shoulder to below the elbow and bulging from dislocated bones. He stuck a needle in, but no blood emerged, and the twins explained that he was just "letting air out."

While the little doctor satisfied himself that the foot was not broken and bound the ankle, women filled a wooden bowl with scalding hot water. Sitting beside the bed, he gently dipped Barber's arm in the hot water for as long as the American could stand it, over and over and over. After several days, the swelling went down, but the arm hung virtually useless.

The physician gave Barber a little bag of stones to carry and instructions to add another rock to the bag each day and carry it until the pain forced him to put it down. Once his ankle had mended enough for him to hobble, the pilot was placed in a bamboo seat, with a strong guerrilla fighter at each end of two poles, and they carried him as if he were ancient royalty. They tramped the road for days, finding shelter in villages and Chinese army camps where Barber sometimes, taking part in a polite local custom for honored guests, sang to entertain his hosts after dinner.

Word of the American pilot with a nice voice preceded him down the trail, and at one camp, his bamboo chair was hoisted to a platform plastered with posters of the leaders of the allied nations, and the Chinese troops called for a song from their guest.

With the twins interpreting, Barber launched into:

When I was a serving lass, down on Drury Lane,
My master was a kindly man, my mistress was the same . . .

Applause and cheers rose, and Barber, feeling like a stage star, continued:

Along came a pilot, merry as can be,
And he is the cause of all my misery,
Singing bell-bottom trousers, coat of navy blue . . .

The long trip to safety became a sightseer's delight, and Barber fell in love with the Chinese people. He never forgot their generosity and how some villages welcomed his arrival with strings of exploding firecrackers. It was dangerous for the Chinese. Earlier, when the Japanese discovered three villages had helped a pilot escape, they destroyed them.

The only setback on Barber's journey was the mayor's wife in one village, who cleaned him out of about a thousand American dollars in emergency escape money during a ferocious card game she called "poky-poky." Rex considered himself a good poker player, but she was better, particularly when dealing the cards. His full house was beaten by her four of a kind, then his four aces impossibly fell to her straight flush. "I knew she was cheating, but she was one of the best card handlers I ever saw," he said. He considered the price an inconsequential exchange for safety and hospitality.

The long trip on foot finally ended, and Barber had a two-day boat ride that delivered him to an American base where General Claire Chennault happened to be visiting. The general loaded him on his personal C-47 transport, and Barber was soon out of China. He had been behind enemy lines for six weeks, from mid-April until July 1944.

His family was notified that he wasn't dead after all.

In a military hospital in San Francisco, orthopedic surgeons were awed by the work of the Chinese doctor. They told Barber, "You can thank him that you're still alive." Without that care, Barber could have lost his damaged arm at the shoulder or died of gangrene. The needle, the scalding water, and the rocks in the sack had stretched the ligaments and given him back about 75 percent of his normal arm motion. The surgeons operated, and the arm returned to 95 percent. Although his right arm remained a half inch shorter than the left, Rex Barber was returned to flying status.

31

The Legend

More than two years of hard fighting passed between the attack on Yamamoto and the end of the war. Germany fell to the Russians, pressing from the east, and the Americans and their allies, attacking from the west. In the Pacific, bloody island battles culminated with atomic bombs being dropped on Japan to finally force the fanatical nation to surrender.

Two more of the American pilots who had flown the Yamamoto mission, Eldon Stratton and Gordon Whittaker, joined Ray Hine on the roster of those killed in action.

John Mitchell temporarily left the testing fields of Muroc to fly P-51 Mustangs during the final Allied offensive against Japan. By then, in 1945, the war was almost over, so it no longer mattered if a pilot with information about the Yamamoto mission might be captured. The passage of so much time and the course of the war had rendered useless anything he might confess to the Japanese. Mitchell shot down four more Zeros and brought his official total to a dozen enemy aircraft destroyed in combat. He was back in California when the war came to a close.

Even before the atomic bombs were dropped, the air force was preparing for its postwar operations, and it wanted to split off from the army and become an entity of its own. A few good hero stories would help.

With the lid about to be lifted on much wartime information, the public relations office prepared a news release that gave Tom Lanphier, now a lieutenant colonel, sole credit for shooting down Yamamoto. He was asked to write up his version for publication, and by V-J Day, everything was ready.

This was done even though the air force had never sent anyone out to examine the wreckage of the admiral's plane on Bougainville that had been in Allied hands for many months.

Lanphier had an outstanding record, and with an official count of five verified enemy shoot-downs, he qualified as an ace. He held numerous decorations, but he also wanted Yamamoto. If he was to have political success in later life, he needed that glittering, one-of-a-kind bauble, something no one else could match, so he sat down at a typewriter and wrote history.

Less than a month after the war ended, on September 10, 1945, the War Department made an official announcement that confirmed Lanphier had indeed accomplished the deed. The following day, Lanphier planted his flag in about the most public way possible. His personal story, blessed by the air force, became a set of lengthy articles that were distributed to newspapers across the nation by the North American Newspaper Alliance, a news syndicate.

In the fifth of the six articles, Lanphier described being overcome by a feeling of determination to make the most of what he believed would be the only shot he might get at the fleeing bomber, which he was approaching at approximately a right angle. He said, "I applied myself to my gunnery," and, although believing that he was still out of range, fired "a long steady burst" in front of the bomber. Such a tactic is used to allow a target to fly into the bullets. Lanphier reported that he saw the right engine on the big aircraft start burning, and then the right wing caught fire, too. That, as far as he was concerned, was the epitaph for the Japanese plane, because, once they were set aflame, they usually blew up. Oddly, Lanphier did not mention his often stated claim that he saw the damaged wing fall off.

In the final article he concluded with a vitriolic swipe at the deceased admiral that reflected the general feeling of the day. The plan to kill Yamamoto had been "as cunning and stealthy" as any conceived by Yamamoto himself. "And he had it coming to him. Had he kept his mouth shut, his sword in his scabbard, and his fleet at home, he would have lived a lot longer."

The long series gave the navy credit for planning the attack, saluted Mitchell for leading it, and complimented Rex Barber for shooting down one bomber by himself and combining with Besby Holmes and Ray Hine to bring down a third one over the water. He actually was quite laudatory in his praise of Barber, whom he said was "a legend among Pacific combat pilots." But Lanphier did not give an inch on claiming personal credit for Yamamoto.

When Rex Barber recovered from the wounds sustained in China, he became commander of the 31st Fighter Squadron, stationed at March Field in Riverside, California.

The squadron was part of the 412th Fighter Group, which was truly a gathering of warriors, blending Flying Tigers with the cream of the Cactus Air Force. The commander was none other than Barber's old China boss, Tex Hill. The group's executive officer was John Mitchell. Other squadron commanders included Jack Jacobson and Bob Petit, the veteran from the 339th whose *Miss Virginia* Barber had flown on the Yamamoto mission. It took someone as strong as Hill to keep everything under control, since these pilots were all about as crazy as he was when they got into the air.

Barber might be a roaring beast as a fighter pilot, but on the ground he was about the most levelheaded man Hill had ever met. Barber simply never got mad. Therefore, Hill was astonished on a September morning in 1945 when a furious Rex stormed into the office. He had just finished reading Tom Lanphier's newspaper stories about what had happened in the sky above Bougainville on April 18, 1943. Barber had never seen the official mission report, and Lanphier was making the remarkable claim that he alone had shot down Admiral Yamamoto! The events had been twisted beyond recognition in the long articles, Barber said as he disgustedly handed the newspaper to Hill.

He asked permission to use the office telephone to call Tom Lanphier right *now!*

Tex Hill agreed to be a witness. He had little use for Lanphier, whom he considered "a real flaky guy." Hill had heard the story of the mission from several of the men who had flown it and figured nobody could honestly say who had brought down the admiral. Barber felt that he could not let Lanphier's account become the accepted depiction of what really happened. *This ought to be interesting,* Tex Hill thought as he settled back in his chair and, at Barber's request, picked up a telephone extension to listen in to what was said.

Barber's voice was tinged with heat as he worked his way through the aggravation of the military telephone system to reach Lanphier, who was in Washington. Once Tom was on the line, Rex proceeded to give his old flying buddy a thorough ass-chewing. Hill, who had a volcanic temper of his own, nodded in approval at the abrupt change in behavior of the normally calm Barber. When Rex got mad, he went all the way. Tex Hill would recall that he had never really heard anyone chewed out any better.

"I told him I had read the story and that if this story was anything like the official report that he had told me that he had written . . . he'd better get some changes made quickly because there were so many inaccurate statements," Barber recalled later.

He was particularly incensed that Lanphier stated Rex had said the tail came off the bomber that Barber had shot. "I told him that I never said the tail came off, that I said that a piece came off the rudder." It was a significant difference, for when the Yamamoto wreckage was examined, the tail was still attached to the broken fuselage. Barber walked Lanphier through everything that he had actually said during the chaos after the mission.

According to Tex Hill, Lanphier apologized and promised to get the official record changed. Barber believed him, and hung up confident the report would thereafter share credit for the lead bomber between the two of them, with Rex and Besby Holmes sharing the second bomber.

But to do so would have meant eliminating the third bomber altogether, and the tangle of events would be more confused than ever. So nothing changed. The issue flared brightly, flickered, and once again dimmed, and the pilots of the old 339th went about their business.

Tokyo

The six Zero pilots who failed to protect Yamamoto were not allowed to commit ritual suicide to exorcise their shame. Instead, they were given fly-until-you-die orders. None expected to survive the war.

The flight leader, Lieutenant (j.g.) Takeshi Morizaki, was killed in a dogfight exactly two months after the Yamamoto mission, on June 16, 1943, near Guadalcanal. His wingmen, Yasuji Okazaki and Yoshimi Hidaka, had died a week earlier over the Russells. Toyomitsu Tsujinoue, the leader of the second flight, was shot down near Rendova on July 1, 1943.

The young Shoot-Down King, Shoichi Sugita, continued to fly like a wild man. He was shot down and badly burned in August 1943, but he recovered and returned to combat. The Japanese credited him with seventy individual victories and another forty shared victories before he was killed during the Okinawa campaign on April 15, 1945.

Kenji Yanagiya was the sole survivor of the war, but not because of a lack of combat. At the end of a dive-bombing attack on American planes refueling at the Russell Islands base, Yanagiya was jumped by two U.S. fighters. Bullets burst through his windshield and exploded against the control stick. His right hand and right leg were seriously mauled, and using only his left hand, he made an emergency landing at a Japanese base on Munda. He was knocked unconscious in the crash landing. Medical personnel stuffed cotton in his mouth and three sailors held him down while his hand was amputated without anesthetic. The pain was so intense that it brought him back to consciousness.

Yanagiya's flying career was over, but not his involvement in the Yamamoto mission.

General Douglas MacArthur was assigned to oversee the occupation of Japan. Many years had passed since his ignominious retreat from

Manila, and the general had restored his reputation with extraordinary leadership. Setting up headquarters in Tokyo, MacArthur virtually ruled a Japan that lay in ruins.

More than 1.4 million Japanese had died in the war: The firebombing of Tokyo alone, in March 1945, took more than 100,000 lives. Another 135,000 perished in the atomic bombing at Hiroshima and still another 95,000 at Nagasaki. Japan wanted no more war, and one of the first things on MacArthur's list was to make it impossible for the country to wage such a conflict again. He would rid the nation of its overbearing military caste. One directive issued from his spacious offices in the Dai Ichi Building, across the moat from the emperor's palace grounds, ordered the destruction of all statues to military heroes in the country.

That included one of Isoroku Yamamoto at the Kasumigaura Flying School, where the mighty little admiral had sharpened his vision of the dawning power of naval aviation. According to author Carroll V. Glines, the statue was dismantled, cut in two, and thrown into a lake, where it remained for a decade. Eventually a scrap dealer fished it out and sold it to some friends of the admiral. They found a place for it in a small park in his hometown.

The United States

Two months after Lanphier's newspaper articles appeared, the air force finally got around to recommending decorations for the Yamamoto mission pilots. A confidential memorandum reflected how deeply his claim had been woven into the records.

The list of recommended awards put the name of Lieutenant Colonel Lanphier at the very top, identified him as "Pilot and Flight Leader," and recommended that he be given a Distinguished Service Medal. Second on the list was J. W. Mitchell, the "Pilot and Formation Leader," who was listed with the rank of major, although Mitchell had been promoted to lieutenant colonel months earlier. He also was to get a Distinguished Service Medal.

A Silver Star was recommended for Captain R. T. Barber, a pilot.

Everyone else was to get a Distinguished Flying Cross or, if they already had one, an oak leaf cluster to show they were receiving the award again.

Some of the men from the mission decided to stay in the air force when the war was done. But despite their war records, they almost had to start their careers all over again because of the excess of available personnel. Wartime rank meant little.

John Mitchell, for instance, had risen all the way to full colonel, owned an impressive combat record that stretched from Guadalcanal to Japan, and had been awarded the Distinguished Service Medal, the Distinguished Flying Cross with Oak Leaf Cluster, the Air Medal with nine Oak Leaf Clusters, a Presidential Unit Citation, and, a rarity for an army officer, both the Navy Cross and a Marine Presidential Unit Citation. He applied for a commission in the regular army after the war, on January 29, 1946, and a month later was approved. He was dropped in rank all the way down to first lieutenant. There was simply no room at the top for everyone who wanted to stay in the demobilizing army.

Rex Barber also decided to stay in. There was exciting and important work ahead for experienced pilots as the air force made its way into the jet age, and Barber would be among those who tested the new P-80 Shooting Star, America's first jet fighter plane.

Clearly, the military services were not going to be big enough for Tom Lanphier. There were a lot of war heroes coming home, and in uniform, even with his reputation and decorations, he would be just another officer to be dropped to the bottom rungs of the peacetime air force ladder. If he wanted to seek political office, a rank of mere lieutenant would never do. It would be better to get out while still a lieutenant colonel. Two weeks after the end of the war, he left the air force.

With his background as a reporter, his celebrity, and the prominence of both his own and his wife's families, he took a top editorial job in Boise, Idaho, with the *Idaho Daily Statesman* newspaper. The smell of hot lead and ink appealed to his journalistic side, but designing pages, writing editorials, and getting the presses rolling was tedious and anonymous work. He wanted to make headlines, not write them, and Boise was a political backwater.

Luckily, he still had the air force. Lanphier joined a fighter squadron of the Idaho National Guard, then helped to organize the Air Force Association, a group created to support air power in the future. It would lobby on behalf of the service, and air force veterans would be able to gather at conventions to renew friendships and talk of old times.

The famed Jimmy Doolittle was appointed president during the organizational phase, with Lanphier among the vice presidents, and Lanphier became the AFA's first elected president in 1947. "It's all yours, Junior," Doolittle said as he handed over the gavel to his thirty-one-year-old successor.

The association's magazine then ran a lengthy story on the new president that emphasized how he "dove in and got the Admiral's bomber." It was another brick in the growing legend, and the endorsement of the veterans' group would itself grow in strength over the years.

Lanphier had found a way out of Boise. He toured the nation to support the air force and was usually introduced as the man who shot down Yamamoto. Through the AFA, he finally found his road to Washington, without having to bother with running in an election. Instead, he was soon giving advice to Stuart Symington, a political insider whom President Harry Truman appointed the first secretary of the air force.

Simultaneously, the air force got its first chief of staff, General Tooey Spaatz, another old and close friend of Lanphier's father. It was not long before Lanphier moved to Washington and became an assistant to Symington. It was his long-sought entrée to the world of national politics and kept alive his hope of ascending ever higher into the political stratosphere. He had told Rex Barber he wanted to be president of the United States, and that no longer seemed impossible, if he played his cards right.

Washington loves experts, and Lanphier had all of the qualifications. The air force used him as a primary source when it put together its official history of World War II, and the Yamamoto mission description was taken straight from the disputed "debriefing" report filed from Guadalcanal. None of the other mission pilots were asked for their input, although many were still on active duty and would have been easily found.

The official history hedged only slightly when it said Yamamoto "apparently" died under Lanphier's guns.

If that was not sufficient recognition, Lanphier made a highly publicized aerial voyage around the world aboard regularly scheduled passenger planes to support the growing civilian air services. A stopover in Japan became a moment he considered so important that he used it as the opening scene of his autobiography, for in Tokyo, Tom Lanphier, who claimed to have killed Yamamoto, met the admiral's widow.

The Pan American plane landed at Haneda Airport before dawn, about 4:40 A.M., on December 6, 1949, barely missing the eighth anniversary of the Pearl Harbor attack. He was met by a number of Japanese newspaper reporters and gave his detailed version of the attack on Yamamoto and sternly reminded them that his brother Charlie had died as a Japanese prisoner of war.

After the press conference, reporters brought forward Reiko Yamamoto, wearing a formal black kimono, for a face-to-face meeting.

She bowed and, according to Japanese news stories, said, "I am the wife of the Yamamoto in your story. I am glad to see you."

"I don't know what to say," Lanphier responded, apparently momentarily flustered, and he handed her a bouquet of gold and white chrysanthemums. There was no explanation of the sudden appearance of the flowers, but since the journalists arranged the meeting, they probably also provided the bouquet. The specific type of flower is so highly regarded in Japan that the emperor's position is referred to as the Chrysanthemum Throne, so a great amount of unspoken honor was involved in the simple presentation, for both the giver and the recipient.

Lanphier asked about her four children and encouraged her to raise them to be "good people."

Reiko Yamamoto, according to the stories, said that while she was saddened by her husband's death, she felt it was good that he died at the time he did. The comment was not explained, but perhaps she referred to the admiral still being revered as a war hero in his country. She told the journalists that she held no anger toward Lanphier.

Their meeting was poignant and brief, and Lanphier's airplane took off at 9:11 A.M. for Hawaii to continue his circling of the globe. Newspapers in Tokyo prominently displayed the story of the meeting between the widow and the pilot.

32

Showdown

The Korean War broke out on Sunday, June 25, 1950, and some of the pilots who were on the Yamamoto mission were sent to face a new enemy. Doug Canning flew once again with the 35th Fighter Group, his original unit, which had been decimated early in World War II, but had hatched so many of the Yamamoto mission fliers.

The war came just at the right time for John Mitchell. He had been faithfully punching his career ticket during the short peace between the wars when he began to accumulate unflattering fitness reports. He lost his job commanding a fighter-interceptor group at the bleak Elmendorf Air Force Base in Alaska, and anger and alcohol-related problems led to his reassignment to a depot job at Travis Air Force Base in California. The man who designed and led the complex Yamamoto mission was reported "lacking in leadership" as a paper pusher.

The fitness reports inaccurately reflected the man's ability. Some of the jet fighters in his group were mysteriously malfunctioning, even catching fire, during landing approaches, so as a safety precaution Mitchell grounded that model of plane until Lockheed factory representatives could figure out the problem. The commanding general demanded that Mitchell put the planes back in the air, but Mitchell stalled, giving the Lockheed engineers time to find a fuel line that would overheat and spray fuel onto the hot engine, causing the fires. The planes were all fixed and returned to duty, but Mitchell had a vindictive general writing his fitness reports.

Then came Korea, and Mitchell volunteered to return to the sound of the guns. Given command of the 51st Fighter Wing, he was back in the dangerous skies, flying F-86 Sabre jets and once again leading his men from the front, not from an administrative position safely in the rear. During the next year he shot down four North Korean MiG-15 fighters, earned more Air Medals, his third Distinguished Flying Cross, and a Legion of Merit.

Mitchell was a warrior, and it is difficult to chain an eagle to a desk and expect it to learn to type. He was not the first soldier to experience the dichotomy of being valued less during peace than in war. Rudyard Kipling, the British poet laureate and voice of the Raj, spelled it out many years before in telling the similar plight of his fictional soldier Tommy Atkins.

> For it's Tommy this, an' Tommy that, an' "Chuck him out, the brute!"
> But it's "Savior of 'is country" when the guns begin to shoot.

Rex Barber flew only three combat missions during his abbreviated Korean War duty. After attending the required service schools, his quiet nature made him a natural diplomat, and from 1952 to 1956, Barber was assigned as the air attaché in Ecuador and Colombia. He wore the eagles of a full colonel.

For almost everyone involved, the Yamamoto episode faded into the "who cares?" category during the Korean War. Tom Lanphier, however, was one of those who *did* care. He cared very much.

He nurtured the legend during the 1950s, with articles giving him credit appearing in every sort of publication. *Wings Comics* profiled him in lurid script and drawings, and in January 1956 *True: The Man's Magazine* quoted Lanphier as saying, "I knew I'd hit the jackpot." *Battle Cry* amplified the story: "*One long burst, then another. A wing of the bomber crumpled in flame. She dipped down into the green forest. The bomber hit the treetops and exploded! Nobody would walk away from that one."*

Man's Magazine headlined "Tom Lanphier's Mission: Destroy the Jap Who Plotted Pearl Harbor." *SAGA, World War II,* and others ran stories, and with each retelling, the Lanphier version gained credence. Rex Barber, annoyed and frustrated, kept copies.

And while the legend solidified, Lanphier's civilian career advanced after he hitched his wagon to the rising Washington star of Stuart Symington. After serving as secretary of the air force, Symington became chairman of the National Security Resources Board and held several other positions before winning a seat in the U.S. Senate from Missouri in 1952. Lanphier worked closely with him and catapulted into a high-profile job of his own as vice president of the Convair Division of General Dynamics, one of the nation's largest defense suppliers.

Convair, in San Diego, made missiles. Lanphier was in charge of selling the Atlas intercontinental ballistic missile, and his aggressive championing of the system during the cold war earned him a bully pulpit in Washington. The newspaper columnist Joseph Alsop wrote in 1960 that important men admired Lanphier's devil-may-care, go-for-the-lead-bomber determination, and some were predicting he had a bright future.

"Tom is the ablest young man I know. Nobody is doing more for his nation, at his age, than he is," Symington told a writer. Headlines, appearances on the nationally televised *Today* show, and emcee introductions at speeches he gave around the country all acknowledged Tom Lanphier as "the man who shot down Admiral Yamamoto."

In Washington, such praise was thinly disguised plaudits for someone regarded as having a political future.

Besby Holmes found out the hard way that there was a heavy price to be paid for challenging the established story of what happened on the Yamamoto mission. Critics faced a formidable wall of the highest-ranking men in the United States Air Force and the Air Force Association and those who wrote the history, and Holmes was the most persistent critic of all. Nobody seemed to care about his version of that long-ago mission.

Holmes never retracted a word, and claimed the alleged debriefing was a total fraud. Just like "debriefers" on Guadalcanal, no reporters or historians talked to him as the years passed, and they tilted military history to give the impression that Tom Lanphier had flown the mission almost on his own. Rex Barber wasn't much better, in Holmes's opinion, because of their disagreement about the attack on the second bomber.

Holmes had risen through the ranks in fits and starts after World War II. Beginning again as a lieutenant, he became a captain, then a major, during Korea, finally making lieutenant colonel in the Panama Canal Zone, but feeling he was never given appropriate recognition for his outstanding war record and status as an ace fighter pilot. There seemed to be some invisible ceiling holding him down.

Many years later, Holmes was in his last duty post, at MacDill Air Force Base in Tampa, Florida, part of the U.S. Strike Command, when he saw the familiar face of an old friend who had just transferred in. He and Henry Viccellio greeted each other warmly. They were not equals, however, for Holmes was still a lieutenant colonel, while Viccellio now wore the three stars of a lieutenant general.

Three days later, as the general descended the stairway at the Officers' Club, Holmes took his wife over for an introduction. But Viccellio disappeared before they could make their way through the crowd. Holmes thought the general had intentionally avoided him.

A month later, Holmes happened to be alone with Viccellio in his office, when Viccellio's eyes hardened, and he gruffly said, "You know, Holmes, I blackballed you eighteen times before eighteen promotion boards."

Besby Holmes was absolutely stunned. "For God's sake, why?" he asked. The general turned on his heel and left the room and never spoke to him again.

From that moment, Holmes believed he had been intentionally held back in rank because he challenged official history. He retired a short time later.

. . .

John Mitchell and Rex Barber could not help but keep track of how the story had been distorted, but they were helpless to stop it. Lanphier was a civilian, outside the system, and free to say anything he wanted, while they were serving officers and did not have that same freedom. They had to go through channels.

Both wrote letters of protest, trying to get the official record amended, but to no avail. Mitchell sent a letter all the way up to the very top of the air force chain of command, to General Spaatz, unaware of the friendship between Spaatz and Lanphier's father. The Mitchell appeal was ignored. That convinced him that the military hierarchy was never going to listen to him.

Tom Lanphier was never going to be president of the United States or hold any elective political office at all. In the political firmament, he was but a faint pinpoint of light among galaxies of giant suns. When he hitched his wagon to the wrong star, his chances disappeared in a heartbeat.

Senator Stuart Symington had become Lanphier's mentor. While still secretary of the air force, Symington presented the H. H. Arnold Award to Lanphier during a Madison Square Garden event in 1949 for outstanding civilian service as president of the Air Force Association, again linking Lanphier to the air force power structure. By 1960, Symington was an experienced senator and decided to run for president himself.

That was the opening Tom Lanphier had been waiting for all of his life. He held to the naïve belief that John Kennedy and Lyndon Johnson would deadlock in the convention voting and the Democratic Party would turn to Symington as its compromise candidate. That, Lanphier whispered to friends, would open the door for him, the longtime Symington loyalist, to possibly become the vice presidential nominee. It was beyond the realm of political reality, because Kennedy stormed to the Democratic nomination.

Lanphier watched his political dream dissolve at the hands of Kennedy, a rookie PT boat skipper who had watched the pilots return from the Yamamoto mission in the South Pacific seventeen years earlier.

The claim that Tom Lanphier alone shot down Yamamoto could not go unchallenged forever. Although the military establishment was content to let the issue rest, men who had left the military service and were no longer muzzled were openly questioning his story. One former crew chief, Robert Pappadake, wrote a long poem that included the lines:

> "I got him!" "I got him!" is what Capt. Lanphier said
> I alone shot Yamamoto dead
> Let no other man make this claim
> He'd steal my honor and soil my name.

So while the generals were content, things were shifting far down at the bottom of the chain of command.

Late in 1960, Airman First Class John Wible, attached to the 355th Tactical Fighter Wing based at Myrtle Beach, South Carolina, read in a base newspaper about the exploits of Colonel Rex Barber, who was also with the outfit. The three-striper airman, only twenty years old, requested a meeting with the bird colonel, and quickly made his pitch. He was an amateur historian and wanted to write an article about the Yamamoto mission: Would Colonel Barber help? Yes, said Barber, and for the next thirty minutes he told the story to the young enlisted man, who was about the only person in the entire U.S. Air Force who would listen.

In Wible's view, Barber felt that it was not right for history to be written without consideration of all of the facts. The barrage of Lanphier stories and the empty promises made during the telephone call from Tex Hill's office had soured Barber on his old flight leader. He furnished some names and addresses, and Wible began a private search for information. It lasted for years, and he accumulated an extraordinary amount of documentation and correspondence from the United States and Japan. Although twenty-eight years would pass before Wible published

his work, a rich monograph called *The Yamamoto Mission,* written for
the Admiral Nimitz Foundation, his early work began peeling away the
layers of deception.

When Wible began his project, retirement was just around the corner
for the men who had flown with the Cactus Air Force on Guadalcanal.

After Korea, John Mitchell returned to California, then attended the
National War College, which is usually a ticket to higher rank and better
assignments. Instead of a general's star, he was assigned to command the
Detroit Defense Sector in Battle Creek, Michigan. The air force was bidding him farewell, and Mitchell retired and went into private enterprise.

As a private citizen, Mitchell was finally free to speak his mind.
The drumbeat of publicity over the past twenty years had irritated
him, and the air force obviously was relying solely upon Lanphier. In a
letter to Wible, Mitchell said Lanphier had written "a strongly biased
version, written to play himself up as the hero and as the planner and
leader of the flight, with me playing a minor role."

Since then, the whole episode had become "a question of one man
taking it upon himself to claim something happened and defying anyone to say it wasn't so. With his father, Colonel Tom Lanphier Sr., being
in the intelligence department in the Pentagon, it is understandable
how a one-sided version of such an account could develop." Mitchell
said he thought Lanphier's chance of hitting Yamamoto was fifty-fifty
at best, and should Barber's version of events be true, then "there is
practically no chance that Lanphier shot down Yamamoto."

In a later letter, he described the situation as "a question of an individual telling a story, retelling it, and with no refutations, it eventually becomes the gospel."

Rex Barber retired from the air force on March 31, 1961, after twenty
years, six months, and one day of service, including more than five
years of overseas duty. It was his choice, because he was not flying as
much as he wanted and saw nothing but desk jobs in his future. He returned to the family home in Culver, Oregon, slipped quietly back into
the community and into farming.

"Rex didn't come home with a bag of medals over his shoulder," said one friend. "He came back as just Rex," said his younger sister, Eileen. "Heroism just wasn't important to him." He served as mayor and justice of the peace in Culver, sponsored and coached a Little League team, was a volunteer fireman, and an elder in the church that his parents had helped establish.

Barber was reticent about talking of the war, unless asked, but the growing collection of stories that lionized Tom Lanphier disturbed him. "He would have preferred not to have a lot of publicity, but the facts had to be established," said his brother-in-law, Arthur Olson. His irritation showed through in a letter to John Wible, in which Barber said Lanphier had been "most unfair and presumptive" to push so hard to claim a solitary victory.

Lanphier also communicated with Wible. In a startling 1961 letter, he admitted that no one knew for certain which plane Yamamoto had been in and that he had not learned he had received official credit until his return to the United States. "The air force had satisfied itself that he [Yamamoto] had been in the aircraft that crashed into the jungle, and that, therefore, the air force had credited his demise to me," he wrote. That contradicted his earlier statement that he received the notice from the navy and his boasts on the day of the mission.

The flamboyant Tex Hill was invited to be a guest at a unique gathering of old World War II fighter pilots in the mid-1960s—not in the United States, but in Japan. "I walked in, they clapped a bit, and tales began to flow," Hill said of his appearance before the Zero Fighter Pilots Association. He noticed that one fellow had only one hand and asked him how he had lost it. Through an interpreter, the former Japanese pilot introduced himself as Kenji Yanagiya and described how he was badly wounded in a dogfight but survived it. He then mentioned that, earlier in his military career, he had been one of the Zero pilots who escorted the Yamamoto mission.

Hill replied that he knew that story pretty well. He recalled how his friends John Mitchell and Rex Barber had described that fight. If the Americans were saying there were three bombers up there that day, Yanagiya said, they were wrong. Only two Betty bombers were on the mission, both had been shot down, and Yamamoto had been aboard the lead plane.

That knocked the three-bomber theory of official history into a cocked hat. Although their versions were substantially different, Barber and Holmes confirmed they both attacked the second, trailing bomber. But Barber had fired on two Bettys. So if Yanagiya's eyewitness account was true, then Barber *must* also have shot at the lead bomber, for there was no third Betty.

Yanagiya had not been hiding the information. Nobody had asked him about it. Some documentation had surfaced earlier that there had been only two bombers, but the emergence of an eyewitness was to turn the tide of opinion.

The respected magazine *Reader's Digest* was drawn into the fray in December 1966 when it published a long story written by retired Colonel Thomas G. Lanphier Jr., titled "I Shot Down Yamamoto." A brief biography of the author credited him with shooting down a total of seven Japanese planes, serving as special assistant to the secretary of the air force, and having a nongovernmental career as president of Fairbanks, Morse & Company, vice president of Convair and Raytheon, and currently president of Plamasyn, Inc.

In it, Lanphier related his usual tale of how he fought off the diving Zero, flipped over, saw the bomber below, came in over the treetops and "began firing a long steady burst. Its right engine and right wing began to burn. Then the wing fell off, and the bomber crashed into the jungle."

He stated that Rex Barber "had splashed the other Betty in the ocean."

When he arrived back at Guadalcanal, Lanphier wrote, "A crowd of fliers, mechanics, marines, and GIs swarmed over the plane, hauling me out of the cockpit and thumping me on the back until I felt like a halfback who had just scored the winning touchdown."

John Mitchell and Rex Barber read the story with even more frus-
tration. The Lanphier publicity campaign never seemed to cease.

Unknown to any of them, the air force was at work behind the scenes,
trying to straighten out many cluttered records of past campaigns and
to assign official credit on who shot down what and when. U.S. Air Force
Historical Study No. 85 would produce a list of official "Credits for the
Destruction of Enemy Aircraft."

The historians examined both Japanese and American records
about the Yamamoto flight and concluded that only two bombers had
been on the mission and only one had gone down in the Bougainville
jungle. They decided that both Lanphier and Barber had shot at the
Yamamoto bomber, and each was assigned a half share of the victory.
The pilots' personal records were changed in 1969, but the report did
not come to light until 1978.

The impact was enormous.

Tom Lanphier had set about writing the story of his extraordinary life
and chose to unveil the draft of his autobiographical manuscript at a
convention of the American Fighter Aces Association in Phoenix in
May 1984.

The Aces were not an insular, lobbying organization for a single
service, such as the Air Force Association; its members included some
of the best army, navy, and marine pilots who had ever flown in combat. They were a confident and competent bunch, and not easily impressed. Nonaviators stepped aside in the hotel hallways as these old
fighters swaggered into hotel bars and coffee shops to refight distant
sky battles. Membership was strictly limited to those who had at least
five victories, which meant many competent pilots never qualified for
that exclusive club.

The Yamamoto mission had been flown in 1943—forty-one years
earlier!—and seemed unrelated to the modern world. Since the end of
World War II, the United States had fought in Korea and Vietnam and
man had walked on the moon. Propeller planes had given way to fast

jet fighters and rockets. The twin-tailed P-38, once a breakthrough design, now was found only in museums or flown by a few aircraft enthusiasts. By the time of the Phoenix convention, Admiral Isoroku Yamamoto was old news.

But the meeting was the first time that Mitchell, Barber, and Lanphier had come together in the same room since rotating out of Guadalcanal and New Caledonia. After more than forty years, the reunion held surprises for all of them.

Prior to the convention, Lanphier dropped by to see Barrett Tillman, publisher for the Champlin Fighter Museum in Mesa, Arizona, and executive secretary of the American Fighter Aces Association. After cordial greetings, Tillman asked, "Have you seen this?" and showed his visitor a bound, light blue copy of the USAF Historical Study Number 85. For the first time, Lanphier learned of the air force decision to cut him out of sole possession for the Yamamoto kill, and as he read, he was plunged into a feeling of deep betrayal and had a fit of anger. He yanked the book from Tillman's hands, shouted, "I've never seen this before!" and threw it across the office. It crashed against a window with such force that Tillman wondered if the glass had broken.

The official records that had so long been the granite base of Lanphier's claim of victory had been changed without notice to him, and now he had to share the victory with Barber! He rented a car and sped into downtown Phoenix, where he plundered the morgue of a newspaper until he found the postwar series that he had written about the mission. He made copies and returned to the convention site to pass them around.

Despite the study results, Lanphier refused to back down, and his autobiography only added fuel to the fire, for in the manuscript, he ended up questioning his own words.

For years, Lanphier had insisted that he had trained a careful, long burst of gunfire on the fleeing Betty. "I applied myself to my gunnery and, taking no chances of missing, began firing a long steady burst across the bomber's line of flight from approximately right angles," he wrote in his multipart newspaper series after the war ended. In the *Reader's Digest*, Lanphier reported "firing a long steady burst."

But his autobiography departed radically from that theme, with Lanphier saying he killed Yamamoto with a lucky shot. With a tone of feigned modesty that colors the entire manuscript, Lanphier first alluded to his lack of formal gunnery training and then wrote that he had merely been "clearing his guns" when he "accidentally" killed Yamamoto "with an impossible angle-off shot from a nervous forefinger."

No one could understand why he made such a switch in a key part of his story.

Lanphier gave copies of his manuscript to Mitchell and Barber during the convention, and they read it immediately. Both were so incensed about the way the mission was portrayed that they refused to be photographed with him in front of a P-38 Lightning. To do so might have been construed as endorsing his claims, and neither wanted to take that chance.

Step by step, over the years, more and more information emerged that cast further doubt upon the original story.

An overall account of the mission, including the viewpoints of the various pilots, had been published in 1969, in *Get Yamamoto*, by author Burke Davis. A keen reporter with a gift for the colorful touch, Davis even interviewed Besby Holmes for the first time and included his contrarian view of the fight. The exciting book made it clear that Rex Barber had attacked two bombers, but it did not go beyond setting out the contrasting claims. The central issue remained unsettled.

Zero pilot Yanagiya gave an interview in 1975 and confirmed what he had told Tex Hill privately a decade before—that there were only two bombers on the flight, and, he said, "P-38s were firing from the rear of the lead bomber into the tail of the lead bomber." The use of the plural was probably due to an interpreting error. Barber had been flying right on the tail of the bomber and shooting into the rear. Lanphier always insisted that he shot it from the side. A book written by Zero pilot

Saburo Sakai, Japan's leading ace, confirmed only two bombers were up that day.

Treks into the Bougainville jungles by private groups of investigators over the years produced further questions about the Lanphier version.

The carcass of the Betty bomber contained bullet holes from the rear, consistent with Barber's method of attack, but showed none coming in from the side, where Lanphier claimed to have hit it. The right wing was disconnected from the fuselage, but it was believed to have been knocked off by impact with a tree, not by Lanphier's bullets. So many years had passed and the crash site had been so disturbed by visitors that definitive conclusions were impossible.

Barber and Lanphier swapped angry letters after the Phoenix convention.

"For the dignity of the Aces Association and the credibility of all fighter pilots, I have wanted to leave this historic event alone. I am satisfied with the fact that under the brilliant leadership of Colonel John W. Mitchell, the mission was successfully completed. The inaccurate reports have served only to enhance an individual, not the result of the mission," Barber wrote on September 12, 1984. "However, you have gone so far in an attempt to discredit me that I can no longer remain silent."

Lanphier shot back within a week that Barber was trying to rewrite history. Whatever bonds of friendship might have remained between the two men who once flew together in combat were severed. "You discredit yourself in your campaign to get off a losing horse and onto a winning one," Lanphier grumbled.

Nothing was settled, and the official score remained one-half credit for Lanphier and one-half credit for Barber.

Lanphier filed a petition of appeal of Study Number 85, and the air force answered by convening a Victory Credit Board of Review in

March 1985. The board was to deal only with those dicey "historical" records and not take new testimony, which ruled out the new eyewitness accounts that were becoming public from Yanagiya.

The decision of the VCBR, which remains the official air force position today, was that Barber fired on the Yamamoto bomber first, "setting it afire and causing a portion of the tail empennage to fly off," but that when Barber pulled away, the Betty was still under its own power, although losing altitude just above the jungle.

It ruled that Lanphier disengaged from the Zeros and struck the Yamamote bomber broadside, severing a wing, and it flipped over and plunged to earth. "Barber, on looking back after his pass, saw the airplane fall and understandably presumed it to be the result of his attack."

The air force has stubbornly clung to that faulty version ever since it was issued. Had new testimony been considered, then the board would easily have found the "smoking gun" piece of evidence in Lanphier's own words.

In a letter to General John Condon on December 15, 1984, Lanphier wrote, "The bomber I shot the wing off of was intact from nose to the tip of its tail when I first fired at it."

However, the air force had said Barber hit the lead plane first and not only ripped pieces off the tail, but left it trailing a plume of black smoke. If so, the Betty would have had to have been heavily damaged by the time Lanphier arrived after his acrobatic dogfight with the Zeros.

But the VCBR did not review Lanphier's letter, has refused to reopen the case, and so has perpetuated a distortion of history.

In a corner of Fredericksburg, Texas, stands a hotel that was once a stagecoach stop between San Antonio and San Diego, so famous in its day that it attracted the likes of Robert E. Lee and the author O. Henry as guests. It was once owned by the German ancestors of Admiral Chester W. Nimitz, and although it is in the middle of the Texas Hill Country, it has a Mississippi River steamship façade, a tribute to the strong links the family had to the sea.

In recent times, the building of sun-dried brick has been home to the National Museum of the Pacific War. The museum sits at the crossroads of a tiny Texas town, but it is also an intersection of history. It is supported by the Admiral Nimitz Foundation and regularly hosts programs to go with the museum's extensive exhibits, theater, and memorial garden filled with plaques that honor the American men and women, ships and planes that fought in World War II.

In 1985, the year after the Aces Convention, the 339th Fighter Squadron held a reunion in San Antonio, and John Mitchell, Rex Barber, and several other pilots drove over to the museum in Fredericksburg, where they saw a film of the 1975 interview with Zero pilot Kenji Yanagiya. It was the first time Mitchell had heard of the Yanagiya disclosure, and it was a startling moment. Rex had been right all along!

The next day, during a presentation to the reunion, Mitchell went public with his definitive conclusion. He had made up his mind. While outlining the mission, he turned to Rex Barber and calmly told the audience, "You're looking at the guy right there who got Yamamoto. Period. I don't care what you hear from anybody else, there he is right there."

He said the Yanagiya interview finally proved the point to him beyond question and "verified the fact that Rex Barber got him." Barber had shot at two bombers, and this Japanese pilot was saying that there were only two Bettys flying that day, not three, so Rex had to have blasted away at both of them. The first one carried Yamamoto, and according to the Japanese fighter pilot who saw the whole thing, the P-38 on the tail of the lead bomber shot it down. Confirmation for Mitchell had been discovered in the middle of a routine visit to a museum in a tiny Texas town.

Years passed and, once again, nearly everyone, including those involved, lost interest. But the controversy remained far from settled. Tom Lanphier adamantly defended his story, although his old friend Jimmy Doolittle cautioned him about how memory plays tricks. Lanphier remained undeterred.

The Nimitz Foundation decided to hold a "Yamamoto Retrospective" in April 1988—the forty-fifth anniversary of the mission—and bring together scholars, historians, and pilots in a comprehensive symposium on one of the unique moments of American military history.

Careful arrangements were made to keep the discourse at the rarefied academic levels recognized by historians, and the moderator would be R. Cargill Hall, the chief of research for the Office of Air Force History. The pilots wanted to solve a riddle that had pestered them for almost a half century and, once and for all, settle the issue of "Who shot down Yamamoto?"

If everything worked out, the event would put all of the pilots on a stage at the same time. Tom Lanphier would meet John Mitchell and Rex Barber face to face in a public forum, and all of the records would be available. Jack Jacobson, Lou Kittel, Doug Canning, Besby Holmes, Del Goerke, and Roger Ames would all be there. The warriors who flew the mission would finally have their say, and the guest of honor would be Kenji Yanagiya, who would be flown over from Japan to repeat his important testimony.

It was not to be, for Tom Lanphier had fallen very ill.

Only five months before the symposium, on Friday, November 27, 1987, the *San Diego Tribune* headlined:

WW II FLYING ACE DIES AT AGE 71

Thomas George Lanphier Jr., famed as the World War II flying ace who shot down the plane carrying Adm. Isoroku Yamamoto, commander in chief of the Imperial Japanese Navy in April, 1943, died yesterday at the Veterans Administration Medical Center in La Jolla. His death, after a year-long battle with cancer, came one day before his 72nd birthday.

The article went on to describe his successful careers in both military service and civilian life. Accompanying it was a photograph taken in 1945 of a smiling Tom Lanphier wearing a pilot's leather jacket and a white scarf at his throat.

A *New York Times* obituary also called him the "fighter pilot who shot down the Japanese airplane carrying the architect of the attack on Pearl Harbor." It noted that Rex Barber of Oregon "has sought to prove that it was he, rather than Lanphier, who should have been given credit for shooting down Yamamoto."

The showdown would never happen.

Epilogue

The Yamamoto Retrospective was held as scheduled five months later, but the impact was lessened by the absence of Tom Lanphier. The long anticipated confrontation, in which all questions would be answered and discrepancies cleared, would now be impossible.

Nevertheless, the meeting was productive, for it not only provided a forum for academic speakers to discuss the history of the flight, and its subsequent importance, but also gave the surviving pilots the opportunity to speak personally, through an interpreter, with Kenji Yanagiya.

John Mitchell believed he finally knew what had happened on April 18, 1943, in the brief fight above Bougainville. He had studied the reports and now had confirmation straight from Yanagiya. The years of having to sit by while Lanphier solidified his claim to fame were over, and Mitchell, the mission commander, planned to set the record straight.

None of the surviving pilots believed Tom Lanphier shot down Admiral Yamamoto by himself, for his story had too many inconsistencies and had changed substantially over the years. Claiming to have brought down the admiral's plane with a lucky shot while clearing his guns was the last straw for some. Still, several were uncomfortable, even embarrassed, that the mission had collapsed into such controversy. It was time to let it go.

Reunions of veterans, particularly among men of specific units, are supposed to be celebrations, but meetings that brought together members of the Yamamoto mission were overshadowed by the dispute. The resulting disharmony strained friendships that had bonded in the cauldron of war.

That the mission had been successful was a tribute to everyone on Guadalcanal, but Lanphier's unrelenting quest for a slice of personal glory meant that he could not attend reunions without encountering acrimony. In the end, his claim brought him neither personal happiness nor the recognition he craved.

Jack Jacobson tried to act as peacemaker, for he considered the entire episode unseemly. He refused to openly enter the argument, for he was friends with them all and was convinced that Barber and Lanphier should share the victory.

When Jacobson talked with Barber, he found that Rex had been willing to split the credit until he read Lanphier's manuscript. After that he had dug in his heels. Barber felt it would be cited as the authoritative account of what had happened.

Jacobson returned home to San Diego and contacted Lanphier's surviving family, who lived in the area, and found they also wanted the debate to go away. They asked Jacobson to read an open letter at the Retrospective. Jacobson described the letter as "an appeal for understanding." Memories had faded, and everyone agreed that on a far-off battlefield, forty-five years earlier, they had been buddies.

Jacobson said that R. Cargill Hall, serving as the panel moderator, convinced him to let Hall read the letter as part of the overall presentation.

But John Mitchell had waited a long time to set the record straight, and his impassioned talk ran long as he pointedly gave credit for the shoot-down to Rex Barber.

"Cargill Hall was just having a fit, and he's writing little notes and handing them to Mitchell—'Lay off, lay off,' and he tried to interrupt him a couple of times," Jacobson said. "Anyway, he [Mitchell] went on and on and on and on, and I was just furious. It just wasn't right."

Hall, claiming the session had run out of time, chose not to read the appeal from the Lanphier family.

Jacobson, frustrated at being unable to quench the fire, admitted that Tom Lanphier had brought it on himself. "Lanphier should not have consistently promoted the fact that he shot him down. . . . He stuck his neck out so far, he wasn't a big enough man to say, 'Well, I guess I maybe made a mistake and we should share'—he didn't want to give that up."

The ultimate tragedy of the saga was that hardened feelings of antagonism overrode the glory that was due them all for flying a very dangerous mission that removed Admiral Isoroku Yamamoto from the field. After his death, the Imperial Japanese Navy never won another major battle, and the allies steadily advanced until Japan was utterly destroyed.

The Retrospective did have one unexpected result, for Hall. The air force historical branch was forced to recognize the Yanagiya testimony, which had not been part of previous examinations of the subject.

Since Kenji Yanagiya insisted that all six of the escorting Zeros returned to base, official credit was removed for Lanphier's unwitnessed claim that he had shot down a Zero in the opening moments of the battle. With that subtraction, Lanphier dropped to an official score of four and one-half enemy planes shot down. He was no longer an ace!

Had he still been alive, the erasure of his name from that elite group of fighter pilots would have been a terrible personal affront for a man of such towering ego, particularly since Mitchell, Barber, and Holmes all remained aces.

John Mitchell was an ace before the mission began, but the muddy arithmetic of April 18, 1943 might someday alter the totals of Rex Barber and Besby Holmes.

Holmes had four confirmed kills prior to being credited with one-half of a Betty bomber and a full kill for a Zero during the Yamamoto mission. Barber confirmed seeing him shoot down one fighter, giving Holmes a total of five and one-half confirmed aerial victories. The two other Zeros Holmes claimed that day were disallowed, and the only possible witness, his wingman Ray Hine, vanished.

Rex Barber had a record of three credited victories prior to the mission, and gained one-half credit for each of the two Betty bombers, for a total of four kills. He was also awarded a full kill on a Zero that day, making his score for the mission a full two planes, and an overall total of five combat victories.

The Air Force took away Lanphier's claim on a Zero because he specifically said it was one of the escort fighters, all of which returned to base.

It was assumed that the Zeros shot down by Holmes and Barber had risen to join the fight from the base at Kahili, and therefore were not part of the escort. Although Holmes never said he witnessed Barber shoot down a Zero that day, official counters never challenged the score. The same U.S. Air Force Historical Study No. 85 that stripped Lanphier's Zero left Barber's claim intact, still relying on the original questionable after-action report. "Iron clad rules aren't always so iron clad," a pilot observed.

The Air Force may some day change the numbers again, and there are many variables. But for more than fifty years, both Barber and Holmes have qualified as aces in aerial combat, that status has never been in dispute, and is a side issue at best.

The fact remained that Tom Lanphier did not have five credited wins, and his claim to the Yamamoto victory was fading like the colors of an old flag.

In coming years, even more proof would emerge.

In 1990 Carroll Glines published an exquisitely detailed account of the mission, *Attack on Yamamoto*. It introduced new material and concluded, "Until any unassailable new evidence to the contrary is presented . . . it is the opinion of this writer that only one pilot can rightfully lay total claim to this epic shoot-down. His name is Rex T. Barber."

The English-language version of *Fading Victory: The Diary of Admiral Matome Ugaki*, published the following year, added still another eyewitness account of the Yamamoto bomber flying just above the jungle, with "flames rapidly enveloping the wings and fuselage" and trailing black smoke. He did not mention a wing being shot off, a prime component of the Lanphier version, and the Ugaki viewpoint further assailed Lanphier's assertion that the bomber was undamaged when he struck it.

A third important force entered the fray in 1988 through the efforts of George Chandler, the former P-38 pilot and fighter ace who met Lanphier and Barber on New Caledonia in 1943. After the war, Chandler became a successful banker in Pratt, Kansas. He struck up a friendship with Barber during a visit to Oregon in 1984 and became intrigued by the murky history surrounding the mission. To dig into what happened, he established an unofficial group called the Second Yamamoto Mission Association, which consisted of people interested in the history of the flight.

What started as a hobby developed into a quasi museum and archive. Chandler's office became a library of carefully filed documents, photographs, and maps pertaining to the mission. He developed contacts with sources abroad and experts who examined the crash site, corresponded steadily with those involved, hired lawyers to study air force rules and regulations and to represent the SYMA, created the most authorotative web site about the mission, and even had a P-38 pilot try to duplicate the maneuvers alleged by both Barber and Lanphier. With unfailing politeness, Chandler compiled evidence that disputed myths, plugged gaps, and presented the SYMA case with quiet, insistent logic to every legal and official body concerned.

In 1997, the SYMA presented its evidence to the Victory Confirmation Board of the American Fighter Aces Association, which interviewed Rex Barber in person and recommended that he be given 100 percent credit for shooting down Yamamoto. It was a significant decision, arrived at by men with extensive personal experience of aerial combat. The Aces Association, however, is not the U.S. Air Force.

Every attempt to revisit official air force history was rebuffed, even when elected governmental officials joined the SYMA cause. Replies from entrenched bureaucrats were tinged with arrogance and usually passed the issue to some other agency or official, who also would dodge the question. Repeated efforts drew repeated evasions.

"It is almost impossible to get a correction made in military records," Chandler said after years of work. "To me it seems that everyone with whom we have dealt has been more interested in keeping the status quo rather than trying to be sure that history is accurately recorded.

There seems to be almost a conspiracy to cover up and justify mistakes that have been made in the past."

The Air Force Victory Credit Board and the Air Force Board for the Correction of Military Records adamantly refused to take another comprehensive look at the situation and consider all available evidence, although today the trail is as wide and clearly marked as that of a big city expressway. These same bodies have already stripped Lanphier of a victory over a Zero on the mission and reduced his sole claim to the Yamamoto bomber to a half share, but they will not take the next logical step and examine whether he deserves any credit at all.

Tom Lanphier had a history of exaggerating his deeds. When he claimed that he shot down his first Zero while riding as a guest on a bomber, the members of the bomber crew never stepped forward to confirm the kill. When he claimed to have strangled a Japanese infantryman in the jungle, no one came forth to verify the incident. He was wrong in claiming to have shot down a Zero during the Yamamoto attack, and no one saw him attack either of the bombers. It is possible that he never shot at a Betty at all that day.

The United States Air Force guards its history with great zeal, to the absurd point where researchers looking into controversial issues are sometimes rudely rebuffed and librarians deny them access to material that is decades old and irrelevant to anything but an accurate historical record.

It is unlikely they will change their methods, for to do so would be tantamount to admitting that it has for many years stonewalled a legitimate complaint. Chandler's perception of a conspiracy at work seems strong.

The appearance of undue influence began with Lanphier's father and his many important friends, including Hap Arnold, Tooey Spaatz, and the army general staff during World War II. Tom Lanphier himself was the first elected president of the postwar Air Force Association, was a protégé of the secretary of the air force, and knew high Pentagon officials through his work in missile production companies. It was an invisible wall of power. Not only were they unwilling to question the claim of the designated hero, but they advanced his career.

One reason given by officials for not undertaking a total, unbiased review of the Yamamoto mission since the 1980s was that Lanphier was no longer around to defend himself. History dating back to the dawn of time is frequently updated and revised, but under this peculiar air force excuse, changes should be confined only to live subjects.

The Yamamoto mission should have stood on its own merit, for every American pilot who flew on it was a hero. It was little more than a suicide flight, and the chances were good that many, if not all of them, might not return alive. John Mitchell made the final plans and led the mission in an impeccable manner. Rex Barber was the only member of the killer flight to stick to his orders and attack the bomber no matter what the opposition, and the one hundred and four bullet holes in his plane proved that he did so. Medals of Honor have been awarded for lesser feats of bravery, but the temper tantrum of Admiral Halsey unfairly stripped away that possibility, and the air force meekly acquiesced.

John Mitchell died of cancer on November 15, 1995, and Rex Barber passed away on July 26, 2001. Each thought the other deserved the Congressional Medal of Honor.

April 18, 2003, the sixtieth anniversary of the Yamamoto mission, was declared to be Rex T. Barber Day in Oregon, and a bronze plaque was unveiled to name the bridge across the Crooked River Gorge, ten miles north of Redmond, in honor of Barber and of all Oregon veterans. The quiet Oregonian would have liked that.

The attack on Yamamoto marked a turning point in the Pacific War. He was a reluctant leader who did not want to go to war but was absolutely fierce once his nation was committed to that path. His fleet attacked targets from California to Australia and from China to New Guinea to Alaska. It is appropriate that he died with a sword in his hand, and there is no imagining what havoc he might have sown had he survived to lead the Imperial Japanese Navy in future crucial battles. The outcome would eventually have been the same. His prediction of American production capabilities had been accurate, but he could have made the cost of war terrible to contemplate.

While there were only sixteen men in the cockpits of the P-38s above Bougainville, the success of the attack was due in large measure to every marine, sailor, solder, airman, and member of the Allied services who served on Guadalcanal. They suffered and died in great numbers in a hellish little war all their own. Living conditions were miserable, and the fighting was the worst sort of combat imaginable—in the skies, on the ocean, and in the jungles. For the Americans, death was a constant companion, and potential defeat a distinct possibility. The Japanese, forced onto the defensive, suffered even worse on what they called "Starvation Island."

For a handful of U.S. Army pilots, the period between Pearl Harbor and the death of Yamamoto was the most important time of their lives. Ill-trained and underequipped, the pilots and the men who kept their balky machines flying were thrown into fierce battles in Java, the Philippines, Australia, New Guinea, and Guadalcanal and sent to protect little islands they had never even heard of because there was no choice. Theirs was a blood brotherhood of shared sacrifice that helped stop the Japanese expansion, and they flew and fought and died when no one thought it was possible to slow Yamamoto's juggernaut. They helped provide the United States with the time needed to start its war machine.

In conducting interviews, the author was struck by a singular theme. These men who served their country in a time of such great peril were overwhelmingly modest and unassuming. They did not, and do not, think they did anything special. It is only when they are coerced into telling their stories, showing an old photo, explaining medals that rest in a dusty little case somewhere out of the way, and talking about their comrades—rarely, and only reluctantly, about themselves—that a certainty emerges for a stranger permitted to glimpse their world: They were the best we had.

In 2004, sixty-one years after the mission was flown, the Veterans of Foreign Wars of the United States unanimously passed a resolution stating that Rex Barber deserved "100 percent credit" for shooting down Admiral Yamamoto. The resolution was accompanied by legislation to clear the path for Congress to finally award Barber the Medal of Honor.

Author's Note

The history of World War II continues to be written, although libraries already devote entire shelves to works ranging from government and military publications filled with every possible statistic to small, privately printed books that overflow with personal memories. More information is easily available in old articles in periodicals, magazines of the era, official Internet research sites, scrapbooks, interview transcripts, manuscripts, and diaries that are available in research libraries and museums. For readers who wish to further pursue some of the subjects covered in this book, the author recommends:

Agawa, Hiroyuki. *The Reluctant Admiral: Yamamoto and the Imperial Navy.* Translation by John Bester. Kodansha International Ltd. Tokyo. 1979.

Bartsch, William H. *Doomed at the Start: American Pursuit Pilots in the Philippines, 1941–1942.* Texas A&M University Press. College Station, Tex. 1992.

Bayless, Charles D. *The Bomber: A Pictorial and Historial Review of Hamilton Field, California, 1940.* The Army and Navy Publishing Co., Inc. Baton Rouge, La. 1940.

Bergerud, Eric M. *Fire in the Sky.* Westview Press. Boulder, Colo. 2000.

Boyington, Gregory. *Baa Baa Black Sheep.* Putnam. New York. 1958.

Brand, Max. *A Fighter Squadron at Guadalcanal.* Pocket Books. New York. 1996.

Brown, Courtney. *Tojo: The Last Banzai.* Holt, Rinehart and Winston. New York. 1967.

Burns, James MacGregor. *Roosevelt: The Soldier of Freedom, 1940–1945.* Harcourt Brace Jovanovich. New York. 1970.

Caiden, Martin. *The Ragged, Rugged Warriors.* Dutton. New York. (Original manuscript, American Heritage Center, University of Wyoming, Cheyenne, Wyoming.)

Connaughton, Richard. *MacArthur and Defeat in the Philippines.* Peter Mayer Publishers. New York. 2001.

Davis, Burke. *Get Yamamoto.* Random House. New York. 1969.

Deacon, Richard. *Kempei Tai: A History of the Japanese Secret Service.* Beaufort Books. New York. 1983.

Doolittle, James H., and Glines, Carroll V. *I Could Never Be So Lucky Again: An Autobiography of Gen. James H. "Jimmy" Doolittle.* Bantam Books. New York. 1991.

Frank, Richard B. *Guadalcanal: The Definitive Account of the Landmark Battle.* Random House. New York. 1990.

Fuchida, Mitsuo, and Okumiya, Masatake. *Midway: The Battle That Doomed Japan, the Japanese Navy's Story.* Naval Institute Press. Annapolis, Md. 1955.

Gamble, Bruce. *The Black Sheep.* Presidio Press. Novato, Calif. 1998.

Glines, Carroll V. *Attack on Yamamoto.* Orion Books. New York. 1990.

Hammel, Eric. *Aces Against Japan: The American Aces Speak, Vol. 1.* Presidio Press. Novato, Calif. 1992.

Harris, Brooklyn. *Bill, a Pilot's Story.* 1995.

Hashimoto, Shiro. *1942: Issue in Doubt.* Admiral Nimitz Museum. Fredericksburg, Tex. 1992.

Hess, William N. *Pacific Sweep: The 5th and 13th Fighter Commands in World War II.* Doubleday. New York. 1974.

Holmes, W. J. *Double-Edged Secrets: U.S. Naval Intelligence Operations in the Pacific during World War II.* Naval Institute Press. Annapolis, Md. 1979.

Hoyt, Edwin P. *Blue Skies and Blood: The Battle of the Coral Sea.* Paul S. Eriksson. New York. 1975.

———. *Guadalcanal.* Scarborough House. Boston. 1981.

————. *Yamamoto: The Man Who Planned Pearl Harbor.* McGraw-Hill. New York. 1990.

————. *Three Military Leaders.* Kodansha International. Tokyo. 1993.

Lanphier, Thomas. "At All Costs Reach and Destroy." San Diego, CA. 1988.

Leckie, Robert. *Challenge for the Pacific.* Da Capo Press. New York. 1999.

Lord, Walter. *Lonely Vigil: Coastwatchers of the Solomons.* Viking Press. New York. 1977.

McCully, Newton A. *The McCully Report: The Russo-Japanese War, 1904–1905.* Naval Institute Press. Annapolis, Md. 1977.

Merrill, James M. *A Sailor's Admiral: A Biography of William F. Halsey.* Thomas Y. Crowell Co. New York. 1976.

Mersky, Peter B. *Time of the Aces: Marine Pilots in the Solomons, 1942–1944.* Marines in World War II Commemorative Series. Marine Corps Historical Center. Washington Navy Yard. Washington, D.C. 1993.

Messimer, Dwight R. *Pawns of War: The Loss of the USS Langley and the USS Pecos.* Naval Institute Press. Annapolis, Md. 1983.

Miller, Thomas G. *The Cactus Air Force.* Harper & Row. New York. 1969.

Prados, John. *Combined Fleet Decoded: The Secret History of American Intelligence and the Japanese Navy in World War II.* Naval Institute Press. Annapolis, Md. 1995.

Potter, John Deane. *Yamamoto: The Man Who Menaced America.* Viking Press. New York. 1965.

Rhoades, F. A. *Diary of a Coastwatcher in the Solomons.* The Admiral Nimitz Foundation. Fredericksburg, Tex. 1982.

Ridpath, John Clark. *Ridpath's History of the World, Vol. 9.: The Close of the Nineteenth Century and the Dawn of the Twentieth Century.* Jones Brothers Publishing Co. Cincinnati. 1894.

Stavisky, Samuel E. *Marine Combat Correspondent: World War II in the Pacific.* Ivy Books. New York. 1999.

Steinberg, Rafael, and the editors of Time-Life Books. *Island Fighting: World War II.* Time-Life Books. Alexandria, Va. 1978.

Spurr, Russell. *A Glorious Way to Die: The Kamikaze Mission of the Battleship Yamato.* Newmarket Press. New York. 1981.

Taylor, Theodore. *The Magnificent Mitscher*. W. W. Norton. New York. 1954.

Toland, John. *The Rising Sun: The Decline and Fall of the Japanese Empire, 1936–1945*. Random House. New York. 1970.

———. *Infamy: Pearl Harbor and Its Aftermath*. Doubleday. New York. 1982.

Tregaskis, Richard. *Guadalcanal Diary*. Random House. 1943.

Tuchman, Barbara. *Stillwell and the American Experience in China 1911–45*. Macmillan. New York. 1970.

Twining, Merrill B. *No Bended Knee*. Presidio Press. Novato, Calif. 1996.

Ugaki, Matome. *Fading Victory: The Diary of Admiral Matome Ugaki*. University of Pittsburgh Press. Pittsburgh. 1991.

Van der Rhoer, Edward. *Deadly Magic*. Scribner's. New York. 1978.

Wegner, J. N. *A Lecture on Communications Intelligence*. August 14, 1946. Nimitz Museum. Fredericksburg, Tex.

Wible, John. *The Yamamoto Mission*. Admiral Nimitz Foundation. Fredericksburg, Tex. 1988.

Index

Made in the USA
Lexington, KY
25 January 2016